Sylvia Plath
Method and Madness

Sylvia Plath

METHOD AND MADNESS

Edward Butscher

Schaffner Press
Tucson, Arizona

Schaffner Press, Inc.
2405 N. Summit Drive
Tucson, AZ 85745

Design by Kay Sather

Printed in the United States of America

Acknowledgments: The author has quoted passages, for the purpose of illustrating his own discussion of Sylvia Plath's life and works, from the following works: *The Colossus and Other Poems,* by Sylvia Plath, copyright © 1957, 1958, 1959, 1960, 1962 by Sylvia Plath; published by Alfred Knopf, Inc. *The Savage God: A Study of Suicide,* by A. Alvarez, copyright 1970, 1971, 1972; published by Random House, Inc. *Half Remembered: A Personal History,* by Peter Davison, copyright © 1973 by Peter Davison; published by Harper & Row. *A Closer Look at Ariel: A Memory of Sylvia Plath ,* by Nancy Hunter Steiner, © 1973 by Nancy H. Steiner; published by Harper's Magazine Press. *Ariel,* by Sylvia Plath, copyright © 1961, 1962, 1963, 1964, 1965 by Ted Hughes; published by Harper & Row. *Crossing the Water,* by Sylvia Plath, copyright © 1971 by Ted Hughes; published by Harper & Row. *Winter Trees,* by Sylvia Plath, copyright (c) 1972 by Ted Hughes; published by Harper & Row. *The Bell Jar,* by Sylvia Plath, copyright © 1971 by Harper & Row; published by Harper & Row.

LIBRARY OF CONGRESS CATALOGING IN PUBLICATION DATA

Butscher, Edward
    Sylvia Plath, method and madness.

    Bibliography: p. 378
    Includes Index
    I. Plath, Sylvia. I. Title
PZ4.B98816Sy [PS3566.L27] 811'.5'4 [B] 75-12828
ISBN 0971-0598-2-9

This book is dedicated to the two women who made its author (their nephew) possible:
Edith and Emily Cutillo

and to my father, *the* Edward Butscher

Contents

List of Illustrations   ix
Preface   xi
Acknowledgments   xv

1. My Childhood Landscape Was Not Land   3
2. I Cast Off My Identity   20
3. A Warm Port   41
4. "A Very Talented Teenager"   61
5. Stillness Is a Lie, My Dear   85
6. There Is Nothing More for Me to Say   101
7. We Are Not What We Might Be   120
8. The Cultivated Act   146
9. All Green Dreams   166
10. The Panther's Tread   166
11. Paring Her Person Down   200
12. In a Well-Steered Country   219

13. You Died Like Any Man   232
14. That Landscape of Imperfections   241
15. A Clean Slate   253
16. I Am Two People Now   265
17. Lady of the Shipwrecked   274
18. The Moon is My Mother   292
19. I Am, I Am, I Am   304
20. Cauldron of Morning   319
21. Words Dry and Riderless   341

Epilogue   364
Afterword: "A Mug's Game"   367
Notes   387
Bibliographical Note   398
Index   403

List of Illustrations

Sylvia's high school graduation picture

Philip McCurdy

Sylvia at the beach

Sylvia in 1953

Sylvia with Jill Modlin and Myron Lotz

Sylvia and Gordon Lameyer

Marcia Brown

Sylvia at Cambridge

The Hughes' London flat

Sylvia and Ted Hughes

Sylvia and Frieda

Sylvia with Nicholas

The cottage in Croton

Sylvia with her two children

Sylvia's tombstone

Editor's Note

Due to the circumstances under which the author originally researched and wrote this book, some names were changed or left out so as to protect those people from legal repercussions. Now that these individuals are either deceased or have been revealed in subsequent biographies, here is a list of names which were either changed or omitted in the original edition along with the pages where they appear pseudonymously in the text.

1. "Richard S": Richard Sassoon, 126-27, 137, 138, 144, 152, 172-3, 184

2. "Olga" : Assia Wevill, 301, 304, 311-315, 318, 322-23, 329-30, 331, 346, 363

3. "Dr. Ruth Jones": Dr. Ruth Beuscher,121, 122, 124, 134, 145,149, 155

4. "Buddy Willard" : Richard Norton, 25-27, 45-62, 85-87, 93, 96, 129, 136, 148, 241, 306, 308

5. "Paula Rothholz": Paula Trachtman, 326

6. "Dr. Gordon": Dr. Peter Thornton, 109, 111

7. "Croton" : North Tawton, Devonshire (England), 271, 275, 278, 282, 282, 290, 337

TS
September, 2003

Preface

To write about an artist's life is to write about his or her art. That is the inescapable truth a critical biographer must constantly confront if he hopes to make sense out of the mass of material, fact and fiction, preserved in the artist's name. When the artist in question is primarily a poet, the relationship between life and art, history and myth, becomes even more intense and less patient of disengagement. When the poet is Sylvia Plath, a "confessional" poet who was consciously dedicated to fusing biography with poetry to create an enduring legend, this relationship can no longer be either split asunder or seriously challenged. And yet, the task remains to trace to their various sources the complex system of roots that led, almost inexorably, to both the later poetry and the suicide of the poet at the age of thirty.

No doubt the appellation "bitch goddess" as occasionally applied to Sylvia Plath in these pages will disconcert some readers, but it struck me as a fitting description of the persona who rages through the poetry of *Ariel* and *Winter Trees*—and several poems as yet uncollected or collected only in a limited edition. The "bitch," of course, is a familiar enough figure—a discontented, tense, frequently brilliant woman goaded into fury by her repressed or distorted status in a male society; and the "goddess" conveys the opposite image, a more creative one, though it too represents an extreme. As a combination, "bitch goddess" has the additional advantage of a long metaphorical association—at least from the time of D. H. Lawrence—with fierce ambition and ruthless pursuit of success.

By necessity, a literary biographer cannot accept a deterministic universe, unlike Sylvia Plath herself at times, and must reject as nonsense any melodramatic attempts to predicate suicide upon some aesthetic imperative, however fierce. And yet, he must also realize that the illusions of art are most vital when attached to the emotional placenta of the artist's past, to childhood, since it is in childhood, at least psychologically, where the artist will discover the greatest creative energies—powered, very often, by crucial traumas in a family setting. Furthermore, as Anais Nin once observed, "The young turn to poetry when the world becomes intolerable"; turn to it initially as a form of escape from the demands and sorrows of a reality that has disappointed or wounded them in some profound way.

But many children have fantasies and many children turn to poetry during difficult periods of adjustment to a changing self, during the development of sexual and social identities, only to drop them later on, becoming "normal," functional, supposedly contented adults. What distinguishes the real poet from these, besides the basic ingredients of high intelligence and extreme sensitivity, is a fundamental sense of being different from everyone else, of remaining locked inside an enormous ego which must constantly alter the given world through language to satisfy his, or her, particular vision of it. For him/her, escapism (or what I term *method*) will evolve into commitment, a vocational dedication to his craft and vision (*method* plus *madness*) that imposes *his* order upon the seemingly random phenomena of the senses.

In a word, he becomes God.

As God, history is his biography, religion and religious ritual his myth of self and craft, and the cosmos itself a mere extension of his own conscious and unconscious perceptions. This is more true for poets perhaps, lyric poets, than other artists, because a lyric poet—whether confessional or not—always proceeds from the narrow philosophical position that reality does not exist, does not have shape or meaning, until filtered through his self. All of which should not cloud the fact that the lyric poet also carries within himself the same ruthless remoteness (Yeats' "cold eye") of every other artist, the ability to stand back from the cauldron of his own life, as if from a canvas, and impose the objective values of an artifice, forging finished products from the very fires of emotional entanglements that are still scalding him.

It can be a pretentious business, of course, one easily distorted by lesser talents into license for self-indulgence, but in the hands of a genuine poet, a major artist, which Sylvia Plath certainly was, it can result in masterpieces of poetic insight and beauty. Obsession is the crucial term, because it is in his obsessions that the poet finds his heart truth, his raw material, and it is in his obsessions that the reader will most clearly see the dynamic interaction between self and art at work.

Throughout this book I have endeavored to keep the academic apparatus to a minimum whenever possible and generally have restricted footnotes to the specification of sources. The Plath poems discussed in the text are not, by and large, identified as to publication dates and source, but the "Bibliographical Note" at the end should answer all questions relating to chronology and provenance. I have attempted to always treat the poems in chronological order whenever the date of composition was known.

Briarwood, New York
January, 1975

Acknowledgments

Besides Winthrop Palmer, who has been a poetic inspiration and literary mentor for many years, the people who were most important to the development of this book were the many close friends of Sylvia Plath who generously opened their homes and memories to me. First on this long list would be Philip McCurdy, who not only took time out to answer numerous queries both in person and by mail, but also guided me on a personal tour of Wellesley. Marcia Brown Stern was equally magnanimous, as were Peter and Jane Davison. A special note of thanks must go to Dr. Myron Lotz, who supplied copies of Sylvia's letters to him and had the courage to be candid about their relationship and himself. He has also allowed me the generous use of his collection of photographs relating to Sylvia. Gordon Lameyer was also frank and generous in supplying numerous biographical details and in permitting me to read his unpublished memoir.

In Wellesley itself, both Wilbury Crockett and Dr. Perry Norton provided valuable information during the course of extensive interviews and became good friends of the author in the process. Professor William Norton and Frank Irish were most helpful in giving background on their early contacts with Sylvia. Barbara Rydell was similarly willing to provide information, along with Sylvia's high-school graduation photograph; and many of Sylvia's teachers from junior and senior high school shared their recollections of her with me, including Miss Helen Lawson, Miss Anna Craig, and Miss Addie Willard. James T. Lape was of assistance as well. More distant figures in Sylvia's life were also generous with their time, notably Alfred Kazin, Stanley Kunitz, and Richard Wilbur.

Cyrilly Abels interrupted her busy career as a literary agent to grant me an interview and subsequently helped track down other contacts from Sylvia's *Mademoiselle* days. Dr. Howard Hirt aided me in many tedious research tasks, took photographs in Wellesley and Winthrop, and allowed me the use of his home in Newtonville during my visits to Massachusetts. He, his wife Muriel and their daughter Viki made my stays comfortable and stimulating. Jane Kopp supplied recollections on tape and also provided a photograph of Sylvia. Mrs. Arthur L. Humphrey, Mr. and Mrs. Floyd E. Orton, and Nancy Boyd offered much assistance, and Professors Robert Gorham Davis and George Gibian willingly shared their memories of Sylvia with me.

In England, Elizabeth Sigmund invited me to her friendly Devon home and spent many hours reminiscing about her friend and one-time neighbor; David Compton was no less congenial and informative. Miss K. T. Burton responded to my queries with thoughtful thoroughness and good-natured patience, while May Targett provided both a delicious meal and much valuable testimony. George MacBeth took time off from his heavy schedule at the BBC to discuss his recollections of Sylvia. Brian and Mary de l'Troath did considerable research on my behalf and transformed London into a friendly refuge for a tired traveler; Timothy O'Grady gave that same traveler much good company. The Roches, Paul and Clarissa, were equally warm in welcoming a stranger into their Aldermaston home. Their insights into Sylvia's character made the time we spent together especially important and enjoyable.

Libraries, of course, are the foundation of any research project, and it is a distinct pleasure to thank the librarians who made them such delightful places to visit and use: Mrs. Theresa A. Carroll, Town Librarian at Brookline's Public Library; David Farmer, Assistant to the Director of the Humanities Research Center at the University of Texas; Mrs. Deva Howard, Archivist at the Archives of the Northwestern University Library; A. Phillips, Newnham College's librarian, Cambridge; I. G. Philips, the Keeper of Printed Books at the Bodleian Library, Oxford; Elizabeth K. Olmstead at the Wellesley Free Library; and William R. Cagle, Assistant Librarian at the Lilly Library, Indiana

University. Especially helpful were Holly Hall, who is in charge of the Manuscript Division at the Washington University Library, and Miss Mary Elizabeth Murdock, Director of the Sophia Smith Collection in Smith College's Neilson Library—this library was by far the most congenial to visit, due largely to the efficient, cheerful service supplied by its student and professional staff. Also, the staff at the Reference Library of the BBC outdid itself in providing me with significant script material. The Cambridge Library was similarly of much valuable assistance.

Although an odd series of accidents and tight time schedules prevented us from ever meeting, Professor Eric Homberger was quick to offer his aid, as was Professor Elizabeth Salter; and, through the mails, Professor Valerie Pitt had much worthwhile information to pass on regarding her former pupil. Other people who supplied leads or helped in various ways were Rosemary Goad at Faber and Faber, Marjorie Hewetson of External Research at the BBC, Professor Malcolm Bradbury, University of East Anglia, Miss M. E. Grimshaw, Registrar of the Roll at Newnham College, and the Superintendent of the British Museum's Newspaper Library.

A special note of thanks must go to the *New York Times Book Review*, which printed my inquiry that resulted in several highly informative contacts, as did a similar appeal that appeared in the *Times Literary Supplement*. The staff at Yaddo was also helpful, and so were Mrs. W. H. Brownell, editor of the *Smith Alumnae Quarterly*, Rhoda Selvin at Stony Brook, Professor Allen Grossman of Brandeis University, Richard Steuble of Wolfson College, Cambridge, and Professor Phyllis Williams Lehmann of Smith College.

Mallory Woeber and Clement Moore Henry were most kind and frank during our talks together. From Israel, Professor Dorothea Krook sent a well-documented memoir and took time to answer numerous further inquiries. Similarly, John Press took time out to write an account of his several meetings with Sylvia.

Another important source of information were Town Clerks like Alice T. Mann of Wellesley and Donald S. McLeod of Winthrop, who responded promptly and accurately to most inquiries, and often not only produced photostats of essential documents but went on to suggest further avenues of research. Ann Johnson at the Oregon State Health Division (Vital Statistics Section) was also of help, as was James T. McEachern, Superintendent of Cemeteries at Winthrop, while Mrs. Rose Brown, Secretary to Winthrop's Public Schools, provided information concerning Sylvia's elementary school experience. Similarly of assistance were: Colean Norton, Deputy County Clerk for Harney County, Oregon; Evelyn Marshall, Deputy County Recorder for Washoe County, Nevada; Shirley Andreasen, County Clerk for Storey County, Nevada; Vaughn Smith, County Clerk for Carson City, Nevada; and the Town Clerk of Reno, Nevada.

Two English poets, Edward Lucie-Smith and Ruth Fainlight, contributed what aid they could; and Professor Sylvan Schendler, who is head of the American Studies Research Centre in Hyderabad, India, shared his knowledge of Sylvia with me through the good offices of Dr. Howard Hirt. Professor Norman Shapiro of Wesleyan University was always cooperative, as was Professor Stanley J. Kahrl of Ohio State University. Also, a few months before her death, Mrs. Olive H. Prouty took the trouble to write of her feelings about her former protegée, and Jonathan Miller responded immediately to my questions. Other people who deserve recognition for their contributions include Mrs. Bert T. Giesey, Mrs. Robert C. Whitten, Mrs. Leonard Sachar, Mrs. Clarence H. Botsford, Gail E. Huggins, Mrs. Frederick P. Cahill, Verna Small, Robert E. Anderson, Jr., and Dr. Ruth Tiffany Barnhouse.

With regard to Otto Plath, Professor George P. Fulton, Chairman of Boston University's Biology Department, was especially helpful; and Professor Norman S. Bailey of Bradford College welcomed me into his home and gave me no end of pertinent data. Crucial academic material and records were supplied by Geoffrey P. Pollitt, Director of Biological Laboratories at Harvard University; Katherine Kraft, Assistant at the Harvard University Archives; Marion C. Belliveau, Registrar of Harvard's Faculty of Arts and Sciences; and O. L. Schlenner, Registrar for Northwestern College, who devoted much time and effort to answering my queries. Professor Elmer Mode, a member of Boston University's History Department, and Professor Stewart Duncan, a biologist from the same institution, were equally generous.

Colonel Robert Modlin and his wife Jill were most cooperative and generously gave permission to reproduce several of their photos of Sylvia, Myron Lotz, and themselves. Andrew Concool supplied valuable technical aid. Other people, not directly involved in the project, who should be mentioned are the various former and present students of mine who freed me from countless clerical tasks: Debbie Phillips, Marian Madden, Donna Wolz, and Julia Leeds. Lastly, George Cohn and my colleagues have to be thanked for often having made writing and teaching conditions so pleasurable.

In the end, of course, the best aid any author can have comes inevitably from those closest to him, who have patiently sacrificed the most during his flights away from home and endless retreats into isolation. In this connection, Amy Rothholz has been of inestimable aid and comfort over the years. Nor can the benevolent, always sane influences of Godfrey, Pudding, and Pussy Willow be slighted. Most of all, however, Paula had to bear the major burden of this book's slow emergence, and she always did so with love and spirited interest.

To all of these people, who cannot be held responsible for either the author's opinions or factual errors, I extend my deepest gratitude.

Briarwood, New York
January, 1975

Sylvia Plath
Method and Madness

> I thought how strange it had never occurred to me
> before that I was only purely happy until I was nine
> years old.
>
> *The Bell Jar*

1

My Childhood Landscape Was Not Land

For Sylvia Plath, as even the most casual reading of her poetry demonstrates, the central obsession from the beginning to the end of her life and career was her father, Professor Otto Emile Plath. His life and, more importantly, his death nine days after her eighth birthday left an imprint upon her imagination that time did not erase or soften. He would become part of the myth projected by the poetry, would surface again and again in varying disguises: as Freud's pivotal father figure, as icon and divinity, as totem and demon, and as ultimate modern monster, a Nazi "panzer man."

His reality, the factual and the impressionistic, the human, have been lost in the process, deliberately so from the daughter's viewpoint; and no critical biography about Sylvia Plath would be complete without some effort to restore that reality. Although the facts are sparse, there is at least sufficient information to provide a rough profile.

Otto Plath was born on April 13, 1885, in the German town of Grabow or Grabowo, in the so-called "Polish Corridor," to Theodore and Ernestine Plath, his mother's maiden name being Kottke. He was one of five children, with two brothers and two sisters. Nothing else is known of his childhood. The family appears to have been solidly middle class. Otto's father next turns up in North Dakota, in a small town named Maza, where he was listed by trade as a blacksmith.[1] The rest of the family seems to have remained behind in Germany.

When he was fifteen years old, Otto too emigrated to the United States, moving west to join his father in North Dakota. On September 28, 1903, he entered the Preparatory Department of Northwestern College, a small Lutheran school where the majority of students boarded. At this time he was a second-year high-school student and obviously several years behind in his education. He would remain at Northwestern for the next seven years, earning his Bachelor of Arts degree on June 21, 1910. Like other parochial schools, Northwestern College had the virtues and flaws of its kind, being superior in its rigid concentration upon fundamentals, but far too severe in its discipline, its conservative standards, and pervasive concern for religious teaching. Otto would always resent what he felt was the school's restrictive orthodoxy and eventually abandoned the Lutheran faith altogether.

During the three years that Otto was in preparatory school, he gained a solid grounding in a wide variety of classical courses.[2] Besides the mandatory English and German, which included exercises in spelling, composition, and grammar, memorization of poetry and readings in many German, American, and English literary masterpieces, he had to take geography and history (taught in German) all three years, along with religion and Latin. Penmanship and drawing were required for two years and Greek was a mandatory subject in the final year. Mathematics was likewise required and in his senior year Otto studied algebra.

Being essentially a liberal arts institution, Northwestern was patently weakest in the physical sciences, although Otto would, during his four years as a college student, devote three years to the study of chemistry and physics. Zoology had been his favorite subject in preparatory school and he had also taken a course in botany. French was optional, but Latin and German were required and put to use in a variety of other subjects. Many years later this grounding in languages was to prove of considerable advantage to Otto when he decided to pursue graduate studies at Harvard University.

When Otto entered his freshman year at Northwestern College, his registration card indicated that he and his father had again changed residence. Their home was now listed as Harney, Oregon, and Theodore Plath's occupation was entered as "farmer." The records of Harney County, however, show no evidence of a deed having ever been made out to any person by the name of Plath, which suggests that Otto's father may temporarily have signed up as a farm hand in Harney until he could obtain work in his own profession. Undoubtedly the older

Plath had to make a financial sacrifice to maintain his son at boarding school, and this, along with the possibility of a business reversal, may account for the move to another state. Regardless, Oregon remained the Plath home for at least the next twelve years. During this time there was never any question of Otto's leaving Northwestern before graduation, though he did resent the "gloominess" of the Lutheran temperament with increasing bitterness. When Otto graduated from Northwestern in 1910, he went immediately to Washington University in Seattle, where he would receive his Master of Arts degree two years later.

The years from 1912 to 1920 are almost blank as far as my information about Otto Plath is concerned, although *The Bell Jar* has the father slicing sausages in a California delicatessen during World War I. As he possessed a master's degree he might very well have earned his living for a while at teaching; but up to this point his educational background had little to do with his ultimate goal, which was to become an entomologist. At some time during these years he married a girl named Lydia;[3] and on November 5, 1918, his father died in the Oregon City Hospital of an abscess in the right lung at the age of 68. Once again the older Plath's trade was listed as "blacksmith." Not long after his father's death, probably in 1920, Otto headed east for Massachusetts, finally determined to pursue his keen interest in entomology. In all likelihood he left Lydia behind, since he was remembered by his colleagues at Harvard as being unmarried during his years there.

Harvard University was in those days the natural destination for a young man intent upon a career in entomology. Professor William Morton Wheeler, head of its biology department, was an energetic, well-known specialist in the study of ants. Otto's chosen field was bees, where his knowledge of German gave him a distinct advantage, since most pioneering monographs on the subject had been written by Central European scientists whose work had not yet been translated into English. Though old for a graduate student, past 35 at the time, Otto more than made up for this by the intelligence and dedication he brought to his studies. While liberal in political and religious matters, he was still the sum of his German background, maintaining a deep respect for knowledge and the immigrant's typical allegiance to hard work. At Harvard he lived at the Bussi Institute, which was part of Boston's Arboretum on the south side in the Jamaica Plain section. The Institute and the Arboretum were the property of Harvard; but the latter, consisting of acres and acres of lush trees, bushes, and plants from all over the temperate zone, was used by the city for a park.

It was unusual for a student to actually live at Bussi, where the university then held classes, but Otto was also a graduate assistant, and an impoverished one at that. Near the end of the month, like many other fellow assistants, he was not above dining on rat stew when short of money. Such hardluck fare notwithstanding, his love of eating is one aspect of Otto's personality which seems to stand out in the memory of several friends and co-workers. Norman Bailey, for instance, whose brother would be responsible for hiring Otto at Boston University in 1928 and who himself took several courses there under Professor Plath, recalls the sandwiches Otto used to eat with gusto at lunch time, huge sandwiches thick with mayonnaise. Bailey remembers this so vividly because he knew that his teacher had a diabetic condition and was supposed to be watching his diet.

Otto remained at Harvard until 1928 when he received his Doctor of Science degree in applied biology, a degree that is no longer granted except for honorary purposes. His field work and thesis were devoted to bumble bees, which he studied at the Arboretum. Devoting so much attention to a single insect and studying them in their natural habitat, as opposed to controlled laboratory conditions, placed him in the tradition of such grand European entomologists as Henri Fabre. This approach required a great deal of time and patience, locating the nests, observing the bees over an extended period of time regardless of weather, making sufficient notes of all pertinent data, and then organizing the material to conform to accepted academic practice. Like Professor Wheeler, his idol and mentor, Otto was something of an American pioneer in his specialty. Dr. George P. Fulton, present Chairman of Biology at Boston University, who once studied under Professor Plath, recalls that "In some respects, Professor Plath was ahead of his times, because of his course and research interests in animal behavior . . . Today, we would call him a behavioral psychologist, or behavioral biologist." [4]

During his career at Harvard and Boston University, Otto wrote a number of essays and monographs on bees and other insects "which are still of interest today," according to Professor Stewart Duncan, also of Boston University.[5] Otto's doctoral thesis was eventually published in 1934 by the Macmillan Company under the title *Bumble Bees and Their Ways*, with an Introduction by Professor Wheeler. Further, as a tribute to Professor Plath's writing skill, the thesis did not have to be revised for publication. Not only did it evince a lively narrative style, but it also established him as one of the country's leading specialists in the study of bees. Later he was to broaden this reputation with his work in ornithology and ichthyology.

None of this really tells us very much about the man. His intelligence and dedication are evident enough, as is that singleness of purpose which impelled him to become a graduate student at an age when most men are already well settled in their careers. Physically, despite an apparently healthy appetite, he was a slender man of regular features, with blue eyes and almost black hair that was sprinkled with gray as he entered his forties. His hair was usually cut short in the style of the era and he wore a small, neat mustache. Professor Bailey remembers him as being "fairly tall" and giving the impression of angularity. "He also had an ambling, shuffling gait and always seemed in a hurry." [6]

All those who knew Otto Plath intimately agreed that he was nothing like the Prussian tyrant later projected by his daughter's writing; but in varying degrees they also felt that there was a certain rigidity about him, a stiffness in his behavior and attitudes, which became more pronounced as he grew older. Another colleague from Boston University, in the mathematics department, Professor Elmer Mode, characterized Otto as "friendly, sort of kindly in a way, gentle," but then went on to add that "I couldn't say he was the kind of personality I could get enthusiastic about." [7] Professor Mode recalls one incident when Otto, while in the backyard of his home at Winthrop, suddenly snapped out his hand and caught a bee flying past; held it cupped, unharmed, in his palm; and then discoursed at length about its habits.

Otto was forty-three when he graduated from Harvard and began teaching at Boston University. It was in one of his German classes that he had Aurelia Schober for a student. She was working towards her master's degree and, having been born in 1906, she was twenty-one years younger than Otto. In fact, Aurelia's future husband was only four years younger than her own father.

Aurelia's Germanic background and great respect for academic achievement and status were two of her most compatible qualities for Otto. Though she had been born in Boston, her parents were Roman Catholic immigrants from Austria. Her mother Aurelia (née Greenwood) came from Vienna and her father Frank apparently from the Tyrol. The Schobers owned their own home at Point Shirley, the extreme tip of Winthrop, facing the ocean but in view of the bay and of Deer Island, the location of a prison. Frank Schober was a waiter and he and his wife had two other children besides Aurelia, a daughter named Dorothy and a much younger son, Frank Jr. The Schobers had lived at 892 Shirley Street since 1918, moving there at the end of World War I, which had been an unhappy time for German immigrants. In *The Bell Jar*, Esther observes, "My mother spoke German during her childhood in America and was stoned for it during the First World War by the children at school." Sylvia herself, exaggerating a bit, would claim she always envied her mother for having been born and brought up in "the same sea-bitten house." [8]

Professor Plath and Aurelia Schober were married early in 1932. During the Christmas recess, they travelled to Reno, Nevada, where Otto divorced his first wife Lydia and wed Aurelia. The couple set up housekeeping in the Jamaica Plain area so as to be near the university where Otto taught and the Arboretum he loved. Aurelia was apparently content to play the traditional role of faculty wife. Her friends appreciated her congenial disposition and recall her as intelligent and charming. She displayed a sincere, if unprofessional, interest in the arts, including literature, and like Otto seemed to prefer people with similar Germanic backgrounds, such as the Modes, who remained close friends.

If she had any ambitions, beyond the vicarious satisfaction of being a professor's wife, she apparently never mentioned them. More than likely she was content to play daughter to her husband's role of paterfamilias and enjoyed the security of it all. Otto had always been a single-minded man devoted to his work, devoid of outside interests and hobbies, a condition which naturally intensified as he grew older.

On October 27, 1932, Sylvia was born in Boston's Memorial Hospital. The child's name was supposedly derived from the herb "salvia" and the adjective "sylvan," which would have suited Otto's classical education and scientific training. Sylvia herself might have preferred a reference to Shakespeare's "Silvia" in *The Tempest*. Whatever its derivation, the name seemed fitting. The baby was pretty, blonde, and somewhat frail, having been born with a troublesome sinus condition that would afflict her for the rest of her life.

Sylvia was an only child, an only child with an elderly father. Years later she would tell a friend that Otto had not wanted a child but, after seeing her, changed his mind and loved her very much. True or not, it was part of the myth of childhood that Sylvia would feel essential to maintain. She was a bright and attractive child and there is no reason to believe that Otto was not delighted with her. Nevertheless, he eventually did let it be known that he also wanted a son, that he would have a son in a few years. Two and a half years later, Warren Joseph Plath was born and created a fissure in his sister's closed world. In "Ocean W-1212," an impressionistic memoir of her early childhood written near the end of her life,[9] Sylvia described the intrusion of a younger brother with amused vehemence:

A baby! I hated babies. I who for two and a half years had been the centre of a tender universe felt the axis wrench and a polar chill immobilize my bones. I would be a bystander, a museum mammoth. Babies!

The wound is thus mocked, but picked at, picked at, never setting. No amount of analysis or sophisticated detachment could conceal this obsessive absorption with a spoiled paradise. As Freud has observed, "The unwelcome arrival of a baby brother or sister is the oldest and most burning question that assails immature humanity." For the parents, the family unit was complete, and life must have appeared satisfying. Though academics were notoriously underpaid, Otto had a secure position at Boston University among people he liked, and a solid reputation—*Bumble Bees and Their Ways* had come out the year before his son's birth.

It was in late 1936 or early 1937 that the Plaths bought a small home at 892 Johnson Avenue in Winthrop, the town Aurelia had grown up in and still loved, the town where her parents and younger brother still lived. The house on Johnson Avenue faced the bay and later Logan Airport, one in a series of similar houses that crowded Winthrop's bay shore, but it had its own small yard, was relatively inexpensive to maintain, and was close enough to Boston to make Otto's trips to the university no great ordeal. More important, from Aurelia's perspective, it was much nearer her parents' home, which lay on the tip of Winthrop. Here in Winthrop Sylvia would acquire her powerful, almost obsessive love and fear of the ocean, envisioning it from a romanticized adult perch as "a deep woman" who spoke "of miracles and distances," but who could "also kill," as a mother, *the* mother, mother of the universe that transformed the ordinary processes of existence into the stuff of myth and poetry.

Sylvia and her younger brother were taken often to visit their grandmother and the sea that clawed at her yard, where their grandfather had built a retaining wall of stone with his own hands. These visits helped to reinforce the stark realization that her "beautiful fusion with the things of the world was over." Moreover, she could telephone her grandmother by herself as she grew older—W-1212 was the number—and walk along the seashore that held so much fascination for her. It was here on the edge of the sea that she first defied her personal demons, foreshadowing another, more purposeful walk years later: "When I was learning to creep, my mother set me down on the beach to see what I thought of it. I crawled straight for the coming wave and was just through the wall of green when she caught my heels."

But, for the most part, the years in Winthrop were years of joy and adventure, years of exploration stretched out upon sunlit memories of bright colors, compounded by "the wailing of gulls and the smell of salt." The sandy beach was a constant source of unexpected treasures, shells, petrified wood, starfish relics, crab husks, and the like. Her memories are, of course, deliberately refracted through rose-colored glasses, but the images of the sea would dominate her poetry and mind. Those early years cannot be slighted, if only because they encompass her formative struggle to absorb a world in which beauty was ceaselessly bound to horror and happiness to pain, the discovery of death. At her grandmother's house she would nurse "starfish alive in jam jars of seawater and watch them grow back lost arms," but there too she was to observe the older Aurelia "drop the dark green lobsters with their waving, wood-jammed claws into the boiling pot from which they would be, in a minute, drawn—red, dead and edible."

Red would be the color of life itself, vibrant but forever tinged with blood, the agony of an existence poised on the painful edge of extreme sensibilities. The other extreme had to be green nature, green sea, green forest, nature herself, who had her own grisly secrets to impose upon a bright little girl's sensitive consciousness. Paradox would become the foundation of her truth, a sea that gave life stealing it back, a womb of poison.

These were the main elements, passive, unalterable settings, off-stage narratives, that went into the background that would produce the artist, along with a factor as yet unknown, perhaps an organic tendency towards schizophrenia, but they would not have been sufficient in themselves. A situation was needed, a plot ripe with secret tension and geared towards a climax of destruction, betrayal, a re-enactment of an ancient tragedy to forge the tragic poet. As always, the family and an adolescent vantage point, primitively intense, provided the focus. Otto certainly played one of the major roles. In an effort to counteract the threat of her brother, Sylvia undoubtedly went out of her way to please her father, who was not indifferent to her efforts. Using her quick, retentive intellect, the daughter memorized the Latin names for various insects, and the father proudly showed off her skill whenever the chance arose, doting on his daughter's apparent precocity.

Otto's obvious delight in Sylvia's performance, coupled with his consistently paternal attitude towards the whole family, created a certain amount of hidden hostility, which was transformed into anxiety by a daughter's awareness of her need to repress negative emotions for fear of losing her father's love. To ensure Otto's attention, Sylvia had to be on stage for him, demonstrating her own worth, earning affection which should have been hers by birthright. It was an unhealthy ambience for growth, encouraging false values. Learning how to recite those polysyllabic Latin labels, and being rewarded by her father's public approval, did have a positive side, an exposure to the reality of competitive relationships, but it also tended to precipitate a vision of knowledge as solely a means to an end, to recognition. Worse, it suggested to the quick-witted child that her major worth as a human being depended upon what she did rather than who she was.

Not very surprisingly, Sylvia early evinced an ambivalent attitude towards both parents, for her mother's seeming passivity encouraged Otto's potential as a tyrant king. As Sylvia developed a more specialized sexual consciousness and began to concentrate her feminine attentions upon Otto, this also meant a more negative concept of her mother as a rival. A cycle had begun, but it need not have become disabling if Otto had lived long enough for his daughter to transcend this crucial phase and shift her sexual energies outside the home.

Meanwhile, there were portents and broadenings of experience. In 1938 Sylvia entered the Winthrop public school system and discovered another stage on which she could display her talents. School records indicate that she maintained a straight "A" profile from the very beginning, impressing her teachers with her intelligence and dedication.[10] Outwardly she was well on her way to becoming a model child. But 1938 was also the year of the hurricane. It struck on September 21, ripping down trees and power lines, causing awesome tidal waves, and costing two hundred lives from Long Island to Canada before it was over. In her memoir, Sylvia recalls the thrill of anticipation, then the thunderous wind and rain ripping at their house all night long; and in "The Disquieting Muses" she would link the storm, retrospectively, with the birth of her artist self and her mother's inadequacy:

> In the hurricane, when father's twelve
> Study windows bellied in
> Like bubbles about to break, you fed
> My brother and me cookies and ovaltine
> And helped the two of us to choir:
> "Thor is angry: boom, boom, boom!
> Thor is angry: we don't care!"
> But those ladies broke the panes.

The following morning's scene of devastation was all a child could ask for in the way of excitement: "overthrown trees and telephone poles, shoddy summer cottages bobbing out by the lighthouse, and a litter of the ribs of little ships." But the Schober home had been the one in real danger, located as it was on the beach, and Sylvia's memoir ripples with pride over its survival, which reflected favorably upon the indomitable quality of her grandparents' old-fashioned life style: "My grandmother's house had lasted valiant—though the waves broke right over the road and into the bay. My grandfather's sea-wall had saved it, the neighbors said. Sand buried her furnace in golden whorls; salt stained the upholstered sofa; and a dead shark filled what had been the geranium bed, but my grandmother had her broom out, it would soon be right." In Sylvia's imagination, the Schobers would always represent an existence whose security she envied and yearned for, but whose very simplicity kept it outside her complex perceptions and needs.

The hurricane was nature without her maternal mask on and it revealed the other side of the sea, the womb as a grave. Both insights would become and remain hallmarks of the later poetry, philosophical obsessions that never lost their infantile base. But life had a fluid surface, the sea returning to a mysterious, friendly presence, which she and Warren now shared during their exploration of the beach in front of their grandparents' home. Each summer, however, they had to be content with a different beach while the frugal Schobers rented out their house to vacationers and lived in a furnished room nearby. Sylvia remembers Warren and herself carrying nails for their young, boat-building uncle, Frank Jr., and "his petite fiancée," and the many fine seafood dishes her grandmother prepared for them.

The outside world intruded but marginally, through the radio. "The Shadow" and "Superman" were integral parts of Sylvia's growing imagination, though the emergence of Hitler in Germany and the invasion of Poland remained little more than baritone litanies from far-away newscasters. For Otto and Aurelia, and most other Americans with Germanic backgrounds, it was a different story, stirring up memories of World War I. Otto in particular was horrified by the Nazi rise to power.

It is not unlikely that throughout his life Otto typically defied his diabetic condition by eating foods which were forbidden him, a minor act of hubris that seemed to go against the grain of his otherwise scientific nature, exhibiting not so much a self-destructive impulse as an almost arrogant self-confidence. This arrogance became further evident when he developed a sore on his toe in the middle of 1940 and neglected it completely until he required hospitalization. Nevertheless, his condition still did not seem too serious, and the college allowed a graduate student to take over his entomology class on the assumption that Professor Plath would return in the fall.

Months passed, dreadful months for Aurelia and Sylvia, and the condition did not improve. Instead there was a slow but steady deterioration. Gangrene had formed and the doctors finally amputated the toe of the left foot in an effort to save the leg. In a few weeks, as the leaves outside brightened and died, it became obvious that the surgery had been too late. The leg itself was amputated, now in an effort to save the patient's life. But the gangrene was arterio-sclerotic, and Otto's body weakened dangerously under its spreading impact. According to the attending physician, Dr. J. A. Holmes, the "diabetes mellitus" worked on Otto for four months, the gangrene for two, but in the end it was the onset of broncho-pneumonia that wrenched away his last strength in a mere four days.[11] Otto Plath died in the hospital at 9:35 P.M. on November 5, 1940.

The manner alone of Otto's death was bound to have a traumatic effect on a girl of Sylvia's sensitivity and imagination. Somehow she had to struggle with the fact that he had left her, that death was truly final, and that his departure was in some way a "deliberate" act of betrayal. Though only a child of eight, Sylvia fell back upon the only defenses available to her. Unfortunately, they were to remain neurotic in nature and intensity. One such defense was to seek compensation in other realms as public approval became a substitute for lost parental love. The drive for success also served as a sort of emulation of the dead father's own discipline and ambition. Another defense which fits Sylvia's behavior in later years would be greater dependence upon her mother for emotional security. But it was eventually to prove an unhealthy relationship; and the very fierceness of the disguised attacks upon Aurelia in *The Bell Jar* and several later poems, such as "The Disquieting Muse" and "Medusa," imply negative feelings too long held in check for fear of losing her mother's essential affection.

Whatever complex psychological forces were at work upon Sylvia's personality in the years immediately following her father's death, one further defense has to be considered. Though uncomfortable to contemplate, the idea of poetry itself as a defense mechanism cannot be avoided. In a child's hands it becomes an instrument of fantasy, and it was no accident that Sylvia's poetry emerged soon after Otto's death.

But Sylvia herself was to claim that her mother's reading aloud of Matthew Arnold's "Forsaken Merman" was the spark that set her poetic imagination aflame; and once in an interview, replying to a direct question on the matter, she said, "I guess I liked nursery rhymes and I guess I thought I could do the same thing." [12] Yet in a previous interview she had conceded that her life was "sealed off" after the age of seven and that her adolescence was "not too happy," causing her to become "introverted" and to write "diary poems" betweens the ages of nine and sixteen or seventeen. Though she never specifically mentions Otto's death, it is obvious that she was quite aware of the link between her initial artistic efforts and that traumatic event.

She was eight and a half when she had her first poem published in the *Boston Sunday Herald* and when her drawing of a plump lady in a feathered hat won a dollar prize in another newspaper contest. Though hardly more than the cleverness of an intelligent girl, the poem is fascinating for its grasp of elementary techniques:

> Hear the crickets chirping
> In the dewy grass.
> Bright little fireflies
> Twinkle as they pass.

The poem has nothing to do with Sylvia's interior reality and in that sense is pure escapism, but its mere existence proves a discontented drive towards harmony. It is disguise, apprentice verbal manipulation of external phenomena written to please a grown-up world, method's first step towards ordering experience with craft, and it is an objectification of fantasy. Though well liked by adults, particularly authority figures, parental surrogates, Sylvia is usually described by her contemporaries from adolescence as "a loner," as "a daydreamer" given to the poet's traditional retreats from the world into a private universe where the self had divine powers.

The problem with this kind of fantasizing is that it usually becomes double-edged. It partially reduces aggressive drives and hostilities, such as Sylvia's repressed feelings towards her mother, but it also, through its heightening of self-awareness, brings about a keener consciousness of faults and failures—all of which helps explain her manic-depressive swings, their suddenness and intensity. Then again, the fantasies and the poetry that resulted were further extensions of her masks, a means of winning approval, that would allow very little release of negative feelings. Yet all of Sylvia's defenses, however neurotic, did prevent any extended periods of dangerous despair, as her whirlwind assault upon the world's good opinion externalized or temporarily diverted many dark undercurrents.

In more general terms, the death of the father confirmed a childish, perpetual division of events, thoughts, and emotions into polar extremes, stark blacks and whites that included a simplistic adherence to the Puritan frame of ethical purities embedded in Sylvia's Protestant cultural commitments. This was not an unusual position for a child of her years to embrace, but like other obsessions and compulsions it was one she would carry with her for the rest of her life, long after it had ceased to reflect her conscious intellectual views. The opposition of antagonistic forces, not yet intentionally ironic, meant a continual awareness of mortality, a dark stain on the brightest day, which would evolve into a fundamental perception of universal process as death in birth, endless images of a dead foetus. Circumstances seemed to conspire to reaffirm these images. In the year after Otto's death, Sylvia first witnessed a marriage ceremony, acting as flower girl at the wedding of her "Aunt Dotty," Aurelia's sister Dorothy, who would eventually adopt two children and move to another part of Massachusetts. A funeral procession had symbolically translated itself into a wedding march; and the mothering sea could, during a moment of hurricane passion, assume monstrous features.

Sylvia did not attend her father's funeral. Aurelia took the sensible position that the children should remain at home, in order that their grief might be softened and the problem of adapting to Otto's loss made that much easier to bear. In later years, Sylvia regarded this as one of her mother's major sins, a sign that she had not really loved her husband. It is also possible that Aurelia had perhaps unconsciously let slip some of her own feelings that Otto had left her in a financial bind, a struggling widow with two children to raise and no income available beyond what she could bring in herself by going out to work. An observation in *The Bell Jar* by a sardonic Esther appears to support this interpretation, while also presenting a rather cruel caricature of Aurelia's tendency to fall back upon banal Christian platitudes for guidance:

> My own mother wasn't much help. My mother had taught shorthand and typing to support us since my father died and secretly she hated it and hated him for dying and leaving no money because he didn't trust life insurance salesmen. She was always on to me to learn shorthand after college, so I'd have a practical skill as well as a college degree. "Even the apostles were tent-makers," she'd say. "They had to live, just the way we do."

The financial situation was, in fact, quite serious. After paying $37.50 for a plot in the Winthrop Cemetery, Aurelia had very little money left over for a tombstone. In accordance with Otto's wishes, his grave marker is the most modest in the entire cemetery, a small stone bearing nothing more than his name and birth and death dates, another cause for Sylvia's rage whenever she visited the grave on the Azalea Path. Moreover, Otto's departure in general did not receive the public attention befitting a man who had achieved an important measure of success in his field. None of the Boston papers carried an obituary, and the two accounts in Winthrop's weeklies were brief almost to the point of seeming curt. The more complete coverage appeared in the November 14, 1940, edition of the *Winthrop Review*:

Funeral services for Dr. Otto E. Plath were held on Saturday, November 9 at 3 p.m. Rev. Harry Belmont Hill, pastor of the First Methodist Church officiated. A large number of the faculty of Boston University where Dr. Plath was a professor of biology at the College of Liberal Arts attended. Representatives of the Boston University Lodge A. F. and A. M. were also present.

Dr. Plath made his home at 92 Johnson Avenue with his wife Mrs. Aurelia S. Plath and two children, Sylvia and Warren. He is also survived by two brothers and two sisters. Interment was in Winthrop Cemetery.[13]

Soon after Otto's death, Aurelia secured a teaching post at Boston University's School for Secretarial Studies, no longer a separate college, and asked her parents and brother Frank to move in with her to share expenses and take care of the children while she was away. For the Schobers it was a sad time since they had to abandon the home they had loved and cared for over so many years. The house would be listed as "vacant" through 1941, not being sold until 1942 to a family named Whelan, who recall "that the Schobers often came to visit the house after they sold it," as if reluctant finally to surrender it. The Schobers are dim figures, but the few survivors who remember them at all refer to Frank Sr. as a sturdy, pleasant man of benign aspect who rarely spoke—his typical immigrant drive for success is reflected in his steady advancement from "waiter" to "head waiter" to "manager" during the course of his residence in Winthrop—and to his wife Aurelia as a near stereotype of the Viennese grandmother, maternal, warm, and domestically efficient.

Other external events continued to intrude, but Sylvia was caught up in the normal, hectic activities of her generation, attending a local school that was "genuinely public," rubbing elbows with Winthrop's diverse adolescents, "Irish Catholics, German Jews, Swedes, Negroes, Italians and that rare, pure Mayflower dropping, somebody *English*." In a slightly fictionalized article about her youth Sylvia wrote for *Punch*

(April 3, 1963) several months before her suicide, "America! America!",
the ambience is captured perfectly: "Education—laid on free of charge
for the lot of us, a lovely slab of depressed American public. *We* weren't
depressed, of course. We left that to our parents, who eked out one child
or two, and slumped dumbly after work and frugal suppers over their
radios to listen to news of the 'home country' and a black-moustached
man named Hitler." Each day in class, Sylvia and her classmates pledged
allegiance to the flag, hands over their hearts, and sang "America the
Beautiful" and other "songs full of powder-smoke and patriotics to
impossible, wobbly soprano tunes." But it was after school, free of adult
restraints, that the children acted out their classic version of American
youth, imitating a pattern of life which could be found in a million other
towns and cities across the country.

What made Winthrop unique, especially for Sylvia, was the sea all
around it, though it did not effect the standard games and pastimes of the
era: "The sea we knew something about. Terminus of almost every
street, it buckled and swashed and tossed, out of its grey formlessness,
china plates, wooden monkeys, elegant shells and dead men's shoes. Wet
salt winds raked our playgrounds endlessly—those Gothic composites of
gravel, macadam, granite and bald, flailed earth wickedly designed to
bark and scour the tender knee. There we traded playing cards (for the
patterns on the backs) and sordid stories, jumped clothes rope, shot
marbles, and enacted the radio and comic book dramas of our day
('Who knows what evil lurks in the hearts of men? The Shadow
knows—nyah, nyah, nyah!' or 'Up in the sky, look! It's a bird, it's a
plane, it's Superman!')."

In another fictionalized memoir, published earlier during her college
days, Sylvia likewise dwelled on Winthrop and her formative years.[14] In
"Superman and Paula Brown's New Snowsuit," she speaks of kneeling
by her room window each night to contemplate "the lights of Boston
that blazed and blinked far off across the darkening water" and to marvel
"at the moving beacons on the runway" of Logan Airport across the
bay, before retiring at last: "All night I dreamed of flying." Daydreams
were obsessed with the same image: "Mother believed that I should have
an enormous amount of sleep, and so I was never really tired when I
went to bed. This was the best time of day, when I could lie in the vague
twilight, drifting off to sleep, making up dreams inside my head the way
they should go. My flying dreams were as believable as a landscape by
Dali . . ."

Ostensibly, "Superman and Paula Brown's New Snowsuit" is a story,
though there was no attempt to change names. Uncle Frank, who was

now living with the Plaths, remained Uncle Frank and was projected as the little girl's Superman in the flesh. But historical reality also impinged upon the daydreamer's imagination, and there is a poignant scene which is pure autobiography:

> That same winter, war was declared, and I remember sitting by the radio with Mother and Uncle Frank and feeling a queer foreboding in the air. Their voices were low and serious, and their talk was of planes and German bombs. Uncle Frank said something about Germans in America being put in prison for the duration, and Mother kept saying over and over again about daddy: "I'm only glad Otto didn't live to see this; I'm only glad Otto didn't live to see it come to this."

This is the same Aurelia condemned in *The Bell Jar* for not having mourned her husband's death sufficiently, and for persisting to search for a silver lining in the darkest clouds:

> Then I remembered that I had never cried for my father's death.
> My mother hadn't cried either. She had just smiled and said what a merciful thing it was for him he had died, because if he had lived he would have been crippled and an invalid for life, and he couldn't have stood that, he would rather have died than had that happen.

Aurelia was possibly quite right in both instances, but it is easy to see why she and her daughter were destined to live out their lives together in two vastly different galaxies.

In school the war became another occasion for Sylvia to demonstrate her superior skills. She earned the fifth-grade prize for drawing the best civil-defense sign. And yet, there was a psychological impact as well, on the school at large and perhaps on the entire generation that would subsequently grow to become the "apathetic" youth of the 1950's: "Every now and then we would practice an air raid. The fire bell would ring and we would take up our coats and pencils and file down the creaking stairs to the basement where we sat in special corners according to our color tags, and put the pencils between our teeth so the bombs wouldn't make us bite our tongues by mistake. Some of the little children in lower grades would cry because it was dark in the cellar, with only the bare ceiling lights on the cold black stone." White and black extremes, juvenile terror, the enactment of a nightmare—all this had an extremely unfortunate impact upon adolescent sensibilities, echoing and enlarging whatever insecurities already lay coiled in Sylvia's young mind.

At home, fantasy was encouraged by Aurelia's reading aloud to the children and generally impressing upon them the significance of art and literature as social graces. Their favorite book was *Wind in the Willows*, and Sylvia memorized every rhyme: "The Queen and her ladies-in-waiting/ Sat by the window and sewed . . ." But another momentous, threatening change was in store. Aurelia had decided that a move inland was desirable, if only to help alleviate Sylvia's sinus condition and her brother's asthma. For a child, of course, any change in residence is disturbing, and for Sylvia and Warren, still upset by the loss of their father, the move must have been dreadful to envision. Classmates and neighborhood friends would be left behind forever, along with the comforting security of familiar places.

It was in 1942 when Aurelia purchased a house in Wellesley and she, the children, and the grandparents departed from Winthrop for good. Addie I. Willard, one of Sylvia's teachers at the Edward B. Newton School in Winthrop, vividly recollects being given a copy of Professor Plath's *Bumble Bees and Their Ways*: "The book was presented to me by Sylvia and her brother when they came to my office, with their mother, to get their discharge cards as they were moving from Winthrop to Boston." [15] Miss Willard's other memories of Sylvia give some idea of the positive impression Sylvia made upon others, particularly teachers, even long after she had disappeared from their lives: "I was always in close contact with my children and remember Sylvia very clearly. She was a beautiful child, very intelligent, interested in everything, did excellent work. I would say she was a normal girl in every way, but was badly wounded by the loss of her father, whom she adored. It is not strange that after all these years I should remember Sylvia so well, for she was truly outstanding in every way."

For Sylvia herself, looking back upon the dual tragedy of losing Otto and Winthrop, losing her entire childhood in a way, the response was another recourse to art and the reassuring order it engendered: "And this is how it stiffens, my vision of that seaside childhood. My father died, we moved inland. Whereon those nine first years of my life sealed themselves off like a ship in a bottle—beautiful, inaccessible, obsolete, a fine, white, flying myth."

Growing up female in America. What a liability! You grew up with your ears full of cosmetic ads, love songs, advice columns, whoreoscopes, Hollywood gossip, and moral dilemmas on the level of TV soap operas. What litanies the advertisers of the good life chanted at you! What curious catechisms! . . . It didn't matter, you see, whether you had an IQ of 170 or an IQ of 70, you were brain-washed all the same.

ERICA JONG

2

I Cast Off My Identity

Aurelia's decision to leave Winthrop for Wellesley was far more than a sensible economic move. It also represented a shift from a lower-middle and middle-class setting to an upper-middle-class college town, conceivably a bid to provide her children with the perfect WASP childhood. In 1942 Wellesley was the third wealthiest town in the state and the richest per capita.[1] Its 15,000 residents, 2,500 of whom were listed as "students," consisted of a large number of professional people and upwardly mobile business types. The town boasted seven highly respectable schools, including Wellesley College and the Babson Institute. Negroes and Jews were notable by their relative absence.

This was the town which would help shape Sylvia's life from the age of nine to the age of eighteen, when she left for Smith College, and would help reinforce the middle-class values filtered through her mother, who regarded Wellesley from the beginning as a paradise of ultimate respectability, financial, educational, and social. This was the environment whose attitudes would be constantly on display in Sylvia's early poetry and stories, particularly the latter, where the heroines are middle-class Americans to their fingertips, despite minor "rebellions" against such things as bigotry and mindless sororities, and the environment that would later be attacked so vehemently in *The Bell Jar*. This was the environment which provided the essential moral and social framework for her entire life, provided not only the main features of her surface masks, but their underpinnings as well, the adherence to domestic cleanliness, Spock-inspired motherhood, and óther public virtues. Sylvia and Wellesley are almost inseparable in their basic New England sense of sin and duty.

The pretty house which Aurelia purchased at 2 3 Elmwood Road was a smallish, white-framed, two-story building with a screened-in side porch on a half-acre corner plot. Neighboring houses were similarly modest in size and generally not as attractive, though pleasantly rural under the shade of countless trees, the whole area, known as Wellesley Fells, having been thrown open during the war to tract housing, primarily for veterans and their families. It offered an opportunity for Aurelia and people like her with limited incomes to become part of an upper-middle-class town not more than twenty minutes away from Boston by car, and to take advantage of the rich resources channeled through the town's many excellent public institutions. Aurelia joined the local Unitarian fellowship (the church she had attended in Jamaica Plain when she was first married) and became one of its Sunday School teachers.

In the years ahead Aurelia would do everything in her power to ensure that Sylvia and Warren would have "high achievement" childhoods. She became, in the words of Clement Moore, Warren's roommate later at Exeter, "a pusher," the chief force behind "a real Calvinist family" in which "the achievement ethic" held sway.[2] This is not an especially winning picture, but one that nevertheless involved many real sacrifices by the hard-pressed mother and a tireless effort to see that her children had all the advantages given their much better off contemporaries. These included summer camps, Scouting, sailing, piano and viola lessons, dance "assemblies," painting and water-color lessons, and numerous other, frequently expensive extra-curricular activities. If Aurelia did not always appreciate the huge gap which could arise between achievement per se and actual happiness, she certainly cannot be faulted for neglecting any activity which she felt would emotionally and intellectually enhance the lives and future prospects of her offspring. They seemed destined to have everything their mother ever lacked as a child, what can only be described as an ideal adolescence, and if it failed in the end to produce the desired result, a contented, secure, fully rounded adult, perhaps it was an inevitable outgrowth of her society's false emphasis upon competitive performance rather than self-realization;

and the tendency, at least on Sylvia's part, to perfect a mask which kept hidden possible resentments against a mother's oppressive bourgeois values.

Sylvia and Warren were enrolled in the Marshall Perrin Grammar School, a large brick building surrounded by several acres of green grounds, which was within convenient walking distance of their home. There the two Plath children soon took up where they had left off in Winthrop, quickly impressing their teachers with their intelligence and agreeable penchant for extra work. They both earned near perfect grades and several awards for excellence in academic and service areas, and their mother continued her own campaign to ensure that no aspect of their education was slighted, often taking them to the tiny, one-room library a few blocks from Elmwood Road on Route 9, the "main" street that led south into Wellesley proper and north towards Boston. If nothing else, Sylvia's childhood would supply her with a deep and abiding respect for books and whoever wrote them.

In September 1944 Sylvia entered the Alice L. Phillips Junior High School as a seventh grader. This was located in the heart of Wellesley, across the street from the Unitarian Church. Her career at Phillips followed the pattern already established earlier in Winthrop and at Perrin, where her brother remained two years behind her, success sparking success in a dizzying profusion of awards and special commendations. Various teachers from Phillips remember Sylvia as a bright and creative young girl who was somewhat socially isolated among her classmates. Miss Helen Lawson, a ninth-grade English teacher, described her as "extremely neat, personally and about her work," labelling her "a perfectionist" and "one of the few who stand out personally—quiet, easy, willing, and good, morally and scholastically." [3] Another English teacher, Frances Baldwin, characterized Sylvia glowingly as a "very intelligent, bright student, interested in creative writing and successful in her classes." [4] And Anna C. Craig, who would also know her in high school, recalled that "she was an avid reader, read in great depth, actually devoured Shakespearian literature, exhibited a very creative ability in expressing herself both verbally and in writing." [5]

The portrait that emerges from these observations suggests a veritable prodigy at work, one who also possessed the tact and literary insights of a much older person. Sylvia was apparently of sufficient sophistication to know precisely what was required of her, how to make adults take notice. But it was in her poetry that she found a means of discharging at least some of her secret anxieties. Her reading of Shakespeare, whether as deep as Miss Craig thought or not, had given her a rudimentary insight into the fundamental poetic process and its mechanics. All of the verses saved from her junior-high days demonstrate a convincing mastery of basic poetic forms. Still the poetry was approached only as another socially accepted avenue to public success, with Aurelia's proud approval, and not yet as a tool for unearthing the remains of a buried self. It earned Sylvia an Honorable Mention in the National Scholastic Literary Contest for 1947, which must have convinced her she was on the right path.

Most of the poems appeared in the school's literary magazine, *The Phillipian*, over the next three years (from 1944 to 1947), although she never became a member of its staff.[6] They are typical adolescent attempts to find images for the standard phenomena of nature, very few of them exhibiting any special aptitude for metaphor, but all of them remaining clever demonstrations of a highly intelligent mind at work upon the problems of method. Her first effort, "The Spring Parade," which appeared in the April 1945 issue, moves from an opening image of moribund vegetation, "Deep in earth they long have lain/ Waiting for the warm spring rain," to the traditional resurrection, "Through the dewy, cobwebbed glade/ Marches Nature's Spring Parade!" Here is the early love for alliteration, a child's delight, as well as the determined insistence upon defeating the challenge of rhyme. In the same issue, she had another poem called "March," which begins with "wind-wolves" who "are prowling about today" and concludes on the same joyous trumpet blast: "And as over Earth the planets sing,/ We'll hear at last the Song of Spring!"

In the June 1945 edition of *The Phillipian*, Sylvia's contribution would be another brief nature poem entitled "Rain," which commences with drought and a farmer praying for rain and ends with "The quiet singing of the rain,/ The silv'ry rain." It was in her second year of junior high that Sylvia's poetry began to move away from this structural allegiance to a rising narrative line and assert, at last, her affinity for a negative climax. Her description of "A Winter Sunset," which appeared February 1946, has to be quoted in full as a prime example of what will become a typical Plath poem:

> Over the earth's dark rim
> The daylight softly fades
> The sky from orange to gold
> And then to coppen shades.
>
> The moon hangs, a globe of iridescent light
> In a frosty winter sky,

> While against the western glow one sees
> The bare, black skeletons of the trees.

There is a nice balance to this poem and a familiar structural tidiness, the slow drift from sunset through dusk to evening, but more important there is also a relaxed, more sure-handed manipulation of language, no great sense of a forced cheerfulness. Despite an absence of originality, the poem's general restraint and visual accuracy bodes well for its young author, as does the precocious command of linguistic resources. Those final two lines are effective metaphorically and obviously better suited Sylvia's own Gothic imagination: skeletons and winter landscapes, mortality's ever-beckoning reaches. "The Snowflake Star," from April 1946, has its moments as well, but there is a temporary return to strained gaiety and a continued pursuit of the conventional. The melting of snowflakes in the speaker's mitten, the "fairest jewels from Nature's Land," leads to thoughts of possible death, disaster, but instead the climax envisions a drop of dew as a mirror where a "happy thought took root and grew" and "still it lingers on."

This determination to be cheerful, a poetic echo of Sylvia's public mask, is nowhere more in evidence than in a memorial poem printed in the November 1946 issue of *The Phillipian*, written for a Miss Catherine Cox, a teacher at the school for twenty-two years who had recently passed away. Young Sylvia turned once again to nature for her imagery and discovered an eternal possibility for hope. After contemplating "leaden" skies of winter and stinging snowflakes, the poet spies "behind the cold white stillness" a reassuring re-birth, "the promise of spring." Another poem from the same edition, "October," reduces autumnal horrors to "spirals of blue smoke" and "tang of russet apples," standard disguises and doubtless real experiences, but the climax implies something else, something less sweet. Ripening in the meadow is a pumpkin, "Lovely yellow" of course, but "Waiting for Hallowe'en."

An interesting poem, which was printed in February 1947, when Sylvia was less than four months away from graduation, is "Fireside Reveries," interesting because it touched, ever so lightly, upon her awareness of herself as a "daydreamer" and a potential poet of importance. A girl is pictured sitting before the conventional fireplace, a book of poems in her lap; sparks leap to "ascend the sky/ And then are lost into the night." Ephemeral echoes of her dreams, her "gold castles in the air," dreams of attainment, "My thoughts to shining fame aspire," betray a skillful capacity for linking an idea and state of mind with a nicely dove-tailing poetic conceit, sparks and dreams, flames and fame.

From a personal standpoint, it expressed (perhaps for the first time aloud) Sylvia's belief that the direction of her life, its relentless appetite for success and public recognition, would involve a literary career.

Her final contribution to *The Phillipian*, which would also publish several rather stiff prose pieces by Warren over the next two years, came in April 1947 with "Sea Symphony," a poem, and "Victory," a short-story—Sylvia had published several stories in earlier issues but none is really worth investigating.[7] The poem is a happy evocation of seashore details that seems genuinely delighted with itself, a string of aural images that commences with "The slap of the waves on the wet sand shore" and concludes: "The hazy nights and the moon's red glow/ All make a glorious symphony." The story is a trick piece which revolves around the dramatic situation of a woman named Judith besieged by a rainstorm, whose car is stuck in mud and who is trying desperately to reach a telephone at a farm house to warn the town that its dam was bursting. Before she can reach a phone—she is herself a telephone operator, the first of many "ordinary" Plath heroines—a stranger grabs her and begins to strangle her. Then, with a nice O'Henry twist, the rain and lightning cease, and Judith arises unhurt and smiling. It is only a movie!

The success garnered by Sylvia through her writing was nothing compared to her achievements in other areas of school life—all duly recorded in *The Townsman*'s school page, which was occasionally written by the students themselves, and clipped out by Aurelia with maternal zeal. Sylvia's name does not begin to surface in these columns until 1947, during her last year at Phillips. The school's assembly period for January 8 was devoted to a demonstration of a photographic memory by William Wallace and campaign presentations by students running for senior class offices. Frank Irish and Barbara Bottsford, both friends of Sylvia, were campaigning against each other for President, and Sylvia herself was running for Secretary against three others. It was the first time she had ever tried for any school post and suggests perhaps that she was attempting to correct her "loner" label. The actual campaign speeches were delivered to the school on January 15, and Sylvia's presentation was remarkable for its originality: "Sylvia Plath's speech was in the form of a parody on *Hiawatha* and was followed by the entrance of a boat with passenger which went across the stage to demonstrate smooth sailing with Sylvia as secretary." None of it helped, however, as Sylvia lost out to a girl named Sarah Bond.

But the following week's assembly, a spelling bee conducted among representatives from all twenty-one English classes, saw Sylvia come in second. Interestingly, the assembly was chaired by her brother Warren, whose status as a freshman, a seventh grader, had not deterred him from already making his mark. Sylvia was also a participant in a special program on February 5 dedicated to "The Spirit of Ancient Rome," but was not in the school play, *A Case of Springtime*, when it appeared on March 20, although she did place fourth in the poster competition for it. On May 29 the Unitarian Church presented books as awards to students who had maintained a perfect attendance record over the year, Sylvia and Warren being among the recipients. The final assembly of the year, which took place near the end of June, was dedicated primarily to awards and Sylvia was triumphant.

Thirty certificates for excellence in oral and written expression were given out, several of Sylvia's friends winning them and Warren collecting one of the ten granted to the seventh grade. But three special students, one from each grade, were selected for the highest awards, a book on a subject they were particularly interested in pursuing. Sylvia was the special student for the seniors and was given Brooks' and Warren's *Understanding Poetry*. She also earned a unique recommendation card for having straight "A's" during her three years at Phillips, and another one for a perfect record of punctuality. Nor was this all: "Sylvia Plath was awarded a sixth letter, which is a junior high school pennant and commendation card for being the only pupil in the history of the school who had ever earned enough credits for a sixth letter." Finally, she "was awarded an achievement certificate for a drawing that was given first place at a national contest at Carnegie Institute."

This kind of recognition, besides further enlarging Sylvia's anxiety-driven narcissism, was public confirmation that she was indeed a golden girl destined for great things. And yet she maintained her friendly mask with studied concentration and dutifully followed her mother's guidance in mastering the cultural and social arts. She took her piano and viola lessons and eventually would join the high-school orchestra, being "forced" into it, according to a later interview, despite her tone deafness, which would prevent her from ever accomplishing much more than woodenly banging out popular tunes on the piano. Even near the end of her life, she would be complaining about her musical deficiency to a friend: "She couldn't feel music. She used to say to me, 'I see it, I see how beautiful it is, but I can't *feel* it!' " [8] The painting and watercolor lessons she loved, because she did believe she had a certain talent for it, as several awards seem to affirm, and enjoyed the satisfaction it brought. The summer camps, too, were pleasurable experiences, the Scout camp, the sailing camp, and the like, but she resented having to participate in

Mrs. Gulliette Ferguson's locally famous "dance assemblies" at the Maugus Club and would never become more than an adequate dancer.

Bicycle riding and tennis were her favorite sports and she yearned to take skiing lessons but knew that was beyond her mother's financial capacity. She did babysit to earn extra money and in her senior year at Phillips let her mother teach her typing, which she mastered quickly. Anything requiring intelligence and only a minimum of manual dexterity were well within her eager grasp. Back in the sixth grade at Perrin Grammar School, she had demonstrated her intellectual ability on the Revised Stanford-Binet Intelligence Test. Dorothy H. Humphrey, a resident of Wellesley and a senior in Boston University's School for Education, was taking a course in "ability testing" during the 1943–1944 school year.[9] As part of her class assignment, she had to administer the test "to a number of subjects of my own choosing" and naturally turned to her own previous elementary school, Perrin, for aid. The school readily gave its permission—I.Q. tests were then still considered of prime significance—and Miss Humphrey remembers the experience clearly: "One of my subjects was a very pretty sixth grade girl—Sylvia Plath. She turned out to be a very unusual and exciting 'testee.' She was keenly interested in the test and seemed to enjoy the whole lengthy procedure. It was lengthy because she continued to answer items correctly at levels far above average for her age. When I scored Sylvia's test I was excited to find that the results indicated an I.Q. of about 160 (I don't remember the exact figure). This is, of course, well into the 'genius' classification."

Such intelligence was the curse and blessing of Sylvia's entire life; as she said later, "there is no escaping the mind." But it did make the business of winning public approval that much easier for her though she was never characterized by any of her teachers as a "grind." Sylvia had gained many friends at Phillips, all of whom would continue on with her to the senior high school, Bradford, in the fall of 1947. Louise Guisey and Barbara Bottsford were her two closest girl friends, although she was on fairly congenial terms with all the girls in class; and Frank Irish and "Richard Willard" were probably her closest boy friends. Irish, who would co-edit the high-school paper with her in their senior year, had no inkling of Sylvia's future fame as a writer. "I do remember her as an excellent student, with something of a bent for things literary, but I had no foretaste that she would succeed as she did. Of course, I had only occasional glimpses of the intense kind of person she probably was." [10]

Trying to define the precise nature of their relationship, Irish goes on to say, "We were friends, and I think once or twice she had a crush (if that is the right word) on me, and, at another time, I on her; but these spells never seemed to occur at the same time, so our friendship never became as deep or as close as it might have been." Richard Willard, whose elder brother "Buddy" Sylvia admired from afar throughout her high-school career for his curly blond locks, good looks, academic brilliance, and athletic ability—qualities that Richard himself possessed in large measure, remembers a similar pattern through junior and senior high. He recalls Sylvia, whom he first met when she was nine or ten years old as "children of friends," as "a very sensitive person" with "an extraordinary intellect," who played to win whenever they engaged in any board games but heaped praise on him if he did succeed in defeating her, which was rare.[11]

He also remembers dating her several times in high school, where they were in the same group, but found himself caught in a dilemma, "quite attracted to her physically" and "fond of her as a person," and yet, "at the same time, I think I was afraid of her, recognized a genius that was running rings around my average intellect." The result was friendship rather than a romantic attachment. Later he would visit with her after she had just returned from school or a summer job: "I would ring her doorbell, and we would go walking in the then undeveloped section of Wellesley Hills. We would talk in a way that I can still remember, having an ability to share feelings that you would like to have with a sister, with a best friend, that men rarely do, sharing our sensitivities, not on matters of humdrum, everyday affairs, but on life goals, etc. And she was a good listener." However, she remained "awkward," a loner "who didn't date a lot, scholastically competitive," and "spent long hours reading, writing, studying." But in high school "she turned intensely, passionately to literature, and I was no foil for her literary interests."

Richard Willard also felt that Warren was "a quiet, studious, sensitive, gentle person," and he remembers Mrs. Plath as possessing some of the same virtues, a woman who appeared younger than she was and "welcomed my dating her daughter." All in all, he found her "a sweet, widowed lady who was beset by more problems than perhaps she could handle, taking care of her parents and the children. I had the impression of a person working under tension and fatigue, providing a great deal of incentive for Sylvia's writing." As for the relationship between Sylvia and her brother, he described it as "close and singularly free of adolescent rivalry," Sylvia bestowing "maternal as well as sisterly attention" upon her younger brother. Willard admits to having "no inkling of her psychosexual make-up" except to note that Sylvia always presented a "very feminine appearance" and came from "the same Puritan background" as he. His sole recollection of any allusion to the dead Otto was an impression that he had doted on his daughter and had been rather autocratic at home.

Another boy who would play a fairly important role in Sylvia's life entered the scene in September of 1946. His name was Philip McCurdy, and he first met her through Warren, who was a classmate of his in the seventh grade. Being two years younger than Sylvia, Philip would not be regarded as a potential suitor by her until college; but he quickly became one of her closest friends and companions, sharing her interest in literature and, in particular, art. Like Richard, he recalls with fondness many meditative walks through the woods at Sylvia's side, discussing large social and personal issues like many other serious-minded, highly self-conscious teenagers. Nature was all around them in beautiful abundance whatever they did. The Hunnewell fields, forest, and pond, a favorite necking spot, was a mere two blocks away from Sylvia's door, and Lake Waban and its own extensive woods were not much further off in the opposite direction, all within easy reach by foot or bicycle.

Philip McCurdy was obviously intrigued by Sylvia from the beginning, perhaps motivated in part by a disruptive family life which had turned him into a self-confessed "school rat," a boy who delighted in every aspect of his school existence to the extent of spending more hours there than at home. Whatever the reason, his warm relationship with Sylvia still was impressed in his memory many years later: "Most of all, it took so little to start off the very intensive, introspective discussions between us—a flower, a frog, a moon, a breeze. If my recall sounds all euphoric, it is simply that I cannot dredge up a harsh or cruel word, gesture or slight. We did not cling together to wall out a hard world, rather we revelled equally in its worries, joys, wonderings and frustrations. Parent figures remained mostly tolerant and bemused. And we each had full, lively *outside* relations to other people—other dates, other friendships which, curiously, rarely intersected." [12]

There may well have been a deeper romantic infatuation than Philip was willing to admit to himself at the time, but in the main his idyllic recollections are not too far removed from the portrait painted by Richard Willard about his own relationship with Sylvia. Philip was her "baby" throughout high school, a safe younger male whom she did not have to compete against or attract, another brotherly type whose sensitivity, intelligence, American good looks, and common interest in the arts made him an ideal companion. Their apprentice exercises with ink drawings in particular kept them together; and the resemblance between their sketches from that time is remarkable—all exhibiting the same love of detail, the same solid black outlines, the same accurate eye.

Sylvia also liked the idea that Philip was set upon pursuing "the natural sciences," which she respected with a Liberal Arts major's awe, partially out of loyalty to her father and partially out of an earlier determination to become a doctor herself, to master a field of knowledge that appeared so alien and incomprehensible to her fantasy-oriented imagination. Her entire background placed a premium on practical skills, as her mother must have preached often enough, and put doctors in a category above the rest of mankind—perhaps almost in the realm of Otto himself. But "puppy love" for Sylvia, when she entered Bradford High School in September of 1947, was little more than a distraction and a pleasant way of occupying spare time. Boys like Richard, Frank, and later Philip were used mainly as tennis partners, conversation foils, and handsome escorts.

On entering high school Sylvia and her classmates were given an entrance exam in grammar and vocabulary, and the twenty or so top students were then admitted into Wilbury Crockett's English 21 course, which concentrated on American Literature. Below them was another college-preparation class run along more standard lines and, at the bottom, two general and vocational classes—purgatory itself. Being in Mr. Crockett's class was both an honor and a guarantee of doing college-level work in a college-like atmosphere, with each class conducted in seminar fashion from the start. The students had to buy their own books, perhaps as many as forty-five in a single year—which must have been a serious strain on Mrs. Plath's tight budget—and there were no such things as formal tests or examinations. But each student was expected to submit four 5,000-word papers a year. After being corrected by Mr. Crockett, these essays then had to be defended in front of the class. In English 21, Sylvia, for the first time, would read such writers as Fitzgerald, Hemingway, Stevens, Twain, T. S. Eliot, Frost, and Dickinson, for whom she would develop a special fondness.

And yet Mr. Crockett's classes were much more than advanced literary courses; they were a world unto themselves. Known as "Crocketeers" by the rest of the school, his students were expected actively to participate in every aspect of high-school life: to run the school newspaper and magazine, to put on the term plays, to arrange special assemblies, and in general to maintain extracurricular programs at a proper pitch. Besides the class lectures and discussions, some of the Crocketeers were taken by their teacher to a theatre or public lecture in

Boston every two weeks; and each fall meant a trip to New York, while spring signaled a trip to Washington, D.C., or a visit to the U.N.

Writing of all kinds was encouraged, and the students were expected by Mr. Crockett to enter their fiction, poetry, and essays in the *Atlantic Monthly* and *Scholastic Magazine* contests. Oddly enough, Sylvia would never win the *Atlantic's* top prize, despite her verse's comparative skill; though she did earn several Merit Awards and would get Honorable Mention in her senior year. Mr. Crockett was struck by Sylvia's creative gift from the beginning, "too talented to believe," and reacted warmly to her obvious enthusiasm for the writers studied in class.[13] Her papers were always perceptive, well-argued, and neatly typed, the latter a trademark by now. An almost compulsive attention to detail was still evident in everything she did and wrote, but her excitement and passion, however exaggerated, for the writers she was reading for the first time seemed genuine. In a class of exceptional students, she stood out as obviously destined for ultimate success.

The negative side of Bradford did not become clear until later in life: either that or Sylvia had not been able earlier to voice her objections out of some psychological need to keep her scholastic universe intact. Whatever the reason, it was in "America! America!", as a woman of thirty, that Sylvia tried to articulate some of the pressures created by high schools like Bradford, and by the parents behind their frantic emphasis on superficial values:

Later, the college obsession would seize us, a subtle, terrifying virus. Everybody had to go to *some* college or other. A business college, a junior college, a state college, a secretarial college, an Ivy League college, a pig farmer's college. The book first, then the work. By the time we (future cop and electronic brain alike) exploded into our prosperous, post-war high school, full-time guidance counselors jogged our elbows at ever-diminishing intervals to discuss motives, hopes, school subjects, jobs—and colleges. Excellent teachers showered on to us like meteors: Biology teachers holding up human brains, English teachers inspiring us with a personal ideological fierceness about Tolstoy and Plato, Art teachers leading us through the slums of Boston, then back to the Easel to hurl public school gouache with social awareness and fury. Eccentricities, the perils of being *too* special, were reasoned and cooed from us like sucked thumbs.

It is obvious that Sylvia is speaking about her own career at Bradford; the reference to the English teachers' fierceness about Tolstoy and Plato fits Mr. Crockett, and it is equally obvious that she especially resented the guidance program: "The girls' guidance counsellor diagnosed my problem straight off. I was just too dangerously brainy. My high, pure string of straight A's might, without proper extra-curricular tempering, snap me into the void. More and more, the colleges wanted All-Round Students." She listened and entered into the necessary circle of winning friends and influencing adults, "my widening circle of activities—chewing orange sections at the quarters of girls' basketball games (I had made the team), painting mammoth L'il Abners and Daisy Maes for the class dances, pasting up dummies of the school newspaper at midnight while my already dissipated co-editor read out the jokes at the bottom of the columns of the *New Yorker*"—the co-editor was Frank Irish.

Sylvia conformed, and with a vengeance. Philip McCurdy has described her as "a super-normal teenager," [14] and she later admitted that "I became a rabid teenage pragmatist," which meant "levelling my bobby-socks to match those of my school mates" and wearing the conventional uniform, "the pageboy hairdo, squeaky clean, the skirt and sweater, the 'loafers,' those scuffed copies of Indian moccasins." She even joined one of the two high-school sororities then in existence at Bradford, enduring a humiliating initiation period, only to discover that the sorority meetings consisted of a brood of prosaic girls who "ate cake and catted about the Saturday night date."

But none of this interfered with her relentless march towards academic victories, and there was enough of the naïve in her to make conformity appear reasonable. Authority spoke and she listened, like a good girl scout. On Thursday, September 4, the superintendent of schools, William Gaige, welcomed the students to a new term with cheerleader allusions to a "happy ship" and their need to keep it "spic and span." A Mr. Pierce followed with a metaphor about casting a fly upon water, which he elaborated into an educational parable. To what extent Sylvia embraced these stock platitudes is impossible to say, though that haunting intelligence must have made her feel acutely uncomfortable at times. Sylvia still clung to the supernatural possibilities posited by the Unitarian Church and the Christian culture nurturing her, listening to her mother's homilies, attending services and Sunday school each week, accepting the framework of the world around her and its promise of deeper meanings. A religious context was as natural as air in Wellesley, though Philip McCurdy believed she had already become an agnostic.

It permeated Bradford's daily life as well. Each morning, over the loudspeaker, the classes were greeted by hymns, psalms, readings from religious books, and other inspirational bromides—despite America's supposed separation of church and state. Mr. Crockett's class naturally took the lead. The "Crocketeers" arranged and delivered the morning broadcasts, along with several other more cultural programs. During the week of May 13, 1948, for instance, the English 21, 31, and 41 classes wrote and produced a series of radio plays that dealt with their particular term's area of literary concentration. Sylvia's class was responsible for putting out three plays, an adaptation of Poe's "Monsieur Bon-Bon," a play about World War II by Norman Corwin, and an original play written by Sylvia in collaboration with a girl named Mary Ventura entitled *The Island*. Other cultural events from Sylvia's first year included various field trips to plays and movies and submission of material to the *Atlantic*'s school contest, which resulted in two "Crocketeers" earning top honors in the essay competition and nineteen others garnering merit ratings. Sylvia won two merit awards for two poems she had submitted, "April, 1948" and "The Farewell."

From almost every standpoint, Bradford was an extension of Sylvia's career at Phillips. Not only were her friends the same but the milieu of competitive yet insular learning experiences was strikingly similar, a smaller version of Wellesley itself, protective, friendly, intellectually rich, if slightly too sweet on occasion. The transition from junior to senior high had been painless; and a glance at *The Phillipian*'s final issue for Sylvia, where her picture and those of the other seniors were displayed, along with a few labels and an identifying sentence, shows that her future was neatly laid out. Her nickname is listed as "Siv," although "Syl" was more common, and her hobby as "writing stories," while it was also noted that she had belonged to the "Booklovers" club and thought of her future prospects in terms of journalism. The identifying tag was an odd reminder of Otto's appetite, perhaps a reflection of Aurelia's generosity at lunch time or Sylvia's desire to imitate her father: "Oh! Those sandwiches!"

Despite her circle of friends and generally congenial relationships with other students, the golden child, the surface Sylvia, could not shake her loner role. As a senior she continued to "pal around" with Frank Irish and Richard Willard, and increasingly with Philip McCurdy, who was now at Bradford in the tenth grade. They took their long walks and bicycle rides together, went on private picnics, played tennis, and pursued their endless discussions about the inner meaning of life's various forces. Sex never intruded, "baby" still regarding her with awe; she was his idealized first love, that inevitable phenomenon of emerging malehood.

Not that sex was taboo, at least conversationally. Like other teenagers with a literary background, they relished an image of themselves as mature adults, capable of discussing sex with intellectual detachment. Consequently, according to McCurdy, "in earlier years, we had discussed the probable effect of intercourse on her menstrual problems, as well as that great teenage paradox: the tampon vs. *the virgo intacta.*" With typical teenage self-absorption, Sylvia worried about her budding breasts, waistline, and thighs, which she felt were too thick. She wanted and needed to be sexually attractive, as her culture encouraged, but the idea of sex itself was somewhat disconcerting for personal and moral reasons. Her home and church emphasized the era's strict commitment to pre-marital virginity, while she herself would retain during adolescence a Puritan conception of sex as disgusting. To make matters worse, the onset of the menstrual cycle in her pubescence was accompanied by cramps and an irregular, copious flow. Given Sylvia's sexual confusion with reference to Otto, it is easy to get a picture of a tortured young girl who must have believed that the simple act of being a woman involved pain.

Sylvia rarely dated in the formal sense before her senior year, when she would snare a Williams boy, whom she "seemed serious about" in Richard Willard's words; but she did engage in the standard rites of juvenile mating, kissing, and petting in proper fashion, sending the boys home in a state of painful frustration. If her enormous curiosity made the prospect of sex intriguing, this was counterbalanced by strong feelings of social and religious propriety and not a little disgust. Only later would she even dare play with *double entendres*, a child's clever naughtiness.

In her junior year at Bradford, English 31 introduced Sylvia to British literature and her enthusiasms increased tenfold, now for Donne, Blake, Milton, Yeats, Auden—who would remain a favorite for years to come—and for Dylan Thomas, whom she imitated and idolized as the perfect example of the modern poet, excessive in language and life, on the road to a romantic doom. Other writers read outside of class were mostly women, such as Sara Teasdale and Edith Sitwell.

Sylvia impressed everyone with her wit and intelligence, and her readiness to laugh, but Mr. Crockett characterized it as "a little too ready." Once in class he was discussing the image of the rising sun used in a poem they had recently read and jokingly remarked that English 31 students could never appreciate the poem properly since none of them would ever get up early enough in the morning to see the sun rise. A few days later on a cold April morning, Mr. Crockett was aroused from his sleep at 2 A.M. by the front doorbell. When he answered it, he found Sylvia and several friends from the class gathered on the front porch, waiting to take him to a nearby hill to observe the sun rise. With a laugh, he agreed, dressed hurriedly, and then accompanied them on their expedition. Sylvia had been the plot's organizer. Playful, touched with wry humor, this unexpected visit demonstrated her sheer delight in accepting a challenge, chasing the unusual in an effort to make life more intense and interesting.

Mr. Crockett was one of the few people in Wellesley who had any conception of the Sylvia hiding beneath the surface. "I had the feeling she was going along for the ride even then," he remembers. In his view, she possessed the capacity both to "seal herself off" from others and to manipulate them "for what they could give her." Although only a teenager, she was already "very adept at role playing." But none of these insights prevented Sylvia and Mr. Crockett from becoming extremely close, as he did with most of his students, although a formal reserve necessarily remained, a reserve which Mr. Crockett encouraged in class by insisting that every pupil address one another by the title of either Mr. or Miss.

Mr. Crockett describes Sylvia at the time as being "very, very pretty," having beautiful skin and teeth, carrying her willowy tallness with studied grace—photographs indicate that she also had the correct "debutante's slouch." Such physical appeal, combined with her willingness to please, helped maintain her position as class star. Sylvia's mother, loaded down with good intentions, pushed her to perform. A few years later, while in the pit of schizophrenic depression after her unsuccessful suicide attempt, Sylvia would complain to a friend that her "mother never allowed me to be a woman."

For the three years that Sylvia was in Mr. Crockett's class, and years afterwards, teacher and student enjoyed "a great intellectual friendship." It is easy to understand how Sylvia might have come to look upon her affectionate, brilliant teacher as a positive father figure, one who had all of Otto's virtues and none of his supposed arrogance and despotism. Late in 1960, she would send a copy of *The Colossus* to Mr. Crockett from England, dedicated to the man "in whose classroom and wisdom these poems have root." Although hard put to make any positive comment about the poems, finding them a bit static and artificial, Mr. Crockett was deeply touched by the gesture.

The second year at Bradford continued Sylvia's exposure to a wide variety of cultural experiences, and her personal pursuit of honors. The year before, she had been among the thirty-two sophomores on the honor roll from the beginning, a position she would never relinquish, and had worked on the school paper, on the dance committee, and with the basketball team. Now she tried to maintain the same pace while further broadening her frame of reference. On September 16 the Crocketeers from English 31 and 41 accompanied Miss Palmer's English 32 class to Boston to see Lawrence Olivier's movie version of *Hamlet.* Three weeks later, English 31 engaged in a class series of panel discussions on philosophical works, touching upon duNoüy's *Human Destiny*, Barlow's *Man Against Myth*, and Toynbee's *Civilization on Trial*, which indicates the respect Mr. Crockett had for his pupils.

As expected, Sylvia was again on the honor roll when it was released on December 2 and again on February 17, 1949. The June results from the *Atlantic Monthly* and *Scholastic Magazine* contests were somewhat disappointing, however, with Sylvia not even earning a merit certificate, although she did win one of the five golden keys awarded to the class by the judges of *Scholastic Magazine*'s art competition. She was also a member of the large group, sixty-eight Crocketteers in all, that presented an end-of-term choric drama to the school. Another consolation was the knowledge that she and Frank Irish would be editing *The Bradford* in their senior year, a fact which earned a front-page story in the school paper, along with a picture of Sylvia, Frank, and several other editors, all friends and all from Mr. Crockett's class. The accompanying story stressed that Sylvia would be a good editor "because of her exceptional ability as a writer. Not only has she a keen critical eye, but also the noteworthy reputation of sticking to a task until it is done." The picture shows a smiling Sylvia in long hair, white peasant blouse, wide skirt, white bobby socks and inevitable loafers.

In September, when Sylvia returned to Bradford for her senior year, she was asked by the local paper *The Townsman* to write its "High School Highlights" column for the September 15, 1949, issue, which she did with near professional polish. Two weeks later, she and Frank Irish called their first staff meeting, and publication of *The Bradford* was under way. A different kind of public notice had been accorded Sylvia some months earlier, again due to Mr. Crockett and his use of the *Atlantic Monthly* in class. In March she and Jean Woods from English 31 had written a letter to the magazine in response to an article by Professor Erwin Edman of Columbia University, which had presented a negative image of modern man as a frail creature lost in a limitless universe. Their letter asked the professor about "the spiritual element" and the need to recognize "a force or creative intelligence above mankind." Edman's return letter simply declined to engage in a debate over a complex philosophical position. In light of the poems Sylvia would be writing in college about a brutal universe of godless process, it is possible that she was either play-acting here, conforming to the conventional belief in deity she knew she should possess, or seriously attempting to convince herself and soothe her own fears.

In English 41, which was a year unit on world literature, Sylvia was reading, analyzing, discussing and writing about Plato, Chekhov, Mann, and Dostoevsky, whose *Crime and Punishment* left an indelible impression. In comparison to these visions of humanity the world of Wellesley must have shrunk in her mind into an antique toy, though a piece of it, its Puritan values, lay embedded in her heart. Mr. Crockett was not only expanding her mental horizons, leaving frightening vacancies where God had once ruled supreme; he was also sticking to his own notion of what the Protestant ethic really entailed: beginning in October, his classes would have to donate a dollar each to CARE for every month remaining, a dollar they had earned, not one wheedled from their parents.

Nor could Sylvia escape the surface demands of her religious culture. On November 24 *The Townsman* noted that "Sylvia Plath read devotionals during the week and also at the assembly on Friday. Besides Biblical selections, she read portions from the article *A Protestant's Faith* by Daniel Poling in the Nov. 6 issue of *Life*." After the devotionals, Sylvia also read Governor Dever's Thanksgiving Day Proclamation and then, following a stirring hymn by the choir, she introduced Althea Kiser to the assembly. It was also her happy duty to announce that $146.81 had been collected for the drive against infantile paralysis at the October Dance for the March of Dimes. Religion and culture, inseparable halves of the whole child, bracketed her remorselessly.

Such extremes only tended to confirm her infantile insistence upon black and white poles, which had further physical confirmation as well in her severe depressions whenever her sinuses or menstrual cramps bothered her. Discipline, like achievement, which was its purest fruit, remained the best antidote for these Manichean intensities of perception and feeling. Since literature had been decided upon—she and Frank Irish were the sole members of English 41 to list their future careers as "writer"—discipline not only prevailed here as well but also bore fruit. *Seventeen* magazine, another Bible, accepted a story of hers, "And Summer Will Not Come Again," after forty-five previous rejections, publishing it eventually in the August edition. As a story it is slight, the title taken from a poem by Sara Teasdale, a stanza of which is quoted near the end, involving a girl like Sylvia, "Celia," who loses the boy she likes because of her jealousy, which drives him away, and leaves her in tears, sitting alone by the silent telephone.

If nothing else, the story demonstrates Sylvia's early effort to write what she believed the market wanted; and it is unlikely that she herself put any credence in this sort of romantic pap, however much she was a product of her time and place as her letters attest, with their stress on finding and keeping a boy friend. In the brief biographical sketch accompanying the story, Sylvia is portrayed as thinking seventeen "the *best* age," while her life is described as "filled with senior activities, helping to edit her high school newspaper, working on the yearbook art staff, college week ends. She plays a lot of basketball and tennis and she pounds the piano 'strictly for my own enjoyment.' Jazz makes her melt inside. Debussy and Chopin suit her dreamier moods."

A better example of what her discipline could accomplish was "Bitter Strawberries," an anti-war poem that would appear in the *Christian Science Monitor*, also in August. This poem was the direct outgrowth of her summer job at Look Out Farm, a produce outlet several miles from home, where she spent each day picking strawberries and packaging spinach, and bicycled the several miles to and from work. The hard physical labor under a broiling sun and among an odd mixture of fellow workers was an unsettling experience that Sylvia would never forget, though she actually enjoyed the harsh newness of it, the sheer numbness that let her fall into a dreamless sleep each night as soon as her head touched the pillow. Set in a strawberry field, the poem is a straightforward narrative that tries to relate farming in America to the war then raging in Korea. The "head woman," the overseer of the women picking strawberries, voices a typical, American, right-wing reaction, "Bomb them off the map." Details of place are used effectively to accentuate the bitter setting, while the taste of strawberries turns "thick and sour" as the horseflies "buzzed, paused and stung" in the manner of bombers. One of the older pickers, a woman named Mary, protests against such callousness, because she "got a fella/ Old enough to go"; but the landscape offers no hope and hints at tragedy:

> The sky was high and blue.
> Two children laughed at tag
> In the tall grass,
> Leaping awkward and longlegged
> Across the rutted road.

"Bitter Strawberries" avoided the trap of propaganda and achieved a genuine coherence that violated neither social protest nor poetic demands, while autobiography supplied the convincing touch.

Sylvia published several other poems in *The Bradford* during her senior year, all anonymously and one of them, "Family Reunion," is a fascinating example of how advanced her art was, at least with regard to metaphor.[15] Interestingly, perhaps because of the aspect of anonymity, this poem also dwells sardonically upon a family scene in a way that none of her other efforts dared to. Its tone is vicious, belittling, and not at all disguised. The first stanza introduces the event, the arrival of relatives, "the clash of people meeting/ The laughter and the screams of greeting." The unknown speaker's reaction is clearly unhappy, "dull drums of my pulses beat/ Against a silence wearing thin," and the second stanza is a cruel gallery of caricatured relatives: Aunt Elizabeth who is "fat always" and gives a "greasy smack on every cheek"; Cousin Jane, "our spinster with the faded eyes" and "hands like nervous butterflies"; Uncle Paul, whose "jarring baritone" is rough "as splintered wood"; and the "youngest nephew," who whines "and drools at the reception line."

Sylvia's last six months at Bradford were a time of celebration and hectic activity. She learned that she had won a scholarship to Smith College in Northampton and need not worry about money. Also, as usual, Mr. Crockett was responsible for putting on the senior play, and the Crocketeers were pressed into service. He selected *The Admirable Crichton* and Sylvia got the role of Lady Agatha, a small but physically demanding part. Never having acted before, she was determined to make a success of it. She practiced long and hard, bringing to the role the same dedication, energy, and discipline she lavished upon her school work and writing, even getting her friend Barbara Bottsford to help her "learn how to run like a boy." [16]

Five weeks of arduous rehearsals concluded at the end of April when *The Admirable Crichton* gained wide praise; the cast's picture appeared on the front page of *The Townsman*, and *The Bradford*'s glowing review included a generous compliment for the two girls playing off the leading lady, Lady Mary Lasenby: "Her two sisters, Lady Agatha (Sylvia Plath) and Lady Catherine (Elizabeth Burdoin) showed interesting contrast, adding a graciousness to the drawing-room scenes as well as pointing up the strength in the character of their sister in the ship-wreck scene." But all of this was not mere back-slapping. Mr. Crockett himself remembers being surprised and delighted by how professionally Sylvia performed. She had proved once again that an audience brought out her best.

The month before her success in *The Admirable Crichton*, at a Friday morning assembly, Sylvia and most of her fellow Crocketeers were inducted into the National Honor Society, receiving a pin and a certificate from the new principal, Mr. Graves. Of course, there had to be doubts. Sylvia would be leaving Wellesley. For the first time in her life, she would be separated from her mother and brother and be isolated from the security of a home. But that summer she picked strawberries and there was no time to think about internal pressures. Mere activity was a virtue; and the trick, as Sylvia well knew, was never to stop long enough to let depression take hold.

Are we not straying as through an infinite nothing?
Do we not feel the breath of empty space? Has it not
become colder? Is not night and more night coming
on all the while? . . . Do we not hear anything yet of
the noise of the grave-diggers who are burying God?

NIETZSCHE

3

A Warm Port

Sprawled among the gentle hills of western Massachusetts in Pioneer
Valley, a mere seven miles from Amherst College and Emily Dickinson's homey retreat from the world, Smith College had grown steadily
since its modest founding in 1875, when it could boast but fourteen
students, six teachers, three buildings, thirteen acres of land, and some
$400,000 in assets, the generous bequest of Sophia Smith, who was
interested in the "more thorough Christian education of women." As its
staff and physical plant increased, along with its academic reputation,
Smith soon became one of the "seven sisters" to the country's seven Ivy
League colleges, attracting many of the brightest, richest, most socially
prominent young ladies in America, as well as some of the most
neurotic: the constant tensions generated by fierce academic and social
competition occasionally led to nervous breakdowns and suicides.

Hard-nosed Protestant money had worked its usual magic, transforming love of God, capital and learning (not always in that order) into a
cultural gold mine. By the time Sylvia entered in September of 1950,
Smith was the largest women's college in the world, with thirty-five
buildings scattered over an impressive two-hundred-and-fourteen-acre
campus, assets near $27,000,000 and an enrollment in excess of 2,000
students. It had indeed come a long way from that thin line of Dickinson

ghosts in full white dresses and plain straw bonnets who had smilingly posed for their graduation picture back in the late 1880's.

The college grounds were nearly perfect in their tutored rural prettiness, in sharp contrast to the grim commercial ugliness of Northampton itself. Besides Paradise Pond, which had been named by Jenny Lind and rather unfairly referred to by Sylvia as an insignificant "frog pool," and the carefully maintained Botanical Garden, there were huge ancient elms and pines everywhere, set amid expansive stretches of grass. The buildings for the most part displayed "polyglot architecture ranging from Victorian to Georgian to Frank Lloyd Wright in style" [1] and exuded New England seriousness from every dark corner. Haven House, Sylvia's dormitory, where she was the only freshman to have a single room and that on the third floor, was one of these sound stone-and-brick structures, which must have given her a strong sense of security. Located just off Elm Street (another security symbol and omen), the campus's main thoroughfare, it was only a short walk from the library, the school observatory, and the Botanical Garden, but quite a distance from the gym and Sage Hall, the auditorium where many special events were held.

The first few days were predictably hectic for the in-coming class, days of confusion and continual uproar, unpacking, making friends, registering for courses, locating the correct buildings, being constantly appraised and approached by the horde of Amherst men who had descended *en masse* to pass judgment upon the latest entrants. One of the most embarrasing freshman experiences had to be the physical examination and posture test: each student was photographed in the nude at the gym, frontwards and sideways, to determine if she needed a special class in posture correction. Fortunately, Sylvia did not, but the whole process rankled, as did the obvious contempt heaped upon her by upper-class schoolmates. She and Marcia Brown, who would become her closest friend at Smith and who was soon characterized as "my alter ego," had to answer the phone at Haven House and endure other minor indignities because of their lowly status. But ritual, no matter how stupid or useless, never really disconcerted Sylvia.

Marcia Brown remembers those early college days well, the exciting phenomenon of "new faces, wondering who you are going to like, who's going to like you, if you really are going to survive, and gradually putting names and faces together." [2] Sylvia, who was residing in the remote attic by herself while Marcia shared a ground-floor room with a friend, struck her as "somewhat physically isolated and, by nature, slightly removed from some of the normal socializing, partially out of shyness and feelings of inadequacy because she felt strange as a scholarship student"—that is, "she didn't have the right kind of clothes, felt gawky and awkward, which she was, and she had an astonishing lack of a sort of general know-how, what I call late teenage sophistication." This naïve youthfulness seemed "almost gauche in some circumstances," but Marcia was drawn to her in spite of herself, perhaps intrigued by the odd combination of social innocence and intellectual precocity, and "early on, we got to be very close in a meandering sort of talking friendship, often discussing things like life goals and the complexities of human relationships."

Haven House was ideal for Sylvia in a way, since its eclectic population included many loners and individualistic high achievers, such as William F. Buckley Jr.'s younger sister, Maureen, who carried on the family tradition of articulate zest for debate and Catholic conservatism. And yet, for Sylvia, the single greatest advantage of Haven House had to be the presence of Marcia. In her she found the opposite, positive self or alter ego she inevitably needed for support, a touchstone of normalcy, someone certain enough of her own identity and desires to prevent Sylvia from slipping too far over the edge during one of her manic-depressive stages.

Their warm relationship, which would last to the end of Sylvia's life, probably gained much of its durability from the fact that Marcia never represented any serious competitive threat, being a bright but not exceptional student whose interests tended in the direction of psychology and political science. She was sincere and unselfish in a manner which must have been alien to Sylvia's whole personality, and her connection with literature remained minimal, although the two girls did collaborate on a piece about Princeton men in their second semester for the May 4, 1951, issue of *The Princeton Tiger*. More important, Marcia's relatively uncomplicated and level-headed vision of the universe encompassed no neurotic ghosts to match Sylvia's own; and, as a result, Sylvia rarely "acted" in her friend's company or felt the need for any extravagant display of artistic temperament. On the other hand, neither did she ever reveal her despair and true feelings about the people closest to her.

Whatever the glue of their friendship, Marcia did help Sylvia adjust to Smith's peculiar society the crucial first year. Intellectually, the college promised to be all that she could have anticipated and more. During the course of two semesters, it offered a more productive and varied cultural menu than a person could expect to find in any fair-sized metropolis. In her first year, for instance, Sylvia was able to hear Vladimir Nabokov expound on Alexander Pushkin, and Ernest Simmons talk at length about "Dostoevsky's Fiction and Western Realism"—both lectures further stimulating her deep fascination with Russian writers, Dostoevsky in particular. Nabokov's address on October 19 must have struck a nerve when he claimed exile as "an almost natural state" for Russian authors, and went on to define it as "the restlessness of the soul, the feeling of not belonging to one's surroundings," [3] which of course could apply to any creative individual but gave precise public voice to Sylvia's personal sense of alienation.

She also heard novelist Elizabeth Bowen, whom she would interview three years later in New York City, lecture on "The Novel on Both Sides of the Atlantic." During Sylvia's first semester Congressman John Kennedy addressed the government classes on January 6 and then stayed over for an evening talk. Vespers, conducted each Sunday evening before a declining audience of believers, inevitably had a guest preacher of national stature, such as Reinhold Niebuhr or Paul Tillich; Ralph Bunche paid a visit to the campus early in Sylvia's second semester. The drama group at school (which Sylvia lacked the courage to approach despite her high-school success) put on a full complement of classics; and musical concerts of a more professional nature were given at Sage or John Greene Hall—the latter named for Sophia Smith's persuasive minister and located right next door to Haven House. Isaac Stern gave a recital there in January.

But Smith's most thrilling feature had to be the sprinkling of well-known literary figures among its English faculty, figures like Robert Gorham Davis, author of numerous reviews for the *New York Times Book Review*; Newton Arvin, biographer and critic; and Mary Ellen Chase, the prolific novelist and old-line feminist, who would soon take a special interest in Sylvia's career. Writers of this stature promised the kind of intense intellectual atmosphere she had always revelled in; and, more to the point, if manipulated properly, they might become influential in aiding her own literary progress. But her ambitions were necessarily vague from lack of knowledge. She wanted fame from writing poetry and fiction, and hoped to go into editorial work or college teaching. She also still nursed a secret conviction that her painting and drawing techniques were moving towards major expression, although her weak color control had not really improved.

In any event, the chance to compete against brilliant contemporaries in a safe academic setting was alluring enough in itself, especially since Sylvia retained the unique advantage of having already been published in two national magazines. However exclusive and sophisticated, Smith

College was but a school, and school to Sylvia meant an arena she fully understood and knew how to master. The separation from her mother was more illusory than real as the physical distance between them remained relatively short—with Sylvia making frequent trips home for holidays—and the campus abounded in surrogate parental authorities. Also, according to Marcia, Aurelia "used to write to Sylvia every single day at school," a record of maternal devotion that is somehow uncomfortable to contemplate.

As a liberal arts institution in the early 1950's, a decade before the student revolutions of the sixties smashed the paternalism behind most such enterprises, Smith College offered a fairly rigid curriculum, particularly for the first two undergraduate years, which were intended to inculcate a Renaissance-like awareness of all major academic disciplines. Little or no choice was permitted as six credits (or class hours) were required in literature, six in the fine arts and religion, six in history, six in government or a related area, and six in one of the physical sciences. As an English major, Sylvia was not required to take freshman English and could select several electives in her field, which she did, along with a few introductory courses and French.

But whether taking political science or the horrendous physical science 192 course described in *The Bell Jar* or History II, one of those catch-all classes that bravely covered "the history of Europe from the decline of the Roman Empire to the present," the results were the same: a superlative mark and the admiration of her instructor. Sylvia's approach to her subjects was still machine-like in its thoroughness as she attended every lecture without fail and took "these extraordinary notes in (they looked like calligraphy) an absolutely, uniformly beautiful handwriting." Then, after returning to her room, she abstracted what she felt was important from this mass of raw data. Marcia was in awe of her "tremendously well-organized study habits" and her great need to excel, "which meant an enormous amount to her, more than hanging around with the kids."

When signing up for her courses at the registrar's office, Sylvia was informed by the clerk that it was customary at Smith for scholarship students to write a note of thanks to whomever had endowed their scholarship, if that person were still alive. Perhaps appropriately in some sardonic way, Sylvia's patron was none other than Mrs. Olive Prouty (Higgens), the popular novelist, then in her late sixties, who had already written ten highly commercial novels and was busily engaged on the eleventh, *Fabia*. An extremely wealthy and formidable woman whose mansion in Brookline was not far from the country club where Sylvia's grandfather had worked, Mrs. Prouty was the successful offshoot of a strong religious, business, and academic background, her father having been the head of the Mechanical Department at Worcester Polytechnic Institute. From the beginning, her career as a writer had been accompanied by financial, if not critical, success, *Stella Dallas* becoming a bestseller in 1922 and then a celebrated movie vehicle for Barbara Stanwyck. The process was repeated with *Now, Voyager* and Bette Davis. All of Mrs. Prouty's novels were "women's books" in the worst sense, didactic, sentimental melodramas whose sole literary virtue was a basic narrative skill.

Ever alert for possible support, Sylvia lost little time in writing Mrs. Prouty a "sincere" letter of appreciation, filled with expressions of gratitude and glowing descriptions of her new life at Smith, and including a closing wish that she could one day write books as fine as those written by her kind benefactor. A return note invited the nascent writer to lunch. In the meantime, Sylvia had secured and actually read one of Mrs. Prouty's novels in the town library. She was appalled by the slushy writing and undiluted sentimentality and once more found herself in an ambiguous relationship with a mother figure upon whom she had to depend for financial aid. Mrs. Prouty represented both wealth and social position, American success at its purest, which Sylvia could easily respect, envy, even stand in awe of; but Mrs. Prouty also personified the kind of literary mediocrity Sylvia's keen critical sense could not abide. The patron-scholar relationship by its very nature, as an echo of the symbiotic relationship with her mother, had to increase Sylvia's frustration and bitterness at not being able to express her true feelings for fear of the consequences. Again she was being made to perform for others and her suppressed resentment, in consequence, only gained momentum.

The fictionalized description of the first luncheon meeting between the two was interjected into *The Bell Jar*, and we hear from Esther how she drank the finger-bowl water by mistake, thinking it was soup, the humor of the situation dominating the scene. But in the real-life relationship Sylvia, as usual, did her duty, even more than her duty, and with outward good cheer and eagerness, writing happy, girlish letters to her patron at regular intervals, occasionally visiting her, and keeping Mrs. Prouty well-informed of her modest protégée's amazing progress.

Academically, the first year at Smith was almost a repeat of Sylvia's entire high-school experience. She continued the same dedication to hard work she had always shown, earning her "A's" with seeming ease.

Esther concedes at one point: "I just studied too hard, I didn't know when to stop." Sylvia was impressing her teachers, often doing more work than required, while attending lectures and chapel regularly; but in social terms she remained something of an outsider. A few of the upper-class girls in Haven House treated her with an ill-concealed derision stemming from their stereotyped American distaste for solitary scholars. The social pressure on a girl like Sylvia must have been immense. According to May Targett, a fellow Smith student and later acquaintance of Sylvia at Cambridge, the typical, bright Smith girl was expected to be both efficient and well-rounded in her traditional role—that is, as someone who would eventually marry a professional man, raise a family, and yet be expected to converse about Rilke over a gourmet meal she had prepared herself.

Near the end of her undergraduate career Sylvia herself would admit in a *Mademoiselle* interview "that at Smith you must sneak in the rear door if you haven't a date on Saturday night." [4] Not only did the Smith girl have to have a date every weekend, but he had to be the right sort, presumably a student from one of the Ivy League schools with either impeccable social or academic connections. In desperation, Sylvia suffered through blind date after blind date, usually a relative or friend of one of the other girls, giving little of herself and getting less in return, while none of the victims ever requested a repeat performance. During the Christmas recess, however, which she was spending at home, the unexpected happened. "Buddy Willard," a former high-school track star and distant idol, suddenly dropped by her house after having run the two-mile distance from his own home in Wellesley Hills. After a few minutes of mumbling awkwardness, he suggested that he might be coming up to see her at Smith one day, and then departed as mysteriously as he had arrived. Sylvia was beside herself with excitement, but doubted he would ever follow through on his offer.

It was three months later, on a crisp Saturday morning in March, that Buddy did indeed appear at her dormitory. He was in Northampton to take Jane Anderson, a physics major a year ahead of Sylvia, to Smith's sophomore prom. But he had called to ask her to Yale's senior prom in June, which had far more prestige attached to it. Having been interrupted in her lonely study of the Crusades for a mid-semester exam, Sylvia accepted with relief and intense pleasure. As Esther observed: "I had never been to Yale, and Yale was the place all the seniors in my house liked to go best on weekends." Yale meant status, instant respect from her fellow students, and Buddy Willard seemed the perfect boy friend, smart, handsome, blond, athletic, intent upon becoming a doctor and serving mankind—she was still determined eventually to marry a doctor.

Buddy's entire background, his academic family, his love of the physical sciences, his occasional insensitivity to certain personal and literary allusions, his close ties with his strong-willed mother and her somewhat jaundiced view of the world, all tended to make him the wrong choice for Sylvia from any sensible standpoint. She, on the other hand, was coldly using him for her own purposes from the start, which were never simple either. For her later protests of despair have to be accepted in light of her need in a mate for both conventional perfection and intellectual respectability. The rage that surfaced against Buddy in the years ahead was part of the neurotic fury that surfaced whenever her ego seemed violated and she felt forced to endure a dependent relationship with a lesser figure (in her eyes) because of external circumstances. She needed Buddy for social reasons, needed his Yale association and obvious good looks, but in time had to come to abhor the solemn, pragmatic, self-confident nature of his rationalist outlook, and his vanity as well, which was almost equal to her own in many ways.

Buddy's faults were hardly monumental, as they derived mainly from a fundamental seriousness about himself and others that often led to deadening blandness. Marcia recalls a joke in which he was compared to vanilla ice cream. Her own reaction to him was negative in a curiously divided fashion: "I really didn't like him. He was so sweet and so good, sort of sentimental, and I thought he was a drip, really, really square, very little sense of humor, as I recall, sweetly bland." But he also possessed the sterling qualities of being "terribly sincere, terribly interested in other people, very, very thoughtful, just considerate beyond anybody."—and these were qualities which would undoubtedly serve him as a doctor.

Sylvia's initial reaction was naturally excessive and romantic and possibly self-deluding, although she would not see much of him before the summer. His academic record and general air of certainty instilled in her an "enormous respect," and Marcia felt Sylvia remained "in awe of him" for quite some time. Of course, Sylvia found the situation itself "very glamorous and exciting" and delighted in the idea that she had attained "the senior, handsome, unattainable male figure from high school." Their subsequent duels were the direct result of fantasy slipping into reality, and Sylvia discovering alternate means of escape and social acceptance. If his unconscious Philistinism interfered with her fantasy life, he too would pay a high price for her company. His brother Richard recalled that Buddy found her "sometimes cruel, sometimes ridiculing" as their relationship evolved. He certainly suffered as much as she during the long unravelling of their romance. Bitchiness was another art at which Sylvia would become adept.

Other people saw this hidden Sylvia from time to time, though usually only when she thought herself safe from potential social consequences. Clement Moore, her brother's roommate in his second year at Exeter and later Harvard, remembered meeting Sylvia for the first time at the Plath home during her freshman year. Like most other boys, he was impressed by her good looks and social grace and by the vivaciousness of her personality. She also appeared very aware of the necessary restrictions placed upon the expression of deep emotion in society. Yet Clement also realized that "like her brother, she had this same compulsion to do everything right" and that there was "a kind of nasty streak" in her which soon emerged in the form of a teasing mockery of him. Where he acted out his rages, releasing them immediately and often over petty matters, his sister suppressed hers with smiling determination—except in circumstances where the young prey of her swift tongue posed no real threat to her guarded public image.

But, above all else, Sylvia remained intensely concerned with her career as a writer, since it still offered the best chance for her to achieve popular as well as intellectual success—both of equal importance. With typical energy, she attacked poetry as if it were an alien fortress that could be breached only through a constant frontal assault upon its myriad defenses. Day after day, page after page, she hacked out villanelles and sonnets and rondels in her bulging notebook, shaping poem after poem with the same joyless persistence she gave to her studies. The immediate result was a collection of artificial, frequently shallow verse that sagged under the weight of their own cleverness. But they were deliberately the type of poem most likely to influence judges and literature professors—esoteric, learned, complex road maps to the sublime. They did not fail to impress.

With the possible exception of "Admonitions," the very titles of these poems give them away: "The Dream of a Hearse-Driver," "Notes on Zarathustra's Prologue," and "Go Get the Goodly Squab." The poems themselves are too obviously constructed around reading, and their remoteness from experience suggests that Sylvia still refused to regard art as a valid method of giving voice to either her father obsession or her inner rages. Her poems, echoing her life to this juncture, had to be and were socially acceptable artifacts, crafty, superficial vehicles of linguistic excellence created almost solely for the purpose of gaining recognition and attention. Their craftsmanship is real and at times impressive, but the heart behind them beats false.

Nevertheless the poems do have the merit of providing a clear picture of Sylvia's early approach to both basic themes and poetic problems. In "Admonitions," for instance, a rondel in the form of a sermon, the refrain and its alternate version—"never try to know more than you should" and "oh never try to knock on rotten wood"—go beyond their own simplistic truism in the last stanza: "For deadly secrets strike when understood/ and lucky stars all exit on the run." There is a hint here that Sylvia possessed enough psychological insight into her own make-up to discern lurking disaster if and when she did reveal the inner self—that any confrontation of her father's specter (and her "unnatural" reaction to him) skirted the brink of a serious psychic problem. And yet the surface message of the poem, a coy warning against introspection, hangs in mid-air without connections or worth.

"Notes on Zarathustra's Prologue" has at least the biographical value of defining Sylvia's personal reaction to Nietzsche's thought and attests to the godless universe that was beginning to expand inside her brain—despite vespers. Structurally, too, the poem is lucid enough. The first stanza paraphrases Nietzsche's credo with several awkward images: man "like a shrill flea" on his shrunken earth and huddling together in fear of the prophet's laughter and "fangs of ice." The second stanza announces the same message to the modern world: jet planes writing the news that "god is dead" across the sky. The poem concludes with the lines "till the womb of chaos spouts with fire/ and hatches Nietzsche's dancing star." But the despair is distinct and insistent, firmly yoked to mankind's new role of victim in an atomic era bereft of spiritual values and innocence. The womb image introduces the notion that birth alone is not the answer and that supermen have their own skeptical burdens to bear.

"The Dream of a Hearse-Driver" is the most fascinating of the four. Its format, a slight variation on the rondel's interlocking rhyme scheme, again maintains the aura of an exercise and suggests that Sylvia required severe formal restraints for confidence's sake. The dream material is, of course, invented, but Sylvia's personal awareness of the latent and manifest content of dreams must have figured in her writing. The male narrator of the poem is speaking to an unknown female "you" and devotes most of the poem to describing his first dream in which he was a hearse-driver on some unknown, surrealistic island. His hearse had gone through a red light and a raving woman accused him of "damaging the whole unseen/ lightning plant of the universe." She demands a fine, but a secret voice tells him to hold her hand and kiss her mouth instead, which would "void all penalty." He stubbornly refuses and pays the fine, thereby upsetting the woman, who now "washed the way with tears." The narrator then "drove to you upon the wind." In an offhand manner, the last two lines mention a second dream that touched briefly upon China, but the narrator refuses to elaborate further.

The poem is often clumsy—"warm wind feathers/ with wet plumage"—and too studiously Kafkaesque, but the core of its nightmare conceit infers more solemn advice not to retreat from life. An awareness of mortal limits is called for and the love affair has the air of a mismatch: poor Buddy Willard no doubt already was being castigated for his Philistine sins and taking Jane Anderson to the prom. Whatever its symbolic nature, the poem never succeeds in communicating the dream's supposed horror. Rather only the problematic or puzzle aspects of the dream are given emphasis. Influences are not easy to isolate, but Sylvia here seems firmly committed to the Auden line and the grand American tradition of Stevens and Crane in which obscurity serves to uncover underlying emotional discord.

Yet in "Go Get the Goodly Squab" there is a pervasive Dylan Thomas influence, especially in the hortative tone and the persistent drive to find human parallels in the zoological realm. The poem is also decidedly different from the other three in terms of craftsmanship. Here Sylvia forsook the easy iambic line in order to accentuate the imperative voice. Line after line commences with an attention-grabbing spondee, although the normal English iambic measure is not really avoided for very long. Furthermore, her use of alliteration, always a special delight for her, now varies between juvenile heaviness and a surprising subtlety. Although the rhyme scheme is still too restrictive, the off lines utilize slant rhymes and alliteration to good effect.

The poem's title is constructed upon a biblical allusion—the birds, beasts, and fishes of Genesis. Its grandiose syntax and diction mimic the King James version, while the title suggests "squire" rather than "squab." In any case, the linear movement throughout is a paradoxical retrogression upon the book of Genesis, descending from the ideal peak, significantly below God, of birds and flight, down through the median animal kingdom to fish life, and thus back to the sea from which men once crawled. There is another contrasting progression at work as well, this one forming an earth-pointing parabola inside each stanza. The refrains, continuing always from the second word of each stanza's last line, give a consecutive representation to the three kingdoms:

Hide, hide, in the safe cave
Lest the blizzard drive you blind.

Hide, hide, in the warm port
Lest the water drag you to drown.

Sylvia has again donned priestly robes to provide a little allegorical instruction and, on the surface, allows the lesson to stay simple. She orders the reader outright to let the wild creatures survive unrestricted in their various elements, although some creatures may be domesticated. But the reader is also to hide at home, cling to the familiar, and not venture out of his depths—how near this is to the warning in "Admonitions"! The wildness in mankind, that ecological wholeness he once possessed before evolution specialized him intellectually, is what the poet wishes to see preserved. Danger for human intruders remains in nature's hands—in the blatant threats of "lightning" and "blizzard" or, much worse, in Sylvia's obsessive metaphor of death by water. Though not yet an apocalyptic poet by any means, she was heading in that direction with Gothic determination.

Although uncertain of her own function, Sylvia could not escape the early conviction that art, as the offspring or adjunct of primeval religious impulses, had once again to assume its ritual function in the Freudian-menaced modern consciousness. Much later she would courageously trace this tantalizing thread to its spider end in "The Moon and the Yew Tree," one of her finest works. For now she seemed content to avoid the problem of mythic antecedents and suggest moral direction. Her final emotional break with her personal childhood myths and the sweetly redemptive religion of her mother was still well in the future.

Myth was important to Sylvia—always, in particular, the myth of her own image. Though not yet a part of Smith's "intensely centralized social organization," she differed little from her cohorts in appearance. Standard dress included "gray flannel Bermuda shorts, wool knee socks, pink Brooks Brothers' shirts for lectures; tweed skirts and sweaters for dinner and faculty appointments." [5] Her public personality, too, was carefully defined and projected. Accompanied by Marcia Brown, she dropped by the Vocational Guidance Office to secure a summer job and made a very positive impression upon its staff. One member (with the initials B. J.) described her enthusiastically as "attractive, tall, good-looking—keen sense of humor, intelligent, a delightful person—would recommend highly for anything." [6] Another interviewer, Alice Norma Davis, wrote her up as "composed, logical, organized and intelligent."

Added to these positive attributes were her notable skill in arts and crafts, canoeing, drama, and tennis, her favorite sport.

The staff did find her a summer position as mother's helper for a Mrs. "May March" and her three children. The March family lived in Swampscott, an exclusive resort area on the coast, which meant that Sylvia would be near the sand and sea she loved. Best of all, Marcia would be working for relatives of the same family in a nearby mansion—there were several huge white houses clustered in a compound not far from the beach. She and Marcia had become close friends over the year, Sylvia having spent the mid-semester break with her at Marcia's sister's house in the mountains of New Hampshire. The only distressing note was that Marcia's branch of the family, a doctor, his wife, and their three children, lived permanently on Long Island and would not be journeying to Swampscott until after the first week in July, which meant that the two girls would be separated for the first three weeks or so.

But Sylvia did not have much time to worry about such matters. Most of May and early June were spent in intensive preparations for the final exams, which she predictably passed with brilliance. She then had the excitement of attending the Yale prom with Buddy—which proved a chastening experience that apparently led to their first disagreement. It was resolved quickly, however, and Buddy and Richard picked up Sylvia and her luggage at Smith on Saturday, June 3, for the drive back to Wellesley. After supper that same night, Buddy came over to the house on his bicycle and walked her around the block. They talked about the international situation, and he made a pass at her, which she blocked coyly. Ten minutes later he had left, though they departed "buddies," and Sylvia was annoyed at herself for demonstrating her ignorance of current events. Naturally, she decided to read the *Christian Science Monitor* more intently in the future.

On Sunday Buddy and Richard took off for a week of camping and fishing in Maine and Sylvia was left alone. She used the day to unpack, mow the lawn, and make a fast trip into downtown Wellesley, where she bought Buddy a record, Franck's *D Minor Symphony*, for his graduation—though at her mother's suggestion—and herself an arm-load of summer reading: John Steinbeck's *In Dubious Battle* and Faulkner's *As I Lay Dying* and *The Sound and the Fury*, along with paper editions of *The Grapes of Wrath*, *Sanctuary*, Hemingway's *The Sun Also Rises*, and Pearl Buck's *The Good Earth*. On the way home, she stopped off at the town's tennis courts, her "favorite hunting grounds," and met Philip McCurdy there. Though still a few inches too short for her taste, he had matured considerably over the last year, and she began to look at him in terms of a boy friend rather than as another brother. She dreaded the idea of the girls in town mocking her for hanging around with a high-school senior, but he had earned a second prize in the state United Nations' essay contest that year, and that increased his worth in her eyes.

On Monday, which was cold and rainy, she met her mother in town and they rambled through the Gardner Art Palace, a kind of mansion museum and exhibition of twentieth-century memorabilia. That night she dedicated to reading Buddy's sociology papers with great care, well over a hundred pages of them; and later she admitted to Marcia in a letter that she wondered if she would be able to keep up with him. The following day, she and Pat O'Neil paid a visit to Mr. Crockett at school; and the rest of the week was devoted to piano practice, gardening, going to the movies, and playing tennis with Philip McCurdy. On Friday night, Buddy and Richard returned to town, and Buddy telephoned to ask if she would like to baby-sit with him and his younger brother "Ronald" and then sleep over so that they could get an early start in the morning—Sylvia was accompanying the family to Yale and Buddy's graduation.

Sylvia agreed and arrived at the Willard home near six. Buddy embarrassed her by cooking the dinner. Ronald, who was only seven years old, was then tucked into bed and his older brother told him a story. Buddy and Sylvia washed and dried the dishes, did some minor necking, and listened to the Franck symphony. The Willards came home early and Sylvia retired almost immediately—feeling awkward because Buddy's father had seen her in her pajamas. Her attitude towards the Willards, as usual towards older people, was complex and swiftly changeable. In a few days she would be referring to Mr. and Mrs. Willard as "Uncle Bill" and "Aunt Mildred" and, in her letters to Marcia, gushing over Mrs. Willard's prettiness and domestic efficiency. Sylvia was impressed by the fact that Mrs. Willard had gotten up at five o'clock the next morning, cleaned the house, packed a big picnic lunch, and prepared a hot breakfast for all six of them an hour later.

At seven o'clock Buddy, Sylvia, and Mr. and Mrs. Willard started out for New Haven. Sylvia sat in the back with "Aunt Mildred." They arrived in plenty of time for the ceremonies and "a neat speech" by Yale's president to the graduating class. The picnic lunch in the hills was less successful; after finding a nice spot, they realized that they had left the lunch back at the room where they were staying. Much of the afternoon was then taken up with "class day." Buddy and his fellow graduates were supposedly to spend their last hours together, however uncomfortable in their warm caps and gowns. Oddly enough, Buddy demonstrated a fine sense of unconventional spirit in refusing to be caught up in sentiment at the prospect of graduation. In fact, he and Sylvia had a tiff because she refused to admit to "Uncle Bill" that class day was a trite affair. Mr. Willard was boyishly excited about the graduation, and Sylvia was probably being both kind and cautious in not revealing her true feelings. She had played her role of charming guest and possible future daughter-in-law admirably, even to the extent of making small talk at a two-hour tea in the master's house with a group of mothers, boys, and fiancées, and was not going to ruin it over such a detail.

A swim in the bay and a visit to Swainrock, the local Coney Island, completed the long day. She and Mrs. Willard retired to the "Y" to sleep, and by eight o'clock Sylvia was in bed. Before she could fall asleep, the phone rang. It was Buddy explaining that he would be leaving the next day for a week's trip to Arizona with family friends. Furthermore, after his summer job was over, a counseling job in Brewster on Cape Cod, he would be heading west again to see some married friends before entering Harvard. Sylvia was furious at being abandoned, but did not let it show, except in a certain coldness in her subsequent letter to him at Brewster and during their brief summer visits.

It was on a Monday near the end of June when Sylvia reported to her job at Swampscott. The first impression was pleasant as three happy children, her new charges, escorted her to her huge, second-floor room with its own bath and a beautiful view of the ocean. The luxurious surroundings, however, and her inferior role as governess and pseudo-maid soon had the effect of accentuating her feelings of loneliness. After unpacking and washing the two older children, "Douglas" and "Winny," she went straight to bed and dozed off. She was awakened at 1:00 A.M. by Winny's screaming over a nightmare, but did not get up until fifteen minutes later to shush him, when it became obvious the child was not going to stop without some adult comfort. At five in the morning, "Clara Bow," the toddler who was not yet two, began howling; and an hour later Winny came in noisily, already dressed and ready to play. This was to be a fairly regular pattern for the rest of her stay at the March home.

The awkwardness of her position was immeasurably increased by her lack of experience. After a while, she adjusted somewhat to the tedious tasks of taking care of the children, which included laundry, making beds, picking up after her wards, and keeping a close eye on Clara Bow, who was constantly trotting off to explore her new world. But Sylvia never felt comfortable with the Marches. As Marcia noted, "they had a very ambivalent attitude towards girls working in the house," treating them as social equals one minute and then as servants the next. As a result, Sylvia frequently found herself in a quandary over some insignificant matter. For instance, she did not know if she should read during moments of calm, or if that would be considered shirking her responsibility. For a girl so concerned about impressions and manners, this kind of problem weighed heavily, as did her guilt feelings because she could not cook. Mrs. March or the maid had to prepare hot lunches for the children.

On the happier side, a letter from Buddy, "a chatty note," had been awaiting her on arrival at the March house, and their relationship was stabilized, at least temporarily. Also, a local boy had tried to pick her up on the beach, after Mrs. March returned to the house with Clara Bow, and this fed her ego. A strange event was a nightmare Sylvia had about Buddy—strange because it followed the same moral guidelines found in her simplistic stories and in her daily life. She dreamed that she had broken a date with him to go out with a rakish man who was only interested in sex, and that she had a terrible evening. On returning home, she was greeted by her mother and Buddy, who had just taken Jane Anderson to the prom in her place. At nightmare's end, she was left holding Douglas and Winny in her arms while Buddy receded mysteriously, step by step, shaking his head sadly and murmuring in reproach, "Oh, Syl." But the end was not the end as she took the two children and entered the March car with them, while thinking herself a fool.

Sylvia may have edited her dream to make it more presentable and less revealing. The pat ending, its didactic heaviness, belies its dream nature. And yet it is apparent that Sylvia feared losing Buddy at this stage precisely because she was beginning to understand that she would never marry him. Also her mask was truly lodged in her consciousness to the extent that its fictions had power over part of her unconscious mind as well. What is fascinating, however, is the pairing of Buddy and Mrs. Plath into a formal tableau of conscience, and the continued jealousy towards Jane Anderson.

Besides the hard work and feelings of discomfort about her role, Sylvia was haunted by the need for companionship. Marcia was not to arrive at Swampscott until July 6. A week earlier she had gotten a few days off and headed for Wellesley to catch up on her sleep. Home had never seemed so silent and peaceful before, and she was happy to see Warren, who had a nice suntan from working at the farm and was learning to drive. During this respite—it was the Fourth of July weekend—Mrs. Willard called to ask if she wanted to drive up to Brewster to see Buddy. Sylvia politely declined, claiming exhaustion as an excuse.

When Marcia did arrive at Swampscott, the situation at the Marches' became more bearable. Marcia's mansion was two houses away, but the girls got to see each other every day when they took the children to the beach. Marcia's family was much more snobbish and formal than Sylvia's and treated her with disdain. But this had the advantage of giving Marcia a greater sense of freedom and less uncertainty about the precise nature of her position in the household. Sylvia remained unsure and uncomfortable, although Mrs. March would eventually write to the Placement Office to report that she had found her "intelligent, well-mannered and pleasant." But Sylvia seethed underneath in her dependent role, and the three children, for all their "adorable" aspects, stirred up deep, dark waters. A poem written in England years later, "The Babysitters," provides a more accurate glimpse at her real feelings about the family, especially about Clara Bow. In it she characterized herself and Marcia as "little put-upon sisters" who "were always crying, in our spare rooms"—an exaggerated portrait, to be sure, of their tearless irritations and spacious living quarters.

The poem also goes into the endless, trivial chores that irked Sylvia, the ironing and laundry, the dressing of and caring for the three children. But it was the infant who dismayed her the most: "I didn't know how to cook, and babies depressed me." Each night, in revenge, she wrote terrible things about the Marches in her diary, her fingers red with "triangular scorch marks from ironing tiny ruchings and puffed sleeves." Her happiest memory, and the heart of the nostalgic poem, was a particular day-off in which the two girls rented a boat and rowed out to Children's Island, a speck of land near Marblehead.

The day was July 24 and they had gotten the "holiday" together, the first in several weeks, only after numerous requests. The two girls borrowed bicycles and set off at 9:45 A.M. for Marblehead, after having stolen a pineapple and slices of sugared ham from the family larder. Marblehead proved delightful, and they navigated its crooked, narrow streets with an air of discovery, wondering at the beautiful restorations. Marcia wrote in her diary that night: "I must live here, air, view, invigorating, stimulating, up-lifting!" At 10:30 they reached the dock and left their bikes in a shed at the transportation cove, where they rented a rowboat.

Their initial destination was undecided, but they soon agreed to try for Children's Island, despite the long row involved. The sun grew hotter and they removed most of their clothes. Sylvia did much of the actual rowing, while Marcia sat in the rear and read aloud from Philip Wylie's *Generation of Vipers*. It was about noon when they reached the island and pulled the boat on shore. To their disgust and semi-frightened excitement, the island appeared dead, deserted, "a gallery of creaking porches and still interiors" in Sylvia's words. Flocks of gulls greeted their arrival with shrill cries and simulated attacks until the girls scared them away with pieces of driftwood.

There were many decaying buildings on the island, and the girls went on to explore each one. The first proved empty and so they followed an overgrown and glass-studded path to the next, where they found "a table set with a jar of strawberry preserves, mayonnaise, a 1951 magazine, other magazines, an ace of spades, radio, some spilled Tide." A bird flew out of the stove, startling and mystifying them. Exploration over, they returned to the boat. In a relaxed mood, they stepped off the steep beach shelf and entered the water: "We kicked and talked. The thick salt kept us up."

The rest of that memorable day has been extracted by Marcia from her own diary: "Many pages tell of rowing back in the late afternoon, buying picnic supper supplies, which we cooked on the beach near Castle Rock, meeting a young man, a friend of Sylvia's, a Canadian who joined us for supper—my rapturous delight over the blue, glistening, pounding sea—the sheer joy of this day, ending with our biking home in the dark and my writing sometime after ten—in speechless, wonderfully exhausted state—of our ever strong relationship fusing into a human chain."

Sylvia worked at the March house until the end of August and during that time saw Buddy only once or twice. A few days before returning home she wrote him a curt letter in which she chided him for his indifference. Unknown to him, Sylvia had discovered her own attractiveness and realized that she wanted much more experience with other boys. But she was really not prepared for an actual break-up, and on September 4 Mr. and Mrs. Willard drove Sylvia and her mother to a cabin in Brewster's woods which Aurelia had rented for a week. On the way, the quartet stopped to picnic on the beach near Plymouth Rock. "Uncle Bill" lectured Sylvia on the history behind it, and found it difficult to believe that she had lived in Massachusetts all these years and had not once paid homage to this famous shrine of freedom. Sylvia resented his tone and the air of commercial patriotism hovering around the Rock itself, "what they had done to the place," but she listened solemnly and repressed an urge to burst out laughing.

Once in Brewster, the first person she met was Richard, not Buddy, and he made a favorable impression on her with his sun-bleached copper hair and rich tan. Because she had been able to talk with him in the same relaxed fashion as she talked with Philip McCurdy, Sylvia had always liked Richard in a brotherly way. Now at the sight of him she felt the stirrings of something more than friendship. Buddy joined the group but appeared cold and remote, and hardly spoke to her all afternoon when they went swimming together. It was Richard who ran with Sylvia up the beach to get dry, while Buddy sat glumly with the three adults; and it was Richard who sat in the sand beside her and caressed her tan skin. That night, it was again Richard whom Sylvia accompanied on a long walk along the dark road near the ocean. Inevitably, they kissed several times and seemed on the brink of something more; but they were hesitant, or at least Richard was, and Sylvia went along. So they discussed Richard's current girl friend and Buddy with profound earnestness. In the end, they promised to remain close friends and confidants, which Sylvia had to characterize as "an odd relationship." She was finding the Willards more complex and less likable than she had anticipated.

The second night in Brewster was equally galling for Sylvia, who hated the continuing purgatory of uncertainty in her relationship with Buddy. Mr. Willard; Buddy; Rit, Buddy's waiter-roommate at Lathams, where they both worked; Catherine, a forty-year-old waitress from the same place; and Sylvia paid a visit to Joe Crowly, a friend of Buddy's who had a restaurant where Buddy wanted Sylvia to work the following summer. Joe apparently amused Sylvia with his antics and stories about summer people, but she was enraged at Buddy for not trying to be alone with her. On the third afternoon, at last, they did manage to spend an hour by themselves on a deserted beach. He had brought a physics book to read, but kept pausing to ask her what had happened to her at the Marches' and why had she changed. She refused to reply, annoyed by his air of civilized bewilderment.

Finally, she addressed him with icy calmness. "I would like to level your skull with this book. Maybe then you would really say something."

"I know," he answered, "that's what worries me."

He suggested that they have "a truth talk" that night, a technique for clearing up misunderstandings he had heard about from some married friends. Mystified and intrigued, she eagerly agreed. They met as planned and walked to the middle of an open field, where Buddy had them sit back to back, braced against one another. He then explained that one of them was to ask a question and the other to reply as candidly as possible. Minutes of tense silence passed before Buddy asked about her last letter to him and explained that it convinced him she did not care for him anymore. Consequently, he could not help acting cold towards her when she showed up with her mother. Sylvia in turn confessed that it was all a misunderstanding. A moment of reconciliation followed, with much kissing and expressions of tenderness.

Sylvia certainly felt pleased at having a regular boy friend again; but, as a letter to Marcia Brown indicates, she also was determined to go out with other boys. More important, she accepted the idea that Buddy was not the man she would eventually marry. Among the things she resented were his positive approach to everything, his tendency to manage her affairs, and his humorless, uncompromising outlook in general. For his part, however, he only wished that she were three years older and could marry him immediately. Letters from his married roommates had made him more eager than ever to do likewise; and in any case, like his two brothers, Buddy had wanted to get married ever since entering college. The next morning, after Buddy came over and made her breakfast, Sylvia left for Wellesley with her mother and the Willards.

On the ride back, she sat in front with "Uncle Bill," while Aurelia entertained "Aunt Mildred" in the rear seat. Sylvia and Buddy had told no one about their new "understanding"—a vague agreement to get married after she graduated; but Mr. Willard made it clear that he would enjoy having her as a daughter-in-law. Sylvia was sincerely moved by the declaration, for all of her contempt, and felt like crying; though part of her sadness might have been for herself, or for the more realistic awareness of a future without Buddy in it.

> We do not content ourselves with the life we have in ourselves and in our own being; we desire to live an imaginary life in the minds of others, and for this purpose we endeavor to shine.
>
> PASCAL

4

"A Very Talented Teenager"

Who was Sylvia Plath? Sylvia Plath was a success. That was the beautiful, bullet-sure simplicity of her drive.

Her sophomore year at Smith was destined to follow the escalating pattern of the first year, with additional, concentrated efforts at being "popular" on campus, at rounding off the golden-girl image. Straight "A's" remained the norm, despite several difficult courses; and she delighted in her Art and Creative Writing classes, which were more pleasure than work. At chapel on the night of September 28 she had the satisfaction of hearing Dean Helen Randall read off her name with twenty-three others, including Louise Guisey's, as the top-ranking students in a class of more than six hundred girls.

But Sylvia had decided that social conformity demanded a more extensive involvement in extra-curricular activities. Besides attending concerts and plays, she participated in the traditional "step sings" on the lawn in front of the Students' Building and taught art as a volunteer at the People's Institute in Northampton, the town's welfare center. She also worked on the school newspaper, a more congenial task, for a few hours each day in the College Hall Tower, where she managed to "filch" reams of official note paper for her endless letter writing. The mask of her public life was finally assuming the kind of proportion between achievement and popularity that her determined ego demanded.

Even Buddy was cooperating, albeit unwittingly. That same fall he was given a scholarship to medical school and entered Harvard University. Sylvia was still intrigued by medicine and doctors, as she was by any vocational skill outside her own field; and lately she had hit upon the idea of using Buddy to learn more about the actual workings of a hospital. She pleaded with him to take her along with him on his daily rounds until he finally consented. It was a bright, coolish Friday afternoon when she skipped her last classes, in a rare act of defiance, and hitched a ride into Cambridge.

That night, after putting on the customary surgical gown, she accompanied Buddy on his tour of duty through Boston's Lying-In Hospital, attending all his classes, laboratory lessons, and intern observations. The experience proved to be crucial for both Sylvia and her poetry—that is, upsetting in a way that would leave deep psychological scars long after. The experience might have been shocking for anyone not familiar with hospital routines; but for a repressed, sensitive, and sexually unsure young girl, it was devastating. The long night's series of traumatic events were faithfully recorded in *The Bell Jar*, where only Esther's characteristic naïveté remains suspect.

Sylvia first followed Buddy and several companions into an operating room where the students were soon busily dissecting a preserved corpse as she looked on from a nearby stool. Surrounding her were tables bearing other corpses. According to Esther, the dead bodies were not horrifying at all because they "had stiff, leathery, purple-black skin and they smelt like old pickle jars"—a realistic touch that was probably meant to conceal their actual impact. Here was death in the raw, the brutal epitome of Sylvia's subsequent warnings against nature's amoral and remorseless processes of destruction; precious human organisms reduced to chunks of meat for callow boys to butcher into steaks. What more confirmation could be given of the universe's capricious evil?

Further confirmation was not long in coming. After the dissection exercise, Sylvia had the opportunity to inspect at close quarters the typical array of jarred fetuses common to any teaching hospital or medical school, where the bottles of unborn infants are arranged chronologically to show their development at various stages. Esther conceded that they were "gruesome things"; and to Sylvia their moon heads swimming and glowing in the false glass wombs became touchstones of horror, empirical symbols of stillborn humanity. They developed in her imagination as *objets d'art* of the central obsession with

Kierkegaard's "fear of nothingness" that would govern her later poetry, *real* symbols springing from the rich soil of her own nature. Perhaps, too, they reminded her of the baby brother who had come to disturb her perfect childhood world.

Other events that night at Buddy's side had to be nearly as disturbing. They included a lecture on sickle-cell anemia, interviews with seriously ill patients by doctors and students, and the witnessing of a live birth. The latter took place some time after a midnight meal, and Sylvia had to wear a mask of cotton gauze for the event. The delivery was handled by one of Buddy's friends, who was assisted by a staff doctor. Everything proceeded normally enough until the baby's head became lodged in the mother's vagina. This necessitated a quick scalpel cut which freed the infant in a stream of blood. Later, as he was being held up, the baby urinated directly into the doctor's face to provide some comic relief. But for a girl of her sensibilities the result could only have been an intensification of hostile feelings towards infants and the whole process of childbearing.

The entire experience was, in fact, a disaster; and her feelings towards Buddy, already undergoing a change, were necessarily affected. According to *The Bell Jar*, Buddy soon attempted to introduce Sylvia to the joys of premarital sex by having her watch him undress in his room. Her savage, witty ridicule of his male parts in the novel as "turkey neck and turkey gizzards" results from an almost adolescent disgust with sexuality and highlights the frozen sexual ambiguity of her make-up at the time. The fact that Buddy may have had an affair with a waitress shortly before this incident, while she "remained pure" in accord with the prevalent double standard, undoubtedly added fuel to her distaste.

Sex would never be a simple pleasure for Sylvia, if pleasure at all, though she was fascinated by the technical details and often approached its mysteries through double-entendre in her college poetry. "Dialogue en Route," for example, which was written during this period, contained the provocative image of "Adam erect in his folderol cloak." Another contemporary poem, "Ballade Banale," presented the artist figure as a wandering juggler with a "pink banjo," who leaves her when she makes the mistake of saying "I loved him with my whole heart." Later, of course, in a poem such as "The Bull of the Bendylaw," she would be able to merge the two prime themes, sexual conjunction and literate allegory, with greater assurance.

Much later, Sylvia had a phone call from Buddy at her dormitory. He announced with solemn stoicism that his annual chest X-ray had proved positive; he had tuberculosis.[1] Fortunately, as a medical student on a scholarship, he would be sent free of charge to a special sanatorium at Saranac Lake in New York's Adirondack Mountains. From her point of view, self-centered as always, it was a blessing. He was going to be effectively removed from her life, but she could continue to reap the benefit of campus identification as his girl friend. She wrote to him with chatty faithfulness, as she did to Mrs. Prouty and many others, partly out of a vague sense of guilt and partly out of that awesome Calvinist sense of duty she could never quite escape. He replied in lengthy letters filled with the melodramatic weight of his condition and the despair it generated in his athlete's heart—despair which was transforming him into a pathetic shadow of his former sure self. He now became dependent upon her in an absurd role-reversal that included amateur attempts to write poetry.

It was during the Thanskgiving holiday that Sylvia met Myron ("Mike") Lotz and Robert Modlin for the first time. Robert was Richard Willard's roommate at Yale, a fellow medical student; and Richard had invited both him and his friend Mike, another medical student, to Thanksgiving dinner at the Willard home. Later that day Sylvia and her mother dropped by for a brief visit. Lotz recalled her "as a gangling, gawky girl, pretty angular, to me not that attractive." [2] Modlin was later to be put off more by the apparent insincerity of her manner than by any physical shortcoming. What did impress Mike, and led to his subsequent pursuit of Sylvia, was her Smith background, her growing reputation as a poet and scholarship student, and the sheer intensity of her creative spirit. He may also have recognized in her the same compulsion to succeed that was dominant in his own character.

Mike had been the second and last of two boys born to poor, hard-working German immigrants in Warren, Ohio. Although uneducated themselves, the Lotzes valued schooling as the surest means to prosperity; and Mike emerged as another second-generation achiever. His intelligence and addiction to work helped him earn a scholarship to Ohio State University in a competition in which he ranked fifth out of 10,000 participants. At the same time, he was attaining local fame as a pitcher on the high-school team. In September of 1950 he entered Yale University on a full scholarship, after having won the coveted New York Yale Club award for that year.

Mike's freshman year saw him move near the top of his class academically, and his pitching skills began attracting numerous professional scouts to the Yale baseball games. Never content with second-best, however, he was already determined to reach the top of his class in the second year. This over-achievement syndrome dominated everything he did. He labored hard to master various arts, studying classical music, memorizing reams of poetry, writing elaborate literary critiques, and in general putting as much distance as possible between himself and his parents' lower-class world. An odd side of his personality also made him susceptible to what he labelled "the Smith-girl type"—brilliant, creative, unpredictable, high-strung girls like Sylvia, who could be counted upon to cause a certain amount of excitement whatever the situation.

It was during this Thanksgiving dinner that Robert Modlin, a candid, red-haired, freckle-faced Irishman with an intelligent appetite for life, let drop a comment about how fortunate the Willards were in having three fine sons and a lovely home in a comfortable neighborhood like Wellesley Hills. Unexpectedly, a serious three-hour discussion ensued in which Mrs. Willard attempted to explain her pervasive sense of frustration and discontent; and her feeling that she and her husband, whom she considered grossly underpaid, deserved much better.[3] Mrs. Willard was convinced that her more affluent neighbors looked with condescension upon her family. She also shared her friend Aurelia's intense concern about money; and it is difficult not to conclude that Sylvia's cruel fictional portrait of the two women in *The Bell Jar* as sister martyrs under the skin is fairly accurate, if selective and unkind.

Sylvia's dislike of Mrs. Willard, which she of course repressed, could only have increased with Buddy's sequesterment and his mother's continued encouragement of future marriage plans. The relationship with Buddy plodded along as before, through the mails for the most part, though Mrs. Willard did make the suggestion that Sylvia work as a waitress in the mountains to be near her son. Whatever fury that may have caused in Sylvia, appearances had to be maintained; and she rarely let on at home that she had any intention other than that of becoming Mrs. Buddy Willard some day. In the Spring, however, Sylvia began to invite Myron Lotz up to several house parties at Smith. He had the same elegant qualifications as Buddy, being a handsome "Yalie" with excellent grades while in pursuit of a medical career—not to mention that he was also an outstanding athlete. Moreover, unlike Buddy, he stood in constant, appreciative awe of Sylvia's literary gifts, often showing off her affected erudition to his friends and exchanging with her a number of literary compositions. The fact that he had received a $30,000 bonus for signing with the Detroit Tigers the winter before, thus enabling him to buy a car, no doubt did nothing to lessen the attraction.

Mike quickly discovered Sylvia's obsessive need to be different from other women—especially her desire to escape the grim, narrow boundaries of their conventional husbands and babies at all cost. Once they passed a wedding in progress while driving through Northampton, and Sylvia could not help blurting out in disgust, "There's another frumpy bride caught up in some meaningless marriage!" This, of course, was play-acting at another level: adolescent shock technique from a "poet" relishing her own alienation; but underneath there was, in fact, an authentic, "obsessive, compelling need to be creative," which meant to be special enough to escape the closet future prescribed by her mother's bourgeois universe. For Sylvia there were always only two extremes to choose between. Life itself was frequently visualized as "a bowl of feces and cream."

Sex was still a guarded treasure, a precious gift withheld; and their physical contact was minimal, little more than extensive necking and petting, which passed for "heavy going" in those days when good girls preserved their virginity until the wedding night. But sex, as a central and unknown experience, beckoned to Sylvia, waiting to be explored, however weak her actual desire. Mike believed that beneath her conventional Puritanism "she would love to get laid," that in a less circumspect age she could have easily become "a sexual libertine." In any case, the inhibitions caused by her upbringing prevented the possibility of experiment in sex as in her poetry.

Weekend dates between Mike and Sylvia were dominated by her "words, words, a torrent of words" and a stubborn refusal to face up to the problems in her make-up. She was always pausing to admire the view of moonlight gilding the tree branches or to note how the sun danced across a field of grass; and she would display her vocabulary in a stagey series of lush images, many of which would later appear in her poems. Surface reality was but a metaphor; and, like many other people, Mike noticed how she never mentioned her mother, though she often rhapsodized over her dead father, saying what a terrible blow his death had been for her and how she had been his worshipped darling. Nor did she trouble to hide her contempt for Mrs. Prouty. During this time Sylvia saw herself as merely another puppet to be manipulated at will.

Lotz also became aware of yet another side to Sylvia—that she exhibited "many, many facets" was part of her charm for him—and this was the "crafty plotter" role, the maneuvering of people and events to suit private designs. For instance, her behavior in groups could vary drastically. At times she was quiet and self-contained, pleasantly tolerant and attentive to her companions. At other times she became almost hysterical with chatter and fought doggedly in a loud voice to gain and keep the conversational spotlight.

To understand Sylvia at this point is to understand the complex nature of her divided personality. Though not yet schizophrenic in any medical sense, she was three persons, three Sylvias in constant struggle with one another for domination: Sylvia the modest, bright, dutiful, hard-working, terribly efficient child of middle-class parents and strict Calvinist values who was grateful for the smallest favor; Sylvia the poet, the golden girl on campus who was destined for great things in the arts and glittered when she walked and talked; and Sylvia the bitch goddess, aching to go on a rampage of destruction against all those who possessed what she did not and who made her cater to their whims. In this last role she was contemptuous of weaklings and passionately despised her own flesh-and-blood ties.

Like other complex personalities, of course, there were other Sylvias as well: Sylvia the sad little girl still hurting from the profound wound of her father's rejection and abandonment of her and wanting to crawl back into her mother's cave-safe womb; and Sylvia the ordinary teenager who yearned for a kind husband, children, and a house like her grandmother's by the seashore. But these were only fitful shadows of the three main configurations, subconscious fragments that never conquered the real world for very long. One sure sign of Sylvia's lurking psychosis, in fact, was the thoroughness with which she shaped and maintained the first two "masks"—abstractions of self that constantly threatened complete emotional detachment or, to use her own effective metaphor, a descending bell-jar. She remained narcissistic and totally committed to self, but the self had become an uncertain projection of a splitting ego.

Her public mask as a sophomore steadily gained prominence, her altruistic endeavors and new school spirit paying off handsomely. Classmates supported her for various honorary posts—the trappings of power in a powerless world. Already a member of the Studio Club and on the Student Council for the second straight year, she was now elected sophomore prom officer (or "Entertainment Chairman" as it was officially called) and helped run the International Students' Day and Charity Ball, which presumably represented an advancement over her minor role on the Decorations Committee for the freshman prom the year before. The plum she wanted most, however, was Secretary to the Honor Board, the student body empowered to deal with infractions of the honor system. The house "reps" from Haven House did nominate her for the position, but then she had to campaign against two other candidates, which she did with her usual thoroughness. Unfortunately that was not enough and a girl named Nanette Walker won the election on March 20, 1952, with Sylvia running a strong second.

The unhappiness of losing did not last long as, a month later, Miss Walker announced that she had decided to spend her junior year abroad. That left the new office vacant. Sylvia received the post by default and thus earned herself a flattering write-up in the *Smith Weekly Current.* Her name was becoming well known on campus, which gave her immense pleasure; and at the end of the year, in a sort of public-relations climax, she was chosen for "Push," the sophomore committee whose members had the irksome but prestigious task of serving as escorts for seniors and alumnae during graduation weekend.

Practical ambition, and her own awareness of the inherent limitations of school politics, caused Sylvia also to seek out more concrete means for advancing herself that might be in line with a possible career. She became a correspondent for the Press Board, which meant writing local releases for a town newspaper, in this case the *Springfield Daily News.* Besides earning her a little money and enhancing her reputation, the job provided needed practice in pruning her writing. Yet all this time her three writing teachers, Alfred Fisher, Howard Rollin Patch, and Mary Ellen Chase, reacted with almost uncritical applause to her prodigal talent—she had a vague crush on the handsome, white-haired Mr. Fisher.

Professor Chase was particularly impressed by the absence of "conceit or arrogance" in Sylvia and found her "thoughtful, generous, humorous and charming." Having been a respected teacher and "name" at Smith since 1926, and a pleasant, erudite individual in her own right, Chase held a unique position in both the school and the English Department.[4] Her prolific writing—memoirs, biblical studies, novels, and the like— also gave her a certain amount of local status. Her house near Paradise Pond, which she shared with her constant companion, Eleanor Shipley Duckett, retired Professor Emeritus of Classical Languages at Smith, was a focal point for many of the college's brighter students. From Sylvia's cold perch, Professor Chase was indeed a valuable ally; but, like Mrs. Prouty, she also represented the dual threat of inferior art and still another clutching mother figure—Chase was in her sixties and destined to retire herself in 1956—who had to be catered to and flattered.

Though Sylvia shared Professor Chase's feminist distaste for marriage and a supporting role, she would callously caricature her as an old lesbian poet in *The Bell Jar,* including her among "these weird old women" poor Esther was always attracting. Robert Gorham Davis was another well-known member of the English faculty whom Sylvia tried assiduously to cultivate by cornering him in the lunch room and hallways to engage him in conversation.[5] She sat in occasionally on his writing class and would later take his lecture course on Modern American Literature. Ironically, Professor George Gibian, Sylvia's subsequent thesis adviser, recalls Davis once remarking how refreshing it was "to have a completely wholesome, healthy, yet creative student" like Sylvia and how he "had never had a talented writer in his creative writing class who was not a little neurotic or something, except Sylvia." [6]

Sylvia could and did deceive the best of them. The public portrait of her that emerges is close to the portrait she obviously wanted to paint, that of a normal, happy, brilliant young girl dedicated to duty, art, and scholarship, an outgoing student who could play tennis, bang out popular tunes on the piano, paint, date Ivy League men, and write sophisticated poems and stories in her spare time. She was the all-American college girl at her best and continued to dress the part with meticulous care long after the fad for loose skirts, bobby socks, button sweaters, and pretty white blouses had disappeared. As one fellow student wryly noted, "you had the feeling that she would be in saddle shoes for the rest of her life." [7]

Even politically her views differed little from those of the brighter Smith girls, few of them being much interested in either history or politics. Although she was no doubt quite sincere in her liberalism, her walled-in ego rarely allowed her to take a deep interest in the affairs of the world. She opposed President Eisenhower, was glad to see the Korean Conflict dawdling to an end, heatedly supported Adlai E. Stevenson's futile presidential bid, and despised Senator Joseph McCarthy's sensational witch-hunting tactics. Along with hundreds of her fellow students, she was in Greene Hall the night of April 10, 1952, when Senator McCarthy himself, accompanied by his inevitable bodyguard and bulging satchel of communist names, addressed the college on "Communism in Government." Like the rest, she listened politely as he spoke about the growing red menace, and then, at the end, instead of applauding, rose to hiss at him. Enraged, the good senator snarled back, "Hiss? That name sounds familiar!", before stalking off the stage.[8]

College in the 1950's was a liberal but quiet place. Protests usually centered around school problems, such as sign-in hours; and the riots then erupting in South American and European universities were regarded with horror and disbelief by most American students. Political views were reflex actions, the result of deep reading and the conviction that progress and America were synonymous, that education itself held the key to most of the country's major problems, that is, poverty and integration. The average college student, who came from a solid middle-

or upper-middle-class background, was geared from infancy towards attaining a better life than that of his parents. Blacks existed only in the abstract since they did not live in white neighborhoods and very few of them ever reached college. Presumably, only in the South were they mistreated.

Sylvia had, in fact, previously attempted to deal with a contemporary problem in "Bitter Strawberries" with some success; and now she confronted McCarthy's America in a brief poem called "Temper of the Time," which would eventually appear in *The Nation* as her first contribution to that influential journal.[9] The effectiveness of the poem stems from the very restrictive nature of its modest goal: to define American dilemmas in the cliché-ridden language of its natives. What makes it attractive as a poem *and* an intellectual exercise is its playful sparseness—that is, playful in Sylvia's demonic understanding of the word. Every phrase has a razor double-edge, a cliché leading to true meaning, and the sixth and last stanza is a fine little twist in strict keeping with the bleak tone of the whole:

> His wife and his children
> hang riddled with shot,
> there's a hex on the cradle
> and death in the pot.

"Temper of the Time" had enabled Sylvia to escape the intense preoccupation with self so evident in her previous poems—if only briefly. But writing was still her main concern, not politics or sociology. Made secure by the anchor of her father's red Thesaurus, she continued to use words to build walls of fantasy to keep the real world at bay. She wrote *New Yorker*–type short stories and Audenesque poems, sending them off regularly to the major "slick" magazines like *Seventeen*, *Mademoiselle*, *Harper's*, and the *Atlantic Monthly*. *Seventeen* soon took several more of her pieces, which added to her reputation at Smith, but she remained anxious and uncertain about her art and its ultimate acceptance. Sylvia still approached writing with the grim determination of a German bricklayer. Later, when speaking to a friend about the many rejection slips she had already collected, she would boast, "I've got hundreds. They make me proud of myself. They show me I try." [10]

Discipline and practical application were the watchwords. They got hundreds of things written, but also prevented most of them from ever breathing freely. Her literary enthusiasms continued to fluctuate as well. Though committed to Yeats, Stevens, and Auden, she was now a Dylan

Thomas devotée and carried his books around like sacred talismans in which she had underlined and commented upon special stanzas and whole poems. Spurred, no doubt, by his recent highly publicized tour through the United States—she might very well have heard him read either in Boston or New York—Sylvia revelled in his convoluted verbal patterns, striking radical imagery, and odd adherence to inherited forms. Perhaps she saw in him a male reflection of her secret bitch self, which was quite masculine in its consciousness of power—herself without sexual restraints and social inhibitions. Then, too, one of her idols, Edith Sitwell, had approved and supported him, which must have given weight to his hazy outline.

Near the end of her second year, Sylvia entered a short story called "Sunday at the Mintons" in the annual fiction contest for college students at *Mademoiselle* magazine. The weary editor, after sifting through hundreds of manuscripts, was impressed by her tale and scribbled hastily across the top of its first page: "Imaginative. Well-written. Certainly superior. Hold." And hold they did until the final board meeting decided during the summer that "Sunday at the Mintons" deserved the award for that year. The story sheds light upon Sylvia's rational, conscious awareness of the function of fantasy and of her own suppressed feelings of hostility towards her brother, who must have appeared like a creature from another planet in her romantic mind from time to time.[11] The plot of the story revolves around the schematic conflict between Elizabeth and Henry Minton, an aging, retired brother and sister now living together again in the old family home by the sea. Narrated from Elizabeth's point of view, the story is slanted against Henry from the start. Elizabeth is presented as a gentle, sensitive, quite intelligent creature who delights in the surfaces of things and often gives them a daydream profundity, while Henry is the brute essence of hard-headed realism, of stuffy details and pragmatic facts. "Always when they were small, Henry would be making charts and maps, copying from his geography book, reducing things to scale, while she would dream over the pictures of the mountains and rivers with the queer foreign names."

Brother is constantly compared to sister in an invidious way. She is "slender" and offers "a soft violet figure" to the world, but he is pilloried with insidious consistency: he is "slow" and "ponderous" and he "moralizes," he oozes "sanctimoniousness like plump golden drops of butter," and his eyes gleam "very cold, very blue." A tiny bit of the secret author comes through also: "There would come a time, Elizabeth thought, as she had thought so many times before, when she would confront Henry and say something to him. She did not know quite what, but it would be something rather shattering and dreadful." It is easy to hear Sylvia speaking here, aching to unleash her howling outrage. But this is only a story, and Sylvia knew how to tell a story and make her audience like it. If her self-portrait is biographically accurate in places—"Elizabeth was cherishing, the way she would a dear, slandered friend, the vague, imprecise world in which she lived"—it is for a purpose, as part of the story's deliberate pattern of thesis and anti-thesis.

Brother and sister clash, with the rock-thick brother expectedly winning until they go to the seashore to watch the tide arrive. Elizabeth drops her brooch, which had belonged to their mother, and Henry climbs down to the rocks to retrieve it for her. While there, a huge wave comes in and takes him away, as his sister looks on "in an ecstasy of horror," then with "a growing peace" while her brother's "flailing arms rise, sink and rise again." Death by water, by drowning, the beloved fear has come true; but the story adds an O'Henry twist: it is all in her imagination. The pair returns to the family house with no change in their lives.

Though hardly a memorable story, "Sunday at the Mintons" is a remarkable artifice for a girl of nineteen to have constructed and controlled; and it certainly earned the $500 prize. But fiction continued to be Sylvia's weak point. Her narcissism could not create any of Forster's "round characters"; and the narrative is too long and obvious at every seam. But the crafty story tells us much about Sylvia, and perhaps about her uncertain though loving attitude towards her brother.

In her fantasy, Elizabeth triumphs and her brother is killed; and that is sufficient to blunt her rage, so that she can docilely return home with him at the end. By imagining him drowned and obliterated, she could now afford to pity him and, as the climactic twist emphasizes, continue living behind the submissive mask of feminine duty. Revenge is accomplished in fancy, not fact, but it suffices as a sort of stop-gap measure. In an ironic last turn of the screw, even the story as an objective whole is just that: Sylvia's fantasy revenge on her brother. Life imitates art in her mirror notebook.

There are other psychological currents in the story that should be touched on too, if only briefly. The fact that the sister is married, for example, a stereotype of the chaste librarian, touches one of Sylvia's terrifying poles: the sterile loneliness of spinsterhood, a feeling of healthy flesh and mind straight out of Wellesley that "the drawing back from any aspect of life was a courting of deformity." Balanced against this fate, in continual opposition to it, is the primal fear: Elizabeth "felt oddly that she was merging into someone else, her mother perhaps." These are further indications of Sylvia's persistent and dangerous unsureness regarding her own identity. Neither alternative was attractive; and the lack of a real solution—from the point of view of her narrow spyglass—is affirmed by the last resort to fantasy. Being a woman certainly placed an additional burden upon Sylvia; and she constantly brooded upon the twin alternatives of spinsterhood and marriage, between the examples of Mary Ellen Chase and her mother—extreme examples for a girl being torn apart by the extreme demands of her own divided personality.

At least in "Sunday at the Mintons" Sylvia was confronting a few comet fragments from her obsession's nova core, though obliquely, which gives the story an authentic feel on occasion. This is not true of "The Perfect Set-Up," a short story which Sylvia had entered in *Seventeen*'s annual contest—she continued to bombard them with work—and which had only garnered an Honorable Mention, although it would appear complete in the October issue under the generous blurb of "A very perceptive story by a very talented teenager." As with all her fiction, it is closely autobiographical in basic detail, being drawn from her experiences the summer before while at the March household. Lisa is the heroine's name, and morality sparks the machine of the endless story, not fantasy, with anti-Semitism providing the plot mechanism.

The story is moral, block by block of it, right up to the brick-wall ending which must be quoted in full for both its characteristic awfulness (its smug condescension) and its equally characteristic aura of muted despair:

> You know how sometimes you could slap yourself for a stupid remark you made or a big chance you missed to do the best you could? Well, right then I wanted to worm my way down into that sand until I was covered all over and couldn't see the line of foam Ruth was making out there in the water. I just sat there with the whole summer turning sour in my mouth.

D. H. Lawrence had observed, as Sylvia herself would come to see in a few years, that American writers are compelled to moral preachments and choices, even at the price of smothering the hidden snake of delicious sin. This, of course, explains the terrible artificiality of most of Sylvia's college writings—not only the sense of a "performance," but the constant attempt to erect ethical frameworks.

The same didactic proclivity pervaded her poetry, too, though never to the extent noted in her fiction. Poetry brushed against lower chords.

But her poems also remained surface contraptions, towers of Babel built upon extravagantly erudite foundations—all still too remote from the bitch self for final conviction. "Mad Girl's Love Song" was described by Sylvia as her "favorite villanelle"; and Philip McCurdy has suggested that it was the crafty outgrowth of their relationship and her intense reaction to Dylan Thomas at the time. The poem is important for the thematic emphasis placed upon madness as a congenital human condition and, from a stylistic point of view, for its relaxed diction. There is none of the awkward straining after verbal showmanship common to other early works. Oddly, in view of Sylvia's always interesting grasp of imagery, the metaphors are its weakest links and sound like a young Poe stoking up his allegorical forge. Bookish allusions, "seraphim and Satan's men," contend with poorly realized abstractions, "arbitrary blackness," for attention.

The two refrains, expected in a villanelle to carry both melody and meaning to some inevitable climax, are far from subtle in their wisdom: "I think I made you up inside my head" and "I shut my eyes and all the world drops dead." These are the unavoidable, poetically banal truths of the child moving from innocence into adult reality with his awesome ego intact. But in the context of the poem's narrative logic and the author's biography, they also represent madness refined to purest self; the empiric world is distilled until it has no tangible value. More significant, a universe—admittedly only literary—is deemed possible in which "God topples from the sky." Again Sylvia has accepted Nietzsche's belief that the old order, the romantic myths of the nineteenth-century's evangelical good and evil ("seraphim and Satan's men"), must now depart. The patent melodrama of the situation, a lover waiting years for her beloved to return, should not obscure either the familiar sardonic wit behind its construction or the seriousness of the despair underlying its philosophic nihilism. Like Nietzsche's madman, Sylvia knew the dangers. The absolute "I" does invite insanity, particularly when abandoned to a frightening secular reality, one of ends and relative ethics.

"Circus in Three Rings," for which Gordon Lameyer supplied the title, hits directly at Sylvia's concern with her aesthetic—that is, with the method of creative process and her self-concept as a performer. Yeats's "foul rag and bone shop of the heart" is the inspiration, but the poem's three magic circus rings lead to a negative concept of sex as dangerous (a motif that would be elaborated upon again and again until the hymen was broken) and a basic distrust of love, which would have dismayed the old Irish mystic. Love, of course, meant commitment to someone else, an extension of self impossible for Sylvia, who remained convinced that only her withdrawal into art could protect her. She had been wounded once by a man, her father, and would never again expose herself so completely.

Although obviously dedicated to Yeats and Stevens, the poem as a whole is strikingly reminiscent of Poe's "The Conqueror Worm"—perhaps because Poe, like Nietzsche, spoke more intimately to her secret will and cynical existential despair. The first stanza, for example, establishes "the circus tent of a hurricane," one "designed by a drunken god," and then concludes to the applause of "angels." Love is, of course, overtly confounded, her "extravagant heart blows up again," and the poem's governing principle is certainly extravagant enough. The last stanza's black magic, partaking of Mephistopheles' pagan evil, is still somewhat unexpected. The disappearance into smoke, as her love develops into "my demon of doom," reasserts the failure of Puritan America to provide a bulwark against a personal sense of disease and lack of belief. If the language remains trapped in nineteenth-century allegory, the despair does not, nor does the refusal to accept love's illusions. Sylvia was almost being honest.

A much better poem from the same period, "Two Lovers and a Beachcomber by the Real Sea," which would appear in *Mademoiselle* during Sylvia's senior year, is also palpably an *objet d'art*, an intellectual exercise dense with conceits; but something organic does emerge, driven, no doubt, by her deep emotional reaction to the ocean in any context. It is this exciting manipulation of ideas, feelings, and images which rescues the poem. The poet has taken on the difficult task, familiar to Wallace Stevens, of providing concrete poetic realities for two complex abstractions: imagination and ideas or thoughts (logically structured conclusions rooted in illogical emotions). In a very broad way, the poem is a metaphysical configuration, since it does try to bridge the tremendous distance between abstraction and *res*. The conceits involved, however, would hardly qualify for comparison with the sophisticated and deeply felt product of, say, a Herbert or a Donne, whom she would imitate repeatedly at Cambridge.

Directly and simply, far too simply, the imagination is symbolized by a summer house being boarded up at vacation's end. "Thoughts," belonging to the observer-narrator, had once been like weeds in the tumbling tide, "a maze of mermaid hair," but now deteriorate into bat wings that "disappear/ into the attic of the skull." The metaphors and similes in the second stanza here are effective in carrying through the metamorphosis of the real into the unreal (and vice versa) which was begun by the title and first stanza. The third stanza is a bald statement of aesthetic intent. Her poetic voice sheds its metaphorical function to phrase unequivocally the problem, hers and her lover's, and to outline in near-prose the poem's philosophical *raison d'être:*

> We are not what we might be: what we are
> outlaws all extrapolation
> beyond the interval of now and here:
> white whales are gone with the white ocean.

This is heady stuff for a college undergraduate to essay and would impress the distinguished panel of judges who eventually awarded it the Glascock prize; but it violates the Poundian dictum against naked declarations of moral convictions and aesthetic preachments. Common sense, and this verse as an example, indicate that such an abrupt shift jeopardizes the poem's nurturing atmosphere and can ruin whatever artistic cohesion the poet has labored to create.

The last stanza (as quoted above) is saved somewhat by the final line, its alliterative, conversational ease reaffirming the poem's pictorial allegiance to an historical awareness of place. In terms of meaning, it supports the contention of the previous three lines that nothing exists beyond the present tense by mourning the loss of Moby Dick and the leviathan allegory of good and evil he represented. As an immediate image, it implies white-caps suggesting humps of white whales. White and sea for Sylvia were dual aspects of the same innocence—not sperm intrusions, but her lost fusion with the things of the real world of the past. Her childhood reminiscence about that "fine, white flying myth" has become Melville's vanished America: disappearing remnants of a century in which nature still held profound secrets and in which gods and demons were still plausible literary monads.

The fourth stanza presents the sole human figure in the poem's bleak terrain, "a lone beachcomber," and introduces yet another lost world. With a stick, the beachcomber is rooting among "kaleidoscopic shells" and "probing fractured Venus." His only company is "a tent of taunting gulls." Sylvia is broadening the scene, shaping a larger perspective, expanding towards a greater and greater spirit of desolation. Gulls, who can fly, in arrogant contrast to man's unaristocratic and slightly comical squat, are represented as passing a moral judgment upon the beach-comber, a low figure in our society who has neither property nor stature but is often associated with a somewhat romanticized perception of life. The reference to a fractured Venus evokes Botticelli's lush painting (the poem evokes a "painterly" quality throughout), while its broken condition symbolizes Sylvia's eschewal of the Italian Renaissance and its grandiose glorification of individual man. Instead of a beautiful allusion to a sensual goddess amid a flared, glorified shell, we get a lowly beachcomber, a prototypical failure, rummaging among discarded shells to the disdain of the bird kingdom. The irony is eloquent, all of a piece with what went before.

In fact, the irony of the fourth stanza acquires an almost diabolical cast when read at the level of Freudian symbolism. "Probing fractured Venus": the language compels recognition of unconscious signs which etch a cruel act of intercourse between an outcast and a dead, shattered goddess. Its terrible reality for Sylvia would be hard to deny in light of her subsequent confinement in a mental institution where, according to *The Bell Jar*, female symptoms of disorder generally manifested themselves in sexual terms. The depressing milieu of squalor under this Freudian interpretation amplifies the poem's dismal mood, which is grotesquely heightened by the fact that the beachcomber "squats" during his performance. As a result, two fundamental acts of existence, fornicating and defecating, both of which the poet regarded with adolescent disgust, are ruthlessly intermingled to stress again the utter destruction of an historic-aesthetic past, and whatever solutions such a past might once have supplied for inescapable mortality.

The images in the fifth stanza are as imaginative as those in the second, but the constrained syntax is too ungainly for full effectiveness. Modern man's helplessness before nature's raw power, the sea, is reiterated as a major motif, "sunken shank of bone," which exhibits a savage animism as it "chuckles in back track of the wave." Thus a vivid illustration, signal of the real, is mated to a deadly allusion. "Shank of bone" echoes Shakespeare's epigram, "a hank of hair and piece of bone," close enough to avoid a coincidence. Womanhood suffers a lack of identity under the threat of dehumanized sex. In a reversal from the terrifying role played in "Go Get the Goodly Squab," death by water has become a rhetorical exercise. The sea will not relinquish its dead, be they Moby Dick or Botticelli, "though the mind like an oyster labors on and on/ a grain of sand is all we have."

"One grain out of an entire beach": the thought is a sublime summary of the Plath canon, the fatal note inevitably ending symphonies of despair. Her sexual preoccupation with the woman, herself, and with coupling actions continues into "labors"—a barren task of giving birth to pearls, which stubbornly remain grains of sand; and into the oyster's resemblance to a woman's moist, mobile vulva. With the mixed language of Thomas and Stevens, the last stanza recapitulates and restores the imagination's lack of power and life, its closed-down state as visualized in the poem's initial metaphor:

> Water will run by the rule; the actual sun
> will scrupulously rise and set;
> no little man lives in the exacting moon
> and that is that, is that, is that.

What is finally significant and different about "Two Lovers and a Beachcomber by the Real Sea" is its absolute evasion of a direct assumption of deity and an appeal for humanistic alternatives. While rejecting prayers to a godhead who does not exist (or have a moral force), Sylvia returns to her stark vision of a completely anti-human cosmos. Previously, she had also negated the possibility of Christian redemption, but always in terms of Christian allegory itself. This poem's intellectual core is, however, foundationally and aridly atheistic, and the despair depicted possesses no saving romantic frame. Process—a dehumanized biological and mechanical process—is everything, though mankind must, like the pitiful oyster, persevere with the only weapon left. In man's case, it is his mind. This conflict involving mind, belief, and imagination will crop up often in Sylvia's poetry as she attempts to utilize her art for personal salvation. The disguises were wearing thin, the method turning towards madness and its heart-felt truth.

"Lament" does not bring madness any closer, but it does touch upon its central hurt, the death of the father, for the first time in a poem. The opening three lines *(terza rima)* clearly define the figure as none other than Otto the entomologist:

> The sting of bees took away my father
> Who walked in a swarming shroud of wings
> And scorned the tick of the falling weather.

It is simultaneously a hymn of praise and a song of rebuke: praise for his power ("wings") and arrogant courage ("scorned . . ."), rebuke for letting that arrogance destroy him. Almost as if afraid of confessional indiscretion, Sylvia removes her mother as well three stanzas later—thus perhaps again using fantasy for revenge:

> A scowl of sun struck down my mother
> Tolling her grave with golden tongs,
> But the sting of bees took away my father.

Dylan Thomas abounds, but he cannot be blamed for the poem's creaking sham, its refusal to step down into the furnace and take fire. As a lament, it fails to convey any sense of mourning or true loss. It is but another stage performance. more legerdemain. Perhaps the closeness of the subject forced Sylvia to retreat into earlier contrivances. Much more interesting, however, is the first step in the direction of a myth, father as god, the insistence upon raising memory into legend. Otto emerges as Poseidon no less, potent god of the sea in Greek mythology: "He rode the flood in a pride of prongs." He is an awesome, inhuman creature who laughed at "the ambush of angels' tongues" and could "mangle the grin of kings." Poetry touches Otto for the first time and he is a deity, a mythical giant; and this sets the stage for a classical resurrection later on. His crime was hubris, a striking back at the vast forces of nature unleashed in Sylvia's other poetry, and she looked upon him as savior.

On April 9, the night before Senator McCarthy's theatrics took place at Greene Hall, Robert Frost had spoken from the same stage. In his usual rambling style, he had emphasized that poetry was not a form of escapism, but a fervent "pursuit" of life—a belief that Sylvia still could not share with him. Nothing in her life or art had happened yet to indicate that her masks and cunning methods were inadequate. She was a success in both and continued to work hard at maintaining her image. After her final Smith weekend as an escort for graduating seniors and families, she headed east for a brief visit at home before reporting to her new summer job on Cape Cod. Again she would be near the sea.

Sylvia had been interviewed by the Placement Office on the same day Frost gave his speech and was supplied with a waitress position at the Belmont Hotel in West Harwich. She became, in her own words, "a hash slinger" with black uniform and all; and was polishing tables when the cable from *Mademoiselle* arrived via her mother which announced her prize for "Sunday at the Mintons."

The job turned out to be much more pleasant than she had anticipated, the demanding routine of physical labor giving her life a purposeful if mindless rhythm. The important fact was that she was on the Cape during its "swinging" season, surrounded by college kids eager to have a good time. As usual she over-did both working and playing and by Saturday, June 28, felt a menacing tickle in her throat. Past experience told her she was in for one of her exhausting illnesses and should stay in bed. Unfortunately, the phone rang in her room and it was Phil Brawner, a friend of hers from Wellesley who would be a senior at Princeton in the fall. Her mother had told him where he could reach Sylvia, and he wanted to take her out dining and dancing that night. Despite her forebodings and a work-shift that did not end until eight, she agreed.

After getting off work, she dressed up and met him in the lobby. They went to a nearby nightclub, and Sylvia enjoyed the meal and entertainment, as well as the general atmosphere of feverish activity. She foolishly made arrangements to meet him and a friend of his for tennis the next afternoon. But Sunday morning she woke up feeling quite sick and made an early trip to see a doctor in Harwich, who advised her to return home for a few days of rest. After informing her employer that she was ill and would be gone for a couple of days, Sylvia packed her suitcase. When Phil arrived in his tennis outfit, she asked him if he would mind her accompanying him back to Wellesley. He and his friend assured her it was all right with them, especially since it had started to rain and tennis was out of the question. On the way, they picked up another friend, another Princeton boy named Art Kramer, who was working as a chauffeur for a millionaire.

The four of them decided to have some fun before leaving the Cape and stopped off to buy some beer. Sylvia, who looked tan and healthy, went along with the idea, although her temperature was well over 100° and she felt feverish. They drove to the beach and sat watching the ocean for a while and drank their beer. Sylvia was very quiet, but the three boys assumed it was from exhaustion—the reason she had given for her abrupt departure. During the long ride home, she lost her voice and became miserably ill. Once at home, she went straight to bed, and her mother called the doctor. He arrived later that evening and gave Sylvia a penicillin shot, which had the effect of putting her in a coma for the next three days.

While she was unconscious the following day, the Belmont called to inquire when she would be returning as they had to hire a girl in the interim. Mrs. Plath, who believed that her daughter needed the rest and really did not want to go back, told them to hire a permanent replacement. When Sylvia recovered and found out what had happened, she was desolate. The idea of being trapped in an empty, hot Wellesley and missing all the fun at the Cape, of having nothing to do under her mother's eye, was too much. She lapsed into a depression and planned desperately how to get back to the ocean and her new friends at the Belmont.

Because it was already the middle of the season, her chances of finding a summer post were almost non-existent, but each day she scanned the help-wanted ads in the papers and phoned friends about possible vacancies. None was forthcoming and Sylvia began to realize that she had to structure her days carefully if she did not want her depression to worsen dangerously. She made out a daily schedule for herself and followed it tenaciously: "Science four hours in the morning. Afternoon, tennis practice, writing. Evening, short-hand or planned intellectual reading."

Phil Brawner, who was working without pay at the Shawmut Bank in Boston to gain experience, helped her get through the weekends. On Saturday, July 5, after playing tennis with her in the afternoon, he took Sylvia to a movie in Boston—a double bill of *Quartet* and *Kind Hearts and Coronets*, which she enjoyed. Sunday night they sat in the cocktail lounge at the Copley Plaza, "the merry-go-round," sipped Scotch and sodas, and talked about their respective problems. She found his company and fine Southern manners—he had been raised in Charleston —rather charming, but was not attracted to him physically. Later she admitted to Marcia Brown that she was using him because "he's a human being, of the Wellesley aristocracy, and a means of convenient transportation and amusement." Marcia had never seen this side of Sylvia, who soon showed that she realized her mistake by asking, "Do I shock you by my pragmatism?"

One local job opportunity did come along, a position with an aggressive real-estate agent who was opening an office in Wellesley. He was operating out of a tent for the moment, which was humid and lonely for Sylvia, who had to run the office when he was away with a customer; but she did get a chance to tour some local houses and talk to a few builders, and this fascinated her. The next day, however, there was an ad in *The Christian Science Monitor* for a mother's helper to work in Chatham—only twenty miles or so from the Belmont Hotel. Sylvia rushed to apply and was hired for the rest of the summer by a Mrs. "Edward Burns," a well-to-do follower of Mrs. Eddy with four children.

The Burnses lived in Waban, but rented a big gray house on a small knoll overlooking Chatham's golf course, not far from the sea. Sylvia reported for work on a Saturday, July 19, and met her three charges: "Joan," age three and rather grown-up for her age; "Susan," about five and a half, a quiet and well-behaved girl in pig-tails; and "Billy," almost four and a problem child with a terrible temper and a tendency to hide under his bed when not appeased. In every way, the Burns household seemed better than the Marches'. Sylvia found the parents a charming and warm-hearted couple who insisted upon treating her as a member of the family, which included elaborate meals of lobster, lamb, beef, and steak, along with an endless supply of fresh fruit and salads.

The negative side of the coin did not become apparent until a few weeks later, when Sylvia began to realize that her role as "a member of the family" also entailed parental-like supervision and interference—a loss of independence that distressed her and reminded her of her own mother's possessive ways. For all her warmth and sincere concern, Mrs. Burns seemed to Sylvia something of a prig. She made her feel uncomfortable whenever she talked to a boy on the phone or went out on a date. Once, when Sylvia had a call after ten at night, Mrs. Burns looked at her archly and inquired, "And where did you meet all these boys?"

Sylvia told Marcia that she felt like replying, "What the hell do you think I am, Red Riding Hood? I think I could fight off any man single-handed, and they're not carnivorous beasts. You married one, didn't you?"

She did nothing of the sort, of course, but repressed her legitimate anger. Back at the Cape again and relatively content, she was not about to let her mask slip, even when Mrs. Burns undertook a subtle campaign to convert her to Christian Science. Aurelia and her relatively more *laissez-faire* home seemed almost attractive by contrast, though Sylvia knew that she had to escape from her mother, especially during times of intense depression: "I love her dearly," she admitted to Marcia, "but she reverberates so much more intensely than I to every depression I go through that I really feel she is better without the strain of me and my intense moods, which I can bounce in and out of with ease."

In terms of actual work, the Burns household was more demanding than the Marches' had been. Sylvia did much more housework, alongside Mrs. Burns, and washed the family sheets and children's clothes each week, in addition to providing snacks for the three youngsters and helping with the main meals. All this meant washing a great quantity of dishes as well, for the Burnses entertained frequently. But Mrs. Burns' superb cooking and the long days at the beach with the children removed some of the strain, as did the Cape's exciting night life. She had many dates and was able to visit her new friends at the Belmont several times. Also Mrs. Burns soon began letting Sylvia drive the family car, a Chevrolet stationwagon, to take the children to the beach and on shopping expeditions into Chatham's narrow, traffic-clogged streets—a gesture of trust which Sylvia appreciated.

One of her most memorable dates of the summer—with Art Kramer, whom she described as "not too beautiful" and far too short for her—involved a visit to the wealthy Mrs. Blossom, who lived in Chatham year round. Although eighty-one and almost senile, Mrs. Blossom was still sprightly in company and, from her bed, told Sylvia and Art, who worked for her, many stories about her adventurous past. She enchanted the teenagers with tales of piano playing before MacDowell, and how she got a pass to see *South Pacific* from Mr. Richard Rodgers himself. Afterwards Sylvia was served sherbet by a servant and given the run of the huge mansion. Success and material wealth had never seemed so closely intertwined.

The job with the Burnses ended on September 16, which aroused mixed feelings in Sylvia. The idea of leaving any "home" was upsetting, but she was glad to escape the hard work and Mrs. Burns' sweetly domineering behavior. Mrs. Burns herself would become and remain a staunch supporter of Sylvia in the years ahead, and a good friend to Aurelia; but Esther's final judgment of her in *The Bell Jar* is one of contemptuous dismissal in which Mrs. Burns is lumped with Mary Ellen Chase and the other old ladies who were always trying to dominate her. Mrs. Burns' visit to Sylvia at McLean's more than a year later would be treated with vicious humor in the novel:

My mother was only one in a long stream of visitors—my former employer, the lady Christian Scientist, who walked on the lawn with me and talked about the mist going up from the earth in the Bible, and the mist being error, and my whole trouble being that I believed in the mist, and the minute I stopped believing in it, it would disappear and I would see I had always been well . . .

As she was being driven south towards Wellesley, in a taxi paid for by Mrs. Burns, Sylvia experienced a vague, anxious sense of loose moorings. As she explained it in a letter to the editors at *Seventeen*, "I was heading back home and realized that, just as I had gotten rooted in my summer habitat, I was cast adrift again." [12] The result was a Shakespearian sonnet in which she "tried to get this across where the solar system tilted and so on." Entitled "The Suitcases Are Packed Again," the poem extends the pathetic fallacy into universal dimensions as the driver "grinds the gears and, with a jerk/ We zoom up into lunatic black sky." The rest of it cleverly develops the basic concept further: stars buzzing "like imbecilic bees" and meteors chirping "in quick chaotic orange"—all because she was departing. Though uneven and not very original, the poem does attempt to translate the terrible anxiety of saying goodbye to a home-like place into a viable symbol, and again reveals some of the dynamics of insecurity driving Sylvia's inner world.

But the major significance of the poem is its continuation of her obsession with cosmic imagery. In fact, it was one of many poems— "Notes on Zarathustra's Prologue," "Dialogue en Route," "To Eva

Descending a Stair," and so on—which insisted upon equating awesome astronomical phenomena with personal states of consciousness. Part of this is quite natural, the expected response of a young poet without systematic convictions to her quite ordinary material; but the extent of its application, its constant, repetitive degree, also suggests a deeper motivation. Sylvia's need "to relate herself to nothing less than the universe," what a psychiatrist would call "the cosmological motive," was an effective method of fighting back against her fear of oblivion.

By summer's end, then, nothing had radically altered in Sylvia's life, at least not in its surface patterns; but exhaustion, mental and physical, was boring through her defenses.

> . . . we want to remove our make-up and take off what is false and be real. But somewhere a piece of disguise that we forgot sticks to us . . . And so we walk around, a mockery and a mere half: neither having achieved being nor actors.
>
> RAINER MARIA RILKE

5

Stillness Is a Lie, My Dear

Winning the *Mademoiselle* short-story contest had polished Sylvia's image at Smith to a mirror brightness, though she herself dared not inspect it too closely. But her junior year began with misgivings. Tuition had been raised another $150, which was not covered by her endowment; and she was forced to leave Haven and move into Lawrence House, a cooperative dormitory for scholarship students where she would have to share the often tedious housekeeping chores (supposedly an hour a day) and serve as a waitress. She was also losing Marcia, which meant a part of her own ego; and the whole concept of moving quarters from the familiar to the strange, of making a domestic change, was upsetting in itself. Happily, her new room, a second-floor suite arrangement with two bedrooms and a common parlor, was large and comfortable, with two windows facing the nearby library and several other resident halls.

Academically, of course, Lawrence was much superior to Haven in the public achievements of its residents, if not in their social pedigrees. During October the house would earn first prize in the Sigma Xi's awards for science students. October was a busy and important month for Sylvia as well. On the seventh, an article had appeared in the school paper about the publication of "The Perfect Setup" in *Seventeen*, along with a highly complimentary outline of her writing career to date.[1] The same issue contained the announcement of two country-wide poetry contests which she wished to enter. One of them, the National Poetry Association's competition for poems to fill its annual college anthology, involved nothing more than a few extra poetry submissions; but the other, *Mademoiselle*'s yearly search for twenty guest editors for its special summer issue devoted to college life and fashions, entailed much more.

As a first step, she had to write a 1500-word critique of the August 1952 issue, specifying likes and dislikes and suggesting concrete changes. This had to be submitted along with a detailed statement of the particular field she was interested in pursuing and why. If successful, she would then be appointed to the Smith College Board and have to complete three given assignments. Her chances of success were rather good since she had won the magazine's short-story contest; and a Smith girl, Jo Ann Wallace, had been an editor the year before. Moreover, Smith was most likely the kind of college *Mademoiselle* wanted represented under any circumstances, in light of its reputation as a leading girls' institution.

Besides a steady stream of submissions and class essays, Sylvia was also busy with her work on the editorial board of the *Smith Review*, which had recently been revived, and with her studies and a large correspondence. She had been admitted to the Honor's Program in English, which meant that she could have greater freedom in her selection of courses, that is, concentrate more on the literature and writing classes that most interested her. Further, the chapel meeting of Wednesday, October 2, had been given over to Dean Randall's announcement of the First Group Scholars, those students whose averages were 3.6 or above. Sylvia was among the 25 girls in her class who fell into this category, a class which now numbered 419 students, 72 of whom were spending their junior year abroad. She was at the top of her class in almost every sense and already well known around campus for both her poetry and scholastic achievements.

Professor Evelyn Page, one of her writing instructors, noted that Sylvia's "fault is to demand too much of herself," being "strict with herself but tolerant of others." A fellow student summed up the school's general view: "I thought she was very sweet—and terribly tired." Driven by a "terrifying fear of mediocrity," she disciplined herself to scale peak after peak, which wore her down physically and mentally, although she would have been the last to admit it. Exhaustion, like illness, represented a surrender of the will. It could also—what was much worse—lead to introspection, a crumbling of inner defenses against the horde of unwanted memories, fears, secret hatreds.

She was writing regularly to Buddy, maintaining the fiction of their unofficial engagement, and seeing Myron Lotz at frequent intervals, and corresponding with Philip McCurdy, now a freshman at Harvard. The latter, whom she saw only during vacations, remained more a congenial companion and admirer than a boy friend in any romantic context. Philip was one with whom she could relax to a certain degree and play the role of loving sister. McCurdy remarks that their long, serious conversations inevitably "came back to Eliot and Cummings again and again." She would introduce him to the subtleties of poetic techniques and he kidded her about her continuing problems with art. As he remembers it, "she made light gently of my superficial rhyming efforts as I often joked with her about her difficulty with freedom, color placement, and balance in painting." [2]

McCurdy had entered Harvard that fall, intent on becoming a teacher, and thus he was later able to open that intellectual sanctuary to her presence by inviting her up to a number of house parties. But Buddy remained a problem. Having no more use for him, she was still reluctant to put herself in the position of rejecting him outright while he was ill. During the Christmas vacation, she paid what was to be her last visit to him at the sanatorium. Although she did not directly broach the subject of disengagement, her mocking, contemptuous attitude left little doubt of her eventual intention. Perhaps only someone with Buddy's childish temperament and innocence, both of which were being reinforced daily by his frightening illness and the threat of an operation, could have stayed unaware of her obvious distaste for both the sanatorium and him. Driven up to the lake by Professor Willard, who continued to regard her as "a beautiful, gifted, happy, wholesome girl and young woman," Sylvia was further disgusted to discover that Buddy had let himself grow quite heavy on the rich diet prescribed by his doctors and a near complete lack of physical exercise. Though still a great lover of food, she could not abide obesity in herself or others and viewed it as a sign of inner deterioration.

In her eyes, Buddy's new flabbiness might also have been a clear confirmation of the self-pity she believed was destroying him. Fortunately, she was boarding with a young couple who had a cottage near the sanatorium, a Dr. Lynn and his attractive wife Emmy. Struck down by TB himself some years earlier, Dr. Lynn had decided to become a writer during his convalescence and was a fluent conversationalist on literary matters, which helped make Sylvia's visit more bearable. But the pressure of Buddy and his frightening sickness was difficult to avoid and, in an attempt to apply her usual cure of salvation through motion, she set out to learn how to ski.

Sylvia was doing rather well in the fundamental stages, her athletic body responding gracefully to each new challenge, when she allowed herself to be encouraged into trying the big hill and took the lift up the mountain's side. With a foolish, almost suicidal kind of abandonment, she then launched herself down the steep incline. After a brief, intoxicating "flash of ecstasy," she found herself rocketing through space towards a distant river in the serpentine valley below. Control was impossible, and she did a dramatic cartwheel before landing in a flurry of snow and frozen earth. Grinning sheepishly, she started to her feet and fell back down. Her left leg was broken in two places.

Dr. Lynn provided excellent care, supervising her recovery, and the immobilization proved more restful than irritating. Unlike Buddy, the young doctor could engage her in long, serious, highly involved literary discussion; and she, in turn, read his massive, unpublished novel with intense interest—a novel she later described to a friend as "a passionate, James-Joycian study of introspection involving every controversial subject from sex to God to modern art." Though personally fascinated by the book, she felt sure that it would never get published. There is more than a hint of disapproval even in her lush compliments, as if she wanted it known that she herself remained determined never to permit her own writing to become so remote from public success. For to her, getting published was not merely important, it was everything. She had no intention of devoting her career to unpopular, experimental enterprises. She would continue to manufacture whatever she believed her specific audience, whether college professors or readers of *Seventeen*, wanted and expected her to produce.

This is all too evident in the poem "Twelfth Night" which was printed in the December *Seventeen*, and in the trite tale about a high-school fraternity, "Initiation," which had actually won the second prize in the same magazine's annual short-story competition and would appear a month later. "Twelfth Night" might be forgiven some of its banalities on the basis of its blatant seasonal impetus, but the crude emotional play upon Poe's "Masque of the Red Death" and the poem's lush romantic trimmings reflect the condescending contempt of the author for her teenage readers. Only in the last two lines—as usual, the climax called her back to the fatal wound—is flesh pared from bone: "As amid the hectic music and gay talk/ She hears the caustic ticking of the clock."

In the following months, while still restricted by the cast on her leg, she would write a much stronger piece, a short story entitled "In the Mountains," that would be published in the Fall 1954 issue of the *Smith Review*. Another story in *The New Yorker* mode, that is, both consciously sophisticated and psychologically subtle, it has a sparse precision of insight and event that is in sharp contrast to her poetry of the time. Much of this results from its patent autobiographical content—Dr. Lynn's name is not even changed—as it recounts the adventures of a young college girl, Isobel by name, when she meets her boy friend Austin in Albany and they take the bus together up to his TB sanatorium in the mountains. Thus, for the first time (if "Sunday at the Mintons" is not counted), Buddy will be symbolically tarred in print, playing a gross Caliban to her Ariel. During the course of the bus ride—and the story is the ride, simple and diary-clear—he emerges as a typical unfeeling lout, while she suffers in silence under his crudeness: "He had always scorned weakness. Any kind of weakness, and she remembered how he mocked her being tender at the killing of the guinea pigs."

As in "Sunday at the Mintons," the stark opposites are cleverly, if superficially sketched in, then reinforced, and the reader has little trouble identifying with and rooting for the sensitive Isobel. At one point, being more real than wise, the heroine makes clear Sylvia's own determination not to be sucked down into marriage: " 'Affairs are one thing,' she said. 'But signing your life away because you're lonely, because you're afraid of being lonely, that's something else again.' " This is out of character for Isobel, but Sylvia still had to depend upon her own interior monologues for material. It must have given her rare pleasure finally to use literature directly in this fashion to state a personal conviction.

The climax of the story—as much of one as a *New Yorker*-type story is allowed—comes when a fellow passenger, an old man, remarks that an open window is too cold for him. Isobel asks Austin to close it, but he refuses, saying, "I will shut it for you, but I won't shut it for him. Do you want it shut?" Then he gives himself away to the Nazi underneath; and the line "He got angry like cold steel" links him with the cold blue eyes of the brother in "Sunday at the Mintons." Isobel sighs patiently and asks him to shut it for her, which he does. Isobel then dozes off on Austin's arm until the bus reaches their stop, and they disembark.

Impulsively, she waves at the old man as the bus pulls away, a true and good heroine to the end. The threat of marriage again intrudes with the appearance of Emmy Lynn, the doctor's young and pretty wife, and reminders of Austin's possibilities as a future husband. The shock now, however, is a reverse one that stems from Austin's suddenly craven acquiescence, as he drinks coffee just to please her and tries to acquire literary values. There was not enough Nazi left in him!

Austin had written to Isobel about Hemingway's *A Farewell to Arms*—a novel he would never have read with sympathy before TB invaded his lungs; and Isobel can wonder that "It was not like him to worry about the girl dying in the book." Like Buddy, Austin had softened, partly out of fear and partly out of need for her; and the change was sickening rather than heartening to witness. At the conclusion of "In the Mountains," the two "lovers" hold hands in front of a fireplace, but hers is described as "cool and unresponsive." It is a solid tale in the will-o-wisp manner, superior to the *Seventeen* honey balls—professional, crisp, perceptive to a degree. More important, it shows that Sylvia did understand herself more than she let on or wanted to and could translate her knowledge of herself and Buddy into viable fiction. The story prevails and a decision had been made. She was not going to marry Buddy under any circumstances.

Earlier he had at least been attractive and rather like her autocratic father—perhaps even strong enough to provide a secure if insensitive existence. She could have played a snug daughter's role and written her poems from the safe haven of the substantial home he would purchase for her. Now that dream was irrevocably lost, and the loss was unsettling in a deeper way than she could have anticipated. It left her unanchored to any definite future. All this and a growing fatigue would make the mask harder and harder to hold up in the months ahead. The danger was not that she would lose control or surrender to the impulses of the raging bitch goddess within herself but that the stiff outward features would become recognizable as parts of a mask.

But method again came to the rescue, at least temporarily, as she returned home early and had a few extra days to spend in Wellesley. Her brother kindly chauffeured her around town and drove her back to school before returning to Exeter himself. The first semester was drawing to a close, and there were examinations to prepare for and papers to be written. Soon after her arrival, the college was inundated by an intense winter storm; snow was "coming down in gulps and blasts and sleetings and icings and softly piling up and always up." It was difficult navigating through the snow banks on her crutches, but Sylvia had to leave her dormitory room only once—to attend her class on medieval literature—before Smith lapsed into its week-long free-study time known as the Reading Period.

As she had no particular worries about the forthcoming finals, Sylvia devoted most of the week to writing two class essays, one on Piers Plowman, "the people's Christ," and another on the Holy Grail; and to working out "In the Mountains" while the gloomy trip to Saranac Lake was still fresh in her mind. She also wrote her usual complement of letters, including a long one to Lotz in which she quoted from *The Rubaiyat*, "one of my favorite poems," and underlined the phrase "I myself am Heaven and Hell." The general tenor of the letter was happy, however, true to the mask, and concentrated on the pleasure she foresaw during the second semester when her status as an honor's student would bring her into closer contact with the English faculty, whose members she continued to regard with almost reverential awe as "lofty geniuses." In fact, the determination to be able one day to teach at their side as an equal had grown into a concrete plan. For a writer, teaching at Smith seemed ideal, a guarantee of the "rich intellectual life" she had always treasured.

Winning prizes, getting published, becoming known, maintaining an "A" average, were the steps to this goal; and, if anything, Sylvia would be working harder than ever to achieve them during the second semester. Early in December, further gratification had come her way with the acceptance of the poem "Crossing the Equinox" by the National Poetry Association for its anthology (her first time between hard covers), and the broadcasting of that news in the school paper. She had also entered two of Smith's own poetry competitions, submitting anonymous contributions to both the Elizabeth Babcock Poetry Prize and the Ethel Olin Prize contests. Near the end of January, she was also notified that she was one of the lucky ten out of seven hundred entrants who had been designated finalists in the *Mademoiselle* competition, which meant that she now had to labor over her three assignments. Even her remarkable, obsessive energy must have felt the additional burden.

What is perhaps most unbelievable about Sylvia's drive was the capacity it demonstrated for a parallel creative force as well. Stories and poems poured from her typewriter in an avalanche of language and form, including many that were discarded whole if they displeased her. Creativity—the certain sign of special fate, an escape from mediocrity— was even more crucial than academic prowess, although she continued to approach art with the same dogged tenacity she gave to her studies. McCurdy's observation about her writing technique is interesting for the insight it provides into Sylvia's whole concept of her art while at Smith and before: "Though we were young, she did not, in retrospect, labor or gush—but very carefully *crafted* her output. I don't remember her straining in actually putting it down, but after lengthy conceptualizing, talking and thinking out, without the agonizing over a line or phrase or word *per se,* it seemed to be there. Actually, I cannot recall her *writing* in my presence as much as working through other authors, ideas, events, and insights." [3]

Such an approach, unusual in an author so young, certainly reflects her dedication to the fundamental principles of her craft but leaves scant room for either taking risks or discovering miracles. As a result, none of the more than four hundred poems written during her years at Smith has much genuine worth. If there are individual lines of great merit, sudden, delightful phrases, startling images, valid insights, the poems themselves cannot be read as well-rounded performances. Mostly they are apprentice exercises laden with too much intellectual weight and derivation from philosophy and literature. Sylvia herself would eventually disavow them completely (along with many later ones that cannot afford to be lost) because of their remoteness from spoken language and true feelings. But during her Smith days she had not yet resolved the fundamental paradox of poetry—that which depends, as it were, upon the pendulum swing between Keats' and Eliot's traditional concept of the poet without an identity "continually informing and filling some other Body" and Pound's idea of the poet as culture hero, the only authentic hero left in the modern world. Her own identity was, too fragmented for her to dare use it as a tool for exploring whatever dark caverns her brilliant, wounded mind forced her to enter. The result was a series of clever disguises; although Eliot's famous comment upon the progress of the artist as "a continual self-sacrifice, a continual extinction of personality" would have undoubtedly dismayed her. Empedocles' leap into the volcano made more sense.

This helps explain why she was "absolutely wild for Auden" at this point in her life, and why the poems emerged as "Audenesque" in general tone and structure. All of them presupposed an urbane, detached voice that refused personal involvement and revelation. In fact, one of the events that excited her about the second semester was the prospect of meeting her idol in person. Beginning in mid-February, a week after the February 14th premiere of Stravinsky's *The Rake's Progress* at the Metropolitan Opera, for which he had written the libretto, Auden would be occupying the William Allan Neilson Chair of Research at Smith for "three whole months." Like Yeats, Thomas, and Eliot, whom she had missed at his famous Harvard readings to her great regret, Auden represented the kind of high art and solid popularity Sylvia so desired for herself.

Sylvia's own poetry was still unable to escape Auden's deadening influence, but it was clearly defining her essential vision of the world. Two of her poems from this period, "Doomsday" and "To Eva Descending the Stair," show some slight improvement over previous efforts. They continue her intense fascination with the darker side of American literature, her Poe-line as filtered through Auden's fine cloth. The fatal note, however, the sense and aura of internal bleakness reflecting life's grimmer alternatives, is still imprisoned by conventional formulas. Her natural taste for the demonic and hopeless, which gave a Gothic cast to everything she wrote, was simply not being given free rein or, worse, seemed too artificial and exaggerated for conviction.

In many ways, "Doomsday" is a continuation of and elaboration upon the negative, unusually romantic perspective established in "Mad Girl's Love Song," with the difference that the narrator is now striving to view the destruction of reality (of scientific *and* religious reality) from a more objective vantage by including herself in the social "we" of the poem's locus. A "universal clock" is the central image, a stereotyped concept lifted from the mechanical universe once visualized by the Deists; but Sylvia cannot, poetically at least, contemplate a truly godless construct; and it is "God's monkey wrench" which destroys "all machines," and not the cynicism or corruption of any human intelligence. Further, the moral questions suggested by the cataclysm do not surface until the end when it becomes "Too late to ask if end was worth the means." Role-playing takes over as ethics masks art. And yet the horror is certainly present, buried deeply under those dry stanzas of careful artifice, her apocalyptic voice whispering through its thin cracks.

"To Eva Descending the Stair" is somewhat more successful primarily because Sylvia had a literal situation upon which to rest her intricately contrived allusions. Depending upon the mythic Eve figure, which had already been used earlier in "Dialogue en Route," Sylvia here transposed self with the allegorical woman of womanhood. Eve is accepted as real and immediate and engaged in the very Freudian activity of descending a staircase. But the poem has an iron cage similar to the prison of "Doomsday" and similarly revolves upon the creaking concept of a mechanical universe: "Clocks cry" and "the universe keeps running." Running is the key as Eva is warned thrice that "stillness is a lie, my dear." It is difficult not to relate this line to Sylvia's own compulsion to run—to achieve constantly—as if stasis and a moment's self-examination might be fatal. Her poetry was still warning herself against herself through its preaching at the world.

On January 13 the student newspaper announced that the House Committee on Un-American Activities had listed Smith as one of the colleges found to have three or more communist members on its staff. An investigation was almost sure to follow.

Sylvia, however, stayed in character and still refused to accept the political or historical part of her persona. Smith was her arena, not the national political scene. Relentlessly, she pursued her studies, wrote stories and poems, and continued to chase after local honors and highly visible school posts. On February 12 she became a junior class representative for the Electoral Board and was also again made a member of the House Council. Far more important in practical terms, she was re-appointed to the Press Board in April. This time she was to work for the *Hampshire Gazette*. A month later she was honored with the school's finest literary plum by being elected editor of the *Smith Review* for the following year.

Auden did finally arrive and gave a reading of his poems at the college on March 8, a Sunday afternoon. Sylvia attended and was delighted by his dry, controlled reading, droll informality, and wrinkled, kindly face. At the reading she met Gordon Lameyer for the first time, although he was a fellow resident of Wellesley, and soon found herself with another boy friend. Nancy Hunter, Sylvia's future roommate, has described Lameyer as "intelligent, articulate, spectacularly handsome, and obviously devoted to Syl," and stressed his height, which was over six feet. This was a natural preference as Sylvia regarded herself as tall; but it may also have had something to do with her unceasing search for a father substitute as Otto had always loomed over her child's-eye view of him and the world.

Gordon Lameyer had other essential qualifications as well.[4] Born in West Newton, the younger of two children, Lameyer possessed a German background similar to Sylvia's, along with unseen scars from the early loss of his father, who had separated from his wife soon after their son's birth. The father had been interned as an alien during the war; and, like Mrs. Plath, the Lameyer matriarch had moved to Wellesley in 1942, determined to make the American Dream come true. Lameyer attended only the best schools, including Sessenden and Choate, and entered Amherst in September 1949, where he was pursuing a liberal arts degree with a major in literature. As he was also participating in the Naval Reserve Officer Training Corps he could become, and already acted like, an officer and a gentleman in the grand old tradition.

When they met, Sylvia was still on crutches, and he guided her back to her dormitory before returning to Amherst. Their conversation was exciting for both of them, his enthusiasm for Auden echoing her own. They also discussed James Joyce, his particular favorite, and Dylan Thomas, whom she had heard read at Amherst.[5] But agreement was not general in the latter case. Lameyer had serious doubts about the Welshman's lush romanticism, and Sylvia refused to abandon her worship either of him or of his poetry. The disagreement, however, was in the kind of intellectual vein that Sylvia could tolerate and appreciate, and they promised to keep in touch. Sylvia now had contacts at New England's big three male citadels, Yale, Harvard, and Amherst, and two highly acceptable boy friends to replace the fading Buddy. Lameyer's literary interest and knowledgeableness must have seemed like a delicious bonus, and the possibility of marriage not as harrowing as it once appeared. If not a medical student, he did have all the other qualifications.

Where Lameyer and Lotz and so many other boy friends would fail Sylvia was in their middle-class backgrounds, in the very respectability which she had learned to court and honor. Influenced strongly by their mothers' intense social aspirations, they were bound to be on the polite, well-mannered side, dutiful towards women, and ever aware of the social amenities and the need to defer to women, especially in unimportant matters. Ravishment did not enter their minds, at least not seriously, and a woman's "no" had to be accepted as final, even when their sensitivities told them differently. They were not Nazi enough for Sylvia, their eyes never growing hard "like cold steel"; and as a result they could never recreate the father-daughter tyranny Sylvia so desperately wanted. Worse, their middle-class respectability reflected her mother's dull world, which she continued to hate with a secret passion.

All of this was internal, however, part of the madness, still remote from the surface method, which went on reaping success. When the committee of English teachers decided upon the winning poems in the Ethel Olin Corbin and Elizabeth Babcock contests, they looked up the real names of the winners and were dismayed to find only one, Sylvia Plath's. Consternation and much serious discussion followed as they wrestled with the moral and educational dilemma of having such an unprecedented honor fall into the hands of a single student. The whole idea seemed to go against the grain of American education and its shotgun marriage to democratic ideals. But wiser heads, including Professor Gibian's, did prevail in the end, and Sylvia was awarded both prizes.

Gibian felt strongly that Sylvia's group of poems were "head and shoulders above all other poems—and some were good too—by others." The group's candid title, "Verbal Calisthenics," certainly describes the type of sheer inventiveness and dazzling intellectual powers on display. They deserved recognition, though destined not to outlast their inception or their author's subsequent, startling growth. "Second Winter," which won the Corbin Prize, is a typical pastoral exercise that could have been written by Sylvia in junior or senior high school— except, perhaps, for some of the sophisticated imagery and the colloquial closing line.

The poem's opening phrase, "And so it goes," is conversationally apt, informal, and relaxed, but what follows is predictable and conventional. Some of the metaphors, such as "bright fireworks of flowers" seen as breaking through their "stubborn shell," are charming in a Marianne Moore manner, without being profound or jolting; but old chestnuts predominate: "phoenix ecstasy of wings" and "the traitor climate." Only the final line, "and so my love has gone, and so it goes," reintroduces the ease of the initial line and betrays a human hand. There is a spoken language at work here that distinguishes it from the rest of the poem's archaic stiffness and makes it nearly modern. Its wry acceptance is also refreshing after all that vegetable display of garden-variety romanticism. Perhaps, at a personal level, the poem also heralded Sylvia's acceptance of her split from Buddy, although fear of self-revelation still prevented her from letting a private voice enter her poetic domain. Another poem from the same time, "Dénouement," encloses the same situation, a lover departing, in another Yeats-like circus, minus the despair. The repetitions of "There is nothing more for me to say" and "The telegram says you have gone away" are further examples of her inability to make refrains work and an absence of conviction.

But poetry as disguise was not really working for Sylvia. As the fatigue wore her down, intense emotional pressure began to build up inside that would vent itself in either freedom or a collapse into failure's blankness. The mask was getting heavier and heavier. Near the end of April, Myron Lotz invited her up to Yale for a special weekend celebration, which was supposed to take the place of the infamous Derby Day, that traditional Yale extravaganza which had led to intense college/town hatreds in the past. While in New Haven, she stayed with

Robert and Jill Modlin, college friends of Lotz who had recently married and were living in a tiny apartment in town.

Sylvia slept behind a curtain in a small alcove and was a perfect house guest in almost every way, while being extremely appreciative of the slightest favor. But the inner uncertainty and emotional turmoil could no longer be completely suppressed. Her splitting personality yanked at her from both sides of the spinster-mother conflict as at one moment she was praising Jill highly for having sacrificed an education and future career in journalism to help put her husband through medical school, and at the next expressing amazement and obvious disapproval of the whole idea.

Both Modlins appreciated Sylvia's neatness and courtesy, the pleasant exterior method, but both also sensed a pervasive lack of spontaneity. Her mask was not functioning well at all. She was "taking too many things in, looking, perhaps feeling, but not participating," acting the loner role, becoming the observer at another foreign spectacle that did not really involve her. Robert remembers thinking "that she was there, kept a smile on her face and said the right things, but was not really there" and that she was "again going through the motions" during the long day of picnics, dancing, and beer-drinking contests. Though ostensibly Mike's "date," she rarely touched or sat near him; and his rambunctious, high-spirited behavior seemed in boyish contrast to her prim remoteness. Once again the Modlins wondered what she was looking for in their friend.

That night, however, things seemed to change radically. It was a romantic evening under the stars on the beach near Look Out Point and its blinking lighthouse. The two couples had separated by mutual consent, and Mike and Sylvia were finally alone together. At first, Sylvia seemed more distant than ever as she lay beside him, watching the light flashing on the water and listening to a mournful fog horn. Their sporadic talk drifted inevitably into literary channels. Sylvia quoted from *Antony and Cleopatra*:

> O happy horse, to bear the weight of Antony!
> Do bravely, horse, for wot'st thou whom thou mov'st?
> The demi-Atlas of this earth, the arm
> And burgonet of men. He's speaking now,
> Or murmuring 'Where's my serpent of old Nile?'

Then she went on to tell him, in a dreamy, distant voice, of how she used to lie in bed at night as a child, unable to sleep and feeling herself floating away, out of her own skin. Always glad of a chance to demonstrate his cultural prowess and memory, Lotz responded by telling her how happy he would be to hold her down in place, become her counter-weight, and alluded to the famous death scene from the same play in which "weight" is played upon by Shakespeare as an expression of Antony's value. Sylvia let Lotz lie on top of her fully clothed and they "dry-humped" in typical teenage fashion, while he fondled her breasts. There was no intercourse in any sense of the word, but his male body pressed into hers kept her locked into the reality she had suddenly found slipping away. Frightened of losing her identity, she needed the sheer weight of him, his masculine, athletic bulk and animal hunger, to pin her spinning universe into the earth, remind her breasts and stomach and outspread legs that she was a real woman in a real time and place. If she could not yet bring herself to accept copulation and the intrusion it represented, she could and did accept this clumsy form of imitation and ritual, just as she accepted her art.

From Lotz's point of view, Sylvia was probably the artist he could not find in himself, the poetess of culture he had always yearned to plunder and master as a strange symbol of his own intellectual and social worth. Whatever its undercurrents, the whole episode had a soothing, beneficial effect upon Sylvia. The next morning, which the two couples spent on the beach reading the Sunday edition of the *New York Times*, she appeared much more relaxed and less self-conscious. Modlin found himself truly liking her for the first time as they soaked up the warm sun, drank cokes, conversed pleasantly about school and current events, and occasionally took a swim. Sun and water inevitably brought out the best in Sylvia, though her sinus problem still prevented her from remaining underwater for very long. The parody of coupling with Lotz the night before had undoubtedly given her a sense of peace and pragmatic awareness, at least for the time being.

But school difficulties continued to harass her in an insidiously quiet way. Besides a difficult Chaucer course, she was taking German and getting a "B" for the first time in her academic career, which would mean the end of her hopes for *summa cum laude* honors. German, the language of her parents, particularly of her father, repelled and resisted her. Even her vacuum-cleaner brain could not sweep up its consonantal toughness. As Esther would complain, "Each time I picked up a German dictionary or a German book, the very sight of those dense, black, barbed-wire letters made my mind shut up like a clam." The language itself subconsciously suggested her hidden hatred of Otto Plath and his authority. Rejecting his language was a defensive gesture, a fairly safe way for her unconscious to vent its real feelings against him.

The other nagging problem was the break-up with Buddy, a less costly one perhaps, but part of a growing uneasiness. Her poetry was obsessed, after all, with departures, the conclusion of love affairs, and an unshakable sense of lost connections. Still the rest of the semester was a successful continuation of her pursuit of public love. Soon after returning to campus, she was notified that her three assignments had indeed earned her the distinction of being one of *Mademoiselle*'s guest editors. This meant further recognition, the excitement of spending June in New York City, and a summer free of demeaning employment in the homes of strangers for $25 a week. The magazine would pay her a regular salary for her month-long effort, besides providing her with a room in a luxury hotel and a well-organized social life. Exposure to New York was enough to thrill Sylvia, who was not unaware of its practical value as well; but the extra benefit of having July and August free was almost overwhelming. As part of her Honor's program, she had definitely decided to write her thesis on James Joyce's use of twin images, which delighted Gordon Lameyer and probably reflected Sylvia's keen and consistent insight into her own dual nature.

She was again chosen as an usher for the Commencement Weekend exercises, which was duly noted by the friendly school press, although she would be in New York when the actual festivities took place. Sylvia was also busy writing her little pieces for the *Hampshire Gazette* and, as a member of the Press Board, was invited to the annual installation banquet at Wiggin's Tavern in Northampton on Wednesday, April 29, where Auden was the guest speaker. Along with the five other fledgling reporters, she listened enthralled as her venerable model expounded upon the problems and tasks of poetry. A month or so earlier, in a March 8th interview, he had spoken more directly about young poets, and his comments might be taken as a deliberate address to Sylvia's personal poetry and her approaches to its creation. "Perhaps the only thing to be criticized," he had said, "is the tendency to be too self-conscious and critical. It's fine when you're older, but young people want to write too much, and, consequently, a lot of it has to be thrown away." [6]

Advice of this sort, however, could have little effect upon Sylvia's rigid *modus operandi* since success was more and more certifying its worth. The string of unbroken awards, including the school's two highest prizes and frequent publication in national organs, had turned her third year into a sort of culminating triumph of art over life, with the *Mademoiselle* invitation the crowning victory. The April 16th edition of the school paper headlined her latest success at *Seventeen*: LAURELS FOR

RECENT POEM/ SYLVIA PLATH AGAIN WINS. Everyone knew who Sylvia Plath was by now at Smith, students and faculty. She was a winner from every angle, and to make sure of it the article began: "One of the most prominent writers on the Smith Campus has once again had her poetry published in *Seventeen* magazine." How she must have relished that sentence, its guarantee of immortality in the moment, its proof of her own value. Surely such an important public figure should not have a vacuum foetus growing so hideously in her virgin cave.

> . . . something very spooky started happening.
> Every time I came to the end of a block and stepped
> off the goddamn curb, I had this feeling that I'd never
> get to the other side of the street. I thought I'd just go
> down, down, down, and nobody'd ever see me again.
>
> J. D. SALINGER, *The Catcher in the Rye*

6

There Is Nothing More for Me to Say

Sylvia's arrival at the Barbizon Hotel must have temporarily relieved her growing sense of despair, or at least tempered it somewhat. None but the most jaded cosmopolite could remain indifferent to the towering building's obvious luxury and enveloping atmosphere of chaste elegance. Twenty girls, many of them from rural areas across the country, were led in a happy glow to their expensively appointed rooms. Sylvia's own plush cell was located on the fifteenth floor and overlooked the Third Avenue El, "rooftops, gardens, and a minute chink of the East River." [1] If she leaned out the window, which she promptly did, she could also see the United Nations headquarters.

Soon after getting settled, the guest editors gathered in the lobby and were herded into New York's streets by Betsy Blackwell, *Mademoiselle*'s editor-in-chief. She guided and encouraged them like a flock of gawking geese through the summer crowds to the magazine's offices on Madison Avenue. Along the way, she turned to smile at Sylvia and Laurie Levy, a bright student from Iowa, as they walked together. "You and Sylvia are our writers," she said. "I expect great things." [2]

Promises of glory, escape with literature from the ordinariness of life—in this highly charged and artificial situation, such dreams were easily shaped. Once actually inside the chattering spaces of *Mademoiselle*'s busy plant, the girls came face to face with the very heart of fantasy. Madelyn Mathers, the guest editor-in-chief, would attempt in the August issue to pin down for posterity's sake the butterfly aspects of the experience: "Still clutching our hats, gloves, pencils, mimeographed date sheets and notebooks, we toured fashionably feminine 575 Madison Avenue and in a daze of pink and green—even to the blush of MLLE's stationery—'The Magazine for Smart Young Women' turned from dream to the *almost* real: live plants on Managing Ed. Cyrilly Abels' office sill; the staccato click of high heels mingling with the rat-tat-tat of unceasing typewriters . . ."

Betsy Blackwell took herself and her task seriously, however, and she saw each girl alone in her office after the introductory tour was completed. Aware of the drug-like effect the whole affair was having upon these impressionable minds, she used the opportunity to remind each of them of the necessity for a good academic background and careful planning in the years ahead. With somber earnestness she threw the same question at each: "What do you plan to be doing twenty years from now?" [3] Sylvia was unaccountably flustered by the straightforward inquiry and answered that editorial work and teaching were her eventual goals—only to have the grim Miss Blackwell conclude with her familiar warning of "health before genius." The appropriateness of the remark is vitiated by its stock application to all the girls, but perhaps Sylvia's inner struggle was already beginning to surface.

In *The Bell Jar* this confrontation between herself and the editor-in-chief is shifted in time, and the paraphrased question is put into the mouth of Jay Cee (Cyrilly Abels), who was supposedly upset by Esther's continuing inability to function. The transposition makes the novel neater and more logical in terms of plot demands, but Esther's vague response might reflect Sylvia's early awareness that the descending bell jar was not going to be halted by any of *Mademoiselle*'s lavish rewards. Although she was frightened and unwilling, her mind was steadily shrinking into a cold and bitter core of self-hatred—far out of reach of both dream and reality. Very soon she would be writing a strange letter to Wilbury Crockett, apologizing for having let him and her other mentors down. But complete collapse was still unimaginable.

Besides providing a few moments for purposeful self-examination, Miss Blackwell also emphasized the brighter aspects of the coming month. With typical enthusiasm, she enumerated the countless joys awaiting the girls: "prizes, luncheons, interviews in fashion, communications, the arts . . ." Nor was she exaggerating. The magazine did not stint in its labors to make June a truly unique and memorable occasion in the guest editors' lives. New York's gilded merry-go-round was swung into motion for them immediately. Fashion was its key tune, of course, the hidden melody of gold that fed the magazine, and fashion naturally dominated many of the planned activities. At the magazine's own "College Clinic" for store buyers, the girls previewed tartans and then went on to the Tobé fall showing, where they had a chance to speak with the famous founder of the Tobé-Coburn School in person. Later, they were taken to see Trigère's fall line as well.

Oddly enough, Sylvia seemed just as fascinated by all this as were the others. In fact, during her New York stay, she bought herself an entire wardrobe, including a dressy veil hat and white gloves, and did make a serious effort to shed her bobby-soxer image. Cyrilly Abels recalls being surprised that a girl with Sylvia's intelligence and literary interests should be so caught up in the fashion whirlwind; but it is likely that Sylvia's behavior here, as with almost everything she had ever done, was a conscious and rather brave attempt to fight despair and mental paralysis—to construct an alternative self, a more sophisticated Sylvia who could laugh at her own inadequacies. To make the picture complete, she and the other girls had their hair done by Richard Hudnut's exclusive salon at the magazine's expense. Sylvia's page-boy cut, described by a companion as "champagne-colored," had the unfortunate effect of accenting her face's German cast—making her appear a little dumpy and much closer in appearance to her mother than she would have liked, at least in photographs.

Despite Esther's heartfelt claim that the other girls made her feel "so jealous I can't speak," Sylvia apparently garnered the special attention she needed and deserved even at *Mademoiselle.* From the beginning Cyrilly Abels—"brilliant managing ed" in Sylvia's parlance—was struck by her talent and had made sure that she was assigned to her own office, where she personally supervised Sylvia's initiation into the complex, often hectic world of the magazine's daily operations. An attractive, dedicated, extremely efficient woman, Miss Abels had always tended to treat her summer guest editors as daughters, having none of her own, and they often kept in touch with her for years afterwards. Her real human warmth was never dampened or exhausted by the dynamic performance that Sylvia witnessed each day as Miss Abels went through her paces of wooing authors, arranging for short stories and feature articles, and taking care of innumerable related details.

Sylvia's own tasks included reading and making comments upon piles of unsolicited manuscripts, typing rejection letters, answering the phone, and running errands. A more pleasant sidelight of the job was her participation at Miss Abels' side in frequent luncheons and conferences with well-known writers: Santha Rama Rau, an Indian woman author who had once attended Wellesley College; Paul Engle, then co-editor of the O. Henry Short Story Collection; novelist Vance Bourjaily; and Elizabeth Bowen, whom she would interview for the magazine as part of her contribution to the August issue.

Miss Abels was intrigued and disconcerted by Sylvia in about equal measure. She sensed something terribly wrong in the very stiffness of Sylvia's mask, in its unrelenting light pleasantness. Twenty years later, she was still amazed. "I never found anyone so unspontaneous so consistently, especially in one so young. She was simply all façade, too polite, too well-brought-up and well-disciplined."

The *Mademoiselle* editor also saw what others could not or did not want to see and realized that such intense control implied a dangerous withdrawal from reality. In desperation, the busy Miss Abels went out of her way to penetrate Sylvia's armor of distant congeniality. She took her out to lunch on many occasions without any distracting third parties present and attempted to share intimacies and childhood memories, trying always to provoke some kind of spontaneous response. Inevitably, her probings and gentle confidences met with empty chatter. In a sort of last-ditch assault, Miss Abels suddenly brought up the question of the Nazi pogrom against the Jews during World War II, since she was familiar with Sylvia's German background. Once again, however, the bait was ignored as the young poet blithely parried the remark with an automatic smile and a few banal, indifferent observations.

But in most social situations that June, Sylvia's mask continued to work effectively. With the exception of her letter to Crockett, her correspondence bristled with exclamations of rapture over her good fortune and joyous descriptions of the delights provided by *Mademoiselle*. Her well-developed social poise helped carry her through the daily barrage of new experiences without too much difficulty; and her relationships with the other girls remained, for the most part, friendly enough. "Doreen" alone—to use her name from *The Bell Jar*—managed to ensnare her in an awkward affair. Described in the novel as "hard and polished," a white-haired, blue-eyed society girl from a Southern college, "Doreen" became the double Sylvia had always had to find or create in fiction and in real life.

Doreen could thus absorb Sylvia's own guilt feelings and act as a screen for negative projections of the hidden bitch self. How real "Doreen" was is impossible to say since Sylvia had reached that juncture in her breakdown where only fiction could maintain her equilibrium. The girl is based upon an actual person, as are the other nine guest editors portrayed in *The Bell Jar*, but her behavior has obviously been heightened and distorted somewhat to fit what was required—an evil second self: "Everything she said was like a secret voice speaking straight out of my own bones." Another guest editor has characterized the original as a "pre-Bunny, platinum blond." [4]

The acidly humorous seduction scene at the disc-jockey's apartment did indeed take place as described in the novel, and Sylvia did cling triumphantly to her virgin status, which had become integrated with her mask's protective shell of normalcy; but "Doreen's" one-dimensional lack of redeeming graces suggests a psychological rather than a narrative or aesthetic purpose. Sylvia's attraction to her with such moth-like tenacity was a peculiar combination of self-love and self-defense—defense against impulses she could not afford to admit; just as her portrayal of "Betsy" in the novel represented the equally false college self—the bouncing blonde with domestic inclinations and a "Sweetheart-of-Sigma-Chi smile" that she had cultivated at Smith.

Sylvia's association with Laurie Levy was much more normal and therefore more remote. Laurie does not appear in *The Bell Jar* at all, perhaps a sign of affection in a book so determined upon symbolic revenge; and she and Sylvia never really gravitated together for very long. One interesting and prophetic discussion they did have concerned Shakespeare's *The Tempest* and Sylvia's insistent perception of Ariel as "male-animal power, fiery depths." Laurie, who would disappear after college into the obscurity of motherhood in Illinois and unfulfilled writing ambitions, stuck to the more conventional view of Ariel as "air, heaven, female . . ."

Laurie had also gone to the disreputable disc-jockey's apartment, under the false pretext of auditioning as a singer before his tape recorder; but she had fled in a panic as soon as his hand slithered across her leg. Near the end of June, she and Sylvia spent almost an entire evening together, drinking warm white wine and sharing their future plans. Sylvia loved this sort of intimate conversation, the kind she had always maintained with Philip McCurdy; and it perhaps helped to stave off the suffocating walls of loneliness her alienation was building. Many topics were touched upon and contrasted, but of one thing they both were convinced: "We agreed that night we would not rush into marriage, if at all; we were never to 'end up in suburban boxes.' "

Frantic activity propelled Sylvia through June, although that now entailed a glass-bowl consciousness of constant public exposure. The magazine's photographers accompanied the girls on all their group excursions, snapping and posing them without relief. A particularly uncomfortable situation arose when it was decided that the guest editors had to have their picture taken in Central Park, with each girl standing and holding the hand of the girl on either side to form a huge star. Laurie remembers that the temperature for the day was a muggy 94°, and that they had to wear Eton caps and "woolen tartans and 40-inch bust-producing long-sleeved button-down boy-shirts" for the occasion. In the picture that resulted, Sylvia is number one, at the apex of the star; and she had the dubious distinction of writing the paragraph-long caption for it—a piece of trite public relations that begins with "We're stargazers" and concludes "with this send-off from MLLE, the star of the campus." Such a "hard-sell" attitude undoubtedly helped to convince poor Sylvia that the worlds of slick magazines and serious literature were too far apart ever to converge.

The photographers were also at the St. Regis Dance given on the hotel's roof—with "a skyline view on all sides"—where two orchestras alternated all night and where the magazine had kindly provided a horde of proper Yale boys for the guest editors to meet. One picture shows Sylvia and Anne Shawber with their tuxedoed dates, crew-cut and clean-cut in the fashion of the period, as they held a "before-dinner confab." Despite her new evening gown, Sylvia sits like a peasant girl under her mechanical smile. The dinner—"chicken a l'estragon in the rose and crystal Mirror Room"—was a rare treat, but real contact between the parties never developed. This was true of all the arranged activities. Sylvia participated with a minimum of emotional involvement. The trip to Bear Mountain, for a picnic and swimming, breakfast in the executive dining room at Macy's, the fashion jaunts to see John Fredericks' fall line of hats and "luxurious lingerie at Vanity Fair," a tour of and luncheon at an advertising agency, sight-seeing at the U.N. (which included, according to Madelyn Mathers, lunch "in the delegates' own dining room, where the view of the East River was as exciting as the international menu")—none of these made much of an impression upon Sylvia's cheerful reserve.

Only the cultural events excited her in any way. On the evening of June 11, for instance, when the guest editors were taken to see the City Center Ballet Company perform *Con Amore, Scotch Symphony, Metamorphoses*, and Benjamin Britten's *Fanfare*, she was almost overwhelmed by the spectacle of music and dancers. She reacted with similar enthusiasm to the revival of Shaw's *Misalliance* and a preview showing of *Let's Do It Again*. But her finest moments in New York, and most psychologically dangerous, were those she spent, usually alone, exploring the city and its endless cultural and social riches. She wandered through Central Park and discovered its carrousel and zoo, and claimed afterwards that she did not hear a word of English spoken the entire time; and she returned again and again to Third Avenue and its famous El, visiting the countless tiny antique shops along the way and stopping at a few of its many bars with a friend, where they discussed philosophical questions and listened to the German-American patrons sing along with the hired musicians. She also found Greenwich Village and toured its annual outdoor art exhibit before having ginger ale in a sidewalk cafe. More familiar landmarks, such as the Empire State Building and the Museum of Modern Art, were also taken in.

Two group activities which she did think intriguing were a visit to a performance of Herb Shriner's popular television show "Two for the Money" and a Saturday afternoon spent at a ballgame as guests of sportscaster Mel Allen and the Yankees. This reminded her of Myron Lotz, who was then in the Minor Leagues at Durham. Depression, however, continued to gnaw at her. She walked alone in the rain and contemplated the vastness of space and time contrasted with the "small and transient" amount of knowledge any single human mind could assimilate. The distance between her ego and the empiric world had widened into a chasm, and the constant parties and excursions and daily work load became more and more a thing apart. Esther explained it in terms of "I felt very still and very empty, the way the eye of a tornado must feel, moving dully along in the middle of the surrounding hullabaloo."

Part of the problem, though in a minor way, was New York itself, which seemed so huge and impersonal to a girl used to the more manageable confines of Wellesley, Northampton, and Boston. The concrete canyons and their rapidly swirling rivers of purposeful strangers reduced her literary and scholastic achievements to mere vanities.[5] Esther admitted that "all the little successes I'd totted up so happily at college fizzled to nothing outside the slick marble and plate-glass fronts along Madison Avenue." And Sylvia herself confided to Myron Lotz her vision of the city as "all strange and other-worldly." She had a terrible realization that "Lives drip away like water here, not even making a dent in the acres and acres of concrete." Like Esther, she found herself sapped of meaning and ambition: "After nineteen years of running after good marks and prizes and grants of one sort or another, I was letting up, slowing down, dropping clean out of the race."

And yet Sylvia had been to New York before with Marcia Brown and had eagerly relished its cosmopolitan treasures and air of liberation. But now she was alone in a new and frightening way. Not only was she expected to be an adult, but she was separated from her mother and that symbiotic relationship with her she so desperately needed as a platform (and possible net) for her fanciful flights. Worse, this separation from Aurelia was occurring at the precise moment when Sylvia's interior self was receiving its greatest challenge, when she most needed her mother's reassuring banalities and middle-class solidity. The vicious cycle that had propelled Sylvia's life since her father's death, the drive towards success and a suppression of hostile emotions that created a continuous sense of insecurity, had reached a zenith where her secret rage against the world and Otto Plath was being turned inward.

Solitude, once so essential and creative, had now become dangerous and unproductive. Esther moves from "The silence depressed me" to "It was my own silence" with deceptive ease. The self-centered personality, whose childhood anxiety could be soothed only by unqualified admiration and love, found that her anxiety was keenly intensified in circumstances where its uniqueness was easily lost amid a crowd of other egos.

The month spent in New York—representing the pinnacle of her achievement—was thus a time of steady deterioration and increasing despair. Method still functioned, but less and less effectively, as Cyrilly Abels' observations testify. With what must have been a titanic struggle, she kept the mask in place and remained a "rather shy, pleasant young woman, in no special way remarkable." On the other hand, Contributing Editor Leo Lerman found Sylvia more artistic in mood and pose, "withdrawn and retiring . . . a poet." [6] She also managed to complete all of her assignments for the magazine. In fact, Sylvia contributed more than any other guest editor to the August issue. Besides those for the normal quota of pictures, she provided the caption for the star picture, an interview with Elizabeth Bowen (selected by Sylvia herself from a list of possible celebrities to interview), her villanelle "Mad Girl's Love Song," an interview article called "Poets on Campus" in which she corresponded with Alastair Reid, Anthony Hecht, George Steiner, William Burford, and her favorite, Richard Wilbur. Sadly, none of it mattered anymore.

One of the more absurd and comic aspects of the August issue involved an attempt by a handwriting expert named Henry O. Teltscher to use the signatures of the guest editors for purposes of analyzing them and their future chances of success. Sylvia's signature—the clearest and by far the neatest—led him to rhapsodize that she "will succeed in artistic fields. She has a sense of form and beauty and an intense enjoyment in her work." The former is certainly true enough, as is the allegiance to form and beauty; but Sylvia was years away from the point where writing would be a pleasure in itself—that is, where creation as process could substitute for creation as the road to acclaim and rewards.

The central symbol of the whole *Mademoiselle* episode, which Sylvia herself would brilliantly isolate with later insight, had to be the photograph of her holding a rose that was published above her signature and Mr. Teltscher's analysis. Knowing she was a poet, the photographer had obligingly supplied her with the perfect prop and asked her to dangle it from one limp hand. It was too much for Sylvia, not only because the rose was paper and so typical of the shallow magazine approach to art, but because her unhappiness had reached the point where she could no longer rely on method to mask reality. *The Bell Jar* indicates that Sylvia well knew what was coming, even if she did not comprehend its cause:

I didn't want my picture taken because I was going to cry. I didn't know why I was going to cry, but I knew that if anybody spoke to me or looked at me too closely the tears would fly out of my eyes and the sobs would fly out of my throat and I'd cry for a week. I could feel the tears brimming and sloshing in me like water in a glass that is unsteady and too full.

The photograph that resulted is a touching one in which Sylvia seems much younger than her twenty years, almost a child again in her high-buttoned, white-collared dress and toothy smile. Although she had broken down and wept before posing, it would be the last time as she moved closer and closer to total stasis. She found the commonest tasks difficult to complete; and her store of physical energy, that marvelous energy which had characterized her every action since birth, appeared depleted. It required a great effort of will to dress herself in the morning, to make conversation, to go through the simplest motions of normal existence. Remote from life in a deadly calm, Sylvia could not care enough about life to exert the slightest effort on her own behalf. When she left New York at the end of June, she was numb inside—trapped in the hurricane eye of mental paralysis and headed for destruction.

Back in Wellesley with family and friends, she thought she would recover with her usual resiliency. She wrote to a friend, however, that the Plath home was "in a state-of-emergency tension." Her beloved "granny" was seriously ill and would hover between life and death for the next few weeks. Worse, her mother's old ulcer was causing her great pain; and Sylvia would have to bear much of the burden of running the house while Aurelia tried to recover and avoid a "costly" operation. The final blow, which almost shattered Sylvia's frail equilibrium, was a letter rejecting her application to a course in creative writing at Harvard's summer school, which she had looked forward to attending. As required, she had submitted some poems to the instructor months earlier and then just assumed she would be accepted as a matter of course—a not unrealistic assumption in light of her previous string of successes in similar situations. The rejection wounded her where she was most vulnerable, namely, in her self-esteem, and it increased the already mushrooming sense of insecurity about her talents and personal worth. Further, instead of providing a definite routine, the rest of the summer stretched out endlessly before her like a wasteland.

All of her friends were away for the summer, and the town had never seemed so desolate. She must have been reminded of the summer before when she had left the Belmont in ill-health and lapsed into a severe depression. It was then that she had first used the metaphor of a bell jar to describe her feelings of uneasy detachment from the real world to Marcia Brown: "Oh, Marty, I never have spent such a queer summer. It is quite amazing how I've gone around for most of my life as in the rarefied atmosphere under a bell-jar, all according to schedule, four college years neatly quartered out in seasons, with summers to be filled in at will, hopefully, profitably, and never more than two or three weeks free at one time to worry about what comes next. Now, although the top would have seemed to have suddenly blown off, if I keep moving time will pass, being as time is but an emptying of waste baskets, a deadly going out and in of doors, a brushing of teeth routinely, a marking off of spaces until the cycle comes round again." [7]

Marcia was spending the summer in Cambridge, a fact which Mrs. Plath told her not to dwell on in her daughter's presence, but she did come down to have dinner one evening with Sylvia soon after her return. Marcia was upset and saddened at what she found. Throughout the meal, Sylvia was "clearly depressed, almost sort of zombieish, and physically exhausted." She talked about the New York City venture with distaste and horror, explaining that it was "a very unsettling experience in many ways, that she hated many of the people she was with there, hated their values, their outlook, their behavior, their falseness. But it really shook her up, about what she wanted to do and why she had been there in the first place."

Although convinced that Sylvia was in a bad way, Marcia felt helpless to aid her in any concrete fashion beyond offering her a shoulder to cry on and a sense of deep concern. She feared telling Aurelia, being fully aware of her continuing hypersensitivity about her daughter's mental condition.

"The last thing I wanted to do was talk to Mrs. Plath," Marcia has recalled, "because Mrs. Plath over-reacted to everything, and I didn't want to stir her up any more than she was at the time." Aurelia had always seen Marcia as the perfect friend for Sylvia, the kind of "sun-shiney" person she would have liked her daughter to emulate; but Marcia found Mrs. Plath difficult to take: "she gushed all over the place, everything was sweet and dear and touching, tears in her eyes all the time." This heavy sentimentality had its worst effect in Mrs. Plath's treatment of Sylvia: "I just had the feeling she was breathing on her every minute."

Sylvia was thus cut off from her mother, the most important individual in her life, at the crucial time when she most needed her.

But school and writing, which had always worked in the past, had to be the answer, along with intense self-discipline. As she had the summer before during a moment of crisis, Sylvia set out to erect her own psychological shelter. She was determined to structure and use her time wisely, to labor over the arduous Joyce paper, and to write a first novel by utilizing her recent sojourn in New York for plot material. She would also rigorously pursue a full complement of physical recreations, hiking, trips to the beach, tennis, bicycle riding, and walks around Cambridge. But the plan was easier to devise than execute, although she persisted in maintaining her old image in other ways, disguising the *Mademoiselle* disaster with ad-man exaggerations in her own scrapbook: "Fantastic, fabulous, and all other inadequate adjectives go to describe the four gala and chaotic weeks I worked as Guest Managing Ed." [8]

The novel never progressed beyond a few disjointed pages, and the attempt to penetrate *Ulysses* was a total failure that only abetted her disintegration into incoherence. Joyce's virtuoso puns, double entendres, and playful, extravagant syntax were the worst medicines Sylvia could have tried to take. She swam in nonsense, pushing herself further away from shore, until absolute nullity loomed: "I was a nothing, a zero."

During the first two weeks of July, Sylvia did have Gordon Lameyer available for companionship. Her brother, who would be entering Harvard in September, was living at home while working as an orderly in a local convalescent home; and both Lotz and McCurdy would not be free before summer's end. She felt useless and incapable of sustaining interest in anything, but still intended to follow her plan. Gordon helped greatly because of his literary enthusiasms; and he, in turn, found her as bright and charming as ever, if a little more taciturn. The only concrete sign of possible trouble he detected was her inexplicable denseness regarding Joyce and her honors thesis.

But on July 13 Gordon departed for the Officers' Training School at Newport, Rhode Island, and Sylvia was left behind to confront the heat and her despair alone. Valiantly, she attempted to adhere to the plan's guidelines and visited the beach several times on her own. Nothing really worked, however, as she felt herself sinking slowly into a vegetable state. Even writing, perhaps especially writing, eluded her suddenly awkward and uncaring grasp. Conscious that her illness was galloping out of control, she took to studying abnormal psychology books, to no avail. Her mind isolated and categorized her symptoms and their clinical causes easily enough, but the knowledge was useless.

Mrs. Plath, not teaching summer school, began to notice that her daughter's odd listlessness was not improving and had indeed worsened. With familiar pragmatism, she suggested several practical courses of action, such as learning shorthand and serving as a candy-striper in the local hospital. Sylvia obediently tried both for a while without much success.

Her symptoms grew more pronounced. She rarely stirred from the house and complained that she could not sleep at night, that her body resisted her brain's simplest commands, that her fingers could not hold a pen or pencil or, when they did, scrawled rubbish across the page. She told her mother how she was letting everyone down—the school and Mrs. Prouty and all the other sponsors who expected so much of her. Finally, uncertain and truly worried about her daughter's health, Aurelia took her to the town's psychiatrist, referred to as "Dr. Gordon" in *The Bell Jar*.[9]

Perhaps because he treated her as a neurotic female rather than as a severe depressive, Dr. Gordon could not begin to rescue Sylvia. When no signs of improvement were forthcoming after several weeks of private sessions, he then recommended that she be given shock treatments at his own clinic. But to be successful at all, and its statistical successes are remarkable, electric shock treatment must be accompanied by intensive parallel psychotherapy. That Sylvia was simply subjected to a series of powerful jolts would only lead to the addition of new fears and another trauma. Besides everything else, Sylvia's frail ego was now in a constant panic over the threat of more shock treatments should she not get better. Her rapidly shifting imagination linked the treatment with the execution of the Rosenbergs, which had occurred during her

New York venture, and convinced her that psychiatrists had to be avoided:

> *By the roots of my hair some god got hold of me.*
> *I sizzled in his blue volts like a desert prophet.*

The flux needed a center, the anchor of an icon from the past. Although unable rationally to relieve her destructive depression, Sylvia did begin to associate the entire process with her dead father. Somehow Otto was the crucial figure at the heart of her black inferno, and the Electra search began in earnest. During the day, she had taken to riding into Boston and strolling aimlessly around the Common, occasionally talking with strangers. Her wanderings were reflex actions, physical motions towards recovering a mental purpose; and food, which had always been so important, could no longer be swallowed, no doubt because the self-love it used to represent had ceased to exist.

Now she extended her trips out to Winthrop, the landscape of a myth-like childhood and the place where a godly father had once dwelled and smiled upon her. Deer Island Prison, the local grammar school, Logan Airport across the bay, all the old landmarks stirred up adolescent recollections and emotional storms she was not equipped to handle. She visited the graveyard where Otto was buried and finally located the modest tombstone after much effort. The unadorned name and stark numbers told her nothing, but it is likely they intensified the sense of depression already smothering her.

Rage over her mother's callous "neglect" of her husband was revived, as was a sharpened awareness of resurrected loss and guilt. She struggled against the terrifying notion that she herself had hated her father as much as she had loved him—that her secret wish for his death could have mysteriously aided the diabetes that killed him. In response to Jay Cee's observation about her inadequacy, Esther trips into the discovery of a different Otto from the laughing father she had created for the benefit of her mask: "It sounded true, and I recognized it, the way you recognize some non-descript person that's been hanging around your door for ages and then suddenly comes up and introduces himself as your real father and looks exactly like you, so you know he really is your father, and the person you thought all your life was your father is a sham."

From this disturbing vantage, there was also no returning to the sham life of achievement. Death beckoned like a womb, and suicide became not an ominous freak occurrence but a definite goal. The single remaining question was one of method. Sylvia had collapsed at last into a psychotic extreme or what psychiatry has labelled "schizophrenia melancholia." Method had shifted to a war footing. Annihilation would be a fit punishment for the sin of hating parents. It would also be salvation from the agony of bearing an unacceptable self. Sylvia read the newspapers carefully for accounts of suicides and thought deeply about the most efficient means of removing herself from the world and making it pay in sorrow for having wounded her. She made a vague attempt at slitting her veins with a razor blade; later she plunged into the fetal ocean at Nauset Beach. But the water rejected her.

Day poured into day as August drooped over hot sands, and the situation became unendurable. School and school routines loomed before her like a steel maze; the prospect of having to reassert the selves she could no longer believe in or trust frightened her further. Gordon Lameyer returned to Wellesley on a pass the weekend before her serious suicide attempt, accompanied by a sailor-schoolmate from Newport. Sylvia and a neighborhood girl friend double-dated with them, spending Saturday, August 22, at the beach. On the sly, she interrogated the sailor intently about suicide in general—how to go about it and which were the most effective weapons. She found the thought of marring her body too distasteful and obscene. There was also a certain reluctance to participate fully in her own death. Sleeping pills were the obvious and traditional method, and she retained her commitment to inherited forms—a gentle drifting into the sweet oblivion of "That good night," the same oblivion she had combatted so furiously since her father's death. Virginia Woolf's experiment with veronal and medinal might have reassured her that the decision was a correct one, properly literary and painless and, more important, often non-lethal, which left the door open for a dramatic rescue.

The place, too, was easy and appropriate. Under the porch of her mother's house there was a crawl space where fire wood was stored—a dark and snug place, as deceptively obvious as Poe's purloined letter, a metaphoric womb for her to return to and perfect.

Dr. Gordon had already prescribed sleeping pills, although Mrs. Plath sensibly kept the bottle under lock and key in a strong-box in the bedroom,[10] doling them out to her daughter one at a time each night. Unknown to her, however, Sylvia was aware that the key to the strong-box was also hidden in the bedroom and knew, in fact, exactly where to find it. She had located it during an earlier search and guarded the knowledge like a secret gift for days. On Monday morning, hearing her mother go out, Sylvia entered her bedroom, found the key, secured the prized bottle, and then removed all signs of her presence. She was delighted to discover that forty-eight pills were still left.

Sylvia was in no hurry and deliberately set about her task with calm precision. First, to forestall an immediate search, she wrote a note and left it on the kitchen table, explaining that she had gone for a long hike and would "be back tomorrow." Then, like a little girl planning an afternoon nap, she took a glass of tap water and a blanket with her (she was dressed in "a light blue skirt and white sleeveless blouse") into the basement. The shoulder-high crawl space was above and behind a wall of cinder blocks. Sylvia carefully placed the water and bottle of pills on a nearby piece of wood, shoved aside the pile of dusty, half-rotted logs and boards, and hoisted herself over the concrete edge. She next took the pills and water with her before pushing the wood back into place, thereby effectively screening herself from any casual inspection. Slowly she crawled across the cold, loose earth to a far wall and wrapped herself in the blanket. One by one, she swallowed the pills and drank sips of water until forty of them had disappeared.

Esther describes the final process. In fact, this section of the novel is almost pure diary:

> At first nothing happened, but as I approached the bottom of the bottle, red and blue lights began to flash before my eyes. The bottle slid from my fingers and I lay down.
>
> The silence drew off, baring the pebbles and shells and all the tatty wreckage of my life. Then, at the rim of vision, it gathered itself, and in one sweeping tide, rushed me to sleep.

So, after the fact and art of it merged, the sea and its shore did return to make a myth of what was a refusal of myths; but at the time nothingness itself sufficed.

While Sylvia lay unconscious under their feet, the Plath family returned home. Aurelia was quite worried about her daughter's disappearance although long hikes were not a rarity that summer and of course she did not think to check the strong-box. By supper time she grew concerned enough to call the police after a quick survey of neighborhood friends turned up no one who had seen Sylvia. She knew that if her daughter were actually off on a hike, she would certainly have telephoned her by evening.

The local police were reassuringly responsive and got in touch with other police departments, including that in Boston. The newspapers were also notified, and reporters converged on Elmwood Road from *The*

Boston Daily Globe, The Boston Herald, and *The Boston Post.* Friends, too, called and offered their services, as did many neighbors. Assisted by a Col. Rex Gary from Wellesley, described in the *Globe* as "formerly associated with United States Army Intelligence," Mrs. Plath and Warren drove into Boston late that same night and cruised around the Common and the Public Garden, desperately hoping to catch sight of Sylvia wandering the streets.

The next morning, the story was given prominent space in the *Globe* under the headline of "Beautiful Smith Girl Missing at Wellesley," [11] alongside a snapshot of Sylvia. In the column accompanying the headline, Sylvia got the kind of attention she would have loved. Besides being designated "beautiful," she was referred to as "brilliant" and "widely known on the campus and among alumnae for her brilliance, creative talent and initiative." Officials at Smith College were quoted as describing her as "one of the most outstanding girls we have." Mrs. Plath, meanwhile, who would make no mention of psychiatrists and shock treatments to any reporters in the trying few days ahead, did tell the press that "her daughter was close to a nervous collapse as a result of extremely intensive activities."

The vagueness of this statement was clarified somewhat further on in the column: " 'It sounds peculiar,' Mrs. Plath said, 'but she has set standards for herself that are almost unattainable. She's made almost a minor obsession of fulfilling what she believes to be her responsibilities to her sponsors, and I am gravely concerned for her.' " Aurelia also told the reporter that Sylvia had been instructed "by her doctor to devote less time to academic activities in the interest of her health"—a true enough comment that reveals nothing of the real depth of Sylvia's mental torment.

The local police and Chief Robert P. McBey had searched the cellar soon after coming to the Plath home, as part of a general search of the whole house, and saw nothing. One of the few comic sidelights to the whole affair would come after Sylvia was found days later, when Chief McBey attempted to clear himself of a charge of negligence. "We searched that cellar Monday night or thought we did," he would tell a *Globe* reporter. "Of course there is the possibility that she might not have been there when we were. She had a blanket with her that was not reported as missing before she was found." The latter part of his statement summons up an absurd picture of Sylvia crawling, semi-comatose, out of her hole to sneak upstairs to filch a blanket before returning to her crawl space, replacing the firewood, and relapsing into unconsciousness.

Other absurdities abounded when the search continued the following morning, Tuesday, August 25, but they were the legitimate result of many sincere people unselfishly dedicating themselves to an unpleasant task. The news spread rapidly, and friends and neighbors responded by offering their services and extending their sympathies to the anxious family. They were organized into several different search parties and sent on their way, spending most of the humid day—it had rained heavily during the night—combing the thick woods behind Elmwood Road and along the shores of Morse's Pond and Lake Waban. The Andover State Police initiated their own more professional hunt for the missing girl and brought along Big Sid—sometimes referred to as Lieutenant Sid, a bloodhound—to the Plath home in hope that he could pick up Sylvia's scent from there. He failed to do so, a fact which the police attributed to the recent rains.

The local Boy Scout troop, Post 80 of the Explorers, led by a neighbor named Bradford Gove and an expert in the region's terrain named Carroll Hunnewell, also participated; and the Cambridge and Boston Police sent patrols on repeated swings through the Boston Common and Public Garden areas. Mrs. Plath was growing more and more distraught, a condition that was hardly eased by innumerable telephone calls, visitors, reporters, and various search groups, many of whom congregated in front of the house. She was quoted in the evening edition of the *Globe* as feeling certain that "some form of nervous exhaustion may have occurred."

Her anxiety had been given added impetus by an early morning discovery that the nearly full bottle of pills was missing from the strong-box. That discovery combined with the fact that Sylvia had taken no luggage or clothes with her seemed to transform suicide from a vague possibility into a real threat. So did Mrs. Plath's own observation to the *Boston Herald* that "There is no question of a boy in the case"—a remark which Sylvia would use for a different purpose in *The Bell Jar*.[12]

"Writer's block" was the crucial line of self-defense as Aurelia faced a ceaseless barrage of inquiries. She admitted to the *Post* reporter that her daughter had been "writing despondently in her diary since about July 1," and also emphasized that Sylvia had voiced frequent concern about losing "her creative ability in writing."[13] The morning edition of the *Globe* for August 26 included a front-page photograph of Sylvia with her mother and brother, as requested by Aurelia "in the hope that it might encourage the girl to report her whereabouts." The same paper carried a more detailed account by Mrs. Plath of the reasons behind her daughter's odd behavior; and again the story is fascinating both for what it says and does not say:

"She recently felt she was unworthy of the confidence held for her by the people she knew. For some time she has been unable to write either fiction, or her more recent love, poetry.

"Instead of regarding this as just an arid period that every writer faces at times, she believed something had happened to her mind, that it was unable to produce creatively any more.

"Although her doctor assured us this was simply due to nervous exhaustion, Sylvia was constantly seeking for ways in which to blame herself for the failure, and became increasingly despondent."

Her brother participated in the search with grim diligence and "recorded on a map of the Wellesley area tonight the grounds searched by Wellesley police, State Police, Scouts, neighbors and volunteers." His mother, besides expressing doubt that Sylvia would communicate with her friends or classmates "because her mood was too much one of withdrawal," had sent a message to Mrs. Prouty's home in Brookline on the wild chance that Sylvia might have tried to contact her rich sponsor; but a return postcard indicated that the "authoress" was vacationing in Maine.

Unaware of the constant turmoil in the world above, Sylvia was careening through her flashing lights towards the bottom well of darkness; but a part of her would not complete the voyage and struggled to survive like a trapped, panic-stricken animal. She moaned aloud, crawled to her knees, and started to rise; but her head hit the ceiling and she collapsed, striking her face against the concrete basement wall. Yet she was able in her unconscious state to gasp for breath and did not sink into a coma.

What was keeping her alive? According to Karl Menninger, every suicide appears to involve three, not one, persons or personalities: the one doing the killing, the one being killed, and the one who is dying; that is, one active attacker and two passive victims.[14] For a terminal suicide, ruling out mere chance, all three must function in unison. But in those countless cases where the suicide is saved from himself, it would probably mean a refusal to die by one of the passive personalities. In Sylvia's case, one may speculate that the hidden bitch goddess would not take kindly to the idea of being murdered by an alternative self—that it would, in fact, fight back fiercely to remain alive to manipulate the world and its puny inhabitants.

On Wednesday afternoon, Sylvia's grandmother went to the basement to do the family laundry and heard Sylvia's pitiful moans from behind the stacks of fire wood. Hurriedly, she returned upstairs to find Warren, who accompanied her to the basement and cleared away the logs. Sylvia's huddled body was soon visible, and he realized that he would need help in extracting her from the crawl space. The police were called and arrived minutes later under the lead of Chief McBey himself. They easily freed Sylvia and soon had her in an ambulance and on her way to the Newton-Wellesley Hospital. Hours later the doctors were able to report her condition as "good."

·Watch these Pearls, these Pearls of modern women.
Particularly American women. Battening on love.
And fluttering in the first batlike throes of dementia.

D. H. LAWRENCE

7

We Are Not
What We Might Be

When Sylvia entered the hospital at Framingham, her "good" condition
was something only a doctor could sense in her steady pulse.

Outwardly she looked in the worst possible state. Sylvia would later
write that maggots had been scraped "like sticky pearls" off her flesh
when she was first freed from the crawl space; and her face was a
swollen mass of multicolored bruises under a mop of dirt-clotted hair. A
scar ravaged her distended right cheek; and two ugly sores punctuated
the corners of her cracked lips. A nurse on duty when she was admitted
described her as "more dead than alive"—a more accurate statement
than she realized if Sylvia's mental state is also taken into consideration.[1]
Her mind had not been rescued, only her determined body.

When she awoke fully and sought the painful light once again, it was
to reaffirm her infantile dependency and the return-to-the-womb nature
of her suicide gesture. Esther makes us experience the intense agony of
this resurrection:

A chisel cracked down on my eye, and a slit of light opened, like a mouth or
a wound, till the darkness clamped shut on it again. I tried to roll away from the
direction of the light, but hands wrapped round my limbs like mummy bands
and I couldn't move.

I began to think I must be in an underground chamber, lit by blinding lights, and that the chamber was full of people who for some reason were holding me down.

Then the chisel struck again, and the light leapt into my head, and through the thick, warm, furry dark, a voice cried,

"Mother!"

Sylvia knew with a kind of instinctive wisdom and dread that Mrs. Plath was essential, the great mother-sea without whom she could not survive, but with whom she could never achieve independent sanity. Upon regaining consciousness, the first question she asked her mother was "Did we lose the house?" [2] Sylvia was still her mother, after all, in the attic of her ego's coral mansion, Lady Rowena and not Ligeia, insecure but convinced that the universe still hinged on coins of the mundane realm. The artist in her might slay Aurelia, and the golden girl disdain her bourgeois preoccupations, but the obedient little girl knew that Aurelia spoke truly about weaving gold from hair-shirts.

"Did we lose the house?" Sylvia and naive Esther are one here.

"Did we lose the house?" This is the primal fear, a loss of shelter and family heart, money mated to sex, an insistent middle-class fear of the lurking poorhouse fused forever with a more ancient turtle panic over a missing shell.

The house was not lost. Mrs. Plath, who never left her daughter's side during those long hours of shifting shadows, thanked the loyal citizens of Wellesley for their gallant efforts in a letter to *The Townsman*, including all the official organizations from far and near that had cooperated in the futile search. The amenities were thus observed despite the disaster; but Sylvia's brooding bitch soul knew that a mere show of manners was not sufficient and that the frail bounds of polite behavior had been irrevocably overstepped.

However, Mrs. Plath was now certain that her bright and dutiful daughter was merely going through a temporary, childish phase. Intent upon protecting the family image, and perhaps inwardly relishing another form of domestic martyrdom, she came often to speak to her daughter with the calm, no-nonsense logic of responsible adulthood. The governing rationale behind her behavior—neither unusual nor without merit—was that acting as if Sylvia were normal would make her so. Aurelia also continued to cite her daughter's writer's block and resented any suggestion that Sylvia might have experienced a nervous breakdown for some other reason. When Cyrilly Abels heard about Sylvia's harrowing ordeal a few days after the event, she immediately called Mrs. Plath to offer sympathy and whatever help she could and to apologize for *Mademoiselle*'s allowing a Boston tabloid to print "Mad Girl's Love Song" alongside news of Sylvia's attempted suicide. Aurelia was pleasant and chatty at first, and emphasized that "Sylvia was in such despair because she couldn't write." But when Miss Abels informed her of Sylvia's unspontaneous behavior in New York and indicated that she might have been concealing serious mental problems, Aurelia underwent a complete change. She became distant and "most uncommunicative" and soon brought the telephone conversation to an end. Miss Abels called back several times after that, but her *faux pas* stood like a closed door between them; and no exchange of ideas or feelings was possible under the circumstances.

Less than a week after she had been found, Sylvia was taken by ambulance to the locked ward in the psychiatric wing of Massachusetts General Hospital. It was free and convenient and would prevent her from hurting herself further, while the resident doctors attempted her rehabilitation. Fo tunately, Mrs. Prouty—due to the efforts of Aurelia—had become aware of and deeply concerned over her protégée's dilemma and decided to pay for Sylvia's hospitalization in a private institution. In fact, Mrs. Prouty's own Cadillac and its uniformed chauffeur drove Sylvia (accompanied by her mother and brother) from Boston to McLean Hospital in Belmont—a prestigious, beautifully rural sanatorium with one of the finest psychiatric staffs in the state. Mrs. Prouty had finally made a contribution to literature.

But in the beginning, even McLean's advanced techniques, individualized attention, and pleasant surroundings could not accomplish much beyond maintaining the physical well being of their charge. As Lotz noted when he visited her, Sylvia was "obviously psychotic" and still suicidal. Shock treatment of some sort or another seemed called for, but her extreme fear of electro-shock therapy caused her doctors to put her on insulin instead—a milder form of the same technique. The only apparent result was a drastic increase in weight and a serious interference with her menstrual cycle, which had never been regular. She looked worse than ever during those initial weeks at McLean's and refused to take care of herself, neither washing nor dressing herself and leaving her hair dirty and uncombed. Most visitors were shocked and somewhat frightened by her savage appearance—the golden girl's worst fears had floated to the surface in the shape of an evil double.

And yet she certainly had moments of insight and lucid purpose, and responded to Gordon Lameyer's letters with sincere gratitude and appreciation, timidly requesting him not to try to see her. Her letters to Lameyer from McLean are fascinating documents both in content and style. The early ones, written while she remained close to death and incapable of erecting defenses against life's demands, are couched in a tiny, self-effacing script that reflects a kind of sweet vulnerability. They are the missives of a scared little girl who is appreciative of the slightest favor and attention—nothing at all like the bold signature printed in *Mademoiselle.*

But as Sylvia reconstructed her mask (what Peter Davison has accurately characterized as her "anthropoid shell"),³ the letters undergo an almost miraculous change. Their frightened handwriting grows larger and larger and recovers its firm self-confidence; and "the gratefulness at having been restored" begins to disappear. Her suitor could once again be manipulated, even treated with a certain amount of contempt and condescension. In the words of Davison, "the tenderness towards Gordon vanished and she began acting, she assumed a persona." The old secret hatred of males reasserted its control and "as the year went on she got tougher and tougher."

Before her public self rediscovered the path towards literary stardom, however, she had touched absolute bottom.⁴ In the first weeks at McLean, language itself failed her. She was painfully cognizant of her inability to formulate words and clear thoughts. "I can only speak in terms of one-syllable words now," she complained to Lotz, who knew how much she revelled in language for its own sake, "and I can't think." But she retained enough rationality to decide that her "English teacher was the one she always wanted to see." And with unselfish loyalty, Mr. Crockett did make the journey from Wellesley to Belmont once a week for the five months that Sylvia spent at McLean's.

Although not an expert in psychological matters, Crockett had sufficient sensitivity and experience with students to realize that language, above all, could rescue Sylvia from the chaos of a fragmented identity. Being a child again, she would have to be led like a child back up the stairway of abstract thought. Patiently, he played countless word games with her and strove to get her involved in solving simple anagrams. He concentrated always on the "game" aspects of making sounds and letters do her bidding once more. It was a difficult task, and frequently an unrewarding one, but he stayed with it and her. Soon, reacting to him as a positive father substitute, Sylvia accepted his guidance with erratic enthusiasm and performed for him as she had once performed for Otto, while delighting in the constant reward of his paternal affection and interest.

Neither the games nor other language exercises were enough, however, since the impulse towards abstraction lacked the base of a coordinated emotional and intellectual personality. Language could not unify experience without the given unity of an effective and integrated identity. But she was fortunate in that "Dr. Ruth Jones" was assigned to her case, and an immediate rapport was established between the two. A young and flexible woman relatively new to the field, Dr. Jones possessed none of the rigid orthodoxies of her male colleagues. She wisely adopted a sort of honor system with Sylvia, explaining in detail exactly what she was doing and why, and also making sure that her patient was no longer upset by a steady stream of well-meaning visitors, including members of her own family.

On the negative side, when the insulin treatment failed to provide the necessary catharsis for Sylvia's entangled selves, Dr. Jones had to put her patient through an extensive course in electro-shock therapy, but accompanied it throughout with intensive psychotherapy. The sessions with the psychiatrist combined with weekly shock treatments, the agony of which was more imagined than real, enabled Sylvia to organize the past and her relationships with her parents in a more honest fashion. Aided by her own perceptive intelligence, she came slowly to understand the emotional and rational truth behind her ambivalent attitudes towards her mother and father.

For instance, as emphasized and perhaps distorted in *The Bell Jar*, once she could admit that she actually hated her mother, could break the ancient taboo, Sylvia could also begin to understand her more as another human being, or at least how to "handle her" without becoming unduly distraught. As for the father, that Oedipal shadow and myth, she would reluctantly concede to a friend a year later: "He was an autocrat. I adored and despised him, and I probably wished many times that he was dead. When he obliged me and died, I imagined that I had killed him." [5] To Peter Davison she would be more casual, dismissing Otto as "a sort of fuddy-duddy professor who dealt with bugs down in Boston." Both views seem to indicate a mental revolution, a demythification of the past in order to take a more reasonable view of the cosmos; but the patness of the quotations, their obvious textbook quality, suggests that this new attitude to the father figure was probably another side of the old mask.

The actual techniques employed by Dr. Jones in her treatment of Sylvia are necessarily shrouded in the medical profession's respect for privacy. Thus the precise approach is difficult to isolate, but it would not be unfair to assume that like most of her counterparts in the 1950's, Dr. Jones remained generally committed to orthodox Freudianism—an assumption reinforced by Sylvia's own comments after the fact and her fictional portrait of the therapeutic process in *The Bell Jar*. This would tend to entail a certain amount of leading analysis, a constant return to the crucial frustrations and repressions of childhood, and an awareness of the key role played by the Oedipal situation in the emerging ego's sense of self.

But Sylvia was hardly an ordinary patient, however ordinary her breakdown can be described in cold psychoanalytic jargon; she was the nascent artist poised on the abyss of discovery. Her multiple selves had been exposed at last, at a very high cost to be sure; and now a courageous plunge into genuine catharsis might have released her imprisoned bitch goddess once and for all. But Dr. Jones was not dealing with the future and could not risk such a dubious undertaking. Instead she diligently served the sick girl and ignored the genius below—that is, she helped resurrect the mask and gave it a firmer fit by letting Sylvia participate in the unearthing of the classic Electra complex governing her repressed feelings towards Otto and Aurelia. Sylvia herself often alluded to her Electra complex with detached amusement.

Indeed, the entire Freudian apparatus became another feature of the mask, a sensible extension of the sensible college girl's enlightened vision of the sensible world. Categories saved her. She would emerge from McLean's as disoriented as ever, still committed to disguise as a fundamental mode of behavior and composition. As the letters to Gordon Lameyer clearly demonstrate, her return to life was nothing more than a return to the manipulative role that had placed her in the sanatorium in the first place.[6] If anything, she was even less capable of real human relationships when she was discharged as cured just before Christmas 1953 than when she had entered nearly a half-year before.

There were changes, startling ones in some ways, but they were the result of Freudian additions to the mask and did not represent any basic alteration in character. Her attitude towards sex, for instance, was an obvious reversal. Dr. Jones had striven to convince her that true escape from her mother's domination had to include a rejection of Aurelia's narrow Puritan strictures regarding the importance of chastity. Sylvia acquired a douche and decided, with typical energy and efficiency, that the common-sense approach to sex was best. Sexual intercourse was but another wholesome sport for the human body to enjoy, just like tennis or bicycle riding. Sophisticated female independence could settle for nothing less. The immediate, most humorous result was a fierce attack upon Philip McCurdy's ambivalent relationship with her.

McCurdy, who continued to idolize and love Sylvia from afar while warmly entrenched in the role of a younger brother, had been profoundly dismayed by her brush with death and hastened to welcome her back. They slipped easily into the old roles of confidants once again and were soon exchanging experiences. Like her mother, Sylvia realized that writer's block was the safest disguise for what had happened to her. Perhaps she even fooled herself to a degree, though that seems unlikely. In any event, she adhered to the Plath family line. "I was physically pooped when I returned from New York," she told McCurdy. "I just got into a vicious cycle of the more I tried the less I could write, the less I could write, the more depressed I became about not being able to produce. It didn't come. It didn't work. I stayed awake. I got to the point where I just didn't think I was ever going to be able to write."

As usual, the truth is here, but a surface truth unconnected to any deeper undercurrents.

Nevertheless, McCurdy accepted the explanation as he accepted Sylvia, completely and without inspection. He suggested they date and she readily agreed. A few nights later, they went to The Totem Pole, the "in" place of the area, for dancing. Although they enjoyed each other's company, the atmosphere and juvenile behavior of the other couples struck them as an "utter exercise in banality." The fact that Sylvia was only a mediocre dancer did not help. They returned early and "went parking" after driving past the house to the wooded area near the skating pond. In a few minutes, as the heavy petting raced towards consummation at Sylvia's urging, McCurdy realized that "she was mechanically starved for affection" after her McLean retreat and that the old rules were out. Abashed, uncertain, caught up in her passion, he surrendered to her demands in a "fitful" fashion, but it "seemed almost incestuous." A part of him was delighted and pleasurably overwhelmed, and he found her and the unbelievable experience "marvellous"; and yet it entailed a painful loss as well, the discovery of a madonna's flesh and estrous heat.

Time passed, and they alternately caressed and made love, "touching and talking," when they were not laughing and weeping. She warned him, "Don't put me on a pedestal"—a little late perhaps; and they discussed with youthful wisdom how trite conventional mores really were. From McCurdy's point of view, all of it retained a kind of childish innocence. Despite the awesome, unsettling alteration in their relationship, at least from his naïve perspective, they were still secret sharers in a pact against exterior chaos and adult misunderstandings. He drove her home, and they parked in front of her house for several hours more, where they necked and talked energetically, before he finally departed.[7]

With the mask back in place, Sylvia was more than ready to return to Smith and her feverish pursuit of honors. Dr. Jones agreed, recommended her re-admission strongly, and praised Sylvia's insights into her own illness and her new-found ability to accept the discordant aspects of herself. Psychotherapy, in short, had been a success. Smith was eager to agree, regarding Sylvia as one of its brilliant stars; and she enrolled for the spring term, which was due to commence on February 1. It would mean repeating a half-year's work, but she would be treated as the golden girl once more, her halo burnished even brighter by her well-publicized suicide attempt. Although Lawrence House would again be her campus home, she would now have a single room; and the infirmary had special instructions always to remain open to her as a sort of sanctuary from the rigors of college existence. Better yet, all her classes were scheduled for the mornings, including Saturdays, and each Wednesday she could depend upon a conference with Dr. Jones.

The courses themselves were exciting to contemplate, as were the teachers involved. She would be taking Early American Literature (Hawthorne, Melville, and Henry James) with Newton Arvin; Modern American Literature with Robert Gorham Davis; Russian Literature (devoted exclusively to Tolstoy and Dostoevsky) with George Gibian; European Intellectual History of the 19th Century "with a magnificent and powerful German woman"; and Medieval Art History. She still loved the idea of associating with "names" and participating in highly intellectual exercises of any kind. This time, however, she was determined to have fun as well—to enjoy her new sexual emancipation to the limit and not become a slave to her writing. Hoping to detract attention from the small scar on her right cheek, she dyed her hair blond—"the most incredibly brass, brash gold I have ever seen," according to Marcia—and bought new clothes for the occasion.

On the Sunday before her departure, Sylvia spent the entire day at the Crockett home, although she refused an invitation to remain for dinner. They discussed Eliot's play, *The Confidential Clerk*, which they had all seen and enjoyed, and then listened to recordings of Robert Frost reading his own poetry. Sylvia was entranced by the way the poet's rough, casual voice and style so faithfully echoed his poems' rustic textures. They also had tea and some of Mrs. Crockett's homemade raspberry tarts while sprawled in front of a crackling fire. Mr. Crockett was "at his intellectual best," and the visit was a pleasant interlude between the recent loss of self-confidence and the new battles for meaning and control ahead.

A few days before classes commenced, her brother kindly offered to drive Sylvia up to Smith. They left Wellesley in light snow and sleet and, as they approached Northampton, the weather took a sharp turn for the worse. By the time they were actually on college property, the car was being rocked by a blinding blizzard. Grimly and calmly, Warren navigated through the sheets of snow and began the descent of a steep, unplowed hill near Paradise Pond. But traction was poor and the car started to skid out of control, turned sideways, and seemed ready to tilt over. A crash seemed inevitable as another car loomed up below them on the hill; and Sylvia, who had tried to destroy herself only months earlier, was panic-striken and frantically moaned to herself again and again, "Oh, God! God! God!" Fate seemed to hear her, at least this time, as the car made a complete spin and came to a full stop without hitting anything or going off the road. But it would be half an hour before Sylvia stopped shaking.

Happily, the near-accident was the only ill omen to mar her return to Smith. The officials of the college went out of their way to welcome her, and the girls at Lawrence House were no less gracious. A fellow student and friend at Lawrence, Jane Truslow, remembers that "everyone made a big fuss over her." [8] Marcia, who was again at Haven, came over the next evening; and she and Sylvia had a pleasant dinner together reminiscing and discussing their new courses and teachers. The gushing, highly affected behavior of her friend convinced Marcia that Sylvia's recovery had taken a strange turn—that "she was obviously trying on a whole lot of different manners and means." The "loner" of old had become a boisterous extrovert.

The next few days were pleasantly hectic for Sylvia as she met her instructors, bought books and "other necessities," and made her large double room homey by filling its two bookcases. On Thursday night she sat down to write a long letter to Philip McCurdy in reply to the one she had from him that same day. After detailing her many activities of the past week, she went into an elaborate and pretentious explanation of the need for them not to let their new erotic relationship destroy the Platonic friendship they had once possessed. She concluded by assuring him of her continued love, while letting him know that both of them were free to go out with other partners without fear of a rupture in their "special understanding." The letter is redolent with self-conscious arrogance.

Besides being the golden girl who had published in national magazines and won Smith's highest honors, Sylvia was now also the romantic poet who had tried to commit suicide and ended up in an asylum. Her manipulative instincts would not permit her to ignore this opportunity to further enhance her own myth. In a short while, she had acquired a small group of devoted drudges, less attractive girls more than willing to bask in her reflected glory by running errands for her and listening to her endless stream of self-important chatter.

The effect she had at Smith may best be gauged by the reactions of another student, Elinor Klein, a junior from a neighboring dormitory where Sylvia was once invited to dinner. Elinor had been asked to join the table—a special honor—and remembered "thinking ungenerously, 'It's too much. She's pretty too!' Admiring her work and her easy brilliance, I automatically assumed that such genius would have the grace to take a clichéd form—the shy, spectacled, unattractive kind in the corner clutching her Dostoevsky for dear life. But Sylvia was lovely, willowy-lithe with great soft dark eyes, wide laughing mouth and a tumble of light hair." The blatant hero worship behind such romantic effusions had its reward when the two girls began sharing afternoons alone together—"talking nonstop until twilight"—although Sylvia undoubtedly did most of the talking.

There were enough Elinor Kleins around campus to make Sylvia's next year and a half at Smith a whirlwind of admiration. "She had come back to Smith after her first arduous illness," according to Elinor, "and celebrated her recovery constantly. She spoke about her illness with insight, honesty and great good humor. Even our most serious conversations were invariably punctuated with laughter."

These same Elinor Kleins were eager to supply their queen with one blind date after another until Sylvia had built up an entire constellation of young male satellites. Her new sexual liberation helped immeasurably, as did her new personality and local fame. Being "easy" in the fifties almost guaranteed immediate popularity—a truism Sylvia had refused to accept when a freshman; and she was making up for lost time in the sexual realm. As Jane Truslow recalls it, "she took the whole thing up with enormous enthusiasm and would astound everybody with her frank approach, dragging the boy off into a dark room on the first date."

Most of her boy friends naturally came from Amherst, the closest Ivy-League school, such as Richard S——, French grandson of a British poet; and someone simply identified as "George," a chemistry major with definite ideas about masculine superiority. The other Ivy-League schools were also well represented, however, and Sylvia maintained her ties with Gordon Lameyer and Myron Lotz. In fact, she seemed to be engaged in an endless juggling act from weekend to weekend, visiting Harvard and Yale, having boys up to Smith. She was like a collector of specimens, in a way, each boy signifying a different aspect of the perfect male: Lotz the athlete, Lameyer the naval officer, McCurdy the educator, George the scientist, and S——— the decadent European.

S——— is the curiosity piece. Short, dark, often rough and indifferent towards her, he was Sylvia's black lover, the closet passion, as un-American as Valentino and much too sophisticated for her wiles. He could not be manipulated as easily as the others and was not above slapping her on occasion, although he had his own share of shy sensitivity. According to Jane Truslow, "he looked kind of Indian"; and Nancy Hunter has given us an interesting portrait of him and of Sylvia's reaction to him: "She saw another young man regularly while I knew her, a dark, brooding, passionate Gallic type whose brilliance and imagination were the equal of her own. She endowed him with the qualities of a Byronic hero: an air of mystery and an almost sinister melancholia that she found fascinating, even though she seemed also to regard him, at times, as an amusing toy. Because he was small and slightly built she admitted to a feeling of physical revulsion in his presence. 'When he holds me in his arms,' she confided, 'I feel like Mother Earth with a small brown bug crawling on me.' "

But Sylvia's statement, typical though it is, has to be accepted with reservations. Sexuality was part of the resurrected mask, an important part in terms of certifying her female excellence in bed; but she had discovered a conventional truth: most American college boys are inept lovers. S——— alone offered a sense of expertise, a mutual sharing of pleasure and interest that did not include only athletic contests of strength or stamina. More important, his certain malehood carried with it the persistent image of vice, of delightful continental corruption. The opposite extreme of healthy American philistinism did have a human form after all.

During her first meal back at Lawrence House, Sylvia had met Nancy Hunter, an attractive, dark-haired education major who had transferred to Smith from Ohio's Wooster College in 1953. Nancy had been given Sylvia's old room on the second floor and was invited to be one of the fortunate six at Sylvia's table—under the housemother's direction, all the tables bore floral bouquets in honor of Sylvia's return. Like Elinor Klein, Nancy was surprised by Sylvia's striking appearance and blurted out, "They didn't tell me you were beautiful!", which brought relieved laughter from the others in the room.

Nancy's description of Sylvia is also like Elinor Klein's in its rose-colored absorption with movie-star details: "She was impressively tall, almost statuesque, and she carried the height with an air of easy assurance. Her yellow hair, which had been lightened several shades from its natural light brown, was shoulder length and had been carefully trained to dip with a precise and provocative flourish over her left eyebrow. Her eyes were very dark, deeply set under heavy lids that give them a brooding quality in many of her photographs. Her cheekbones were high and pronounced, their prominence exaggerated by the faint, irregular brown scar that was the only physical reminder of the suicide attempt. The face was angular and its features strong, a fact that may explain the dark shadows that seem to haunt it in photographs."

Nancy would eventually become for Sylvia another campus alter ego to replace Marcia Brown, who would be graduating and getting married in June. "She referred to me in letters to her mother as her alter ego and often remarked that we presented a mirror image or represented opposite sides of the same coin." Nancy's practical turn of mind was supportive and essential, and acted as "a filter through which the inspiration passed, qualifying and tempering what she initiated." Sylvia lost little time in getting Nancy to agree to be her roommate next year.

Jane Truslow recalls that Sylvia, Nancy, and their small clique of House friends tended to regard themselves as members of a "fast crowd," superior to and more sophisticated than the rest of Smith. They rejected the extreme of rebellion exemplified by Lawrence's handful of determined non-conformists, but also revelled in their own women-of-the-world airs by dating Ivy League boys and going to the right places. As usual, politics did not intrude; and, like "shopgirls, we worked long hours, and the diversions we sought when we relaxed were pedestrian. We pursued boys, clothes, and entertainment as energetically as we pursued an education."

But Sylvia and Marcia remained close in a way that Sylvia and Nancy never could, perhaps because Nancy's healthy selfishness would never permit her fully to accept her alter-ego function as Sylvia's mother figure in crucial situations to come. A few days after returning to Smith, Sylvia and Marcia went into town and shopped for more books to fill Sylvia's two bookcases. Despite Marcia's lack of a literary background, Sylvia did not hesitate to use her as a sounding board, particularly regarding her new-found enthusiasm for Dostoevsky. One Sunday, February 14, they had breakfast in Northampton and discussed Dostoevsky's theories of crime and insanity for hours, before hearing a Unitarian sermon on marriage and the Kinsey Report, which Sylvia appreciated because of the minister's subtle wit.

A few days earlier, on Thursday night, Sylvia had gone to Mary

Ellen Chase's lecture on "Imagination in the Old Testament" and afterwards was one of the select few invited to the reception at President Wright's house—a special "first" that thrilled her immensely. Her ego continued to feed on the attention shown her by faculty and students alike, but her new self-concept retained its romantic aura of safe despair. While on one of her book-buying binges, she secured a copy of Tennessee Williams' *Camino Real*, which she had seen in New York the previous spring before its hasty closing and which she regarded as her favorite Williams' play. One line in particular stuck in her mind, and its nihilistic absolutism suggests a return to Nietzsche: "And these are the moments when we look into ourselves and ask with a wonder which never is lost altogether: Can this be all? Is there nothing more? Is this what the glittering wheels of heaven turn for?" Other lines memorized from the same play further confirm her familiar inability to escape the empty universe carved from reality by her scalpel-like mind, such as "We have to distrust each other. It is our only defense against betrayal" and the more pretentious "We are all of us guinea pigs in the laboratory of God. Humanity is just a work in progress." Like Williams, she savored her terrible insights with a romantic passion.

Marriage remained a sore point. A senior girl from Lawrence was married early in the semester at Northampton's Congregational Church, which Sylvia attended—her first wedding since her aunt's nearly twelve years before; and she would, of course, serve as a bridesmaid for Marcia in June. On a rainy Friday, February 26, the two girls had gone into town to purchase Sylvia's dress. Still haunted by the need to be normal in every respect, as a woman and an artist, she had to have at least the prospect of marriage always in front of her to fence off the horrible alternative of spinsterhood. With Byronic affectation, another penchant reinforced by Tennessee Williams, Sylvia had spoken to McCurdy of her new conviction that the wedding ceremony should be a stark but poetic affair performed on some cliff overlooking the ocean—a pure pagan ritual inextricably linked to nature's great forces of birth, death, and re-birth. But she also felt desperate and wanted an official fiancé to replace the abandoned Buddy Willard, if only to certify that McLean and her suicide attempt had not rendered her unattractive as a marriage partner.

After her return to Smith, Sylvia had made sure to write Myron Lotz a warm letter, letting him know of her complete recovery. The letter itself has unfortunately been lost, but Lotz remembers that it was filled with good-natured frankness and represented, in his eyes, "an amazing renaissance." Despite the recent tragedy, she spoke of herself as "an optimist" and admitted that she had "at least seen places that I never knew existed." Several weeks later she invited Lotz and his friends, Bob and Jill Modlin, up to Smith. They collected her at Lawrence and drove over snow-covered roads to a small Italian restaurant she loved, where she munched through her favorite dinner of hamburger, onions, and pizza while talking endlessly and confidently of her plans to be a writer. Then she directed the party along another snow-covered road through the woods to a bar six or eight miles outside of town. There she once again took center stage, saying solid, sensible things about the serious writer's need to have other people support her during her apprenticeship, as well as planning for an alternative career, such as teaching.

Intrigued as always by her mask of bubbling assurance, Bob Modlin began probing at her statements in a quiet way, asking question after question. As Jill Modlin recalls it, "She started off with a lot of confidence about her future, asking, 'How can you sit around and not know what your life is going to be like?', etc., but when Bob pinned her down it all came out, a lot of doubts." It became clear that "she had this tremendous anxiety about her creativity" and that in her heart "she didn't know whether she could write." Her ambivalent attitude towards marriage surfaced as she again remarked to Jill how wonderful it was for her to be a housewife and have definite future plans—only to negate her own enthusiasm a little later with the sincere query, "How could you give up a career in journalism?"

It was probably during this time, when still unsettled by Bob Modlin's questions, that Sylvia told Lotz how she yearned to make someone a good wife and hinted that Lotz himself could be the fortunate husband. Caught off guard and not particularly enamored of the prospect of being married to a recent mental patient, he replied fast and furiously and "gave her triple talk." The rejection had to have hurt deeply, striking at the soul of her basic insecurity and its balancing shell of enormous self-pride. As Lotz himself had observed, this was the girl who "really felt she was something," but whose new adjustment to life he could only describe as "fragile."

In April, again at Sylvia's invitation, Lotz made another visit to Northampton, but found a much different Sylvia waiting for him there. Rejection had stirred self-doubts into overt hostility. When she greeted him, she did so as the queen bee surrounded by several eager, buzzing drones, including "George" and Richard S——, and treated him with ill-concealed contempt, eventually accusing him of attempting to compete with her. The two arch manipulators and fellow over-achievers had finally struck the right match and ignited a series of explosive recriminations.

Soon after returning to his own college, Lotz scribbled angrily in his journal, under the date of April 23: "saw Sylvia today—no soap, acted like a snobby bitch, knowing that four mongrel dogs were sniffing around her bottom—nasty harpie!" However superficially accurate the description of Sylvia's behavior seems, it has to be read in light of Lotz's earlier painful rejection of her and the fact that both parties had been using one another for their own not always clear purposes from the beginning. Honesty and love had never been important elements in their mercurial interaction, and were not now in the abrupt termination of that relationship.

Lotz was more or less out of the picture, but Sylvia's covey of male admirers helped to soothe whatever sense of disappointment was involved. Men had become central to her, as had the sex act itself in a different, more intense way, but only as a perpetual audience for her verbal display and constant Wife of Bath mastery over them, and perhaps also unconsciously as proof against the ever-threatening night of nullifying madness. Wrestling with their clumsy bodies, proving her superiority even in bed, leading them on a leash to Harvard and Yale weekends, displaying them like trophies to the other girls—all this sufficed to guarantee the golden-girl aura.

Maintaining that aura also meant a continuous dedication to her physical appearance. She kept her hair dyed and paid strict attention to her clothes, always dressing to suit the occasion in the most feminine way possible. As soon as the warm weather arrived, she spent long hours on the griddle of the alumnae gym's roof, which was next door to Lawrence House. Here, day after day, she anointed herself with baby oil "beyond the bounds of the normal—she was going to be tanner than anybody else on campus." The old Sylvia was functioning with an iron will once more: whatever needed to be done to ensure success was done with total dedication, regardless of the physical or mental toll.

According to Nancy Hunter, Sylvia was writing again during the spring semester, but it was primarily revisions of critical essays, since no poems have yet been identified as having come from this period. In May she did have the pleasure of seeing "Doomsday" appear in *Harper's*, but her intense social, intellectual, and scholastic pursuits left her little time for creative endeavors. Each course seemed to demand and get her undivided attention in and out of class; and for every book assigned she read many ancillary texts, either borrowing them from the school library

or buying them in paperback editions. The high level of her performance as a student can be seen in the following observation of Professor
George Gibian, her Russian Literature teacher: "I came to know her
hand-writing—very clear, rounded, quite legible. Her exam was
excellent—and then later I got to know her in person: she was, it turned
out, that good-looking girl who stared intently, out of the crowd of
students, when I was talking to the class. Her work was absolutely
outstanding—a brilliant student of literature who wrote brilliant essays
and exams."

Sylvia's excitement over her courses and her professors was real, and
she found herself discovering new favorites among authors, although she
retained a literary crush on Dylan Thomas and still tried to imitate his
use of the sea for metaphorical effects. Richard Wilbur, the young,
handsome poet whom she had interviewed for *Mademoiselle*, was another
new idol; and, as Nancy Hunter has testified, "She read every word he
wrote and showed me every article about him and every photograph of
him that appeared anywhere in print." An interesting sidelight to this
fascination with Wilbur, and a later effort by that poet to restore her to
life, would be a fine poem of his written in 1972 that succinctly isolates
the last ten years of Sylvia's life and art:

> Outliving Sylvia who, condemned to live,
> Shall study for a decade, as she must,
> To state at last her brilliant negative
> In poems free and helpless and unjust.[9]

Other near-contemporaries did not fare as well. Adrienne Rich, for
instance, whose collection of poems, *A Change of World*, had won the
Yale Younger Poets Award in 1951 and who attended the more
prestigious Radcliffe, was regarded with envious dislike—Sylvia believed
her own work to be superior.

But classic authors also came to the forefront of her consciousness, due
largely to the intense re-reading of them necessary for her classes.
Melville and Dostoevsky, whom she had first met under Mr. Crockett's
perceptive tutelage, suddenly acquired new significance. The biggest
discovery of the term, however, would be D. H. Lawrence. When
preparing for an examination in her Early American Literature course in
mid-April, she took down her unread copy of *Studies in Classical
American Literature* to check over the chapters on Melville for
Lawrence's comments concerning *Billy Budd*. The book was a
revelation, and she read it from cover to cover, underlining furiously as
she did so.

Lawrence had not been a stranger to her, Lawrence the novelist, that is; but now she felt she understood him, and probably her own literature and being, as she never had before. His insights into the American soul—"hard, isolate, stoic, and a killer. It has never yet melted"—and unique understanding of the sea's pull—"The greatest material mother of us all is the sea"—must have given her a sense of comradeship. Above all, Lawrence appeared to comprehend the linking of mother sea with the artist, and to realize the despair and failure ultimate in any parallel creation: "The further extreme, the greatest mother, is the sea. Love the great mother of the sea, the Magna Mater. And see how bitter it is. And see how you must fail to win her to your ideal: forever fail. Absolutely fail." Mrs. Plath, suicide, art as Ahab's obsession with revenge and final meanings, which would become the hallmark of Sylvia's later literature, are here brought together in a blinding, brilliant synthesis.

In the next few years Lawrence's poetry would become equally important to her, having a definite influence upon her own work; and his insights into women and the artist, among other things, remained central to her own concerns. But that semester was one of discovery in almost every field as she read heavily in philosophy, sociology, comparative literature, and psychology. She was finding huge gaps in her knowledge, even in literature, which her compulsive drive towards total command would not allow her to ignore. On the day after discovering Lawrence the critic, Hans Kohn came from Columbia University to lecture her Intellectual History class on Ibsen. She was so absorbed by his brilliant presentation that she uncharacteristically forgot to take notes and smiled knowingly at the professor in a kind of trance as he described what a *roué* was. He happened to catch her smile and nodded, "Ach, that girl, she knows, she's had experience!", which caused her to blush.

After class Sylvia went across the street to the school bookstore and used more money from her rapidly diminishing bank account to buy books, twelve in all. Besides the collected plays of Ibsen, she also purchased the plays of George Bernard Shaw, Eugene O'Neill, and the Greek tragedians. Other books bought included Fry's *Venus Observed*, Delmore Schwartz's *Vaudeville for a Princess*, Whitman's *Leaves of Grass*, and Sterne's *Tristram Shandy*. The Ibsen plays she started to read at once that very afternoon, but most of the rest were marked off for summer reading. The long novels from her two literature courses, *Moby Dick, War and Peace, Crime and Punishment*, several of Henry James's works, and the critical texts that went along with them, left her scant time for much outside reading. But the stimulation was always there, given an added boost by the attendant excitement of academic and social competition.

One day in particular—Wednesday, March 3—can be looked at, not as a typical day in Sylvia's school career that semester, but as an indication of the way she constantly drove herself to take advantage of every opportunity to master her world. It was a cold, rainy day, but she arose early, peeled potatoes and sliced carrots for the House, had a light breakfast of coffee and hot cross buns, raced to the library to return an armful of overdue books on Dostoevsky, attended the 8:30 Chapel where she heard President Wright read a letter from one of the Buckley family about the need for Smith alumnae to stop supporting the college because it was harboring several communists on its faculty (one of whom supposedly was Newton Arvin, Sylvia's mild-mannered and brilliant professor); then to the 9 A.M. class of that same professor to take a one-hour exam on the theme of guilt and retribution in Hawthorne. After the exam she had a free study hour, as Intellectual History had been cancelled for the day, before going to her Russian Literature course and taking another exam, this one on Dostoevsky.

Sylvia returned to Lawrence House for lunch and a game of bridge with some of the girls, but she was bothered by the familiar symptoms of a sore throat and menacing cold. She then went to see Dr. Jones for their weekly consultation, although according to Sylvia their friendship had developed to the point where they spent most of the hour gossiping about college affairs. After the session, Sylvia bought a bottle of anti-histamine tablets and returned to Lawrence to take them, along with much water and some apples. That night she attended I. A. Richards' lecture on poetry and was again invited to the reception at President Wright's house. Needless to add, she finally tumbled into bed exhausted and wracked by a severe cold.

This was the way Sylvia drove herself and, if nothing else, it at least had the benefit of keeping her mind and body fully occupied. Even when sunning herself on the gym roof, she never failed to read one of her required books. The only problem looming ahead, and it was a real problem considering her previous experience, was how to fill her summer. She still wanted to spend it in Cambridge, attending Harvard, but a scholarship was essential since money remained difficult to obtain. She had spent all her surplus funds on books, records, and clothes and knew her mother would not be able to afford to send her to summer school. The only possibility was a scholarship, and she applied for one in German, hoping that her superlative scholastic record and the strong recommendations of her teachers would prove effective. Such would prove to be the case, but before that time she had an unexpected opportunity to improve her chances.

Philip McCurdy had invited her to a dance at his dormitory, Adams House, on Saturday night, March 27, early in her spring vacation, and Sylvia had accepted. Besides the dance, which would take place in the dining hall on the ground floor, McCurdy and his tutor-friend Norman Shapiro, a poet and translator whom Sylvia admired, had arranged a party in a room upstairs. Sylvia, in fact, came early on Saturday to help Shapiro mix his locally famous punch of gin and grenadine. Like most of McCurdy's other friends at Harvard, Shapiro was intrigued by Sylvia. He writes about her and their first meeting with obvious affection: "I think the first time I met Sylvia was at her home in Wellesley. I was doing some translations from Old Provençal poetry for a course, and I had gone with Phil to visit her on some pretext or other. I took one of the translations along to work on, and Sylvia was quite taken with it. She asked to see more of my poems—which really weren't very voluminous —and I sent a few to her through Phil. I'm afraid her critical powers were less developed then than they were later to be. The poem that she mentioned in her letter to Phil was hardly a masterpiece. But she was very generous and sweet, and probably told Phil how much she liked it because she knew what good friends we were." [10]

After visiting the dance downstairs for a while, McCurdy and Sylvia went up to the party. Some forty-odd people, mostly Harvard graduate students and tutors, were crushed into the small room, and many of them were already familiar with Sylvia's reputation as a successful poet and prize winner. She delighted in the sudden glow of their attention as they crowded around her, literally sitting at her feet to listen to her and soon she was playing her favorite role of queen bee.

Along with everyone else, McCurdy was overwhelmed by the charismatic glow of her radiant presence in his room. "This is a beautiful girl," he recalled, "she was nothing but strikingly beautiful, beautiful hair, beautiful carriage." A few hours later, they returned to the dance downstairs, and McCurdy was soon pointing out to her a man named "Carl Scot"—later Professor of Government who was then an Assistant Senior Tutor at Harvard and, most impressive of all from Sylvia's viewpoint, the administrator in charge of the school's summer session. Never one to pass up an opportunity, Sylvia was dancing cheek to cheek with him in minutes, using her athletic, well-tanned body as an implement of insistent persuasion. McCurdy described her act in terms of amused admiration: "Sylvia put him through a bump and grind the likes of which you have never seen in your life." A grotesque overtone of sorts was added by the fact that Mr. Scot's wife was then in the process of beginning a painful labor in one of the upstairs rooms.

Although it's unlikely that Sylvia's sexual ploy had much to do with it, she was granted a full scholarship to study German at Harvard that summer. Better yet, she was elected president of Alpha at Smith, and the college would decide at semester's end to grant her its largest scholarship for the following year, and thereby relieve her sense of guilt about not working during the summer. She had also convinced Nancy Hunter that she too ought to attend Harvard's summer program and room with her off campus in Cambridge. Nancy had needed very little persuasion once she learned that Hans Kohn was going to give two courses in her field during the summer. She applied for her own scholarship and got it. Her decision and acceptance cheered at least two parties: "Both Mrs. Plath and our housemother expressed pleasure at the news that I would be with Syl that summer. Both were concerned that the anniversary of the suicide attempt, which would fall during our stay in Cambridge, might prove a difficult hurdle for her to overcome."

But summer and suicide were remote from Sylvia's mind as she continued her dual existence as bright scholarship student and frantic social coed whose sanity and romantic charms were taken for granted. The spring vacation was spent at Harvard and back in Wellesley for the most part, and in Philip McCurdy's company. He often took her driving, and they visited an art exhibit, played much tennis, and generally reverted to the easy comradeship of earlier days. He remained in love with her, more so than he perhaps realized, always delighted by her presence; and she treated him tenderly as "Baby," a beloved younger brother. Sex rarely intruded, although McCurdy recalls: "Once, during the spring vacation period in Adams House, we were quite close, despite earlier agreements, to edging into the bedroom when a college policeman intervened by battering on the hall door. (I had forgotten the far less casual visitor procedures in force during the holidays.)"

With the temporary dismissal of Lotz, Sylvia seemed to feel the need to identify at least one of her many boy friends as a "steady" companion who would serve to demonstrate her normalcy. George was the choice for the next few weeks since, like S——, he would be graduating from Amherst in June. He was a pleasant, masculine, stimulating WASP type whose interest in the biological sciences satisfied Sylvia's taste for solid mastery of difficult fields. His "shop talk" impressed her and her friends, as had Buddy and Richard Willard's at one time, and he himself was not averse to squiring her around to various cultural events and keeping her weekends busy.

The first (and last) sign of a deep disenchantment with George came during the weekend of April 14–15. Nancy and Sylvia had gone to Yale and attended a religious-center lecture and discussion on sex and conception. Afterwards they met George and several others for the return trip to Northampton. George was in an irritable mood because of a severe cold and fever, and Sylvia resented his callous public treatment of her and sensed the basic sexist prejudice behind his behavior. Though hearing Andres Segovia play that night at Smith eased the situation, Sylvia had apparently decided that George as a marriage candidate was untenable. His independence could not be tolerated.

The formal break, if it could be called such under the circumstances, came a week later. Sylvia spent the next weekend in George's company, and the highlights of their final period together embraced activities as divergent as seeing the movie version of *Pygmalion*, starring Leslie Howard and Wendy Hiller, and climbing Smith's 830-foot-high fire tower during the middle of the night with another adventurous couple. While on the tower, Sylvia was squeezed nearly breathless by terror, but chattered on gaily and refused to panic in front of the others. Cowardice, as her later poems certainly prove, was never one of her faults.

The rest of the week George was too involved with his honors thesis in chemistry to pay much attention to Sylvia; and she, in turn, devoted most of her free time to Richard S——, whom she was enjoying more and more. Other recreations also helped fill the gap left by George's defection. There was a trip home where she was treated by Mrs. Palmer of Wellesley High, along with Pat O'Neil and Louise Guisey, to a dinner of "jack august lobsters"; and a formal Phi Beta dinner back at Smith. Plenty of good food and a constant spotlight were still among her main needs.

The following Wednesday was to have seen another, smaller Phi Beta dinner, this one at Lawrence House, to which Sylvia would have the honor of inviting four of her teachers. She had looked forward to the event for weeks and intended to wear an expensive silver-and-white ball gown. One of her devastating sinus colds developed, however, abetted again by exhaustion, and she ended up in the infirmary instead. The housemother then had to disinvite the four faculty members. Resting in the sun and reading Tolstoy and James had not prevented fatigue from once again breaking down her body's frail defenses.

A happier episode from this upside-down week was the announcement in the school newspaper that Alfred Kazin, critic and author of *On Native Ground*, would be appointed to the Nielson Chair for the next semester. It was now a full year's assignment, and Kazin would be teaching short-story writing the first semester and the twentieth-century novel, the second. An extra course, General Literature 291, was to accompany each. Here was another literary star Sylvia could cultivate, a solid connection who had both fame and scholastic respectability to offer. Elinor Klein would subsequently claim that she talked Sylvia into attending Kazin's short-story writing class, but it is doubtful that Sylvia needed much persuasion.

There was another announcement in the school press which must have been less pleasant for Sylvia to contemplate. On May 6 a girl named Amy Remondelli was installed as the *Smith Review*'s new editor. Although Sylvia was on the magazine's board again, and contributing regularly to its pages, she could not help but feel a little upset by the reminder of the high post she herself should have held, and would have held if the events of the previous summer had not intervened.

But the new mask was wearing well, the two surface Sylvias were firmly back in control, and nothing else could have really mattered very much. Even her pet obsessions had returned full force like primitive rituals to protect her against unseen menaces. She continued to regard her personal possessions as sacrosanct extensions of herself, and all violations were viewed with furious horror. Gordon Lameyer, who was still on his cruise, tells of the time she went to Yale with a boy and left her clothes and books in the trunk of the car while they were in a nightclub. When they returned, they found the trunk broken open and Sylvia's suitcase gone. Her underlined copies of Dylan Thomas and Dostoevsky had been among the stolen articles, and her rage knew no bounds. She made such a terrible scene, and blamed the boy as if he had been the actual thief, that he felt compelled to reimburse her in cash for the losses.

But such outbursts were rare, and the spring term was counted a success. A sad note was the imminent departure of Richard S——, who would be sailing for Paris as soon as he graduated; and Sylvia promised to spend a final weekend with him in New York City. They left on Saturday, May 8, in S——'s Volkswagen and reached New Haven in time for a late lunch. The rest of the journey along the Merritt Parkway into New York was much less enjoyable because of the heavy rains and traffic.

They reached the city with only enough time to register and drop off their luggage at a hotel on Forty-fourth Street before running out to buy theatre tickets and have a hasty dinner. The play, which was being staged in Greenwich Village, was a preview performance of Chekhov's *Seagull* featuring Montgomery Clift. Sylvia was not greatly impressed, and they had to return through the rain to the hotel bar. They then spent most of the long evening reading French poetry, Rimbaud and Baudelaire, drinking wine, and making love. The whole experience was deliciously Baudelairian from Sylvia's vantage point, another putatively dangerous step into murky continental waters. S——'s sophistication had never seemed more attractive—such a heady contrast to the sunlight pastimes of her other boy friends. His dark charm would be sorely missed.

Unfortunately, their intense lovemaking left them little time for sleeping, and Sylvia needed her sleep whatever the situation. They arose at noon on Sunday and checked out, but Sylvia was still groggy. It did not prevent her from gorging herself at Reuben's with herrings in cream, onion soup, ice-cream eclairs, coffee, and liberal doses of white wine—a feast which consumed some two hours of time as well. On the drive back, she lay in the back seat and dozed off. She awoke to discover a crowd of curious people staring through the rear windows at her. Richard had pulled off the parkway to get a cup of coffee and left her peacefully sleeping in the parking lot. Embarrassed, she staggered out of her cramped bed and rode the rest of the way in front.

The next two weeks were a time of intense study and review as she prepared for final examinations and wrote a number of papers for her various courses. *War and Peace*, *Anna Karenina*, *The Ambassador*, and *Moby Dick* were but a few of the thick, small-print volumes she had to confront day after day, often for a second time; and she tumbled into bed each night in a state of agitated, cerebral exhaustion that made it difficult to sleep. Sylvia desperately needed physical activity, like a game of tennis or a swim in the pool, and occasionally she would think back nostalgically upon her laborious days at Look Out Farm and the simple pleasures of a dreamless sleep.

The only interruption in her rigorous academic schedule was a weekend visit (May 15 and 16) of her mother, her brother, and Clement Moore, whom she entertained with her usual air of enthusiasm. On May 27 she finished her last exam, packed, and headed for home, content that her talents had not been diminished in the slightest by last summer's tragic events. Once again her marks were perfect, Smith had been re-conquered, and she had proved to all and sundry that Sylvia Plath was back on the trail of success. More important, her new air of extroverted sophistication also demonstrated that she had matured in social and sexual ways as well—that her femininity was as spectacular as her intellectual and creative gifts.

Sylvia looked forward to the summer, not only for the Harvard experience, but as an opportunity to read the many books she had bought during the term and to work at her poetry. She had already decided that her last year would be much less social and devoted more to her studies. Graduate school was essential since she really had no idea of how to use her particular talents, and college teaching was impossible without another degree. And since she was going to attend graduate school, it also had to be both the best and free, which meant a scholarship of some kind or another.

The whole month of June, however, lay before her like a present. Free of school pressures and not due to report to Harvard until the middle of July, she could afford to relax and socialize to her heart's content. There were two weddings of friends to attend. Marcia's would be near the end of the month, and Sylvia had invited Nancy Hunter to her Wellesley home for a weekend stay at the beginning of the month.[11] Nancy's birthday was June 3, and Sylvia wanted to celebrate it as impressively as possible. She had asked Philip McCurdy to arrange a date for Nancy with Norman Shapiro, while McCurdy would be her own escort that night. McCurdy agreed but had to withdraw at the last minute because of an exam and asked Andrew Jamison, a Byzantine scholar and the House Librarian at Adams, to stand in for him.

The Wednesday before Nancy's birthday, the two girls went to see Mrs. Prouty at her Brookline mansion. Nancy recalls that Sylvia "was grateful to and indulgently fond of her famous patron, as well as obviously impressed by the financial success of *Stella Dallas.*" In any case, the two girls were properly awed by the matronly novelist and her butler, who served them tea and a tray of canapés. In less than half an hour, they had devoured a platter of tiny cucumber sandwiches and were at work on a second. Nancy's account of their behavior, which was more high-spirited than rude, captures the atmosphere perfectly: "We talked importantly with Mrs. Prouty about her literary career, about Smith, and about ourselves in the best approximation of small talk we could manage, punctuating our remarks with the incessant, audible crackle of crisp, paper-thin, sour-creamy cucumbers." The embarrassment did not come until after their departure.

Thursday morning, the day of her twenty-first birthday, Nancy was greeted by Sylvia carrying a breakfast tray and a present, which turned out to be a small copy of *Alice in Wonderland*—a book that Sylvia herself must have relished for its metaphor of a little girl lost in an insane world.

Later the two girls drove to Cape Cod and spent most of the afternoon at Nauset Beach. Sylvia enjoyed introducing the sea and its treasures to her friend and necessary double, who came from Akron, Ohio. With precision and enthusiasm, she described the various relationships between sea and shore: "transformed a shard of clamshell or a starfish into a miracle of craftsmanship and design." Sylvia was not now playing the role of ingénue, but merely expressing the little-girl awe she had always experienced in the presence of the great mother.

That night was the double date with Shapiro and Jamison, and Sylvia had planned it carefully as she wanted to expose Nancy to Boston's night life with professional aplomb. Although almost engaged to an Amherst student, Nancy was not averse to dating others, and she found Norman Shapiro "brilliant, urbane, and irresistibly handsome." She also noted that Sylvia treated him "in a tolerant and patronizing manner." He was, in a temporary way, Sylvia's prized possession which she could bestow upon her friend like a grand dame who knows the full value of her bequest: "He had accumulated a string of graduate degrees, spoke seven languages fluently, and had lived all over the world."

In her memoir, *A Closer Look at Ariel*, Nancy rhapsodizes about the evening in Boston and marvels over the rich program: "The night's activities introduced me to a variety of delights, ranging from Armenian cuisine, complete with baklava, to Turkish belly dancers and Vaughn Monroe's The Meadows." But years later, all Shapiro could remember was dinner and a movie. The one thing that did stand out had nothing to do with Nancy: "I remember that Phil was a little miffed when my friend came back with a trace of lipstick smudged on his collar. He had quite a crush on Sylvia and assumed it was hers. But as I recall it was all very innocent."

The rest of the month was no less pleasant and busy. Gordon Lameyer had returned from his cruise looking tan and handsomer than ever, and Sylvia decided that he was indeed the perfect marriage candidate. She saw him frequently during the next few weeks, and they tried to re-establish the old relationship. But problems emerged as Lameyer began to resent her attempts to direct and shape his life. Arguments arose and they broke up. Lameyer returned to the naval base at Charlestown, Maryland, where he was now stationed. The split was brief, however, and Sylvia was soon writing to him as if all were as before. Shortly thereafter, she paid a visit to him in Maryland, having gone to Washington, D.C. to stay with a friend named Sue Weller. During the summer months, he would come often to Cambridge on weekends to take her out, still convinced that she was a virgin and that marriage between them was an actual possibility.

But other potential mates needed tending, and Sylvia did not ignore Philip McCurdy. In fact, she was hoping he could find a job in the Boston area and be near her, but instead McCurdy and Shapiro were hired as counselors on the Cape. They would be coming into Cambridge only on weekends when possible, which was convenient enough, since Sylvia would be studying her dreaded German once again and might need extra study time.

The biggest event in June was Marcia's wedding. It stirred deep waters and brought about a dramatic breach in Sylvia's façade of resurrected and improved golden girl. The marriage ceremony was being held in New Hampshire, and Sylvia went up a few days early. She then proceeded to behave in an odd, "exceedingly manic" manner, giggling, talking constantly, using her charms on the male guests with dance-hall boldness. Years later, Marcia recalled her actions as "terribly flirtatious and very emotional." She also recalls that Sylvia "drank too much one night and wept and carried on." The climax came on the eve of the big event: "I remember the night before the wedding I helped put her hair up, and she had hiccups and tears." Thus Sylvia had effectively reversed their roles and perhaps assumed Marcia's unvoiced fears and doubts in true "double" fashion.

No doubt Sylvia was also expressing a deep sense of hurt at losing an alter ego. And she was possibly giving vent to her own fears about marriage. The mask had slipped loose because of her intense joy and sadness to the point where she could not handle her personal sense of womanhood. Whatever the roots of her irrationality, however, they disappeared back into the soil of her unconscious during the actual ceremony. Sylvia behaved with proper decorum. Perhaps the reality had proved less threatening than its anticipation. Besides, the immediate future did hold its special promise of Harvard and Nancy Hunter—another double to hold her hand when and if the darkness fell again.

The problem of the double personality has been of central concern to men from primitive times to the present. In essence, the appearance of the Double is an aspect of man's eternal desire to solve the enigma of his own identity.

Sylvia Plath

8

The Cultivated Act

"Ich. Ich. Ich."

The barbed-wire tongue of the father was like an enclosure that summer in 1954, but Sylvia could and would hurdle even that obstacle. Lameyer remembers how she strove to impress her German teacher by submitting extra translations of Rilke's poetry that had been cribbed from MacIntyre's translations.[1] But if her German studies brought back memories of Otto and World War II, and intensified those of a year ago, Cambridge itself was sufficiently exciting to act as a neutralizing agent. Here were Harvard and boy friends and a new adventure in communal living away from her mother and Wellesley's dead summer streets. In mid-July she, Nancy, and two other girls from Lawrence House sublet a three-room apartment on Massachusetts Avenue, not far from Harvard Square. Sylvia and Nancy took the bedroom for themselves and relegated their co-tenants to a parlor couch. But they agreed to do the cooking in return, since the other two girls were working full time. Sylvia and Nancy had only morning classes.

Sylvia was still a mediocre cook at best, but with the aid of a cookbook she found little trouble turning out delicious and often elegant meals. As usual when confronted by an unknown practical art, she paid strict attention to details and was satisfied with nothing less than perfection:

"as though she actually believed that anything worth doing was worth doing well."

The relationship between Sylvia and Nancy, which had been pleasant and mutually satisfying to this point, now faced the severe test of prolonged close contact. Signs of strain came early but seemed minor. Nancy noticed that Sylvia used her share of the cooking money—the four girls contributed a dollar a day to the common larder—to buy luxury items, such as anchovy paste, capers, and walnuts, and left Nancy the unappreciated chore of purchasing necessary staples. But the crucial irritation stemmed from Sylvia's well-established obsession with personal property—her need to keep separate and immaculate her own possessions, even if they were merely a bottle of cheap nail polish or a left-over bag of potato chips from a recent party.

Nancy's narration of her roommate's idiosyncrasies, and her acid reaction to them, makes for depressing reading, although her memoir is undoubtedly accurate "in letter and spirit," as both Marcia Brown and Peter Davison have observed. Sylvia's odd, somewhat childish sense of personal property had, after all, a painful logic and history behind it, which inspires pity rather than censure, while Nancy's smug tone smacks of a cold cattiness that chills the reader with its dispassion. Thus when Nancy once commented upon Sylvia's penchant for arranging her drawers with precise tidiness, Sylvia admitted with pathetic candor, "if anyone ever disarranged my things I'd feel as though I had been raped intellectually." And yet Nancy could only write in retrospect, "The reaction was extreme and it frightened me."

In other ways, however, Sylvia proved a delightful, informative companion. She enjoyed her role as leader in their explorations of Cambridge and exposed Nancy to the university town's well-known highlights as she had exposed her earlier to the seashore's secrets. They adopted a cat, named Nijinsky by Sylvia because of his graceful movements, kept the apartment clean and congenial, and generally enjoyed themselves. Boys were still the main preoccupation, and Sylvia had little time for writing. McCurdy showed up for several weekend dates, as did Lameyer, whom she continued to speak of as her fiancé. But, as Nancy noted, "I never heard Syl express strong feelings about any of the boys she dated; she enjoyed male company and blossomed in its presence, but she did not appear to care deeply about any of the men she had met up to that point." [2]

Myron Lotz, her discarded athletic hero, was still playing baseball in the minor leagues, and her dark lover S—— remained an ocean away.

She needed him the most because he represented an extreme of danger, largely metaphorical, which could help keep negative emotions and memories in check. Perhaps that was why she would become so involved with Edwin, called Irwin in *The Bell Jar*, the closet rapist ugly enough to repel (and thus fascinate) her middle-class self. Besides his ugliness and great intensity of purpose, he also had in her eyes the most prized of gifts, namely, intellectual brilliance. Nancy and Sylvia met him on the steps of the Widener Library and, after detailing his physical faults with prim cruelty—and these included a tall emaciated frame and thick glasses—even Nancy had to concede that "Syl and I knew that he was probably the most brilliant man we had ever met."

What Nancy failed to mention is that he also had a wife in St. Louis, where he was a professor at a local college. In her view of the events that followed, Edwin is the villain and she the perceptive, suspense-building onlooker: "For all his affable good nature there was something sinister about him that I couldn't define." Edwin became one of Sylvia's regular beaux and even drove her to her weekly appointments with Dr. Jones. The crisis came when Nancy awoke one morning to discover Sylvia's bed unslept in, and a subsequent call from Edwin confirmed her worst suspicions. He informed her that Sylvia had hemorrhaged during the night, had seen a doctor, and was now all right. If she was raped, as Sylvia told Nancy later, she was not about to let it ruin her day.[3] After returning home briefly, Sylvia went with Edwin to the beach for a picnic and did not get in again until 5 P.M. This time she was pale and shaken.

The hemorrhaging had started again, and when Sylvia arose from the bed after talking to Nancy, "a large dark stain had spread across the place where she was sitting." The same frightening stain darkened the back of her skirt, and a thin trickle of blood snaked down her leg and into her shoe. At this juncture, Sylvia was more annoyed than upset, for she had grown accustomed to her irregular period, and simply changed into a nightgown to have dinner with the girls. Midway through the meal, she staggered from the table and raced to the bathroom, where, still bleeding, she collapsed. Fear took over, especially her fear of the medical profession. "Her horror of doctors and hospitals was so profound that it almost seemed she would rather bleed to death than encounter them again."

Sylvia gave Nancy the name of the gynecologist she had seen the night before at the hospital, but could not remember the pseudonym she had used. Nancy telephoned him and explained her friend's predicament. He sympathetically told her how to prevent further bleeding.

With admirable calm, Nancy did as instructed. For the next three hours Sylvia lay on the bed, which had been covered with an old plastic tablecloth, and talked with Nancy, who would occasionally check the padding between Sylvia's legs for signs of further bleeding.

The remedy did not work. When Sylvia arose at last, near ten o'clock, the tablecloth was thick with blood. She had obviously lost too much and Nancy desperately called the doctor. He agreed to meet them at the hospital emergency room in ten minutes. Transportation was now the problem, and Nancy did not hesitate to telephone Edwin and demand that he take them to the hospital. He appeared five minutes later and drove them the short distance required. An orderly wheeled Sylvia into the emergency room, accompanied at Sylvia's request by the very nervous Nancy. The doctor had little trouble stopping the blood. Nancy then asked the hospital to send Edwin the bill—a move that Esther would assume credit for in *The Bell Jar*. Edwin, who had remained in his car all the while, drove the girls back home and promised at the door to call tomorrow about Sylvia's condition. Nancy recalls: " 'Don't bother,' I said vehemently, 'you've done enough.' "

Sylvia recovered and continued to see Edwin. In fact, Gordon Lameyer claims that Edwin subsequently gave her a present of a navy blazer, which she accepted but which her mother made her return. Whether Sylvia was actually raped is difficult to tell. She was not a virgin at the time, and not averse to sex, although it had always been in the context of acceptable partners.

Whatever led up to the episode, Sylvia may have enjoyed the whole experience, not the "rape" so much as the consequent attention it engendered. But it also had the effect of forever altering the relationship between herself and Nancy. Nancy had seen far too much of her friend at close quarters and had become involved more deeply than she wanted to with Sylvia's passionate need for a mother figure. Further, the incident served to reveal that Sylvia's readjustment after the breakdown of the year before was an uneasy one, "as if her emotional problems had not been solved but had merely been lifted from her and hidden away in some antiseptic storage room, to be clamped down upon her again in an unsuspecting moment."

In discovering the "real" Sylvia, Nancy also now knew that being her friend's "alter ego" entailed much more than just a mutual sharing of pleasant social and academic activities. Sylvia expected her double to be a true other self, quite willing to sacrifice her own needs to Sylvia's more important ones. Nancy wanted none of that and subtly began to limit her participation in Sylvia's activities.

Her resolve was hardened one evening when Mrs. Plath telephoned from Wellesley. It was the anniversary of Sylvia's suicide attempt, and Aurelia wanted to speak with her daughter and reassure herself that Sylvia was all right. It was an understandable gesture of concern, but Nancy resented Mrs. Plath's assumption that she was somehow Sylvia's keeper. Nevertheless she did agree to try to locate her. Lameyer had taken Sylvia out for the evening, and they had planned to stop off at a number of different parties before reaching Lameyer's family home and dinner. Nancy quickly began calling all of Sylvia's friends in Boston. Before she actually reached Sylvia at one of the parties, Mrs. Plath had called back several times, which only increased Nancy's state of tension. Finally Sylvia was located and telephoned her mother to assure her that all was well.

The experience convinced Nancy that her decision to back off from Sylvia's chaotic universe was sensible in the extreme: "A chill settled along my bones as I allowed myself to imagine the consequences if I were wrong—if Syl was approaching another breakdown that I had failed to anticipate." Sylvia was not approaching another breakdown, of course, but merely "racing from experience to experience with a recklessness that asserted her invincibility." Nancy soon realized that Sylvia's "almost pathological dependence was draining me." Near the end of August, during final exam time, Sylvia awoke with a headache and screamed that she was dying. Alarmed, Nancy kept phoning doctors until she found one who would make a house call. In her memoir, Nancy claimed that Sylvia "had little tolerance for physical pain; using all her energies merely to exist, she had no reserves from which to draw in an emergency." The patness of the statement tends to elicit easy agreement, but it does not take into consideration Sylvia's long history of suffering, which she had not only endured but overcome time and again. Sylvia, sensitive to her roommate's growing disenchantment with her, was perhaps testing Nancy here as a child tests his parents or teachers.

Sylvia begged Nancy to wait with her until the doctor came—an unreasonable but essential request, even though she knew Nancy had to take her examination. Instead Nancy asked one of the other girls to remain and hurried off to school, full of doubts and guilt. In her absence, the doctor arrived, gave Sylvia a few pills, and departed. Soon after, Sylvia felt well enough to leave for class. It was a trivial episode certainly, but Nancy's invisible moat had widened. Unable to risk serious emotional involvement, and not willing to shoulder any consequent guilt, she "drew back instinctively, allowing some distance to come between us like an invisible barrier."

Thus the summer ended under a cloud of change and reassessments. Marcia was gone, living in Boston with her new husband; Lotz remained away, still estranged; McCurdy, her own special "baby," had met and was courting his future wife; and Sylvia and Nancy were destined to become little more than congenial roommates during their senior year together. A sad reminder of another lost relationship had been introduced as well. One day while at Chatham's Beach, Sylvia and Lameyer ran into Buddy Willard, who was working in the area as a camp counselor. The aftermath of tuberculosis and a successful operation had left their mark, and Buddy seemed like a pathetic husk of his former self in Sylvia's pitying eyes.[4]

Academically, the summer had been a great triumph. Another "A" earned Sylvia the right to proceed further in German; and she remained determined to devote her last year at Smith to studying, writing, and winning more prizes, particularly the prize of a full scholarship to graduate school. Her social life must and would be severely limited. She would continue to see Gordon Lameyer; but their romance, which had already endured two fairly serious breaks, would slowly falter as Sylvia's energies were drained by her research and writing exercises. Years later he would remark rather ruefully that she then "became so interested in her work that she had little time for anything else." She even dyed her hair brown and considerably toned down her public image. The result of all this stern settling down was, to quote Nancy again, "a serene year for Syl and a productive one as well."

Her class load was hardly heavy when Sylvia returned to college in September. Besides auditing a philosophy course, she was taking Shakespeare 36 with Professor Esther Dunn, short-story writing with Alfred Kazin, and a German class with the department chairman, Professor Paul G. Graham, that entailed a study of selections from Lessing, Goethe, and Schiller.

But the major portion of her senior-year program was designed to permit maximum time for preparing an honors thesis. Joyce and his dual images were out as far as Sylvia was concerned; Dostoevsky seemed a better subject with his frequent use of split or double personalities. Professor George Gibian, her thesis adviser and friend, has kindly provided an account of the whole process: "After the course, she wanted to write a thesis on Dostoevsky. (Undergraduate honors thesis.) She came often to my little office on the top floor of a weird physics building—Lilly Hall—a little wooden cubicle, really, under the eaves. It was she who chose the theme of the double. No, it was not clear to me at the time that her interest in it was so personal as I now know—but it was equally clear that she was very much involved in the subject. The psychological side interested her as much as, if not more than, the literary. She read a lot of the psychoanalytical and also anthropological literature on the mirror image, the twin, the double."

Sylvia's impression upon Professor Gibian was positive in every way. Physically, she always seemed to him "as if she had just come back from skiing in Vermont or swimming in Bermuda—healthy, good-looking, tall, good posture—like the non-intellectual, un-tormented Smith girl stereotype!" As a student whose thesis he had to direct, she was no less impressive: "ideal; a wish-fulfillment student. It was enough to make some lame suggestion about what she might read, look into, —she was off, and a week later brought back a beautifully developed chapter that showed much more understanding than one ever had in making the suggestion to her."

Although Sylvia would wisely restrict her thesis to a study of two of Dostoevsky's novels, *The Double* and *The Brothers Karamazov*, the entire subject obviously meant a great deal to her as it reflected her continued intellectual awareness of her own schizophrenic nature. Earlier, of course, her private research into abnormal psychiatry and her subsequent treatment under Dr. Jones's care had framed an objective model for a reliable if incomplete self-portrait; but she wanted to press on, move further outside of herself in a search for literary, historical, and social instances of the double's existence. Myth-making was still important to her as an artist, but the major thrust of her search was for external confirmation of her own dual reality. In her later poetry and sole novel, she would utilize this knowledge as a means of structuring objective worlds upon intensely personal existential states. The masks of her life would become the mythical body of her art.

Marcia and Nancy were living examples of Sylvia's realization that the double had to possess both interior and exterior features in order to survive and flourish. As mirrors for an anxious queen, they alone could certify her reality (and its uniqueness) in the "real" world. Only thus could she accept her frightening vision of constant poles in constant opposition as the universe's primary mode of existence and artistic tension. Only thus could she resign herself to being endlessly stretched on the rack of negative extremes she had already established in the major areas of her life.

Her own writing, however, could not take advantage of this growing self-awareness, mainly because its author still insisted upon the importance of appearances and moral commitment over emotional content.

The poetry from her senior year remained locked in the airless cell of traditional formulas, both physically and emotionally.

In fact, none of the poems from this period emerges as a complete and satisfying experience, though, as usual, they do betray a deft hand and individual lines of striking force. But if they are "academic poetry" in the worst sense, they almost never settle for easy answers or sentimental simplism. Part of the problem had to be her continuing identification with poets such as Marianne Moore and Elizabeth Bishop who, for all their technical brilliance, remained trapped within the context of defining reality rather than seeking a transcendental method of escape. In the final analysis Moore and Bishop, along with other Plath favorites like Wylie, Teasdale, and Gardner, were "women poets" who reinforced Sylvia's own penchant for dry cleverness in spinster-like fashion and an unremitting allegiance to the well-made poem above everything else—a poem without blood or power or even the Dostoevskian willingness to sacrifice order to feeling. Sylvia would have been better off listening to Ezra Pound's dictum that "emotion alone endures."

But emotion had not yet become an acceptable element in the Plath scheme of things, at least not true emotion or emotion unfettered by endless hair-splitting. Winter held her fast and drew the most accurate sketch of her mind and heart's dilemma. In a poem called "Ice Age" she comes closest to her bleak vision and strong sense of arid reality—"the heart of the earth grows harder, harder"—and dour endings—"O the eyes of my lover/ are shut with snow/ and all, all is frozen over." The poem also has the virtue of leanness, as the three-line stanzas never overtly stall the steady progress from images of winter "vault of ice" to the death of love and "natural order." As an analogy it is commonplace, but in terms of craft it functions smoothly. .

Another poem, "Winter Words," operates on the same premise of a barren, white still-life, but is more directly concerned with the artist's own perspective. As such it is intriguing, and, like "Ice Age," it points back to "Second Winter" of a few years before and forward to "Spinster"—her Cambridge attempt to define the self's withdrawal into winter when love proves inadequate or non-existent. There is no "I" in "Winter Words," no suggestion of a human hand or heart, and in that sense it regresses to earlier efforts at preaching sermons.

Yet the artist here is a romantic imitation of a romantic poet—a slick version of a Wordsworth in his conservative dotage. This kind of nature mated with a castrated don presents a perfect echo of precisely the way in which Sylvia approached her creative task. She was writing at a frantic pace this year. Nancy recalls that Sylvia "worked furiously, slipping into her spot behind the typewriter in every spare moment," and that she had to be pried "away from it for meals and for sleep"; but the results were further deceptions, further retreats into disguises. Apart from writing itself, her main subject was romantic love, which she hardly conceded existed in her universe of tugging extremes, and an attempt to find in it some harbinger of salvation. In short, she seems to have been even less honest than prior to the suicide attempt, for her earlier poems had at least the grace to admit love's danger and inevitable failure.

That she was aware of this duplicity might be guessed from "Love Is a Parallax," which is dense with academic allusions and vocabulary. It presumably encompasses a dialogue between two lovers upon the nature of love itself. Beginning with "Perspective betrays with its dichotomy" and concluding with "suspense/ on the quicksands of ambivalence/ is our life's whole nemesis," which takes up the first two stanzas, the male presents his case for relativity and ambivalence in all things human. The rest of the poem another eleven stanzas, presents the female view of them as they leave a restaurant and walk home. The couple pause occasionally to kiss, while "the drunks upon the curb and dames/ in dubious doorways forget their Monday names" and until "our strict father leans/ to call for curtain on our thousand scenes."

All the familiar elements are here in abundance: the cynical intellectualism, the pile of negative images, the relentless insistence upon the ultimate meaninglessness of living in a meaningless universe, and the poet's perceptive self-insight into her "cultivated act, a fierce brief fusion/ which dreamers call real, and realists, illusions." What is missing is the acceptance of the final, fatal note. At poem's end Sylvia refuses the old Yeatsian image, "let the blue tent topple," accepts passion's temporary quality, and then plunges into pure escapism: "Yet love/ knows not of death nor calculus above/ the simple sum of heart plus heart."

Time, of course, is the villain running through each of the poems during the unravelling of material (self) and spiritual (love) values. And the moon returns again and again, only to be ironically stripped of its patina of romantic distortions in "Moonsong at Morning." It begins as "moon of illusion" and concludes with "the angel's frame" blasted by facts and "the radiant limb" twisted by "stern truth." This is a touch of the *real* Sylvia, who refuses the stale delusions of a romantic past and exposes them to the cold-eyed scrutiny of science and logic: "each sacred body/ night yielded up/ is mangled by study/ of microscope."

The climax leaves little doubt as to her obsession with both the terror of naked reality and a consequent need to maintain a double:

> Reflect in terror
>   the scorching sun:
> dive at your mirror
>   and drown within.

Like the moon, the mirror is an anchor—a personal metaphor ever at hand to drive home its Gothic point. In "Epitaph in Three Parts" the speaker, a girl trapped on an island, is told by telegram to destroy "your mirror and avoid mishaps." The poem itself seems based upon her romance with Gordon Lameyer and has for a climax to each section the refrain: "There is more than one good way to drown." Drowning, Otto, the sea, death by water, Gordon her sailor-lover, "all the ships go down"—the notes are familiar and will become remorseless as Sylvia swings closer to her father and a deeper self.

For now the poem can only play with surface designs, but in "Epitaph in Three Parts" more was revealed than intended. The first part has "a flock of bottle battleships" deliver the three telegram warnings, and the remark about the mirror is followed by advice to live "on a silent island/ where the water blots out all footsteps." Sylvia seems to suggest an awareness of her drive towards total isolation of the soul. The second is the most interesting command, however, as it tells her to take in "no roving gallant/ who seeks to dally in the port till dawn" (a delightful *double entendre* only she could fully appreciate) because "your fate involves a dark assailant"—possibly an invocation of Richard S——.

The second part of the poem shapes a grisly central image beneath its glittering rhetoric—that of a dead sailor rolling in the surf as gulls eat his eyes out, which may represent another revenge-through-art technique. Lameyer is paying for his blindness—perhaps the poem was written after one of their arguments, although Sylvia's contempt for him, so evident in her manipulation of him to suit her own purposes, was now consistent. Moreover, Sylvia is playing with a kind of horror motif that must have tickled the imprisoned bitch goddess to laughter, sardonic or otherwise. In any case, the last part returns the speaker to her room, "a twittering gray box," and a window that reveals, behind the sky's "rigmarole," "the lid of one/ enormous box of gray where god has gone/ and hidden all the bright angelic men." Grim, sullen, absolutely without hope or color, the real world was always threatening to swallow Sylvia—all her fine nature poems to the contrary.

The future must have appeared much too close for comfort. She was a senior, and adulthood—the finish line—loomed that much larger as she approached. Adulthood signified marriage, children, human demands, the suffocating paraphernalia of her mother's middle-class world. But babies, which she accepted as inevitable signs of a complete and normal Sylvia, still perplexed and frightened her. For they threatened to intrude upon her body and soul, to violate her sacred self, her most prized possession. Professor Gibian, who had Sylvia babysit for him on several occasions, remembers with awe her peculiar reaction: "She did not seem to have any direct human rapport with the children; I don't mean to say she was a bad babysitter, but she just sort of sat at one end of the couch and stared at the child at the other—as though it were some strange creature, someone from another world, not a common, fellow little human being."

Yet Gordon Lameyer recalls an incident in which Sylvia told him she had experienced a great desire to nurse the child she was babysitting. This sharp divergence of response was characteristic of Sylvia's ambivalent approach to life. Bald baby heads haunted her in their moon-like aridity, but they also beckoned her towards the boundaries of real selfless love. As a foreign experience, like being raped or cooking exotic meals, nursing had to have a built-in attraction for her, although babies themselves remained negative images. They suggested the intrusion of her infant brother, severe physical agony, and great future demands upon her as a woman, which she was not sure she possessed enough female identity to satisfy.

Being a woman had been and always would be difficult for Sylvia in any context. While at McLean's and still in the disassociative grip of depression, Sylvia had confided to a visitor that she believed her mother had never wanted her to become a woman, but rather remain a neuter creature dependent upon her for love's nourishment. How literally true Sylvia's statement was is difficult to assess, since she was irrational at the time, but it fits the obvious psychological pattern of the mother-daughter relationship: extreme dependence on the one hand, possessive protectiveness on the other. In a sense, Sylvia and Aurelia would remain frozen in their attitudes towards one another, like a statue of mother and child, until Sylvia's death.

Babies, marriage, adult responsibilities, a passive woman in a masculine society were still in the future, however, and Sylvia adhered to her rigid schedule without regard to ultimate meaning. She would escape them, at least for now, become a famous writer and dazzle the world, even if it meant loneliness and isolation. Kazin's memory of her in his short-story course is fragmentary, but it confirms the price Sylvia was paying in her senior year for her fierce work ethic: "She attended a so-called creative writing class that I gave at Smith in 1954–5; she was then already a professional writer, and when I expressed my surprise that she wanted to take a course with me, she replied that she was lonesome and wanted to talk. We did talk a few times, but I have no very precise recollection of what we talked about." [5]

The only problem involves Sylvia's complexity of intentions. Kazin was a "name" for her to pursue, and her plea for conversation might have been nothing more than a ploy—which would have been successful as he supported her writing enthusiastically and later endorsed her application for a Fulbright Fellowship to Cambridge. Yet she would also have delighted in conversing with a man of Kazin's astuteness and learning. The loneliness might have been simply the inevitable loneliness attendant upon any person foolish enough to sleep with a muse.

Whatever the inner uncertainties, the outer plan was executed with smooth certainty. Sylvia expended intense energy to the point of exhaustion. Gordon Lameyer has said, "she worked feverishly hard that year"; and both Nancy Hunter and Jane Truslow agreed. In the second semester, it all had to merge both into solid achievement and a public testing of that achievement. Sylvia took the comprehensive examination in English Honors and a special qualifying examination for the Fulbright fellowship in the spring of 1955: long, grueling tests that filled her with awesome anxiety and a sort of gleeful determination not to make a false step.[6] Nancy remembers her preparation for the Fulbright well: "Examinations were not usually a worry, but this one was particularly important, and she prepared for it with a nervous flurry, trying to cram a few more facts into a mind that could already disgorge enough literary detail to fill an encyclopedia."

The test itself took half a day to complete and "when she returned to the house at its conclusion, little wrinkles of concentration were etched around her eyes and she looked indignant. While she had obviously done well on the test as a whole, certain questions had bothered her because they concerned authors whom she did not know." One of these was C. P. Snow, and Sylvia went that very afternoon to the school library to do research on him. Jane Truslow's recollection of Sylvia's senior year includes a similar incident. During the course of the comprehensive examination for English Honors, which apparently encompassed much of an entire day, the girls were given a fifteen-minute break for milk and crackers in another room; but Sylvia refused the opportunity and stayed behind to mull over her paper.

Success, of course, was the just reward as she was destined to graduate *summa cum laude* in June and win the Fulbright. Her application had been warmly supported by strong recommendations from Dr. Jones and the best of the English department at Smith. Also her thesis, which was finished on time and entitled "The Magic Mirror: A Study of the Double in Two of Dostoevsky's Novels," earned her favorable comments from the faculty for its concise insights and consistent professional polish. No doubt the author of *Bumble Bees and Their Ways* would have been proud of his daughter's unpedantic directness.

In fact, Sylvia's thesis seems hardly to have been written by the same person whose poetry at the time was so freighted by academic baggage. But prose for Sylvia had always been a plain instrument of communication (as is evident in her earliest fiction), ever since she admitted to Philip McCurdy during their high-school days her ambition to state large ideas in the prose of an Eric Hoffer. Unlike poetry, prose did not have to bear the burden of its creator's self; it could settle for the more humble task of bringing forward key concepts. In *The Magic Mirror*, fittingly dedicated "to George Gibian to whom I am indebted for counsel, critique, and inspiration," Sylvia lets her natural affinity for structural analysis have free play. Her familiar and strong sense of organization has restrained whatever impulse she might have had to wax poetic on a topic so close to her heart and mind.[7]

In the Introduction Sylvia takes great care first to define the ancient nature of her subject, the existence of the double from primitive times to the present, while emphasizing its significance at different levels and across different disciplines; and then narrowly to lay out her particular interest and interpretation that whenever the Double represents "evil or repressed elements in man's nature" it "usually results in a duel which ends in insanity or death for the original hero." Finally, she stresses her intention to limit her study to only two of Dostoevsky's novels, but indicates that they come at the beginning and end of his career and that a study of their two main characters and their doubles, Yakov Petrovitch Golyadkin and Ivan Fyodorovitch Karamazov, "should serve to indicate the vast range and vital relationships in Dostoevsky's development as a writer."

The rest of the paper is a pleasant, highly readable essay more commendable for its research and organizational ability than its original critical perceptions. Sylvia manipulates her readings of critics and psychologists with considerable skill and balances Dostoevsky's treatment of the double against that of other writers like Sherwood Anderson, Edgar Allan Poe, Nathaniel Hawthorne, Franz Kafka, and

Thomas De Quincey. Nowhere does she attempt more than an expansion of ideas advanced by earlier critics, though she does not hesitate to take a stand in matters of literary taste and vigorously defends Dostoevsky's genius. This, too, hints at the deeper currents stirred up by the whole *Doppelgänger* concept, but also demonstrates how far removed her critical insights were from her self-image. Yet there is one sentence quoted from Alfred Kazin's Introduction to an edition of *A Raw Youth* which must have had special meaning for Sylvia: "One of Dostoevsky's greatest insights into the disordered personality is his realization that there are people who will do anything to avoid disarranging the fundamental conception they have of themselves." Furthermore, her own follow-up, the idea that Golyadkin could not tolerate recognizing his alter ego for fear of disturbing his self-image and thus projects a double instead to relieve the intense inner conflict, seems to be a brilliant self-analysis. The final paragraph of *The Magic Mirror* is fascinating in retrospect as a summary of what Sylvia knew and did not know about herself:

However, our paper will conclude here with a reassertion of the psychological and philosophical significance of the Double in Dostoevsky's novels. Although the figure of the Double has become a harbinger of danger and destruction, taking form as it does from the darkest of human fears and repressions, Dostoevsky implies that recognition of our various mirror images and reconciliation with them will save us from disintegration. This reconciliation does not mean a simple or monolithic resolution of conflict, but rather a creative acknowledgment of the fundamental duality of man; it involves a constant courageous acceptance of the eternal paradoxes within the universe and within ourselves.

The pity of Sylvia's thesis, which definitely deserved its high praise from Professor Gibian and others in the department, thus lies in its reflection of Sylvia's own split nature. Her emotions and intellect remained leagues apart, and it was fear of cracking open her masks that would not permit her to translate Dostoevsky's magic mirror into a real one. Like Dostoevsky himself, she lacked the "constant courageous acceptance" of interior and exterior paradoxes.

Achievement, then, still had to suffice. Sylvia had the pleasure in her last semester of winning two distinguished poetry prizes. The group of poems touched upon earlier in this chapter was submitted under the pen name of Robbin Hunter—in honor of her now-distant roommate—and garnered the Academy of American Poets' Award at Smith for 1955;

while "Two Lovers and a Beachcomber by the Real Sea" won her half of the Elizabeth Glascock Prize—*Mademoiselle*'s annual poetry contest for college students. In the interview for *Mademoiselle*, Sylvia is pictured as "bothered little by the pressure to conform"—a laughable observation—and "impatient for graduation, feeling she had already left Smith." Indeed she had. With the Fulbright and some seven hundred dollars in prize and commission money, Sylvia was freer than she had been in years and relieved of that relentless financial pressure which had characterized her entire college career and which had kept alive suppressed feelings of animosity towards her many well-intentioned benefactors.

Gordon Lameyer, who was stationed in Boston and whose tour of duty was coming to an end, remained her fiancé and occasional weekend escort. They had another altercation and grew sullen and apart, but she did write to him while he was at sea to patch up the relationship. Meanwhile, Myron Lotz had experienced a crisis of his own. After reporting to the Detroit Tigers' spring training camp, he was ordered by the organization's general manager to abandon medical school and concentrate on baseball. It did not take him long to realize that the vague success of a possible major-league career did not measure up to a life-time medical vocation. Mike left camp with few regrets and pitched the rest of the season in Bismarck, North Dakota. Like Sylvia's, his final year of study consisted of one triumph after another. He took Part I of the very difficult National Board of Examiners' Exam and came in fifth nationally. He also earned a Henry Fellowship for a year's study at Oxford's Dunn School of Pathology, a truly remarkable achievement since only four such fellowships were awarded that year. Both he and Sylvia would be crossing the Atlantic at summer's end, though on different ships.

A new romance of sorts had entered Sylvia's life briefly in the spring, soon after she finished her thesis on Dostoevsky. Peter Davison, at Alfred Kazin's suggestion, had dropped in on her at Smith and eventually found her sitting alone in the infirmary where she was resting up after an exam. In his autobiography *Half-Remembered*, he describes her during their first meeting as "dressed in the saddle shoes, the kerchief, the simple skirt-and-sweater combination of the time, but, in her, conventional prettiness and intensity of concentration formed a curious, even a disturbing alliance." [8] Sylvia's initial reaction to him was much more positive.

Davison did represent, after all, a distinguished literary past, as his father had been a minor British poet, and he knew many writers. Also his good looks attracted her. Though only twenty-seven, he had already been through Harvard, Cambridge University (where he attended his father's college), the United States Army, and several passionate affairs; and currently he was an editor at Harcourt, Brace—a fact of central significance for Sylvia. She immediately projected her very real enthusiasm for literature and asked him "hundreds of questions about publishing." On a second visit to Smith and Sylvia later that spring, Davison took her for a drive through the country, but romance never entered the picture as she resumed her intense interrogation. He returned to New York without any great desire to see her again.

Sylvia's last year at Smith was to see a number of other dramas acted out, however. According to Nancy Hunter, the final few months at Lawrence House witnessed a miniature conflict between Sylvia, the house's resident celebrity, and "Gloria Brown," its resident radical, who had surrounded herself with her own coterie. As Nancy describes it, the conflict was not a war for leadership, but the inevitable division created by opposing life styles in close quarters. Sylvia's whole persona was geared towards social conformity and success within the context of her culture's surface mores. Though quite capable of intellectually challenging the basic assumptions of her American environment and middle-class background, she would never think of ignoring or flaunting its superficial code of manners and dress. Intricate rhyme schemes and white gloves were both inherited traditions.

Gloria Brown, on the contrary, revelled in being her own woman and anticipated the feminist revolution of the late 1960's by imitating the bohemian life style already being championed by Jack Kerouac, Allen Ginsberg, and others. She was bound to find Sylvia unsettling, a publishing poet forsaking her craft's hallowed trappings of alienation; and Sylvia, in turn, discovered that her "good girl" mentality, her mother's mentality, was shocked and disgusted by Brown's public acts of defiance, sloppy clothes, and drinking in the dormitory without permission. That same "good girl" mentality drove Sylvia to consider and threaten petty acts of "good girl" revenge such as snitching to the authorities. Aware of Sylvia's obsession for personal tidiness, and her sacred belief in the life-line connection of her possessions to her own integrity as a human being, Brown retaliated by having Sylvia's dresser drawers and her room disarranged.

What is interesting about this essentially petty war of wills was its startling conclusion. Keeping to her romantic author role, Nancy brought the conflict to a Lassie-like climax. On commencement day, Sylvia awoke early and complained of severe stomach cramps. Nancy suggested that Sylvia ask Brown for some of her left-over rum. Sylvia doubted if her arch enemy could be forgiving enough for such generosity, but Nancy persisted and went in search of the rum. Brown's reaction to Nancy's request was heartwarming in the extreme: "Without hesitating she reached under a pile of dirty clothes in the corner and pulled out the bottle, which was still half full. 'Tell Syl to take what she needs,' she offered." Sylvia was touched, drank some of the rum, and the girls donned their caps and gowns for the ritual ahead. Another little drama was also in store for Sylvia. Her mother was sick, perhaps wracked by her old ulcer, but she insisted upon being present at her daughter's graduation to see Sylvia receive her *summa cum laude* certificate and poetry prize. The details are unclear, but Mrs. Plath ended up being carried on some kind of litter to the ceremony.

The Smith girls had chosen Adlai Stevenson for their speaker. He emphasized the girls' roles as prime movers in the lives of their future husbands and children, and their need to use their education as a tool for preventing these same husbands and children from becoming too parochial—a reasonable, if somewhat innocent, speech. Nancy's summary of the graduating class's attitude towards it seems accurate: "The speech was eloquent and impressive and we loved it even if it seemed to hurl us back to the satellite role we had escaped for four years—second-class citizens in a man's world where our only possible achievement was a vicarious one." Sylvia would probably agree, but not aloud.

Back at Lawrence House after the ceremonies were completed, Sylvia initiated her counter-move. She asked Nancy how she could repay Brown for her unexpected act of kindness, and her roommate naturally told her to write a note since that was her forte. Sylvia agreed and put a note to Brown inside a lace-trimmed handkerchief. "She handed me the handkerchief and the note, which said simply, 'Thank you for teaching me humility.' It was signed, 'Sylvia.'"

Another summer spread before her. She told the Vocational Guidance Office that she would not be able to work—because her mother was due to have an operation, which was probably true—and had decided to enjoy the Cape's fine beaches and pursue her poetry. Soon after returning to Wellesley, she had a telephone call from Peter Davison. He had left Harcourt and was now an assistant to Thomas J. Wilson, the director of Harvard University Press. Consequently, he had moved to Cambridge, where he rented a small apartment and went about renewing old acquaintances. Sylvia was delighted by his call. She knew he had been at Cambridge, and still had many friends, as well as a sister, living in England. He asked her to have dinner with him at his apartment a few days later and she eagerly agreed. Although Sylvia's penchant for interrogation had not subsided, the experience turned out to be more gratifying than he could have hoped for from past contacts. She arrived in a white dress and a full tan and her hair dyed blonde by the sun. "She asked more and more questions, she seemed strangely elevated, and she hardly waited to be asked to slip into my new bed."

Davison recalls that Sylvia "was, outwardly at least, voracious about sex during our relationship. It was very athletic. She was quite proud of her hard muscles and sun tan. I must have been a sloppy disappointment to her by comparison." But the sex seemed also part of the mask and he "couldn't help feeling that she was pretending to a good deal more intensity than she actually felt." In fact, during one of their intimate conversations, she discussed her past bed partners with distaste and characterized two or three boys as "mostly blah," with the exception of one unnamed fellow, "probably S——, with whom she could have a certain mutuality, a certain capacity for give and take, for joy."

The pretense was not restricted to sexual matters either; and Davison felt, throughout their summer-long affair, that "she was never spontaneous really, never fully herself, always trying to create an effect, to make an impression." And yet, like so many other previous lovers, he was drawn to her and saw her as "volatile, alert, intelligent and interesting" and "full of energy that was sort of distorted, directed towards concrete achievement." The only time her mask slipped was near the end of their relationship when, after having made love, she lay rigid upon his bed and talked about her breakdown and suicide attempt and their frightening aftermath—"talked like a human being, full of self-understanding, compassion and pain, illness and recovery from illness to health, gratitude for having been reunited to life, gratitude to her patroness."

Davison recounts the episode more fully in *Half-Remembered*, which is marred only by his misinterpretation of *The Bell Jar*:

Her narrative at this stage, only two years after the original event, lacked the clumsy irony, the defenses, the semifictionalized characters, the nastiness of temper that mar the novel for me. What I heard was a simpler, less poised, and more touching story. As she came to the end, shock treatment in the hospital and her subsequent slow convalescence, she expressed her gratitude for the help she had had, she was glad to be well again; but the episode still seemed to be the only period of her life that she could invest with any real emotion in retrospect. I was deeply moved; yet I was alarmed too by so dedicated an attention to the approaches of death, so molten an obsession.

But before this revelation, the two young poets had shared many happier moments together—"we saw a lot of each other that summer"—and had discussed their craft without end. She introduced him to Dylan Thomas, loaned him her records of his readings, and told him "what poets she read and adored, like Elizabeth Bishop and Isabella Gardner." He also recalls her attempts "to get the sound that Dylan Thomas was embodying." In return, he told her about Cambridge and whom to see when she arrived there, and wrote her letters of introduction to his sister and friends in London. They were mutually using each other, but the price was not high on either side. Sex, good talks, long days together were standard fare for two young people who were incapable of going beyond themselves at this juncture in their lives.

In the interim, Gordon Lameyer was kept in ignorance regarding the true nature of the affair. Davison, who has since read Sylvia's letters to Lameyer from this period, puts it simply: "She lied to him, about who I was, what we were doing." She told Lameyer that Davison was a prospective agent whom she was trying to convince to handle her work, although she was actually thinking of Cyrilly Abels for that role. When Sylvia and Davison went off for a weekend to Martha's Vineyard in late August, she again told Lameyer she was going to keep an appointment with a literary agent. He remained convinced that his exasperating, unstable Sylvia was still chaste and totally committed to him alone and that he was the one who would have to make a decision regarding their future.

Davison had no such delusions, but even he would be shocked by Sylvia's abrupt and hostile dismissal. It came soon after their trip to Martha's Vineyard. Sylvia had invited him to dinner at her home in Wellesley, ostensibly to meet her mother. The event was depressing for Davison from the beginning when he entered the white frame house on Elmwood Road "with the screened porch, and the shrubbery around it, and the round rugs (Oriental) on the floor, and the dining table in an alcove, and we talked about the *Christian Science Monitor*, which they were serious about." Aurelia herself made an odd impression. He thought her "terribly correct" in her behavior and mannerisms, and quite formal as though he were an ultra respectable suitor.

He also had an example of how Sylvia "handled" her mother; she "was cozy with her and would talk one way in her presence, another outside." After dinner they decided to go for a walk. It was late Sunday but still bright. They reached a gully not far from the house, and Sylvia proceeded bluntly to tell him that their affair was finished. In effect, she no longer needed him. The summer was ending, she would be sailing soon for England, and he had already supplied her with letters of introduction and other contacts. Although older and more cosmopolitan, he felt much younger at that moment and his feelings were hurt. "I was not unhappy about it, really, just very baffled," he conceded years later, and suspected that her earlier confidences and his awed reaction to them may have made her despise him.

Whatever the reason, she "made me feel used, as I later discovered others in her life had felt used." It was certainly an appropriate conclusion to the end of Smith and Wellesley, and the beginning of a new struggle in a much bigger arena across the ocean.

> The whole conviction of my life now rests upon the belief that loneliness, far from being a rare and curious phenomenon, peculiar to myself and a few other solitary men, is the central and inevitable fact of human existence.
>
> THOMAS WOLFE

9

All Green Dreams

Sylvia left for England in early September on the new *S.S. United States*.

In many odd, contradictory ways, her first ocean voyage was a culmination and a regression, a return to the sea and childhood, the mother sea that now frightened her with its unlimited power, vast distances, sense of absent landscapes, and an escape from the lace-narrow confines of her middle-class mentality. As the miles heaved and slipped away behind her, along with her mother and sparkling white Wellesley and the safe school playground of Smith College, she must have experienced terrible spasms of insecurity. She had never been beyond Albany and New York City before, never really been outside the benign academic towns of a polite New England world where her name and face had achieved a certain worth, distinction, almost fame. And she had never been so far away from her mother before.

Matthew Arnold's "sea of faith" apparently failed her during the five-day crossing, as it had failed him and his generation, and she turned desperately to love's simulacrum for consolation. A fellow passenger, a medical student, later reported to both Myron Lotz and the Modlins with obvious disapproval that Sylvia "spent the whole trip on her back" and that the shipboard joke consisted of variations on the theme of Sylvia never getting a decent meal because she was always in her cabin sleeping with someone.

However exaggerated the report, its truth is the truth of Sylvia herself. Facing the prospect of a new life in a new universe where the golden girl was as yet unknown and unappreciated, she had to feel an overwhelming emptiness. Sylvia thrashed around in her narrow berth under the bodies of strangers because it seemed the sole available means of staving off despair, depression, another panic-stricken flight into madness and total negation. Sylvia is real here, and touching, pathetic, a lost little college girl wanting male strangers to reassert her illusions and dreams. Reckless love-making was another form of poetry, a mocking echo of the sea's rhythmic cradle, a necessary therapy until she could reach shore and reassert her masks.

London was delightful, by and large, and she energetically savored it. Museums, monuments, parks, Soho, bookstores, art galleries, cheap theatre tickets, all lived up to expectations.[1] The only disappointments were human. She had gotten in touch with Peter Davison's sister soon after landing and that cordial lady immediately asked her over for dinner, and also invited Peter Shaft as an interesting third party. The dinner was a disaster for everyone concerned. Both Davison's sister and Shaft were startled by Sylvia's outmoded formal attire, in particular her hat and the ubiquitous white gloves; and, as the evening awkwardly progressed, they found her "very prurient," to the point where neither "liked her, though for different reasons." Sylvia, in turn, claimed that all the friends Peter Davison had asked her to look up in London were homosexuals and thus presumably useless. Moreover, she thought Davison's sister quite mad and felt uncomfortably normal in her dynamic presence.

Sylvia's attitude towards Davison himself remained distant, perhaps because of repressed guilt; and, while at the Victoria and Albert Museum, she bought a postcard with a picture of a satyr to send to him at Cambridge. On the reverse side she remarked the close resemblance between "this charming chap" and her correspondent. Again there is a suggestion of a childish distaste for sex, which would seem to belie the report that she had been the initiator of sexual relations with Davison in the first place. As in so many other areas, Sylvia still seemed ambiguous about sex, although she would continue to practice and preach the "sensible" approach of complete hedonism in sexual matters. The latter certainly reflected her intellectual estimate of life's secular finiteness, but deeper emotional currents ran contrary to its pragmatic assumptions. In fact, she may have hated sex as much as she hated the men who asked it of her and, from her perspective, demeaned themselves in the process by letting her use them.

After ten days of sightseeing in London, Sylvia left for Cambridge. It is not difficult to imagine all that must have passed through the mind of a literarily minded young American going to Cambridge for the first time: the intense excitement Sylvia must have experienced taking the train from London—a civilized contraption with dining cars, polite conductors, and friendly passengers—into Cambridgeshire, watching the open fields (blighted now by housing developments) roll past copses of trees and lonely country roads, alighting in a town quaint and ancient enough to be *the* college town for *the* college (though much more crowded than ever expected), being driven by taxi into the university grounds and passing through the "tutored" landscape of its seven colleges, solemn stone walls, ancient with gray and green tear stains, high turrets, cathedral-like spires, quadrangles where the rich grass dare not rise above an inch, long, mournful, comfortable library windows, hints of gargoyles in the slate roofs and hanging eaves, acres and acres of gardens and tamed woods, through which snaked the ultimate college river, the sedgy Cam, punts already visible on its darkish waters.

Here was tradition personified for the sharp New England mind that had thus far to be content with imitations, some of them magnificent in their own right, but imitations nonetheless. Sylvia apparently tried not to be overwhelmed by it and to maintain her special brand of cool sophistication. She had also used a significant portion of her generous fellowship money to purchase a new outfit and a matching set of expensive luggage, only to find herself standing out conspicuously as her fellow students tumbled from the train in untidy and casual attire with their battered suitcases and duffle bags and knapsacks.

Sylvia's college was Newnham, one of the less prestigious, and her dormitory was Whitsted, a large, upper-middle-class house which the college had acquired in the 1920s for women students from overseas. Located on the far side of the college's playing fields, Whitsted could comfortably accommodate only fourteen people: twelve students, one faculty resident, and a Scottish housekeeper named Mrs. Milne, who was short, plump, and had gray hair—"a sort of everyone's granny figure" in the words of May Targett, who would come to Whitsted the following year.[2] The students tended to be evenly divided among Americans, Indians, and English, although there would be two Canadian girls the next year and Isabel Henderson, a Scottish visitor, had come down from Aberdeen University. The four American girls never really gravitated towards one another. Only Jane Kopp would get to know Sylvia at all, sometimes to her regret, and she never became a close friend.

As an official residence of the university, Whitsted functioned with paternalistic thoroughness—a British version of Lawrence House. There were the typical regulations regarding male visitors, clock-in times, and the like, with a porter to watch the books and make sure that no young men called before ten o'clock in the morning and that no one came in later than midnight. The students were also supposed to wear their gowns to every meal and on the streets after dark, though the small number of female students made it difficult for the authorities to catch them when they did otherwise—which was often. In Whitsted itself, where the residents had breakfast, the girls were permitted to eat in dressing gowns, if they had brushed their hair, and the atmosphere was a pleasant, relaxed one in which tension and personal competition were at a minimum.

Sylvia's own room was on the third and top floor, a small, warm place with a high dormer window, a two-seater sofa, the inevitable gas fire which required constant shillings, single bed, coffee table, and a drop-front desk, which was referred to as a "bureau." Although she had to stand to look out of the window, Sylvia liked her room because of its warmth—an extremely important feature in view of her sensitive sinuses, especially after she discovered just how wet and cold English winters were. Writing to Elinor Klein she said that the wind seemed to come from the Russian steppes and that the cobbled streets actually consisted of detached, frost-bitten fingers. A few months later, upon her return from her Christmas trip to Paris, she would plaster the walls with postcards of Renaissance paintings like a patchwork quilt and fill a bookcase with expensive art books.

Sylvia fitted in reasonably well at Whitsted, kept to herself for the most part, and concentrated upon writing, studying, and boy friends. The other girls remember her as a bright and cheerful girl who seemed to fit the mode of an outgoing American coed. The few incidents where she stood out were minor, comical episodes that tell more about the restricted confines of Whitsted's "sweet world" than about her. One involved the house rule that all male guests had to use the bathroom on the first floor. As related to May Targett by Isabel Henderson:

One morning Mrs. Milne came to Sylvia and said, "Yesterday, your young man (Sylvia winced because she did not like the boy very much) used the toilet on the top floor."

"Yes, well, I live on the top floor, my room's on the top floor."

"Yes, but you know very well the rules are they are to use the toilet inside the front door."

"It's two flights down, you know, and it seemed a bit inhospitable to ask him to walk two flights down and two flights up again."

"But, Sylvia, you must admit it just isn't right."

"Why?"

"Sylvia, you may not have noticed but beside the toilets on the first and second floors there are cannisters, eh, for your sanitary towels. There isn't any on the ground floor."

"Oh."

The second tale about Sylvia at Whitsted is told by Jane Kopp, who would involuntarily become Sylvia's essential *Doppelgänger* at Cambridge, and who characterized the Whitsted residents as "a very strange collection of girls" in which several distinctive, high-pitched personalities were evident.[3] One of them was a South African student (white), a revised version of Virginia Woolf physically and emotionally, who was greatly offended by Sylvia's American ways. This girl refused to speak to Sylvia at all during breakfast. One morning, however, she coldly eyed Sylvia slicing her fried eggs into squares as usual and could not help blurting out in exasperation, "Must you cut your eggs in that fashion?" In response, Sylvia put down her knife and fork and replied with icy calmness, "Yes, I really must. What do you do with yours, swallow it whole?"

Slicing eggs into squares is, at once, deliciously practical and oddly compulsive—a culinary summary of Sylvia's mask at Cambridge. Uncertain and needing attention, she played the role of the American on campus, much to the annoyance of the other Americans. Besides her elaborate set of matched white Samsonite luggage, which she took on her vacation jaunts, she "always dressed in the *Mademoiselle* idea of American couture" and, as Jane Kopp observed, "she had a way in those days of gushing and gurgling in the most typical American tourist style." One incident in particular stands out with embarrassing clarity in Jane's mind. The first few nights at Whitsted, Sylvia and Jane would bike (Sylvia's bicycle had been shipped to her from America and had its Smith plate on it) into town in search of a restaurant. Once there Sylvia did not hesitate to ride up to a bobby and ask in ringing tones if he could suggest "a very British and very picturesque place to eat."

Other mannerisms included repetitions of key words and phrases like "enjoy" and "I can't help it but . . ." For instance, she "enjoyed" her new coffee table and she "enjoyed" Mallory Woeber, one of her first boy friends at Cambridge; and, in concert, she might sometimes blurt, "I can't help it but I just enjoy that boy!" Verbal compulsions had their physical counterpart as well. Jane noticed that Sylvia "had a great deal of physical restlessness" and that some part of her body had to be continually in motion—whether a leg swinging under the table or fingers and thumbs nervously dancing. All her little eccentricities had at their core the driving energy of a frustrated will to power which still had to maintain a presentable mask. Though disturbing to Jane and "most people she came into contact with," she was nevertheless looked upon as a quite normal student.

The relationship between Sylvia and Jane (Baltzel) Kopp is itself a fascinating one. In a way, Jane was supposed to replace Marcia Brown and Nancy Hunter and become Sylvia's double, but the attempt here is darker and more frightening. As a mirror image, Jane represented nothing positive to Sylvia. Rather she was a pure projection of Sylvia's hidden ego—a true "double" as found by Sylvia herself in Dostoevsky. Physically Jane fitted the role as she was about the same height, weight, and build as Sylvia, and had the necessary blondish locks and German-American background. Sylvia used the actual phrase *"Doppelgänger"* and, according to Jane, "it bothered her that I would say something that she had just been about to say, claiming it gave her the creeps." On another occasion, Sylvia told her "Cambridge wasn't big enough for both of us" in a humorous manner that suggested "she sort of meant it."

But such insights into the secret Sylvia were rare as she continued the journey towards public success and tried to pick up where she had left off at Smith. Once again she attended all the lectures, went out of her way to cultivate her teachers, and acquired another string of boy friends, which was relatively easy in a society where men vastly outnumbered women. She even managed to get accepted by the ADC, Cambridge's most prestigious dramatic company, although again the limited number of women available helped somewhat. Appropriately, she played the role of a mad poet in her first play and then had the honor of playing a whore briefly in *Bartholomew Fair*, which subsequently ran for nine months, including a London performance. Though efficient and professional in her acting chores, as she had been back in Wellesley High during her sole previous acting stint, Sylvia kept her relationship with ADC remote and temporary. She would show up punctually for rehearsals, do what was required of her, and then disappear; she never attempted to make the acquaintance of any other member of the cast and appeared intent upon maintaining her independence. Perhaps she realized early that no amount of labor would ever make her into anything more than a competent actress—the kind of mediocrity she had always rejected in the past. The single clear memory of her retained by the rest of the company consisted of little more than the rhetorical inquiry, "Wasn't she self-contained?" Jonathan Miller, the company's brightest star, had even less to say and recalled her only as "a tan, blonde sophomore" who appeared on the set from time to time.[4]

Sylvia resigned from the ADC after several months and never again acted on a stage. Her other extracurricular activity centered around *Varsity*, Cambridge's student newspaper, for which she wrote a few immemorable articles, as well as for the many college literary magazines which were constantly springing up and dying several issues later. She also contributed to the more established *Granta* and *The Cambridge Review*. She had her first real taste of public criticism when a fellow student reviewed one of her poems from a student magazine and condemned it for being too imitative of John Donne. The review rankled and made her more hesitant, or at least more selective, about submitting to the local literary journals. Cambridge was literary to a self-conscious degree, to be sure, but criticism was something Sylvia's poetry sorely needed at this point in its development. Soon after arriving at Cambridge, she had submitted a batch of her poems from Smith to John Lehmann at *The London Magazine* and stressed that she had had poems published previously in the United States in the *Atlantic Monthly*, *Harper's*, *The Lyric*, *Mademoiselle*, *The Nation*, and *The New Orleans Poetry Journal*.

Lehmann and his two assistant editors were unimpressed, however, and rejected all of the poems two months later. One of the editors liked "Ice Age" and found "Dance Macabre" "not ineffective," and another went along with the positive verdict on "Ice Age"; but the third tipped the scales in favor of total rejection. All three men quite rightly felt that Sylvia's poetry exhibited an estimable talent which the cleverness and academic acrobatics repressed rather than released. The most telling remark may have been the scrawled comment by one unknown hand that Sylvia seemed "frightened of her feelings." [5]

Rejections always hurt, but Sylvia was completely professional in her approach, as she had been since high school, and wrote and sent out her poetry and occasional stories with efficient dispatch and energy, while keeping detailed, accurate files. The acceptances did come with enough frequency to prevent real depression, though she remained committed to the idea that getting published in *The New Yorker* would be the pinnacle of her career.[6]

But poetry was only part of the Cambridge experience. Of the many boys who came into her life during the first six months at Cambridge,

Mallory Woeber was undoubtedly the most impressive and interesting. A tall, dark-haired boy of nineteen, Woeber had come originally from Darjeeling, India, and his family was now residing in London while their son attended Cambridge. His Jewish background, heroic proportions— Sylvia referred to him as an "Old Testament Hercules" and Jane, as "a great big bear of a guy, tall, florid complexion, nice looking"—his interest in music, and obvious intelligence, made him an exciting companion at any level. He hauled a small organ up to her third-floor room, and she passed many afternoons listening to him play Bach, Beethoven, and popular folk ballads. He reminded her of Dmitri Karamazov.

Sylvia was proud of Woeber, as she had been proud at one time of Lotz, Willard, Lameyer, and McCurdy. He was a possession—a reflection of her great worth as a woman and a mind. He was different from the others, however, in being more sensitive to her awesome drive towards success and the egotism necessary for artistic creation. Thus he writes of Sylvia at this juncture of her career: "Her physical presence was tangible—I swear that on one occasion I entered King's College Dining Hall with her, it was arranged for a concert, full of people looking *away* from the door, and at her entry, *not* cued by noise or other of the conventional senses, many people turned around to see who entered. Not me, of course. Her eyes, a medium brown color, really burned. I very soon came to feel that I had been privileged to encounter a genius, and never desisted from that view. She was, however, at least at that time, possessed by a total determination to serve—perhaps control and master (here perhaps hits a fount of conflict, with its creative as well as destructive aspects) her muse. This presented her as self-centered, with its selfish and hence sometimes personally insensitive behavior, depending upon circumstances." [7]

Woeber has also tried to define the immense energy that seemed to emanate from Sylvia at all times: ". . . she felt she could intensify her performance by Living through Experience, and threw herself at it with an enormous great strength (momentum, should one say?) as well as sensitivity. Intensity seems a key quality she exemplified, and re-spected." Even Woeber's Jewishness had a special appeal because it was different, almost exotic to a Wellesley-bred girl. Davison was half-Jewish, of course, but only Elinor Klein remained close; and to her Sylvia had once admitted, "Everybody today seems so rootless. I know I do. Only the Jews seem to be part of something, to belong to something definite and rooted. I'd like to have that feeling. Maybe I'll marry one someday and give birth at a plow in Israel."

Sylvia had always been uneasy about her German background and the World War II decimation of Jews in Nazi Germany. Years later, as she searched for a persona with which to contemplate her dead father, her selection of a Jewish guise was almost automatic, a stroke of unconscious genius, precisely because the Jewish role offered both intense victim status and a sense of family. As a poet, she was Jewish in spirit: alienated from her environment and ceaselessly viewing reality through the telescope of an outsider, and not above the touch of hauteur only sorrow can bring.

But Woeber and the other young men in her life during that first year at Cambridge were diversions, nothing more, and she "enjoyed" them the way she "enjoyed" her Samsonite luggage and Smith bicycle. Jane Kopp noticed early that Sylvia "had an enormously exaggerated sense of herself" which led to "her almost terrible need to be published and be famous, known as a writer," and an equally "terrible drive to be wife and mother and teacher." She was "not able to be modest even in the number of directions her life should follow." And yet, despite this and the general critical attitude then prevailing in an academic hot-house like Cambridge, Sylvia and Jane could and would look back upon the whole experience as "happy years, years of excitement, glamour, joy and pleasure." [8]

One interesting sidelight to Sylvia's first few months at Cambridge was her attempt to master horseback riding. In the company of Dick Wertz, an old boyfriend of Nancy Hunter's from Yale, she went for her first ride on a powerful stallion named Sam. Suddenly, Sam bolted. Sylvia lost the reins and held onto the horse's neck as Sam galloped through the streets of Cambridge, scattering people left and right and convincing his rider the end was near. Interestingly, Sylvia was both frightened and exhilarated. In her mind it summoned up memories of her ski accident and that near-fatal plunge down the mountain. Fortunately, after two miles, Sam came to a sweaty halt and Sylvia was able to dismount, unharmed but exhausted. The event had thrilled her beyond fear, and it soon became part of the Cambridge experience. Happier realities drew her back into the whirl of her career.

For the first time in her life, Sylvia was under no pressure for money. Nor did she have to cater to sponsors, such as Mrs. Prouty, since the Fulbright endowment was an impersonal thing which simply provided her with checks on schedule. Her only obligation was to do well scholastically, which she would have done under any circumstances, and thereby gain a second year scholarship to finish her tripos and earn a degree. In fact, Sylvia's "luxurious" financial status grated on some of the other Whitsted residents' sense of thrift (and their smaller purses), though they continued to regard her as "a peripheral, amusing figure." The money was spent by Sylvia on the two things dearest to her—books and travel.

Her original ten-day exploration of London had only sharpened her appetite, and she decided to revisit the city on her way to Paris in December during Christmas vacation. But her New England past was not entirely confounded as she traveled by the cheapest means possible, in this case a special Folkstone Tour to France. Unknown to her, Jane Kopp had booked for the same tour, and they would fall into each other's company at the terminal. Before meeting Jane, Sylvia saw two Cocteau films, one of which was *Orpheus*, and stage performances of O'Casey's *Juno and the Paycock*, Shakespeare's *Troilus and Cressida*, and Euripides' *The Bacchae*, as well as Vaughan Williams' opera, *Sir John in Love*. During the first London tour she had also been exposed to Beckett's *Waiting for Godot* and noted the association with Joyce's work.

But Paris lay before her, and a meeting with Richard S——, who had promised to meet her at her hotel. She was delighted to run into Jane because the Folkstone Tour was turning out to be a third-class disaster. The weather was miserable; and every depot, terminal, airport, and railroad station entailed endless delays in grubby buildings for other passengers to arrive and be counted. The crossing was the worst ordeal of all for the two girls as rain and wind churned the Channel. While people vomited around them, they held raincoats over their heads like tents and chatted. Jane could describe it as nothing but "pretty disgusting and harrowing."

They reached Paris near midnight, wet, cold, and exhausted, only to discover that their hotel was a sordid pile of stones and that their room was four flights up. "Characteristically, Sylvia wanted to see Paris immediately and left on her own," but Jane sank wearily into bed and fell fast asleep. She was awakened at about eight or nine in the morning by the sounds of Sylvia and the proprietor beating frantically on the door. Unknowingly, Jane had left the door locked with the key inside. Sylvia had returned early in the morning but could not rouse Jane from her fatigued slumber, finally desisted, and slept the rest of the night on the floor.

When Jane opened the door at last, she saw a new and frightening Sylvia, one in the grip of a fierce, unforgiving rage. "Pale, almost shaking with anger," Sylvia berated her traveling companion mercilessly and regarded the incident as somehow deliberate—"a deep, deep affront, a terrible insult." Jane could not answer in kind, still groggy from lack of sleep and totally surprised by her friend's outburst, but the episode left her "very shaken and full of thought." Although Sylvia "recovered pretty quickly" from her rage, Jane thought it better to leave her alone for a while and departed to explore Paris as Sylvia slipped into bed. When she returned many hours later, she walked in to find Sylvia in bed with S——, a disconcerting moment for Jane, which Sylvia dismissed lightly.

The girls parted company at this point, and Sylvia went on to tour the south of France with S——. Before leaving, however, S——, who was attending the Sorbonne, showed her the Paris he knew and loved, taking her to plays, the Louvre, the Grand Guignol puppet show, and along the Seine for miles. It was in France that Sylvia's enthusiasm for painting first took root. S—— then took her by motor scooter along the Riviera and to Vence, where Sylvia was particularly excited by the Matisse chapel. She would soon be "gushing" to Jane and the others at Whitsted about Matisse and Picasso and many more, buying expensive art books, and trying in her own sketches to duplicate some of their effects, though her own work remained rigid and realistic.

As Woeber remembered it: "She went to France in December, and met the Sun in the South, especially being struck with Vence and Matisse's work in a small chapel." When she returned to Cambridge there was neither soft, golden light nor warmth without end. The cold was unbearable, and the students could see their breath when they talked. The classrooms were too crowded, and her body reacted as if on cue. She came down with a bad case of the flu and was bedridden for days. On two separate occasions she had to report to the infirmary; the first time when severe cramps had given her the impression that she was having an appendicitis attack. The second time was more serious. A splinter was stuck in her eye, and she was almost panic-stricken by fear of blindness. In the ward she mumbled incoherently about Oedipus and Gloucester—while the doctor calmly went about removing it and paraphrased Housman in the process with "if by chance your eye offend you, pluck it out, lass, and be sound."

Private and public life at Cambridge was a balance between tragedy and cause for rejoicing. By early May, there had been two suicides; though earlier, on October 22, 1955, the Queen and the Duke of Edinburgh had honored Newnham with a ceremonial visit. Sylvia and her classmates turned out in the rain to cheer the royal procession. Sylvia also had a surprise visit from Myron Lotz, who was doing as well at Oxford as he had at Yale. Mike was working in the same lab with James Gowans under Sir Howard Fleming and Sir Paul Fields and playing for the Oxford basketball team. The visit was a pleasant interlude for both students. No longer actively involved with one another, they could afford to forget past differences. Lotz was struck by the coziness of Sylvia's room—fresh nuts and apples scattered everywhere amid the piles of books—and by the warmth of Sylvia herself. After a while, they went to dinner at one of Sylvia's favorite restaurants, an Indian place, and discussed the past and future without rancor or regret. At peace for a moment with their incredible drives to achieve, both were able to appreciate the other's truly exceptional gifts. They parted cordially with a promise to correspond.

The latter was easy for Sylvia as extensive letter-writing had been an integral part of her life since Smith. She still wrote faithfully to her mother and brother, who was at Harvard, and kept in regular contact with many other friends back in the States. It was in one of the letters from her mother, who planned to visit Sylvia in June on a first trip to Europe, that she learned her grandmother was dangerously ill with cancer. But it was a sorrow that she seems to have borne rather lightly—at least on the surface, or until "Point Shirley" years later, when she finally tried to encompass the meaning of her grandmother's life and death. As usual in her letters she assiduously cultivated her mask as the bouncing, brilliant, deliriously happy coed and only hinted occasionally to a close friend like Marcia Brown at some of the darker forces ever present in the background of her charade. Elinor Klein remembers: "The letters came every month, documenting bouts with acting, trips to France, forays into the countryside and love, love, love. Like a heroine of an eighteenth-century French novel, she was constantly in love."

The search for a perfect husband and future father of her many children—she would have to have many children—proceeded as before; but none of the prospects satisfied her and secretly she remained terrified by the whole idea of marriage and, above all, of giving birth. Sylvia dreaded the pain and remembered all too clearly the incident at Boston Lying-In with Buddy, the blood, the woman's agony. Jane Kopp recalls one night in which she and Sylvia were returning across a field from the Newnham dining hall to Whitsted, and Sylvia was talking intently "about childbirth, which she was fascinated and horrified by." She mentioned having seen a baby born once and described it as "an incredible mess"—and went on to compare the procedure to "a watermelon through a keyhole," repeating the phrase several times in terrified awe.

During another night walk across that dark field separating the dining hall from Whitsted, the autumn breeze was stirring up leaves and shaking branches. Suddenly, a vague shape, probably a small animal, jumped into the girls' path, and Sylvia leaped behind Jane for protection. Jane was "irked and astonished" by her friend's action, but nothing was said. Socially, the girls never really became very close, perhaps because Sylvia continued to regard Jane dismissively. Also, there had been another divisive incident.

Sylvia had lent Jane several of her books, and Jane had lightly marked them up with a pencil while taking notes. It was not the kind of thing she would have normally done, and she still cannot understand why she did it, although unconscious hostility might have played a role in her behavior. In any case, having forgotten about the marks, she returned the books to Sylvia near the term's end and thanked her for their use. Moments later, Sylvia was rapping furiously on Jane's door, "white as a sheet and shaking." Sylvia screamed at her, "Jane, how could you? How could you mark my books?" Jane did not know what to do beyond apologizing profusely and offering to erase the marks, which she did. Once again Sylvia's "extraordinary sense of self," her obsessive belief that personal possessions were extensions of her ego, had been violated with predictable results.

The two girls would remain together, but never again would they be more than casual acquaintances. Sylvia could not have regarded the loss very highly, since she continued to spend most of her free time in the company of men—"dating constantly" and preparing for a threefold career as writer, teacher and wife-mother. However, she conceded in a letter to Marcia that she hoped to find her voice as a writer before becoming a teacher. Jane remembers that Sylvia was a serious student and writer who arose at six every morning and worked and typed until breakfast, which she took at nine or ten, and generally followed "extremely regular work habits."

The results in creative terms were spotty. By March 21, 1956, Sylvia had managed to write only a few poems, a story, a news article, and a sketch of Cambridge for the *Christian Science Monitor*. The article, entitled "Smith College in Retrospect," appeared in the May 12, 1956, issue of *Varsity* and is a competent if superficial account of Sylvia's *alma mater* in which she details Smith's social scene in the flippant style of *Mademoiselle* or *Seventeen*: "Men at Smith, by the way, are almost as ubiquitous as they are at Cambridge." Three weeks later, in the May 26th edition, Sylvia had another, flashier piece of trivia in the same paper: "May Week Fashions." Sylvia is pictured on the front page (in a bathing suit), which invites the reader to peruse the article in the centerfold. Once there the reader finds more pictures of Sylvia—in a strapless gown and another bathing suit—and a piece of florid journalism that begins, "Sylvia Plath tours the stores and forecasts May Week Fashions."

The story "The Day Mr. Prescott Died," which appeared in the October 20, 1956, issue of *Granta*, is a more serious effort but no less superficial. It was built upon an actual event—a return to Winthrop for the funeral of an old neighbor.[9] Most of the story is devoted to the ritual of mourning and the inevitable discussion in muted tones of how the deceased actually died—polite, properly reverential chatter that falsifies experience in the end. Sylvia was not content to have created a cogent, if prosaic, insight into one aspect of death and survival. Instead she once again seemed compelled to return to the mode of her *Seventeen* tales and ended with a heavy moral:

I thought of Mama, and suddenly all the sad part I hadn't been able to find during the day came up in my throat. "We'll go on better than before," I said. And then I quoted Mama like I never thought I would: "It's all the rest of us can do." And I went to take the hot pea soup off the stove.

Happily, the poetry is more interesting and perceptive and rather less self-conscious. It still smacks of influences, voices overheard in the classroom, sentences underlined in books, but it also demonstrates an unrelenting ability to learn. As A. Alvarez has noted in discussing the poems from the Cambridge period, "Everywhere there is evidence of an unwavering artistic seriousness; she seems to be preparing herself carefully to do battle with the heavyweights."[10]

One of the more successful poems is "Spinster," perhaps because it touches upon the central conflict between aridity—which was supposedly fated for any woman who sought an intellectual career—and the more acceptable role of motherhood. Sylvia wanted and believed she could have both and resented in particular the idea of unmarried dons—she regarded most of the female teachers at Cambridge as grotesque relics from the Victorian era. Wendy Campbell, a friend of Dorothea Krook's who would first meet Sylvia in that lady's lecture class, has preserved Sylvia's conviction that "a drawing back in the face of any aspect of life was nothing less than horrible, a voluntary courting of deformity. It disgusted her, filled her with angry contempt."[11]

Two other poems from this time are interesting for their diverse effects, and for the fact that Sylvia would choose to keep them, while discarding many others, in her first collection, *The Colossus*, several years later. The first was called "Faun"—a title which it would retain in *The Colossus* (originally "Metamorphosis" in *Poetry*, January, 1957). Although a metamorphosis of one kind or another almost always lies at the heart of Sylvia's verse, this is the only time it constitutes the whole poem. "Strumpet Song" is more vivid and varied in its stylistic effects, complementary images, and general energy—all this despite its melodramatic concentration upon the stereotype of the whore in the gutter, who is the spinster's opposite but equally sterile number. Sylvia here castigates her own self-righteousness and refusal to recognize the whore as a sister. The poet, too, who "looks up," is judged guilty of using the body's brute being without regard for the soul's price. Her song, which is her poem, and a Catholic hymn at that, is also the strumpet's song, no more or less—a means of personal satisfaction which does not entail a loss of virginity. Perhaps due to the vehemence of the disgust behind it, which may have reflected her mother's attitude, Sylvia's poem is technically flawless and at the same time thematically simplistic.

The impossible perfections of both love and art lured Sylvia's divided mind into poem after poem; the tension of strict opposites provided her with most of her literary material. Miming Stevens, she often turned to writing poetry about poetry: art confronting its own impulse and being. Two complementary pieces, "On the Plethora of Dryads" and "On the Difficulty of Conjuring Up a Dryad," approached the creative process typically from two different sides. In both works the plant represents art's fecund possibilities, and it is accepted as a magical power. Dryad as cognate of druid reflected Sylvia's definition of the artist as a medicine man of sorts.

Later she would also discover that art could not help to heal her own mind's tortuous fragmentation, just as she would reason out art's incapacity to replace religion's old ritualistic and mythical functions in "On the Decline of Oracles," "The Death of Myth-Making," and similar poems.

Mallory Woeber disappeared from her life in February, and she must have felt an intensification of the pressure to find a husband. Gordon Lameyer was a possibility, and he had agreed to meet her in Germany during her Easter vacation—ostensibly to look for a university for himself at her suggestion. But Easter was a distant promise, and so was Gordon. As Peter Davison once said, Sylvia "was very, very hard on the men in her life" and "the hatred involved in these erotic relationships was very intense." Though Sylvia and Gordon's affair could hardly be characterized as "erotic," the prospect of marriage to so "ordinary" a man could not have filled her with much joy. He lacked the tyrannic boot of her father, without having the sweet humility to play martyr to her talent. He was available, however, and that was sufficient for present needs.

As attested to by "Spinster" and "Strumpet Song," Sylvia had lost none of her belief in the world's unfairness towards women. There were no female models at Cambridge for her to follow, and she resented the implication by male and female professors that scholarship for a woman necessarily meant surrender of femininity or motherhood. In May of 1956, *Isis*, Oxford's student magazine, published a letter of hers in which she castigated the Cambridge men for their antiquated attitude towards the women in their midst: "Apparently, the most difficult feat for a Cambridge male is to accept a woman not merely as feeling, not merely as thinking, but as managing a complex, vital interweaving of both." She went on to point out that Cambridge men tended to put all women in two categories as either "pretty beagling frivolous things and devastating bohemian things" or "esoteric opponents on an intellectual tennis court where the man, by law of kind, always wins."

And yet Sylvia herself, in a letter to Elinor Klein, with whom she had promised to spend the summer touring Greece, cattily dismissed the "ghastly" women at Cambridge as also being of two types: "the fair-skinned twittering bird who adores beagling and darjeeling tea and the large, intellectual cowish type with monastically bobbed hair, impossible elephantine ankles and a horrified moo when within 10 feet of a man." But her *Isis* letter, since it was a public performance and had to maintain a pleasant mask, concluded on a more reasonable note by admitting that the small number of women at Cambridge put them "in an artificial position" and by calling for co-educational public schools in England.

Sylvia was torn again. She found herself in the familiar position of being isolated like an island from the masses of faces and names and bodies that flowed around her daily existence. Her genius and sensitivity were both curse and gift as they inevitably put the majority of fellow human beings in a pit of lesser intelligence (real or imagined) where she could regard them only with contempt—while at the same time having to go through the motions of winning their favor, support, and friendship. In the case of men, the situation was even more severe since she also had the measuring rod of her father—already an internalized myth—with which to rap them across their knuckles for being such naughty children, thinking they could replace *him* in her life.

But she needed men more than ever. Sylvia could not possibly leave Cambridge and become a teacher without a husband, or she would then be nothing more than the stereotyped spinster schoolmarm she had always despised. Furthermore, the women around her in teaching gowns, such as Miss K. T. Burton—a warmly efficient, highly intelligent, unmarried don who would become her Director of Studies in the second year—offered no example of anything beyond the stereotype. She was as terrified of Miss Burton as she had been of Mary Ellen Chase, and for the same reason. In them she sensed a negative possibility of self, as she did in her own mother, and dreaded their influence on her career. Above all, she did not want to end up like them—incomplete and "abnormal."

Relief, in a measure, came near the end of the dark winter. Sylvia attended a lecture by Dorothea Krook—a young Jewish professor from South Africa who would be Sylvia's supervisor in philosophy the following term—on the redemptive powers of love in D. H. Lawrence's story "The Man Who Died." Sylvia was overwhelmed, not only by the lecture, which was brilliant and unconventionally frank, but by Miss Krook herself—her beauty, intelligence, wit, and feminine grace. She wrote to many of her friends in the States to praise Miss Krook in the most complimentary terms possible; Jane Kopp recalls that "she was extremely enthusiastic about Dorothea Krook. In fact, Miss Krook was one of her gushing and burbling subjects, to the extent that, to be frank, none of us listened."

Though divorced and childless, Miss Krook obviously offered the model Sylvia was seeking. And yet the excessiveness of Sylvia's reaction—even taking into account her propensity for excessive reactions—gives the impression that part of her interest in her new supervisor of philosophy was sexual: a sign of a deeply buried (probably never faced) androgynous strain in her own make-up. Some evidence for this view lies, of course, in the death of her father at a crucial time in her sexual development and her unusual dependence upon her mother, as well as in her attitude towards Virginia Woolf's classic tale *Orlando*.

In Sylvia's copy of the Penguin edition of this book, which she used at Cambridge, her underlinings are fascinating for what they reveal about both Sylvia's insight into that novel and into her own psychological profile. Some of them are blatantly done as references for a later essay, but the rest all touch upon Sylvia's own biography. Many of the phrases so underlined will appear, directly or somewhat disguised, in her own poetry, while some of the comments regarding "self" patently relate to a self-image. The book itself, as it follows Orlando through three centuries and a miraculous sex change in pursuit of elusive poetry, may have led her to regard the author as a previous (and dangerous) self. Sylvia underlined the following from pages 119 and 120:

The difference between the sexes is, happily, one of great profundity. Clothes are but a symbol of something hid deep beneath.

Different though the sexes are, they intermix. In every human being a vacillation from one sex to the other takes place, and often it is only the clothes that keep the male or female likeness, while underneath the sex is the very opposite of what it is above.[12]

The statements would seem to conflict, but they come from the same discussion in *Orlando*; and, from Sylvia's viewpoint, they would tend to emphasize the same truth about herself: underneath the other selves, the public masks—and in *Orlando* she has also underlined statements concerning the many selves in any one individual and the existence of a "Captain self," which is hidden but controls all others—lay the driving masculine urge of her bitch goddess, who wanted power and could possibly conceive of another woman as a sex object.

But there is no need to dwell on the matter at any great length here, since an almost school-girl crush on Dorothea Krook is not as significant as the fact that Sylvia very rarely was what she made other people believe and that much of her life was a deliberate myth foisted by her surface selves upon the world to ensure sanity and public acceptance.

A good example of the latter was her continued adherence to the libertine mask she had been wearing since her recovery under Dr. Jones's care. On several different occasions she complained to Jane Kopp about Cambridge's palely loitering males: "I can't help it, Jane, I just feel that what all these English boys need is to go to bed with somebody, and I was just wondering if you had the same impression." Another time, Sylvia phrased her attitude slightly more chauvinistically: "I can't help it, I just enjoy our good old American sensibleness about sex, I can't help it, I really enjoy it, and I can't understand these English types."

True or not, Sylvia's wandering sexuality was about to be curbed. It was in February, in the midst of her dark winter, that she met her future husband. Edward Hughes, known always as Ted, had taken his degree in 1954, a second, and returned often to Cambridge to be with old friends and participate in the university's varied literary life. At the time he met Sylvia, he was living in London, in a modest building once occupied by Dylan Thomas, and working for the Rank Organization: "I graduated in 1954. After a spell of teaching here and there, and another driving an uncle around the continent, I took a job as a rose-gardener, then as a night watchman in a steel factory in London, and later as a reader for J. Arthur Rank at the Pinewood Studios." [13]

The son of a carpenter, Ted had been born (August 17, 1930) in a small town called Mytholmroyd in the West Riding district of Yorkshire, the youngest of three children. The family had moved to Mexborough in south Yorkshire when Ted was seven, his father switching professions and buying a tobacconist's and newsagent's shop. Ted attended the local grammar school and then, in 1948, won an Open Exhibition in English to Pembroke College. Before reaching Cambridge, he served two years in the Royal Air Force at a three-man radio station in east Yorkshire.

The poetic air was dry and dead to Ted in Cambridge, as was most of contemporary British poetry with its stiff accent on formal design and civilized classicism. The only poet at Cambridge who stirred him at all was Thom Gunn; and, in his second year, Ted abandoned English and read in archeology and anthropology for his tripos. Cambridge's reaction to Ted, official Cambridge that is, was no less negative. Wendy Campbell writes: "Ted had apparently posed a certain problem for the college for a part of his time there. He lived with such vehemence, and such a perfect absence of self-consciousness, and such a total indifference to the modes of the Establishment that it was not always easy to both preserve Ted and the appearances which were thought to be necessary." Largeness was the key, whether physical or spiritual—an almost primitive lack of restraint in minor matters of public taste that made Ted stand out from the other undergraduates, though he had developed a coterie of fellow radicals and wrote professionally polished poetry.

Sylvia had read some of his poetry in a few of the Cambridge magazines and undoubtedly knew of him, while he too had heard of her and already respected her considerable artistic achievement. Ted's best friend at Cambridge while Sylvia was there was E. Lucas Meyers, from Sewanee, Tennessee—a cousin of Allen Tate. Meyers, Ted, and several of their friends had decided to found a new magazine, called *St. Botolph's Review* after Botolph's Priory where they roomed; it was destined not to survive its initial issue. A party was obviously in order to celebrate the magazine's launching, and it was fittingly held at the Priory. Sylvia came with an unknown boy, and Jane appeared in the company of Bart Wyett-Brown, who was also a good friend of Lucas. It was a small gathering centering around lunch and much beer and cheap wine. Jane's impression of Ted was favorable: "I liked him instantly." She found him "an extremely interesting and strong figure," though she also sensed that "he was violent" in some vague manner—"just to look at him, it seemed to me he had a violent nature."

Sylvia's reaction was more intense. His height alone would attract her, not to mention his casual bearing and good looks. When she finally engaged him in conversation and discovered he was a poet she admired, the combination must have been irresistible. He was, for her, Dylan Thomas incarnate—strong, romantic, literate (he would quote much of Shakespeare by heart), lyrical by nature (he knew and sang old English ballads), and totally dedicated to his craft. Later she would claim that she decided immediately he was to be her husband—but he is not mentioned in her letters until after they were married some months later. Jane Kopp, however, felt she was serious about Ted from the first meeting: "Sylvia had always, in her way, gushed and gone on and been very public about all the men she met and was spending time with, but this was not so with Ted. I remember thinking she was serious about Ted because she didn't talk about him, had absolutely nothing to say about him."

Sylvia's plans for the Easter vacation, which would begin on Friday, March 23, involved London, Paris, and a meeting with Gordon Lameyer, her putative fiancé, in Germany; but very little of Ted, although he and Lucas would accompany her to London.

It now seemed to her that the whole world was ringed
with gold. She went in to dinner. Wedding rings
abounded. She went to church. Wedding rings were
everywhere. She drove out. Gold, or pinchbeck, thin,
thick, plain, smooth, they glowed dully on every
hand. Rings filled the jewelers' shops, not the flashing
paste and diamonds of Orlando's recollection but
simple bands without a stone in them.

VIRGINIA WOOLF, *Orlando*
(underlined by SYLVIA PLATH)

10

The Panther's Tread

The week before Easter vacation Sylvia received word that her
Fulbright grant had been renewed for the following year, which meant
she could now take Part II of the English tripos—the only part on which
she would be examined—and earn her degree by June 1957. Miss
Burton would now function as Sylvia's Director of Studies, and in that
capacity she was charged with arranging her student's course of study,
advising her on the possibilities available, and appointing supervisors in
each major category.

Sylvia's program for Part II would be both a struggle and a challenge
of the kind she relished. Part I had been more in the nature of a survey,
involving six final papers that dealt with broad literary topics—medieval
through twentieth-century literature, and, finally, more specialized
papers on Shakespeare and literary criticism. But Part II concentrated
on specific areas and included several required papers, as well as critiques
of unprepared texts. Each student was also expected to submit "a bit of
writing" (no longer than 5000 words) on his own, usually of a creative
nature, which could abet but not detract from his final standing. In
Sylvia's case, she would submit a group of about fifty poems, most of
them from her Smith days.

Besides "The English Moralists," which she would be taking with
Dorothea Krook, Sylvia would also be working with Valerie Pitt in

French, where the set texts were *Phèdre, Les Fleurs du Mal,* and works by Montaigne, while Miss Burton would personally be handling "Greek and Classical Tragedy." One of Sylvia's options was to choose between either a brief period paper, covering about fifty years, or a paper dedicated to a single major author. She chose the Chaucer seminar, which was given by Elizabeth Salter.

Miss Burton, who had no idea of Sylvia's distaste for her as the typical spinster don, found Sylvia a model student.[1] She conceded, however, that "although our relationship was extremely good, I never knew her in depth." What Miss Burton recalls particularly about Sylvia was her "sunny" disposition—"the image, always, of a very happy and very poised person, with perfect manners." Moreover, "she was not the kind of person who did any kind of personal leaning on her supervisors"; her submitted work, which was neatly typed from a written draft, "was a pleasure to deal with." Its quality was first-rate without being extraordinary: "As a literary critic, she was very good. I wouldn't say she was brilliant, she wasn't as far as the Cambridge tripos go, but produced a sort of steady first-class material, very sensitive, very much aware of how literature worked, not as cogent as, say, Margaret Drabble, who was also at Newnham at the time, but I have no doubt that she had a very good sensibility and a fine mind . . . and I never worried about her."

But Miss Burton and the hardships of another Cambridge winter still lay in the future as Sylvia prepared for her Easter trip to the continent. On Friday, February 23, she went to London, accompanied by Ted Hughes and Lucas Meyers. She then joined another Fulbright fellow, who attended the London School of Economics, to Canterbury and then on to Paris, where she hoped to spend most of the April vacation. Probably it was at this time that she saw Richard S—— for the last time, breaking off with the past in the conviction that her and Ted's lives were to be forever joined. Later, she met Gordon Lameyer in Munich on her first visit to her father's native country. Germany upset and disturbed her much more than she had thought it would. She and Gordon fought constantly over petty matters. At one point Gordon had cut his finger and leaned against a wall—a memory which would be resurrected in "Munich Mannequins" near the end of her life.[2]

It is difficult to tell at this late date whether the arguments between Sylvia and Gordon during their European rendezvous were solely her responsibility or not—that is, whether she was attempting to extricate herself from a relationship that was no longer viable or whether the squabbles helped convince her of Ted Hughes' desirability. Germany had to have depressed her to the marrow, and her irritation was probably genuine. She was fond of Gordon, and must have appreciated his own sensitivity and his deep feelings about her enough to have been able to work out a more congenial and less painful method of parting. Even in her most manipulative moments, she had rarely resorted to acts of overt cruelty. Indeed she had endeavored to hide any negative feelings behind a cloak of extroverted pleasantness. She must have also realized that she could not simply "drop" Gordon, as she had Peter Davison, especially since his whole trip to Europe was at her suggestion.

Their stay in Germany was no more than a day or two, and they then headed for Italy, eventually reaching Venice. The springtime beauty of the city had no effect on their quarreling, however, and Gordon even made a joke about them in a reference to Mann's *Death in Venice*. The final argument, petty as all the others on the surface, stemmed from Malcolm Brinnin's book *Dylan Thomas in America*. Thomas as a literary topic had always been a point of conflict as Gordon never shared her enthusiasm for him or his poetry. The argument revolved around Brinnin's role in the Welsh poet's death. Sylvia felt that he could have and should have prevented it, and Gordon took the opposite position that no one could have prevented Thomas's relentless march towards self-destruction.

Neither won the argument, of course, but Gordon had at last reached the point where he "wanted to get rid of her." In disgust, on April 13, he sent her back to London on a plane.

Sylvia's return to London led almost immediately to her engagement, as Ted spent all of his modest cash reserves courting her. They agreed to a June wedding, which would coincide with the term's end and Aurelia's expected visit; and Ted abandoned his original plans to earn enough money to join his older brother Gerald in Australia. At Ted's suggestion, they also decided that they would spend their summer honeymoon in Benidorm, a small Spanish fishing village on the Mediterranean, where they could live and work cheaply. Ted left his job at Rank, and they returned together to Cambridge.

Sylvia was happy in a way she had not been since she was a child. In an interview years later for the BBC, she would precisely date the period of her adolescent and teenage unhappiness from the death of Otto to the age of nineteen or twenty. More likely, Ted had provided final salvation. From the beginning of their relationship, he was an amalgam of lover, father, and rescuer from persistent social pressure to get married. Their marriage vow above all was a mutual protection pact *against* the world and *for* poetry. However temperamentally unsuited they might seem in retrospect, they complemented each other perfectly in their belief that poetry was not only important but absolutely central to their existence. Ted would give her the means and encouragement to move more deeply into her unconscious and free her real self from its stifling inhibitions; and Sylvia would help shape his life into a purposeful whole and see that his work (which she would type and submit for him) reached the proper outlets and that he met the right people.

As with all marriages, Ted's and Sylvia's began with the conviction that it was a conjunction of two unique forces. In their case, however, it was. Both were destined to become major poets in England and America, thought Sylvia's impact would be posthumous, and leading exponents of modern poetry's return to roots and sources in the subconscious. The idea of two such tremendously self-centered persons occupying the same house for any period of time without a disastrous explosion seems now almost impossible to contemplate; and what is amazing in the end is not that the marriage was to fail but that it lasted as long and as happily as it did. It also provided two of the more original minds of their generation with an unprecedented and productive opportunity to feed and grow upon one another's stores of poetic insight.

Necessarily, the world was much with them, dreams and ambitions aside, and their marriage had to survive that fact first. A reminder of this perennial truism came soon after Sylvia's engagement. Her grandmother died on April 29, following five months of agony for herself, her husband Frank, and her daughter Aurelia. The woman Sylvia had always envied in a peculiar fashion because of her domestic bliss and joyous acceptance of a narrow female world was gone, and perhaps the granddaughter could now assume that same role.

The wedding between Sylvia Plath and Edward Hughes, which was unannounced to the public, took place on June 6, Blooms Day, in London, with Aurelia acting as a witness and giving the bride away. Aurelia was somewhat dismayed that they would miss the pomp of a more elaborate ceremony, but must have rejoiced at seeing her daughter married only a few months after her mother's death. After Ted and Sylvia toured London and Cambridge with her and escorted her to Paris, she went on alone to Austria to visit the places her mother had known as a child, while Ted and Sylvia departed with knapsacks on their backs for Benidorm, travelling from Paris to Madrid and then south. Sylvia's recent year of modest affluence was over as money once again became, and would remain, scarce. Every decision from now on regarding their way of life would have to include serious consideration of this disheartening, if familiar, factor.

But Benidorm itself, then still unspoiled, required very little money. They were able to rent very cheaply for five weeks a large white stucco house, with its own grape arbor and a fig tree, and they found food prices amazingly low. At Ted's insistence, Sylvia resumed her pen sketches and soon had developed a solid portfolio of Benidorm scenes—the plaster tenements with their cracked walls, the impressive palm trees and stately pueblos set upon the rock cliffs overlooking the harbor and Angel's Bay, the arched stairway leading down into Castillo, the busy market place, and the quaint, ever present sardine boats in dry dock.[3]

The sketches are painstakingly done with an eye to minute detail, but betray no apparent interest beyond the externally pictorial. Sylvia's poems from Benidorm are equally innocuous, though likewise impressive in terms of craft. For the most part, as in "Fiesta Melons" and "Southern Sunrise," they are scene-setters in which details like "quartz-clear dawn" and "bump-rinded cantaloupes" must carry all the weight. The best poem about Benidorm would come many months after the fact when Sylvia could look back upon the area and consider its local scenery in terms of manifest symbols for the human process of endless endings and departures.

"Departure" mates the bitterness of an idyll's conclusion with the blunt fact that the "money's run out." Actually, it was a series of normal responsibilities that called them back to Cambridge; but pressing financial worries, which were more in evidence when the poem was composed, become a neat and highly charged symbol in the poem of the fate that decrees all human paradises must end. Operating from the vantage of a rueful retrospect throughout, the poem can be seen as another example of a deliberate romantic fallacy laboring, with great persuasion, to demonstrate man's corrupting influence on nature. The personal note steadies and concentrates the poem by leading to a few powerful images. Also Sylvia lets alliteration rather than full rhymes bear the technical burden of her message—an advance that signaled a continuation of her slow progress towards a more natural, less obvious form. Imagery was still her strongest point, and it too inevitably improved when closely related to her deeper emotional undercurrents. Like Virginia Woolf, whom she so eerily resembled, Sylvia would learn in time to apply her sensitive intellect to the drama not of material or multiple reality, human characters and complex physical actions, but of the single grand ego that struggled for meaning in the labyrinthine corridors of its own complex self.

"Departure," like "Temper of the Time" and the later "Mushrooms," remains a miniature masterpiece of precise proportions—a set piece in which, however, the finely controlled details and allusions are ultimately stunted by the one-dimensional nature of their content and its lack of complex alternatives. Two other poems undoubtedly written in Benidorm, although concerned with other parts of Spain, were "Alicante Lullaby" and "The Goring." In the former, pretty details dominate the scene as a pair of lovers move through the town, where barrels are rolled "Bumblingly over the nubs of the cobbles" and "Kumquat-colored trolleys ding" as they trundle passengers "under an indigo fizzle"; and loudspeakers blare out rumbas and sambas. The tenor of the poem is ironic: its modern cacophony like a "goddess of jazz and of quarrels" ends with the persona's head on her pillow, "Lullabyed by susurrus lyres and viols." Though also a tourist reaction, "The Goring" has the advantage of the bull-fight ritual at its center. Here Sylvia compares the ceremony with art and finds the picador's savage task "cumbrous routine."

The honeymoon itself, from all appearances, had been a great success, and Sylvia and Ted reluctantly returned to England in August—crossing the choppy waters of the Channel without a shilling between them and in the throes of sea-sickness. They spent the rest of the vacation at Ted's family home on Heptanstall Slack in Yorkshire. A description of this dark, dour Brontë country and how it must have struck a young American like Sylvia on first sight has been provided by Elinor Klein, who would soon be visiting the young couple there: "The rolling English countryside at Heptanstall is cobwebbed by tiny, precise stone fences, sharply marking off property lines, and small houses huddled at the peaks of hills like exclamation points." Sylvia refers to Ted's parents as "dear" more than once, but later would confess to a dislike for their informal ways.

At the moment, however, Sylvia was intrigued by the entire setting, and particularly by the fact that her husband, for all his literary learning, fitted the countryside—shooting rabbits, which she soon knew how to stew, fishing, and generally demonstrating a sympathy with nature's unsentimental realities. It was also a sympathy that would permeate many of the poems in his first collection, *The Hawk in the Rain*, which he had already begun to write. She, in turn, seemed to adapt easily to her new role as country wife and secretary, although secretly she hoped to influence her "staunchly English" husband into abandoning his homeland altogether in favor of America's more comfort-oriented ways.

Elinor Klein, who had toured Europe with another friend, came to Yorkshire near summer's end. When she arrived in a taxi, Ted and

Sylvia were waiting to greet her. Sylvia's first words to her are odd in their concentration upon a seemingly irrelevant facet of local life, and yet quite in character with her obvious concern that the world realize her marriage had to be and was the epitome of bliss: "You've got to see the great pigs they've got around here. They're wonderfully fat and happy. Of course, so are we!"

Ted discussed the history of the area while they accompanied Elinor to the nearest inn, which was two miles down the road. His final words are interesting for the light they shed on his particular insight into rural undercurrents. "It's a funny place, this," he told her. "Every once in a while one of these farmers ups and commits the rawest act of violence, butchers all his animals, then his family and finally himself. Comes from living in such small quarters, I think." Sylvia's next comment touched upon her own feeling of isolation among temporary neighbors—a deep and probably disturbing intensification of her "outsider" mentality, despite her jocular tone: "And watch yourself," she warned her friend laughingly. "They know everything you're doing. Every house is armed with a mirror looking out on the street. You can't see them but they see you. And they'll be watching you. I'm the first American I think they've ever seen. They think I'm some sort of freak."

But Ted and Sylvia were good hosts and made Elinor feel at home. On her first night there, Ted arranged for a special treat—a visit at midnight to the local witch, who lived in a lonely cottage in the valley below. Like his sister Olwyn, Ted possessed a keen interest in mysterious forces, which included a taste for astrology that went against Sylvia's grain of secular skepticism. The journey itself, however, was a rather tame affair. Ted's great bulk gave the two girls an air of confidence as they treaded their way safari-fashion behind him in the darkness. The witch was a gnarled crone glad of their company, who talked at length about such mundane topics as "farming, neighbors, and wildlife."

The next morning, all three took a bus to Haworth Parsonage, where the Brontës had been born, and then walked the rest of the way to the remains of Wuthering Heights, "a small heap of bricks sitting on a piece of undistinguished land." Sylvia, who had brought along pen and paper, sat down and began to sketch. Fifteen minutes later the sketch was finished, and the glum, dilapidated reality of unromantic Withens—the actual name of the place—perfectly captured. Having prepared themselves with Wellington boots, the three decided to forego the convenience of the bus and walk the ten miles back home across the moors. Once in the moors there "is nothing for miles except the soft earth tufted with long waving grasses and everything appears to spin and undulate"—and people were lost every day, as Ted cheerfully noted. He himself had difficulty keeping them on a straight course. As twilight approached, they became somewhat apprehensive.

Finally, they did meet a farmer, who kindly took them home for tea and headed them in the right direction. That night Sylvia "made rabbit stew and we ate like starved prisoners." The rest of Miss Klein's stay was less dramatic but equally entertaining as Ted and Sylvia introduced her to the area's customs: "we hoisted a few with the local mill hands, walked for hours along the bottom where a small but plucky stream pushed the mills, and stared transfixed at the local pigs rooting joyously around in their mucky heaven." Sylvia informed her about the local farmers keeping their chickens in lighted coops so that they laid eggs constantly—a fact which must have given Sylvia a shudder because of its human implications.

Elinor Klein's account cannot be taken entirely at face value, however, since she was interested in presenting a lighter contrast to the dark picture of Sylvia she felt critics and others had painted after her friend's death. But the details ring true, and she was obviously not the type to distort what was said among them during her stay. Sylvia's comment about Ted, for instance, "He's the most magnificent man I've ever met, and a poet, yet," is similar to remarks made in conversations with and in letters to Jane, Marcia, and other companions. Also Sylvia's enthusiastic prediction about the children they would eventually have fits the scheme of her mask's delight in motherhood, the last and most essential experience: "I want a lot—as many as possible. God! Won't they be marvellous—giants in the earth!"

Sylvia leaped into her marriage with the same energy she had devoted to every other experience. Now finally harnessed to the category of "wife," she seemed determined to lift that category to a transcendent peak. "We" and "us" replaced "I" and "me" in her vocabulary, as if only complete submission could affirm the seriousness of her endeavor; and her husband's career became the fulcrum of their mated existence. She knew that his unorganized, uncommercial approach to poetry would only delay his eventual acceptance and that her "unpoetic business streak" alone could guarantee him some of the attention he deserved. Besides being his secretary and typing up his work and sending it out along with her own, Sylvia acted as his agent and tried to get American editors interested in her poetry to look at his as well. In the months ahead, her strenuous public-relations activities on their behalf began to produce results as both of them gained acceptances from *The Nation,*

Poetry (Chicago), and the *Atlantic Monthly*, where Peter Davison was now working.

Behind this portrait of a selfless helpmate, which was supported by a realistic awareness that Ted's verses were indeed superior material, beat the heart of more unconscious life forms. In several poems written towards the end of 1956, Sylvia adopts the totally alien (to her at least) concept that an old-fashioned marriage of dominant male to submissive female best suits both, and nature itself. In "Wreath for a Bridal," for example, she uses Dylan Thomas to show that the marriage pact has nature's approval ("love's proper chapel") and must lead inexorably to an imitation of nature's abundant reproductive powers—"children most fair in legion." Another poem, "Snowman on the Moor," commences with a domestic quarrel. The young wife flees from the house and taunts her husband to "Come find me." He does not stir, and she is warned not to continue her flight by "her winter-beheaded daisies, marrowless, gaunt" (which owes a debt to Emily Dickinson's odd little poem "Apparently With No Surprise"). As always in the Plath sphere, at least before the bitch goddess is released, hubris is the central theme—here of a rebellious bride. Nature punishes such hubris with terrible results; and the fleeing bride, after traversing "stiles of black stone," reaches the "world's white edge." This is Poe's whiteness—the terrifying absence of all value as envisioned in "Ms. Found in a Bottle" and *Eureka*—versus the natural order imposed by mortal limits and fears.

However bad they are as poems, although "Snowman on the Moor" has a certain linguistic charm, these two marriage hymns might have been magical ways for Sylvia to adjust to the demands of a role which had to strain her narcissistic personality to the brink of rage. They assert what has to be true, and give its unpalatable reality a gloss of romanticism; but they also reflect fear of the chasm on the other side of marriage—the far extreme of spinsterhood. Soon after her marriage and back at Cambridge, Sylvia admitted to Jane, "You have no idea how marvellous it is to be relieved of that dreadful social pressure." This vision of the terrible alternative had, of course, found full expression in "Spinster"; but Sylvia wrote two other poems that confront the same sterile perspective, although with different results.

In "Ella Mason and the Eleven Cats," one of four poems later accepted by *Poetry*, the rejecting and rejected figure of "Spinster" has ripened (that is, decayed) into dotty old age. Having shunned a basic aspect of life, she has become a creature beyond the pale, isolated, ridiculed, married only to lesser beings—to cats, ancient female symbols of evil, definite proof of Ella's barren witch status. What is interesting about the poem, besides its Puritan return to clumsy didacticism, is its final judgment that spinsterhood was a form of selfishness—self-love. "Vanity Fair," which appeared with "Spinster" in the first issue of *Gemini*—a brave literary magazine launched in the spring of 1957 by Oxford and Cambridge faculty and students—elaborates upon the same theme, though with more success as Sylvia begins to show the positive influence of her husband's aesthetic. Here Thackeray's world of puppets and Sylvia's vision of witches as spinsters are wedded in a severe portrait of another aging beauty, "Crow's-feet copy veining on stained leaf," who sidles through "frost-thick weather" and bears the raven mystery of how conceit "Waylays simple girls, church going." Although this particular sorceress "sets mirrors enough/ To distract beauty's thought," she represents all the foolish females who choose "to blaze as satan's wife"—as spinsters who pay a terrible price: "Housed in earth, those million brides shriek out./ Some burn short, some long,/ Staked in pride's coven."

Love, of course, must play its part, as it did in "Wreath for a Bridal"; but love had always carried with it the overtones of danger and of sexual intrusion in the earlier poems. "Pursuit," the single poem accepted by *Atlantic* and given an impressive full-page spread, revives the theme and, despite its absence of clear poetic value, presents the central dilemma of Sylvia's concept of herself as artist and woman. The Racine quote heading the poem—*Dans le fond des forêts votre image me suit*—is relevant to the prevailing allegory of the female being hunted down by a panther, an aspect of herself. The climax echoes faithfully the climax of every previous Plath poem: the vision of evil forever lurking in the abysmal darkness of our interior selves, waiting to pounce. Horror is wedded here to sexual love and hate:

> The panther's tread is on the stairs,
> Coming up and up the stairs.

Love, marriage, and art, the triad that Sylvia was trying to support, appears in every one of these poems, although sometimes by their pointed absence; but in the penultimate meditation upon their relationship and meaning, namely, in "Epitaph for Fire and Flower," the summary resolution is negative. The two lovers and art are considered in conjunction, with the human pair condemned to death by time and the flesh's unavoidable corruptions. The couple in this instance are patterned after Dante's doomed lovers Paolo and Francesca and the dual Dantesque universe is clearly planted by the title itself. Not only is

Sylvia working with the familiar motif of two doomed lovers, but she has also returned to the seashore.

The initial two stanzas rephrase the imperatives of the earlier "Go Get the Goodly Squab" in order to stress both love's inevitable quality and its equally inevitable destruction in a system of reality where even "Stars shoot their petals," and suns run to seed. Nature's disinclination to be contained inside any mere human scheme is again at the core of Sylvia's poetic concern. The first stanza denies Stevens by emphasizing the sheer impracticality of trying to string a wave's "green peak on wire" or to "anchor the fluent air/ In quartz." The next-to-last line resurrects Poe, another old friend, and his "Annabel Lee" version of "two most perishable lovers" kindling "angels' envy." Her development closely paralleled Poe's in that they both lived with a sense of imminent doom and ceaseless time, insisted upon translating time into concrete images, were concerned with the evil double, and had a love of and fascination with the bleak despair concomitant upon deep psychological probings into self and into the ultimate nothingness behind the universe.

"Epitaph for Fire and Flower" at least proved that Sylvia had not completely stilled her inner doubts, insecurities, and sense of impending disaster. Her return to Cambridge was less happy than she or her husband could have expected. In the words of Miss Burton: "The one episode I remember vividly was when she came back from vacation saying she had had a wonderful holiday in Paris and it had been a honeymoon. And there she was with Ted. We were all slightly surprised. It had never struck her that when you are a member of an English college, especially in those days, and wanted to get married, you had to first get sanction."

The one happy aspect of the affair was its interesting effect upon the relationship between Sylvia and Dorothea Krook, whose memoir treats it with perceptive detail:

The more personal side of our friendship developed, I seem to recall, from the time of her marriage to Ted Hughes. I became involved in this for reasons serious enough for Sylvia at the start, though in the end amusing as well. At the beginning of the Michaelmas term 1956, her second year at Cambridge, Sylvia appeared, extremely agitated, to tell me that she had "secretly" married Ted during the long vacation, that they had had a marvellous summer in Spain, ecstatically happy, wonderfully productive—happy, obviously, because they adored each other, productive because (she said) they had both managed to write a great deal. But now the hour of reckoning had come: she had got married without tutorial permission, and had to now keep it from tutorial knowledge (this is what she meant by saying she had done it secretly, which I had at first not understood), she was afraid now that her outraged college would recommend that her Fulbright scholarship be taken away, in which case she would have to leave Cambridge and come away without a degree, and please *what* was she to do?

I was a little taken aback, I remember, by the intensity of her fear and agitation, and, even more perhaps, by what I sensed to be a strong suppressed resentment: presumably, at Cambridge rules and practices, Cambridge dons and their demands, the Cambridge set-up as a whole perhaps. It was the first and the only time I glimpsed in Sylvia (without, of course, at the time recognizing it for what it was) a small touch, oh ever so small, of the passionate *rage* which Elizabeth Hardwick and others have come to see as a dominating emotion of her later poetry.

Having turned to Professor Krook for help was the wisest thing Sylvia had ever done. Too enraged to maintain her mask, she was on the point of confronting the authorities with unaccustomed directness and taking the part not of the contrite sinner, but of the outraged victim of unfair regulations and narrow conventions. Fortunately, Professor Krook mollified her and suggested that she approach the proper parties, such as Miss Burton, with "a decent (though not abject) regret about not having asked permission, and plead love, passion, the marriage of true minds, and so on, as the irresistible cause. She was not however (I urged) to 'criticize' the immoral rules or moralize about their iniquity."

Cambridge, which maintained a strict paternalism that would have put Smith to shame and had only that year permitted, for the first time, male and female students to take their examinations together, was not merely surprised by Sylvia's marriage, it was outraged, particularly since her husband had not been one of its favorite sons. But Professor Krook's advice proved to be shrewd: "Within a day or two Sylvia came back, happy and beaming. Her tutor had been completely charming and kind and understanding; she would not have her Fulbright taken away; and she could now go and live with her legally recognized husband in any convenient place in Cambridge." Several months later, looking back upon her plight, Sylvia would be able to treat it lightly and even boast of the fact that she was the sole married undergraduate on campus. The marriage itself seemed to flourish and emit a glow of mutual dedication. Professor Krook observed that her student "was passionately, brilliantly happy . . . I remember at least once experiencing a thrill of fear at the idyllic pitch and intensity of her happiness."

Miss Burton also noted that Sylvia "seemed happier than before and, as far as I could tell, all was going well in the early stages, though I do remember A. P. Rossiter, the late medieval and renaissance writer, saying of her husband, 'I wish he could learn to keep his hands out of the placards,' which didn't suggest to me that Ted was exactly concentrated on Sylvia." Like many others at Cambridge, she had some reservations about the marriage—not the marriage itself so much as the man Sylvia had chosen. Miss Burton had met Ted once, when he appeared with Sylvia in her office, and recalled him only as "a slightly gangling, not altogether couth type, who was certainly tough." The marriage appeared odd "because Ted, at that stage, was very definitely a provincial, while Sylvia had a very wide range of European culture and was totally civilized. She could have passed anywhere without putting a foot wrong, and I was quite sure Ted couldn't."

Another of Sylvia's instructors, Valerie Pitt, had similar reservations about the marriage, and specifically about the choice of partner: "The odd thing is that Miss Plath appeared to me so unmelancholy in herself that her relationship with Mr. Hughes then seemed to me to be out of character." [4] Miss Pitt did know Ted better than Miss Burton had, however, and recollects that Sylvia "told me one extraordinary story about Mr. Hughes smashing the top from a bottle of wine and drinking from it . . . the fierceness implied in her account of this was something I was well able to believe since I had just encountered Mr. Hughes at a party given by one of my students and attended by a group of rather wild young men, whom I was assured were Irish and poets. At the point at which one of them was gesticulating and appeared about to embrace the late Morgan Forster, I left; the party was later raided by the Proctors."

What is interesting about Miss Pitt's general reaction to Sylvia, her marriage to Ted aside, is how closely it parallels those of all of the poet's early teachers, from elementary school to Smith, in its every detail—a tribute to Sylvia's brilliant ability to develop and maintain the precise image necessary for academic and social success: "The selection processes at Oxford and Cambridge Colleges for women produce a situation in which any given group of students includes a number of extremely 'high flyers' with all the difficulties and problems of over-intelligence and over-sensitivity. The group of undergraduates in Miss Plath's time was, in fact, very high strung—they were over-dramatic about themselves and their problems. By contrast—though I emphasize that I would not have had the personal contact with her which might have led her tutor and her Director of Studies to another conclusion—Miss Plath appeared a model of steadiness. The phrase one finds oneself using is 'the All-American Girl'—with all that implies of a kind of brightness. I think, perhaps, this might be right too, for Miss Plath *did* show me some of her verse, which seemed more in the Frost than the Lowell tradition, talented but not more than much undergraduate verse is—and certainly without the special quality of perception apparent in her later work."

Critical reactions were not all from the faculty or just from Sylvia's side. Many of Ted's friends found the match inexplicable. Lucas Meyers, perhaps his best friend, who had earlier evinced a "head-shaking" attitude towards Sylvia, was surprised and somewhat dismayed by his friend's choice of a bride. He confided to Jane that he "had never expected Ted to marry an American"—meaning, according to Jane, such an American American. Perhaps that was another binding element of the marriage—the partners being so closely identified with their native countries; although the major factors remained always their mutual passion for poetry and their shared belief in their own literary careers.

Their immediate problem was still locating a place to live; and day after day, usually in the midst of autumn downpours, the young couple searched for a flat, while ever conscious of the unpaid bills piling up around them. Finally, they found an extremely cheap flat, partially furnished, for about $11.00 a week at 55 Eltisley Avenue, near the Grantchester Meadows and Dorothea Krook's place. Their good fortune was the result of the original tenants' misfortune, for an aged couple had reached the point where they could no longer take care of themselves and had to be removed to a nursing home.

The flat was tiny, cold, and run-down, but its location was ideal and it did represent their first home together. Their good fortune continued as Ted soon found a job teaching English and drama at a boys' secondary school. His salary, coupled with Sylvia's Fulbright money, would at least allow them to clear up all their old debts. None of the other problems facing them seemed very important as they set about establishing a new way of life.

I shall gather myself into myself again,
I shall take my scattered selves and make them one,
Fusing them into a polished crystal ball
Where I can see the moon and the flashing sun.

Sara Teasdale

11

Paring Her Person Down

The impetus behind Sara Teasdale's poem "The Crystal Gazer" was one with which Sylvia undoubtedly sympathized at this critical juncture in her young life: a dying woman's wish, the need to fuse her scattered selves into a single, whole, healthy, efficient, contented entity, and perhaps to use that new and final self to penetrate the future and remove all insecurities. She wrote two poems at Eltisley Avenue around Miss Teasdale's motif, one actually called "Crystal Gazer" and the other "Recantation," but the former rejects the dead poet's autumnal sentimentality.

Sylvia was trying to be both poet and poet's wife—she would type up and send off almost a thousand sheets of work, hers and Ted's, in the next six months or so, by her own estimate—and gain her degree at the same time. Ted's job helped their financial situation immensely, although he was teaching classes of rowdy adolescent boys without the slightest interest in drama or literature of any kind. His towering physical presence and forceful personality worked their magic on the reluctant boys; and he soon had them writing ballads, building bull rings for plays, and reading Russian history. But the job itself had to have been ultimately depressing, if for no other reason than it distracted him from concentrating on his poetry at a crucial period in his development. Unlike Sylvia, he was never one for disguises or undue obeisance to social amenities, having scrawled "writer" boldly on their wedding certificate in contrast to her more modest "student"; and he fought against the idea of teaching as a profession.

Meanwhile, Sylvia had returned to the routine of school work, bicycling to classes, often ten miles a day, spending countless hours in the library, attending lectures and seminars, having conferences with her supervisors (Dorothea Krook, now her closest female friend at Cambridge, gave her an extra hour each week), writing papers, and generally laboring hard to master Part II of the tripos. All of this was in addition to putting their little flat into order. Sylvia had found the place grimed by dust and dirt and many years of neglect, and lost little time in attacking its accumulated filth. In letters back home she complained that England's history was written in dust and that the English themselves were secretly the dirtiest race on the face of the earth.

Ted worked with her to make the flat presentable by helping to paint the living room and the myriad of fireplace bricks a pale blue, and building a five-shelf bookcase out of pine boards. They also purchased a secondhand, indigo-blue sofa and yellow lamps and polished the dark brown woodwork and furniture already there. It became a charming and comfortable first home for them, although far too cramped for two such tall people; but Sylvia resented the fact that she had to spend so much time simply battling the dirt and keeping warm. She deeply missed conveniences she had taken for granted in America like central heating, frozen food, stoves with heat regulators, refrigerators, carpet sweepers, and pipes that did not fall apart. Thus she looked forward eagerly to June and the end of her Cambridge career, when they would be returning to Wellesley for a reception at her mother's house and, if at all possible, jobs teaching in the United States at the college level for both of them.

The cold is what bothered Sylvia the most, as it had the year before—the damp British cold that ate into her bones and forced her frequently to walk around the flat in heavy sweaters or to sit for hours on end before the coal fire in the living room. It was at this coal fire that she had to heat water for the weekly ordeal of her bath—one that never really warmed her in any significant way as her breath came out in clouds as she took it. The cold, and the nagging belief that nothing ever became totally clean or dry, helped convince her that America was where they had to live. She had the added excuse that England was no fit place in which to raise children (as bad teeth and poor dentists proved); and in addition it groaned under the burden of a dead literature presided over by academics.

The problem was securing jobs in America. On December 17, 1956, she wrote a letter to Robert Gorham Davis, then chairman of the English department at Smith, asking if there would be an opening for her on the staff for the 1957–1958 semesters.[1] Her request was eventually answered in the affirmative, due in no small measure to her extraordinary record at Smith and the warm recommendations of former teachers such as Mary Ellen Chase. As for Ted, the chances were less sanguine. His British education, and lack of American reputation as a poet, were against him—a situation Sylvia thought scandalous, although his work was already beginning to appear with fair regularity in American journals.

Another cheering prospect before them constantly that winter was a five-week vacation in a cabin on the "blessed Cape" near Orleans, paid for by Aurelia as a belated wedding present. That, the job at Smith, and simply the whole idea of returning to America—she looked forward to the time, or so she wrote to friends, when she and Ted could share their active social life with her mother—thrilled Sylvia so that none of the exhausting demands of her new role could do more than temporarily depress her. Further, she and Ted were writing and discussing poetry, sharing technical knowledge, working out exercises on set themes, reading aloud to one another. Ted, whose poetic talent was far more mature than his wife's at this juncture, wrote several of the poems, such as "Famous Poet" and "The Martyrdom of Bishop Farrar," that would help make *The Hawk in the Rain* an unusual first collection. The latter, in particular, with its accent on the gruesome details of the Bishop's flaming demise and stubborn will, helped shake up the staid, neo-Georgian world of British poetry: "out of his eyes,/ Out of his mouth, fire like glory broke."

Ted was fortunate in another way also. He had managed to secure freelance work with the British Broadcasting Company by reading the poetry of Yeats and his own work on the air. The rates were generous, if uncertain—about $3.00 a minute in actual reading time; but more important, the programs were providing him with an outlet to a much larger audience than the one which read *Gemini* and other Cambridge magazines. His unique use of fierce metaphors and concentration upon what Philip McCurdy would accurately characterize later as his "biological shock technique," went over well on the air, especially as delivered in Ted's restrained, deeply masculine voice.

Sylvia herself was rapidly moving beyond the banal acquiescence of her "bridal bouquets" in the closing months of 1956, discovering stronger and less artificial ways of yoking her negative insights into the universe's soul-destroying processes to the ordinary flotsam of daily existence. Three poems from this period are worth looking at for their ability to endure as literary compositions on their own merits, irrespective of their author's biography: "Watercolour of Grantchester Meadows," "Black Rooks in Rainy Weather," and "All the Dead Dears"—three extremely effective poems having their original locus in familiar Cambridge scenes.

In the first poem, the universe's malevolence is located in the attitudes of rural complacency so evidently cloistered in the tame landscape outside her flat's window; in Rupert Brooke's nostalgic, sentimentally hazed meadows; in Cambridge's tradition-haunted "lawns and willows, the old trees in the old gardens, the obscure bowling greens, the crooked lanes with their glimpses of cornices and turrets, the low dark opening out on to sunny grass," which Lytton Strachey had so lovingly celebrated a half-century earlier. "Watercolour of Grantchester Meadows" is precisely that, done in quiet pastels to suit the terrain—pale, restrained, almost motionless. The careful phraseology perfectly captures the pastoral setting as in "a country on a nursery plate." Innocuous elements, more pretty than true, hold sway until the final two lines. For the last stanza is a slap in the face and denies everything preceding it. A water rat is introduced first, and he does not quite fit the pervading atmosphere; but he slips so naturally into place, sawing down a reed and swimming lazily "from his limber grave," that the poem's still surface is only slightly disturbed. Unaware of his existence, nearby students "stroll or sit/ Hands laced, in a moon indolence of love." They have restored the scene's reflective calm. But their black gowns clash with the pallid pastels already imposed. With restrained skill, Sylvia has subtly prepared the reader for the tragic, albeit "natural," climax:

> How in such mild air
> The owl shall stoop from his turret, the rat cry out.

It is an effective slashing apart of the entire pastoral scene established by earlier lines. Love, like evil, cannot exist in such a *real* milieu, which is why the students remain unaware of the murder at their feet. Imagination, too, which is actually the major subject of the poem, remains helpless before the brute fact of nature; and the painting prior to the final two lines is false because it does not touch upon the reality beneath.

The excellence of "Watercolour at Grantchester Meadows," as well as of "Black Rooks in Rainy Weather," indicates a maturing of Sylvia's art after marriage, either as the result of her husband's influence or perhaps simply as the next organic stage of growth. And yet true brilliance does not emerge until she mates her serious thematic concerns and technical mastery with an obsessive center point, as will be seen in the poems dealing with her father. The first indication of the kind of intensity which could result from such a mating is evident in "All the Dead Dears," one of the few genuine masterpieces from the late stages of her relentless apprenticeship.

During several jaunts into the town of Cambridge, Sylvia had spent time at the Archeological Museum, an interest she shared with Ted, and was struck particularly by an exhibit on the main floor—a huge stone coffin, face-up, covered by glass, in which lay the remains of a woman. It had been found among the Roman burials at Arbury Road in Cambridge in 1952. The catalogue card attached to the exhibit explained what it contained: "Apart from some fragments of textiles remaining from the shroud in which the body had been wrapped, and the skeletons of a shrew and a mouse, no objects were found with the bones of the woman buried in this double coffin of stone and lead. A.D. 400." A further message instructed the viewer to "note distal end (near foot) of left tibia, which has been gnawed."

Sylvia noted all, and new emotional chords were set humming in her own mind and heart by the pathetic skeletons of the woman and her two tiny coffin-mates. The exhibit's grisly impact drove Sylvia's inbred sense of craft to reach beyond the "well-wrought urn" and touch her strong, if ambivalent, feelings about father and mother, about woman's role in history and society, and about life's intrinsic absurdity. The point of the tableau emerges in the second stanza, where the poet envisions the three skeletons as bearing "Dry witness/ To the gross eating game." A Darwinian evolution outside human control is again the evil villain that Sylvia wants to impress upon her reader. It is a process he might wink at if he did not, like the poet, hear the stars "grinding, crumb by crumb,/ Our own grist down to its bony face." The image sharply conveys the central horror of a death-masked universe gnawing away nightly at human flesh and consciousness. Here the language, organic in Dylan Thomas's and Ted Hughes's use of it, is sparse, kinetic, viciously capable of leaving the poem behind; it is the language of a different Plath. Politeness and academicism are entirely absent. The next stanza shifts with pathological logic from kinship to the narrator's terrified perception of the female skeleton reaching back, ancestor upon ancestor, mother upon mother, "to haul me in." The phrase suggests fishing and Sylvia wisely elaborates on it. An image "looms under the fishpond surface," and the murkiness of its mirror is not completely dispelled by identifying the spot as where "the daft father went down/ With orange duck-feet winnowing his hair—."

The father figure is thus dramatically introduced, drowned of course, as in "Lament" and many later poems—a fragment of Sylvia's fixation; but his appearance and peculiar situation have only a tenuous thematic connection to what went before, that is, as a "natural" expansion of the family trinity to include mother, father, daughter.

Later, after she had fashioned her own highly individualized conversational style, Sylvia would make known her abhorrence of any poetry which came straight from the heart without the benefit of mediating intelligence or craft. To avoid the unfiltered personal experience in poetry that could easily become "a kind of shut box and mirror-looking narcissistic experience," she always maintained that her own work, while confessionally concerned with a private "vision of the apocalypse," was intrinsically involved with the world's endless apocalypses, whether at Auschwitz or Hiroshima; that her poems about "a child forming itself finger by finger in the dark" and "about the bleakness of the moon over a yew tree in a neighborhood graveyard" were actually attempts to preserve and re-emphasize the value of "loving" and "making in all forms" in a nurturing environment constantly menaced by awesome convulsions.[2]

In "All the Dead Dears" birth and death, the poles of nature's catastrophic electrical reality, are fused; both have equal value and lack of it. Life itself possesses no solid meaning; and the museum's scientific detachment, like more immediate funeral rites, cannot protect us from the death-grip of the dead, no matter how intently or dryly it tries. Not only are people and their frail existence belittled mercilessly here, but they are relegated in the end to the same category as mouse and shrew. The poem's negative function as truth-teller and soothsayer indicates Sylvia's growing understanding of a need and desire for personal revelation. Reversing Kant, she wanted revelation without religion; and the result was a complete and moving poetic expression that took full advantage of her sardonic wit.

Departures, changes, an alien society—these were some of the factors that probably helped move Sylvia closer to a personal voice, along with the more positive influences of a poet-husband and the prospect of a return to Smith. But leaving Whitsted had to have its own disturbing impact, for it was both a real and symbolic step away from cloistered femininity and a college mother into the hands of a male stranger and father figure. By strange coincidence, the girl taking over Sylvia's room at Whitsted was May Targett, a graduate of Smith in 1952 who had worked briefly with her on *Scan*, the college newspaper. They had never really known each other, but May recognized Sylvia immediately when they lined up for dinner and introduced herself. The two girls laughed over the fact that they were both wearing Bonnie Doones, brightly colored, knee-length socks. Even back at Smith during their brief contact, May had always sensed in Sylvia "a more normal kind of person trying to emerge, being bright, pretty and efficient all at the same time."

Sylvia was leaving Whitsted before the end of the first term, and May called on her to discover the precise date. Sylvia was friendly and obviously happy over having found the flat near Grantchester Meadows. She talked briefly about her writing and mentioned that she was working on sketches of Cambridge life for *The New Yorker*. She also emoted over the fact that she was proud to have a husband and that he "was going to provide for her" and "had talent of a caliber she could actually look up to."

May met Ted himself in Sylvia's room on one occasion and immediately sensed "he wasn't my cup of tea." But she also felt he was rather appealing, "a large, gangling, pretty British" fellow who never seemed to know where to put his feet. To her his whole attitude was "informal" in a way that clearly clashed with Cambridge's reserved atmosphere. The marriage, however, seemed to May to have a necessary kind of balance to it as Sylvia "with this American calm about doing things" complemented her husband's more erratic approach to life and literature. "I always had the feeling that Ted needed her more than he realized, that the growth of his poetry could use someone like her to talk a lot of things over with."

The marriage was certainly productive as the young couple arose each morning at five to work on their own poetry before leaving for work and school. That "ruthless efficiency" which had carried Sylvia so successfully through a busy academic, social, and literary world in the past now saw her easily through the exhausting hardships of her new life. She approached her many duties with good-natured discipline and envisioned herself in undramatic terms as a "good, plain, very resourceful woman." Wendy Campbell, who had dinner with the Hugheses at their flat on more than one occasion, was impressed by the apparent ease of Sylvia's shifts between the menial reality of her marriage and the rarefied atmosphere of scholarship: "If she wrote an essay it was effortlessly good, if she kept house it was done easily and well, and she even cooked superbly, with enthusiasm and discrimination, and she enjoyed it almost as much as she enjoyed eating."

But opposition to the marriage continued to be something of a social problem. It was during Sylvia's second year at Cambridge that Mary Ellen Chase and her companion Miss Duckworth suddenly appeared on campus after having detoured from their continental destination to see how their brilliant protégée was doing.[3] Miss Chase was dismayed to find Sylvia married, though she tried not to show it; and Sylvia sensed in her "an enemy to her marriage" whom she would still have to court and associate with back at Smith. Miss Chase had finally retired after more than thirty years of active teaching, however, and Sylvia would at least not have the additional burden of her as a colleague in the English department. Again, in Sylvia's mind, her kind mentor was but another image of Miss Burton and the countless other elderly spinster figures who had always tried to impress their sterile life styles upon her own.

To Jane, Miss Chase seemed slightly unfriendly "to the idea of Ted Hughes" rather than to Ted Hughes the person; but Ted himself did nothing to relieve the old professor's anxieties about Sylvia when he laughed at the notion of himself working at anything other than writing. Back home in Northampton, Miss Chase would let her true feelings about Sylvia's husband become well known. As Professor Gibian recalls: "First came the report from Mary Ellen Chase, who visited her in Cambridge. Miss Chase was an old-school feminist. Teaching was the highest thing a woman could do, and getting married the lowest. . . . Chase came back from her visit saying not only had Sylvia gotten married, but that when she asked her husband whether he too would teach, Ted is reported to have said: 'God no, no! Well, maybe I will teach some day, but only as a last resort, if I am starving and find nothing else.' "[4]

Formal opposition aside, and Miss Chase did generously support Sylvia's application to teach at Smith despite her serious reservations about Ted, the marriage was a success on almost every level. Sylvia relished the idea of being married to someone she could not dominate— who even might manhandle her if sufficiently aroused—and Ted savored the benefits of having a young and attractive wife who could talk with him about his first love, poetry, and act as his private secretary and press agent as well as cook and housekeeper. Both of them built up a collection of poetry in the hope of a first book, and Sylvia continued to promote her husband's work with all the guile and determination at her command. An interesting example of how she worked on Ted's behalf concerns *The Hawk in the Rain* which, by October, was already in final form.

It was a cool evening in October, while still at Whitsted and presumably unmarried as far as the authorities were aware, that an unescorted Sylvia attended a party given by the English Speaking Union at Cambridge. John Press, a young man in charge of the local British Council office, was there with a view to keeping in touch with overseas students for the Council, and he has provided an account of what took place:[5]

The room was crowded, the noise terrific, and at about a quarter to seven I reckoned that I'd done my duty, and could take my leave. Then, somehow, I found myself talking to a delightful girl, with long fair hair and big eyes. All thoughts of leaving the party were abandoned. We talked for a few minutes about nothing in particular, and then we got on to English literature. The girl's name was Sylvia Plath; she had come over with a Fulbright; she was at Newnham reading for the English tripos; and she was particularly interested in poetry.

She asked me if I knew of a young English poet called Ted Hughes, and when I answered that I didn't she laughed and said there was no reason why I should as he hadn't been published in England. "But he's had a few poems printed in good American periodicals. I send them over to the States for him. He really is a very good poet. He's my fiancé, but that's not why I say he's a good poet."

We suddenly noticed that it was about 7:15 and that most people had gone. My companion looked a little bit worried. "I shall never make it back to Newnham for Hall." So I told her that we were living not far from Newnham, and I was sure that she'd be welcome to come home for supper. I telephoned my wife, who said there wasn't much in the house, but she could dish up some scrambled eggs.

As we walked through the streets of Cambridge, Sylvia Plath asked how a poet could get published in England. I explained that the only way was to go through the routine of sending poems to periodicals, getting some of them accepted (with luck) and after a while submitting a collection to a publisher. Then I asked her if she was going to send Ted Hughes' poems to the New York Poetry Center, which was offering a prize for the best collection of work by an unpublished poet under thirty. No, she'd never heard of this award, but could I tell her all about it? I said that I'd give her the details when we reached home.

We had supper and I looked up the announcement of the Poetry Center award in, I think, the *London Magazine*. I can't remember what we talked about, but I can vividly recall the impression she made on me—I thought her intelligent, vital and charming. My wife said that she seemed clever and attractive, but that she slightly over-played the eager, wide-eyed American girl, and put on a bit of an Alice-in-Wonderland act.

Early in 1957 I got a letter from Sylvia Plath, in which she announced that

Ted Hughes had won the Poetry Center award and that Faber were bringing out Ted's collection. She was sorry she'd deceived me on one point—she had been married and not engaged to Ted when we met, but she was afraid she might lose her Fulbright if it were known that she was married. But everything was fine now, and I must call on them for coffee one morning and meet Ted.

The judges of the contest, an Anglo-American event, were Stephen Spender, W. H. Auden, and Marianne Moore; and Ted got the telegram notifying him of the award in March 1957. Winning the prize also meant publication of *The Hawk in the Rain* in August by Harper's. Even more exciting, the Center's Director stressed how enthusiastic everyone concerned had been about the book. From Ted's point of view, equally exciting had to be Faber's decision to handle English publication, for it was the firm where T. S. Eliot still functioned as an editor—Ted and Sylvia would come to know him a few years later when he worked with Ted on a children's book.

It was in April also that Sylvia officially learned that she had been given a post as freshman English instructor at Smith. The idea frightened and enthralled her in even measures. On the positive side, she enjoyed the prospect of teaching authors who had meant so much to her own development and the realization that she would no longer have to depend upon the financial uncertainties of grants, prizes, and the like for maintenance. But she was also nervous about returning to Smith, where her students would be only six or seven years younger than she, and her colleagues the same idols she had once worshipped and cultivated.

The Hugheses' general future plan, or at least Sylvia's version of it, called for them to work hard in America for a few years and save money in order to travel to Italy or Spain where they could live cheaply for a whole year and concentrate exclusively on their writing. Afterwards, they could begin having children—many of them. The latter was one of Sylvia's obsessions and Ted appeared to tolerate it; but the enthusiasm was all hers. Years later it would become a crucial element in the disintegration of their marriage.

Ted himself remains a vague, perhaps distorted figure during the Cambridge year of their marriage, and most accounts of him are either from hostile sources or from people who did not know him personally. Sylvia herself appeared to delight in emphasizing his wilder, bohemian aspects, as is evident in her relating to Valerie Pitt the incident about his drinking from a broken bottle. This incident, which took place in Whitsted immediately prior to or right after their marriage, was witnessed by Jane Kopp. Ted had come over to Sylvia's room after a bout of drinking with Lucas Meyers, during the course of which they had fantasized about constructing their own utopia. Ted brought along a bottle of wine to share with Sylvia. Once there, however, he discovered that she had no corkscrew available, and went barging down the hall in search of one. He banged on the first door he came to and yelled out, "Do you have a corkscrew?"

He was, unfortunately, disturbing Christine M. S. Abbot, "an exceedingly severe and correct little woman"—in fact, a rather terrifying moral watchdog of the dormitory who had a hatred for drink and did not hesitate to let her feelings be known. She opened the door and replied with a very cold negative. Ted stared at her in dumbfound silence for a few moments and then suddenly brought the neck of the bottle down on Miss Abbot's doorknob, shattering the top and spilling some wine on the floor at their feet. With that, he turned and slowly walked back to Sylvia's room. Uncharacteristically, Miss Abbot never said a word or reported Ted to the authorities—either too shocked by the unexpected violence or frightened at what such a barbarian might do to her in retaliation.

It is a minor anecdote, though perhaps not from Miss Abbot's perspective, but it does give some insight into Ted's personality. Being used to the rough folkways of Yorkshire, where farmers and mill hands accepted violence as a natural expression of the wildness all around them, he could not adapt with Sylvia's facility to the refined and frequently remote mores of an academic society generations removed from nature—at least not without rebelling from time to time.

Rebellion is the key word. Ted Hughes's poetry is riddled with rebellion, and he was attempting to instill the same vigorous directness into his young wife's poetry—sensing, no doubt, that the brittle verbal convolutions of her early verse reflected the thick layers of Audenesque culture she had absorbed at Smith and Cambridge. The success of his attempts is clearly evident in the three poems discussed earlier and in several other poems written during the first year of their marriage, particularly "Hardcastle Crags," "Sow," and "Dream with Clam Diggers."

To relieve the oppressive confinement of their tight daily schedule, and the smallness of their cramped little room, the Hughses took frequent trips into the English countryside. Naturally, Ted's Yorkshire and its moors were a favorite locale for their nature walks. One of the places visited there was Hardcastle Crags, a narrow valley in the Pennines of West Yorkshire which, significantly, marks the southern boundary of the moorland used by Emily Brontë in *Wuthering Heights*, a novel which comes closest in freakish intensity to the poetry of *Ariel* and *Winter Trees*. The poem that resulted is an effective conflation of the two themes which had streaked through Sylvia's poetry from the beginning: vast natural forces beating down feeble human individuality and the private dilemma of a sensitive female captured in the talons of a universe without meaning or redemption. The images of "Hardcastle Crags" are sharp and organic in the best sense, and carry the poem's growing sense of panic and despair without the least strain. The sudden alterations of accentual rhythms and the frequent harsh stops and clotted consonants simulate the ominous visual and emotional setting.

Sylvia has once more made explicit her conception of nature as a hostile, foreign force too vast for human interference or ultimate comprehension, but this time she has also shown a disinclination to succumb to its overwhelming power. The frightening despair so evident in the climaxes of many previous poems has been shifted to the main body of the work and then denied, though somewhat weakly, in the abrupt conclusion, in the persona's escape. Her voracious mind and its secular awareness of amoral infinity has found a moment's peace, perhaps because of the security engendered by her marriage and apparently bright new future life.

Not far from the old village used as a backdrop for "Hardcastle Crags," a local farmer took great delight in exhibiting his prize, massive hog for all interested visitors, among them Ted and Sylvia. The sight of the huge beast inspired Sylvia to write "Sow," a self-conscious but generally efficient poem that moves naturally from the simple courage of "Hardcastle Crags" to a determined effort at structuring a human myth about a gigantic villain capable of being understood (where nature could not) and thus opposed by a human mentality. Yet here too she is creating a monstrous analogue for the anility of nature, imposing not the imagination of science, relativity, but of art, allegory. With the same tight control of imagery and meter shown in "Hardcastle Crags," but without that poem's occasional lapses into unconvincing abstractions, Sylvia uses "Sow" as a sort of showcase for her linguistic talents. Phrases such as "Mire-smirched, blowzy" and "Brobdingnag bulk" playfully convey the animal's rough dirtiness, its gross "grisly" being recalling the giant in "Snowman on the Moor," while other, more conventional onomatopoeic images, "a jocular fist thwacked the barrel nape" and "Prodigious in gluttonies," emphasize the pig's grandiose, omnivorous rotundity. The language brutally clogs the reader's palate until his mind's tongue can barely contain its burden, which parallels the whole poem's determined progression from a human-scaled reality towards a larger-than-life myth.

In retrospect, "Sow" appears as the first in a series of poems striving to create a central myth of evil for the complex powers of the old enemy nature and its massive processes of life and death. Sylvia may have felt the need to begin formulating a poetic, mythic equivalent for nature's vast reality, a human configuration dramatically huge enough to replace Milton's and Dante's obsolete Satan; and, in the crude Yorkshire farmer's pig, she sensed the initial step. After "Sow" and "The Bull of the Bendylaw," she would shift the essence of her massive demon from the animal world, already remote to the twentieth century, to the modern machines of "Night Walk" and then, with psychological logic, complete the final step of identifying this mechanical evil with nothing less than her own titanic father obsession in "The Colossus" and a group of related poems.

There would be many other intervening poems, of course, and poems that strayed into other themes; but the underlying pattern is there: a straightforward progression that helps explain the final stages of Sylvia's first phase as a poet, the development of a personal voice that permits a confessional impulse its mythic dignity and power. "Sow" concludes with another transformation, of the prize hog, whom the owner treats so cavalierly throughout, suggesting alternate themes of women being mistreated as mere breeding stock by a male society and a mocking of the marital order celebrated in the bridal poems:

> A monument
> Prodigious in gluttonies as that hog whose want
> Made lean Lent
>
> Of kitchen slops and, stomaching no constraint,
> Proceeded to swill
> The seven troughed seas and every earthquaking continent.

The references are clear and deliberate, and the central symbol has been fleshed-in with all the trappings of classical legend. Christian allegory and ritualistic belief cannot contain the devil-like hog's vast proportions, and the entire earth has become but "kitchen slops" for his voracious appetite. Here is a magnificent titan of an enemy we can hate and fear with sanity. For if he is relegated to the class of childhood ogres, he can then perhaps be comprehended with the remnants of our innocence—an innocence which the poet must preserve for us. If Satan is dead along with God, Sylvia's sow can replace him by being projected into closets and dark corners. From a stylistic point of view the poem is torn between the patently literary method of the bridal poems and countless previous endeavors and the more personal voice sounded by "Black Rooks in Rainy Weather" and "Hardcastle Crags." Sylvia's fear of the sexual reality and demands of love, as well as of its arrogant implication of defying fate, had not been completely subjugated by marriage, however, and in "Dream with Clam Diggers" she strives to face this fear in the context of a dream. But the dream façade or situation does not hide the harsh reality of the speaker's predicament, and perversely stresses its inner horror instead. Sylvia succeeds in bringing her poetry in line with atavistic fears and achieves thereby at least a portion of its dark potential. Moreover, she has allowed her natural Gothic bent full rein.

This impulse or steady undercurrent—which might be called "the American Gothic" for want of a better term—entailed a sense of life that brooded remorselessly upon the horror within and behind the American Dream and its vision of "an almost chosen people." It was aware always of the possibility of sin, of Indian massacres and slave cargoes, of corruption and decay as the normal processes of existence. Allegory and melodrama were its natural forms of expression, and the idea of original sin its main motivation in art—that is, a concept of human imperfection, or unseen psychological demons who originated not in hell but in the souls of men. Constructed upon the terrifying incapacity of admirable social and political intentions to eradicate either life's basic futility or man's innate corruption, the American Gothic has consistently provided a metaphysical concept of the universe which, though negative, did leave room for transcendence and did provide American literature with several authentic masterpieces: Poe's existential short stories, Melville's *Moby Dick*, Hawthorne's *The Scarlet Letter*, Lowell's *Life Studies* and, more recently, several of Joyce Carol Oates' chilling tales.

Sylvia was no doubt cognizant of this strain in American literature, and pursued it relentlessly on both a conscious and unconscious level, finding its dark insights congenial to her own psychological and aesthetic disposition. Though often clumsy (and too frightened of ultimate social and personal cost) in the early stages of her development to confront and utilize all its deeper aspects, Sylvia's poetry never swerved from the idea of the road to the sublime as being that through hell, which is why she had reacted so enthusiastically to Lawrence's *Studies in Classic American Literature* at Smith and why Robert Lowell would become such a potent force in the forging of her final style. Her particular demon was the absence of real demons, or rather her need to look into a mirror to find the demon of another self. Her purgation, as "Dream with Clam Diggers" begins to suggest, would have to come in the metaphorical flames of her own mind's self-devouring fury at a world without meaning.

Sylvia's future aesthetic during her second year at Cambridge was as yet unanchored to a firm personal voice. The bitch goddess was repressed as she had never been before by the young wife enjoying the advantages of her new role and the pleasures of a shared future. Sylvia even began attempting to make up for her lack of a social perspective and to overcome her lack of knowledge in such fields as anthropology, archeology, politics, and history. In November of 1956 England was convulsed by arguments over Anthony Eden's move into Egypt, the invasion of that country by England, France, and Israel. At Cambridge, the debate was particularly furious as moral and political realities tended to separate partisans from their original positions. Conservatives and Liberals often reacted according to nationalistic motives rather than party ideology.

Sylvia saw the whole complicated and intense situation as a straightforward morality play and took John Foster Dulles's own self-righteous attitude towards the crisis. To her England was wrong and should have withdrawn immediately as it had violated another country's sovereignty for mere material gain. Her whole American education, and personal liberal convictions, told her that the English and French position was abhorrent in the extreme, and she let her feelings be known. Stanley Kahrl, Lameyer's old friend from the Navy whose wedding Sylvia had attended, came to Cambridge in the fall of 1956 to pursue a B.A. in English. Sylvia looked him up and renewed their friendship. "By then she had broken up with Gordon, and was seeing Ted Hughes. I remember her telling us that she had married him, and that she hadn't told her College authorities, as she might be thrown out if they knew."

The most vivid scene involving Sylvia that remained in Kahrl's mind was in connection with the Suez crisis: "We had invited a few friends to a sherry party. The group included some English rowing friends in Trinity College, graduates of Eton, all quite unintellectual Tories, and Sylvia and Ted Hughes. Either that day, or the day before, I forget which, the Suez War had broken out in earnest. Sylvia was completely appalled at the callous attack launched by the French and English, and arrived full of indignation. . . . antagonism towards the invasion was just as widespread among Conservatives as it was among Laborites.

However, at that party most of our English friends had completed their National Service, some in the Navy, some in the Rifle Brigade, and tended to support the invasion. Sylvia got into a flaming argument with one of the men in particular. . . . It created quite a scene, a scene repeated many times in England that evening, however." Kahrl indicated that Sylvia's debate at the party was "in such strong terms" as to stop all other conversation.

There is a startling contrast here between Sylvia's behavior at Cambridge and the total lack of interest in politics and world affairs evident during her Smith days. Although hardly significant at this point, this attitude does indicate a growing awareness of the need for a more rounded intellectual life. In the years ahead, she would view political commitments as personal extensions of herself and become a dedicated Liberal. Her last phase as a poet would also demand and utilize just such a political awareness—a sense of suffering as a community experience rather than something merely personal. Thus came her eventual realization that a revolt by the Algerians against the ruling French government in the early 1960's and the massacre of the Jews in the 1940's could and did have direct links with the private agonies of a modern lyric poet.

Ted shared Sylvia's liberal leanings. His working-class background had instilled a permanent distrust of Tory policies, but he was less likely to project his views in a public gathering. Kahrl's only memory of him is as a "tall and silent" figure who faded into the crowd, or as much as such an imposing figure could manage to become unnoticeable—always "rather quiet" when around Sylvia's friends at Cambridge. Sylvia herself, he noticed, "didn't seem awfully at ease with English girls"; and he thought her "supercilious," if "rather quiet" herself, on most occasions. But she talked easily and was "intellectually sharp." Sylvia and Kahrl attended several lectures together, and he recalled that "her response to some of the lectures was acute." Oddly, having taken the English Moralists course with her, and that on tragedy as well, he thought that her strong reaction to Dorothea Krook was not all favorable. Kahrl felt that Sylvia "respected her" a great deal, but also condemned her for being "all intellect, an Aristotelian who didn't give any room to the spirit." [6]

Sylvia's poetry helps to define her inner dynamics, since it remained central to her and Ted's marriage and separate existences, but it has to be viewed cautiously. What is fascinating, and occasionally amusing, is how Sylvia's poems and stories from the first year of her marriage often deny her public humility and suggest that the erasing of selves was not as complete or sincere as it seemed. In the poem "Soliloquy of the Solipsist," for instance, which might be seen as a good-natured reply to her husband's "Soliloquy of a Misanthrope" from *The Hawk in the Rain*, Sylvia returns to the total subjectivity of "Mad Girl's Love Song"—it, by the way, appeared on the same page as "Soliloquy of the Solipsist" in the May 1957 issue of *Granta*. The "I" here carefully establishes its powers to create and destroy the world at will, to "Make houses shrink," and to "boycott color and forbid any flower/ To be"; and then uses the fourth and final stanza to affirm supremacy: "All your beauty, all your wit, is a gift, my dear,/ From me."

Such a response to Ted's domination, however playful, does imply a continued awareness of the necessity for preserving some ultimate self against the eroding forces of both love and myth-making. Sylvia realized that Ted's genius and growing success, which she was laboring so hard to ensure, carried with it always the threat of complete absorption in the very realm—art itself—where identity remained crucial. Two complementary pieces—a poem, "The Shrike," and a short story called "The Wishing Box"—attacked this theme from the same perspective: that of a young wife jealous of her husband's obviously superior imaginative powers. In the poem, which is a fierce and direct effort evidently influenced by Ted's language and use of compounds, Sylvia's "envious bride" is the vampire-witch who lies beside her husband in a jealous rage, "Twisting curses in the tangled sheet/ With taloned fingers," while his dreams remove him from her "to wing, sleep-feathered,/ The singular air." In the morning, her response is to devour him with true shrike determination—to "Spike and suck out/ Last blood-drop of that truant heart" with her "red beak."

The parallels are easy enough to see. There is the metaphorical motif of revenge that will dominate her final poetry, and a warning to her husband of the hellish possibilities behind her dutiful mask. The fear of effacement was patently real, but in the story it has a different resolution, one that harkens back to Sylvia's suicide attempt. The bride (Agnes) in this case, only three months married, lacks the shrike's male ("red beak") sense of power; and, when her husband Harold, an accountant with literary aspirations, leaves her each night for his vivid dream world, she can only brood and feel left out as a strange jealousy grows on her "like some dark, malignant cancer." Desperately, she turns to Harold himself for aid. He tries to help her by getting her to participate in an exercise. She must shut her eyes and imagine a goblet, and then embellish it with colors and rustic emblems. But this effort does not succeed. Agnes tries other stimuli, like reading book after book, only to discover that "as soon as she lifted her eyes from the printed matter at hand, it was as if a protecting world extinguished." Visual images are no better. The movies merely lull her into a "rhythmic trance" and the television set, which she cajoles Harold into purchasing on time payments, is superior only in that "she could drink sherry" while watching it. Agnes rapidly becomes an alcoholic, and Harold consults a doctor on her behalf, who dismisses insomnia as "a bit of a nervous strain" and provides a bottle of sleeping pills. At story's end, Agnes takes the inevitable last journey, swallows fifty pills, and lies on the sofa to die. Here Harold finds her when he comes home from work: "Her tranquil features were set in a slight, secret smile of triumph, as if, in some far country unattainable to mortal men, she were, at last, waltzing with the dark, red-caped prince of her early dreams."

As a story, "The Wishing Box" is competent, though somewhat over-written and thin on characterization; but as a seismograph of the subterranean tremors in Sylvia's unconscious it vibrates with ramifications. The touchstones from the past are easily recognized—the insomnia, the inability to create, the incompetent male doctor, the bottle of fifty pills, the final escape as an act of revenge. All this might simply be the result of Sylvia's innate inability to invent narrative structures, but the contemporary elements suggest much more. Though Harold seems remote from Ted Hughes' powerful figure, Sylvia insists upon the correspondence: Harold's most frequent dreams deal with a fox and a giant pike. Also, eerily, the story foreshadows Sylvia's actual response to Ted's abandonment and betrayal less than six years later. First there will be the shrike's violent attacks through her poetry and then the ultimate revenge of suicide itself. Character and fate here, in the Greek sense of their absolute binding, are certainly one.

On the other hand, success remained important to her; or in Jane's words she was still "very dependent on external measures of success." An aspect of that dependence may have been the public effort to paint her marriage as a union of two literary giants. Thus she wrote to friends about the perfection of her marriage and the Herculean proportions of her husband—the man she could not boss around, "a big, handsome bearish brute of a man." Thus she mounted the platform at parties and in private conversation to preach his virtues and the virtues of their creative life together—breeders of art and an eventual race of similarly gifted offspring. Wendy Campbell was convinced that the young pair "seemed to have found solid ground in each other. Ted's gusto took more constructive forms and Sylvia had found a man on the same scale as herself." The remark is perceptive enough, but in the same memoir Mrs.

Campbell has characterized Sylvia as being "incapable of any sort of falsity or affectation or exaggeration." This could hardly be the same girl that Cyrilly Abels, Myron Lotz, and countless others had seen a few years earlier, all of whom had remarked on her lack of genuine openness. It was not the same girl Peter Davison admitted was "never spontaneous really, never fully herself, always trying to create an effect, to make an impression."

Yet it should be recognized that Sylvia did change in many ways after her marriage, becoming more direct and less cautious in revealing her true feelings, as witness her bold behavior at the party Stanley Kahrl had attended in October. Under the blanket security of Ted's commitment to her, she was less constrained, even while taking on all the self-effacing chores of wifehood. Jane Truslow would remark a year later that it was "quite a surprise to me to see how totally domesticated she had become with Ted." Although even in playing the wife Sylvia wore a mask, or at least approached the task with unusual intensity and "made a big thing out of it," she seemed to enjoy the final result.

In June of 1957, when she and Ted sailed for New York, the wheel had come full turn. She was back in a subordinate role, a child again in the protective arms of a father figure; but she was also still Sylvia, the emerging artist, who had already written several important poems and was about to embark upon a teaching career at the school where she had first tasted real success. In her wake, she abandoned the more prosaic masks all girls leave behind when they complete their degrees and marry—whether that of spinster, promiscuous young flirt, or uncertain wall-flower. Jane Kopp conceded that Cambridge had never really known Sylvia at all and lamented "how little I or any of us had of her stature or, much less, of her potential tragedy." She also tried to explain the effect of Sylvia on her in that particular time and in that special place: "Sylvia, for me, was a disturbing person, and I think she was for most people she came into contact with, but disturbing only in a way, at the time, that seemed normal. Being young, affectedly sophisticated and quite absorbed in ourselves, we were all somewhat unkind to others, to ourselves."

I never wanted to get married. The last thing I
wanted was infinite security and to be the place an
arrow shoots off from. I wanted change and
excitement and to shoot off in all directions myself,
like the colored arrows from a Fourth of July rocket.

The Bell Jar

12

In a Well-Steered Country

The Hugheses stayed only a few days in New York City, that once frightening metropolis now "beloved" in Sylvia's eyes, before heading north to Wellesley and the white frame house on Elmwood Road. Aurelia was delighted to see them and eager to show them off to the neighbors and her limited circle of academic friends. A reception for the couple was given near the end of June in the garden. Sylvia and her mother glowed in the company of familiar faces, but Ted retreated behind his dour Yorkshire screen when confronted by so many strangers and said very little. Wilbury Crockett recalls that several of the guests felt there was an air of condescension in his attitude.[1]

A few days later, Ted and Sylvia departed for a cabin in the pine forest of Eastham, Cape Cod, near Rock Harbor. Their life in Eastham echoed the pattern established at Benidorm as they relaxed into a serene cycle of unpressured creativity. As usual, the mornings were reserved for writing and Sylvia's sketching; and the afternoons usually consisted of a few miles of bike riding, followed by long leisurely hours at the beach. The early evenings were devoted to reading.

The poem that emerged from this pleasant interlude was "Mussel Hunter at Rock Harbour," which re-engaged Sylvia's poetic persona with the teeming marine life of the seashore she loved. Technically, it marks an important advance in her progress towards a more natural idiom. And despite the familiar plot, a return to a bleak situation in which nature again asserts its potent prerogative over lesser creatures, there is an intrinsic sense of joy informing the work; and even God, the Unitarian God of her childhood, has reappeared.

At one point in the poem, the speaker wonders if the fiddler crabs feel the mud as pleasurably under their claws as she did "between bare toes." As Sylvia already well knew, in her function as human God and artist, there is no hope for comprehension, and she ceases probing at the "passage of their/ Absolutely alien/ Order." But she also cannot cease her Eve-like transgression, namely, her search for meaning and knowledge. When the husk of a crab is discovered, she returns to the hopeless task of projecting human manifestations upon an alien life form, and wonders if it had died "recluse or suicide" or if it had been an intrepid explorer—"a headstrong Columbus crab." To grasp the emotional background of Sylvia's odd reaction here—odd in its opposition to the negative philosophy of earlier verses—it is necessary to consider a subsequent remark of Ted's about this period: "Her reactions to hurts in other people and animals, and even tiny desecrations of plant-life, were extremely violent." [2]

The existence of such an intense, broad-based sensitivity helps explain Sylvia's continual rage against what she viewed as nature's perpetual brutality. In "Mussel Hunter at Rock Harbour," probably because of the general aura of contentment inspired by her summer holiday, she rejects at least momentarily all that she had ever preached and gives in to more natural feelings of compassion and empathy. She envisions the crab-face as "etched and set there" deliberately, the way "skulls grimace" and with an "Oriental look," which leads imaginatively to the poem's best moment:

> A samurai death mask done
> On a tiger tooth, less for
> Art's sake than God's. Far from sea—

But the final stanza cannot be denied its dark resurrection of an old Plath truth as the sea's waves heave endlessly under their burden of "red-freckled crab-backs, claws/ And whole crabs, dead, their soggy/ Bellies pallid and upturned." These dismembered bodies lose even their forms, but lose them ironically "to their friendly/ Element." Only "this relic" of a crab husk left on shore manages "to face the bald-faced sun." Bald, like black, is a part of Sylvia's signature, an immediate token of sterile emptiness and oblivion, which represents the final result of

Sylvia's high school graduation picture, taken January 1950.

Philip McCurdy in 1951.

August 1952, in Chatham on Cape Cod.

Outside the Yale Bowl, in early 1953. Sylvia poses in front of the car Myron Lotz bought with his bonus money.

Late April 1953, Saturday of Derby Day weekend at Yale. Sylvia sits primly beside Jill Modlin and Myron Lotz.

Gordon Lameyer with Sylvia at Lawrence House, Smith College, 1953.

Marcia Brown, Sylvia's best friend at college, taken at Smith in February of 1954.

Sylvia standing in a field near Whitsted, at Newnham College, Cambridge, December 1955.

The flat on Primrose Hill in London (third house from the left, third floor) where the Hugheses lived before moving to Devon and where Frieda was born.

Sylvia and Ted Hughes shown featured in a January, 1959 article in *Mademoiselle,* entitled "Four Young Poets."

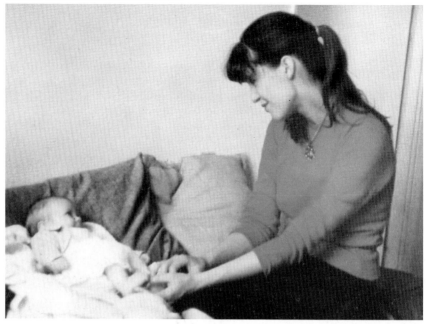

Sylvia and Frieda, taken in the summer of 1960 in their London flat by Myron Lotz.

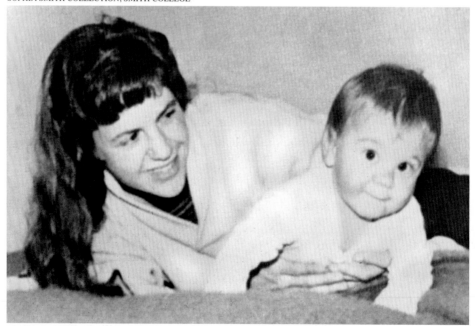

Sylvia with Nicholas, taken in the Devon house, 1962.

A rear vew of the Hughes' thatched cottage in Devon.

Sylvia with Nicholas and Frieda in the yard of her Devon cottage. Taken in August 1962, the day after the telephone incident.

Sylvia's tombstone, set amid the grass and flowers of Yorkshire, reads: "In memory / Sylvia Plath Hughes / 1932-1963 / Even amidst fierce flames / The golden lotus can be planted."

physical creation as well as the artist's central fear. The crab left on shore, an emblem of the poet's own crusade against nature, has escaped the mass indignity of its companions' fate and now must confront a worse punishment, namely, destruction by the merciless sun; *but* (and this conjunction defines Sylvia's entire poetic career) it does so in its own form and on its own terms.

It is interesting to compare "Mussel Hunter at Rock Harbour" to "Green Rock, Winthrop Bay," which was written somewhat later in the year and seems to deal with the same return to Winthrop encompassed by "Dream with Clam Diggers." Although much weaker than the other two, "Green Rock, Winthrop Bay" has the value of suggesting that Sylvia's return to America might have led to a further maturity of the awareness that myth, like childhood, cannot survive in contact with reality. The speaker in the poem presents her Winthrop Bay in negative terms from beginning to end—which explains the singular absence of dramatic tension—in an obvious catalogue of disgust at what has happened to the childhood shore she had departed from fifteen years before, the place of so many happy memories and dreams. Everything is smaller, "periwinkles, shrunk to common/ Size," and less impressive. The gulls sound thin in "the traffic of planes" from Logan Airport across the bay, and Sylvia is left with the scant consolation, a "loophole" really, that time could be blamed for "the rock's dwarfed lump, for the drabbled scum,/ For a churlish welcome."

Sylvia is reminding herself that you can't go home again, but her life at this point was predicated on just the opposite proposition. Disappointment was inevitable. The first signs of trouble came early. After leaving Rock Harbor and arriving at Northampton in late August, Ted and Sylvia soon realized that even the simple matter of finding an apartment was in itself a major undertaking. Memories of their dreadful flat-hunting days at Cambridge the year before must have returned to haunt both of them as they went from agent to agent in search of quarters that would be reasonably cheap and not too far away from the college.

The apartment they finally found was on Elm Street, across from the town's high school. Although the rent was far too high in Sylvia's view (she still had not adjusted to the sky-rocketing prices which had greeted her return to America), she felt the $85 a month was worth it, especially as utilities were included and the landlord had recently redecorated the place and installed a "very tiny" new kitchen.

It was not home in any sense, particularly since they were once again living with a stranger's furniture, but the addition of their own books helped to give the rooms a more comfortable feeling. Very few apartments would have really suited them, but it did seem as if the first few years of their marriage were to be haunted by tiny, cramped flats. As Elinor Klein recalls: "During the next few years [after Cambridge], I visited Ted and Sylvia at their various teaching posts in Northampton and Boston. They always were too large for their quarters—huge, handsome people crammed into tiny, peaked rooms."

For Sylvia, the fact that their apartment was in the town and within walking and biking distance of the college was its main advantage; and in September she was back on the familiar campus and teaching from the same platforms in the same rooms where she had sat as a student several years earlier. Now she conversed as an equal with the same professors she had once stood in awe of, and confronted seventy "eager and intelligent" girls five days of the week with the kind of nervous dread and excitement only a new teacher can appreciate. She had been given three Freshman English 1 classes—a not unusual assignment for a starting instructor, but one that involved an inordinate amount of work. Characteristically, she approached the task with tireless dedication and seriousness, which meant that the work load was even greater than it would have been for a less earnest teacher.

Rosalie Horn, one of her students, echoed the opinion of almost all her students when she characterized Sylvia as "a marvellous teacher" [3]—an opinion shared by the rest of the English faculty as well. One colleague has described her as "one of the two or three finest instructors ever to appear in the English Department at Smith College," and another remarked that she was "an astonishingly good teacher, with great warmth and generosity."

But the very nature of Sylvia's intense and sincere involvement with her students meant a loss of valuable time and energy in her development as a poet. She was discovering, like so many creative writers who accept a faculty position as a means of earning a living while writing, that serious teaching demanded enough emotional and intellectual effort to make writing almost impossible. In the first place, the seemingly short hours were unrepresentative of the enormous time spent in preparation and marking papers outside the actual classroom. Then there was more time devoted to personal conferences with individual students. It did not take Sylvia long to realize that teaching, which she had been preparing for through most of her short life, was simply not an occupation for a poet. It is a mark of her courage (and Ted's) that she accepted this fact—and its implications of continued poverty and constant scratching for funds—completely and honestly by the end of the first semester, when she announced her decision to leave. A great deal of pressure was put on her to remain, but this she stoutly resisted during the remaining six months of her contract.[4]

Other problems at Smith were of a more personal nature. Her tendency to mythify the past, and the people who had figured importantly in that past, now led her to the inevitable disappointments of a reality seen at close range—just as had the reality of Winthrop when she returned there in a foolish effort to recapture a lost childhood. Clarissa Roche, the American wife of the British poet and translator Paul Roche, remembers that Sylvia was intensely disillusioned to find that her idols at Smith were flawed human beings. Paul was on the faculty with Sylvia and shared her dislike of bureaucratic nonsense ("I felt at once a bond of sympathy between us"). He saw that she could not tolerate the "failings of all these people" whom she had once admired from afar, "the pettiness, the jealousies, the boredom of endless discussions at department meetings" which are, of course, typical of any college.[5]

Sylvia and Paul Roche used "to look at each other during those meetings and sigh." The Roches were, in fact, perhaps the closest friends that the Hugheses met during their year at Smith and had been invited by them to their house for dinner three days after Sylvia started teaching. Paul recalls vividly the initial impression Ted and Sylvia made on him and his wife. When he opened the door, he found a "striking, unusual and beautiful pair of human beings standing there." Sylvia's beauty and own height complemented Ted's great size with almost movie-like effect. The Roches found in Ted and Sylvia the same British and American combination and love of poetry that characterized their own marriage. Clarissa, in fact, became one of Sylvia's intimate friends, as important to Sylvia as Marcia had been (and still was through correspondence), although their paths would separate for several years after the Smith experience.

Other friends were made at Smith, usually from among the younger faculty members, though Sylvia was still not averse to cultivating celebrities as such. One of them was the critic Daniel Aaron, who had not been at Smith when Sylvia was a student. Ted and Sylvia met him early in the term, before classes had actually begun, when they had found him typing in his office. He was cordial and responsive, despite the interruption, and invited them to his house. During the course of their subsequent conversation, besides reassuring Sylvia about the chore in front of her, Aaron mentioned that he was a good friend of Leonard Baskin, the young engraver and sculptor who had arrived at Smith during Sylvia's last year and had since set up his own printing press.

Baskin, like the Roches, would become an important friend in the years ahead, his peculiar, powerful vision of dark forces suiting Ted's and Sylvia's own Gothic imaginations perfectly.

Another gratifying aspect of the year at Smith was the increased public notice both Ted and Sylvia were receiving. Ted in particular was finding the American audience highly receptive. He had fifteen poems published in magazines between June and September, including a few in *The New Yorker*—Sylvia's unattained goal. The appearance of *The Hawk in the Rain*, and many complimentary reviews, had opened a series of hitherto closed doors to him—although most people at Smith had never heard of Ted Hughes before meeting him as Sylvia's husband. It was a situation she protested against without success.

One fortunate result of Ted's sudden, albeit limited, fame was an invitation to give a reading at Radcliffe College on Friday afternoon, November 14, which he did to Sylvia's and her mother's delight. The latter had come from Wellesley for the occasion. While Ted read several of the animal poems which would go into his second collection, *Lupercal*, Aurelia sat in the back of the Longfellow Hall auditorium with Philip McCurdy, who had not seen Sylvia since she left Smith as a student. After the reading Mrs. Plath and Philip went up to congratulate the poet. McCurdy was eager for an opportunity to renew his friendship with Sylvia. They "hugged and kissed and chatted for a while," but he made the mistake of kidding Sylvia about her husband's penchant for the same "biological shock words" she had once loved. She responded gaily to the notion but, as McCurdy later admitted, "I think it hurt." He had intruded upon her marriage and consequently was banished from her life.

Though not as dramatically as her husband's, Sylvia's own career was beginning to gain impetus too. In November, *Poetry* magazine awarded her the Bess Hopkins Prize. But the distressing fact was that she was not writing, or not writing very much, as the demands of teaching intruded to an alarming degree. Only at the cabin in the woods near Rock Harbor had she been able to concentrate enough to maintain her steady advance towards a personal voice—and to write several "women's stories" as well, aiming at the lucrative *Saturday Evening Post* market. Throughout her life, Sylvia was infatuated with the idea of becoming a professional writer of short stories for the "slick" magazines, which paid well and could give her the independence she needed.

One poem from this period, which she would characterize as "a favorite" to A. Alvarez—though she had said that about many others earlier—was "Night Shift." It demands the kind of critical attention it has not yet received because it is the next link in the chain of poems Sylvia wrote in an effort to create a Satanic myth; that is, it is a natural evolution of the process begun with the threat of "Hardcastle Crags" and then carried through the biological variations of "Sow" and "The Bull of the Bendylaw." "Night Shift" propels her central metaphor into the age of the machine. Using a sparse syntax, a minimum of adjectives, and a constant dependence upon present participles for mobility, the poem itself moves like a well-oiled machine towards the disturbing climax: human order is reduced to "undershirts" tending "those greased machines." The chilling atmosphere of dread enveloping the men in the factory has become civilization's bell-jar; and Sylvia shocks her reader as she has never shocked him before by rubbing his face in the excrement of his own uselessness. The nineteenth-century Gothic trimmings so prevalent in previous endeavors have been modernized to create a prosaic, daily reality which, because of its recognizable immediacy, strikes a deeper note of desolation.

Moreover, the huge hammers and turning wheels in "Night Shift" suggest the universal clock metaphor Sylvia had used in much earlier poems like "Doomsday" and "To Eva Descending the Stair," and remind the reader that she had yet to abandon her mechanical interpretation of reality. Paul Roche realized at Smith that she was quite elementary in her philosophical outlook. Mindless and mechanically regular process was still the cosmological villain, but she had brought it closer to home. In language brutally suited to its coarseness, Sylvia now located some of its oppressive features in "the silver factory" which might be found on any "Main Street" in America. She was again equating, this time directly, the machine's immense size with "blunt/Indefatigable fact." Fact for Sylvia, as part of the string of nihilistic images that began with bald and black, represented the terrible, undeniable presence of the aborning and decaying world surrounding fragile human life.

Perhaps the poem might also help explain why Sylvia would eventually give in and decide to live in England after all—the one alternative she had steadily rejected during her Cambridge days. Her new political awareness, which was undoubtedly strengthened by her constant contact with liberal intellectuals at Smith, must have made the whole idea of America somewhat unbearable. Nuclear fallout, the Cold War, automation, the military-industrial complex, which President Eisenhower himself would warn against at the end of 1960—all seemed like specific American diseases that were beginning to infect the rest of the globe. But the immediate problem was still how to find enough time and free energy to continue Ted's and her apprenticeship in poetry. Once having made her decision to give up teaching—a difficult decision that must have made her feel guilty and somewhat inadequate—she at least had the prospect of a full year devoted to her art. The Hugheses planned to leave for Boston at the end of the second semester and try to survive there on grants and whatever they could earn by writing. What apparently infuriated her most was the lack of recognition given Ted's work; and Paul Roche believes that this, more than anything else, was influential in her decision to relinquish a teaching career: "At Smith, what bothered, what really made her furious and was, I think, the cause of her leaving, was the degree to which Ted was neglected, not the slightest notice being taken of him."

Ted himself was not overly concerned, particularly as the good reviews of *The Hawk in the Rain* continued to come in, from England as well as America; and he now found himself with sufficient time to give *Lupercal* the attention he felt it needed. He would have liked to teach—though only for economic reasons—but it seemed obvious that his background and lack of contacts were against him. Near the end of the first semester, however, Ted did find a job at the University of Massachusetts at Amherst, thanks to Sylvan Schendler. Professor Schendler had also come to Smith in September 1957 to teach freshman English, but he was older than most instructors and, according to a colleague, "was a little bit 'not the Smith type,' a little aloof, having taught several other places previously, and didn't quite enter into the center of departmental affairs." [6] Presumably this was a mark in his favor in the eyes of Ted and Sylvia.

Professor Schendler made Sylvia's acquaintance at the beginning of the first semester when she came to him for advice on how to organize her freshman classes and he told her simply "to be a teacher and not worry about it"; but he and the Hugheses did become fairly good friends. His impression of the young couple had been favorable: Sylvia was "a dynamic woman" and "a whole woman," and she and Ted were "a whole couple." [7] Later he would be very "surprised and saddened" to learn that they had separated. When Ted asked for help in finding an academic post, Professor Schendler contacted friends at the University of Massachusetts.

In many ways, Ted's teaching appointment was better than Sylvia's in that it was more varied and less demanding. He taught three days a week and had four classes—two "great books" courses, a freshman composition class, and a small senior class in creative writing. Ted was surprised and delighted to discover that he actually enjoyed teaching, a contrast with his earlier experience at the English grammar school in Cambridge. During a *Mademoiselle* interview, Sylvia tried to define both of their attitudes towards teaching: "Ted and I had similar reactions. It was exciting and rewarding to introduce students to writers one particularly enjoys, to stimulate discussions and to watch students develop, but it takes time and energy. Too much, we found, to be able to work at any length on any writing of our own." [8]

The dilemma for the Hugheses was real and disturbing, especially for Sylvia, as older members of the faculty, such as Miss Chase and Mr. Fisher, pressed her to remain. There was also the inducement of working with "many fine, brilliant and creative people" and fellow artists, amid an admittedly "paradisical" setting, as well as the prospect of an Edenic seclusion from the real world and a permanent sense of home. Near the end of February, after the second semester had begun—she was teaching three classes of Freshman English 11 and embarking on a four-week unit dealing with drama—Sylvia wrote to Jane Kopp, who was teaching at the University of New Mexico and hoping for a position at Smith. [9] The letter makes clear that Sylvia had already begun transforming her Cambridge experiences into another myth. Though aware of the reality, the gray, wet weather and the personal misery, she pictured herself as more attached to Cambridge than she could ever be to Smith—drawn by the former's antiquity and tradition.

Again it would seem that she was preparing herself for an eventual return to England, perhaps in the awareness that her husband could never really be happy in America, or in any urban center for that matter; his own past and poetry demanded a return to rustic tranquility. Roots, too, were crucial. Sylvia wanted and needed roots, not temporary flats and constant changes of residence; she wanted a home like her grandmother and mother had had, where she could feel part of a world that found its deepest nourishment in the springs of the past and in rituals that kept that past alive. Like many sensitive Americans of the 1950's, Sylvia was dismayed by a way of life in which mobility appeared to be the only certainty and change the sole goal.

Sylvia did enjoy Smith, and enjoyed meeting Aaron and Baskin and the Roches, but she could no longer abide the artificial environment of a country and a college where the human pettiness inspired by Establishment hierarchies went against the larger values of an old-fashioned familial solidarity. Divorces, broken homes, casual adultery had become a norm. It must be remembered that waste and sin were equally abhorrent to Sylvia's critical mind, and the idea of family absolutely essential. No amount of intellectual development would modify this; which is why she could and did remain faithful to her husband from the day of her marriage to her death. It was part of the code, the set of standards she had inherited, however unwillingly, from her mother, perhaps along with her childish distaste for sex itself.

Smith, then, was a testing ground for Sylvia. It was there during the academic year of 1957–1958 that she believed, as she admitted in her letter to Jane, that she had come of age. Without a doubt, she felt that writing was her life, that her husband was her life, and that the children they would have would be the completion of that life. Her narcissism had, oddly, found full expression in subjugation to marital demands, and to the discipline of her craft. The paring away process commenced at Cambridge seemed finished, and she regarded herself as "a whole woman." During that spring vacation, which Sylvia said "was the only time I had to write for a very long time," she produced a handful of poems (or saved a handful of poems) that indicate the continuation of a divided method—a split in herself and in her poetic development, as her aesthetic was still caught between her earlier academic voice and the more recent thrust towards less restricted personal idioms.

On April 18, 1958, Sylvia gave an informal reading in Springfield, Massachusetts, which was recorded for the Library of Congress—actually a combination reading and interview since Ted was in the room with her and responded occasionally to her comments.[10] One of the inquiries concerned her method of composition. Sylvia replied that several of the poems had been written "pretty much in the space of a day or two, doing nothing else," then she paused, laughed, and said, "He was howling for supper." She went on to explain why "I'm not teaching next year. I found that it was impossible to write while I was working and teaching. And also the kind of analysis I do with my classes is somehow inimical to the sort of work I do myself. So that I feel, actually, that I have to spend the year writing, eating and sleeping when it happens most of the time." As to whom she was reading, Sylvia named "Yeats, Ted Hughes continually, Yeats, Eliot, John Crowe Ransom especially. I have started reading Robert Lowell. I like a good deal in Robert Lowell and, let's see, Shakespeare, Chaucer. Who else? Thomas Wyatt. Who else, Ted? Yes, Hopkins. Let's see. I think Yeats I like very much."

On a direct question dealing with influences, Sylvia found herself itemizing familiar icons and attempting to explain how her recent work was beginning to extricate itself from the straitjacket of traditional formulas: "Yeats, I wouldn't say this last poem ["The Disquieting

Muses"] is influenced by Yeats, but I first learned changing in sound, assonance, from Yeats, for instance, assonance and consonants from Yeats, which, acutely, I mean, is technical. I was very excited when I discovered this. I read Dylan Thomas a great deal for the subtlety in sound. I never worked at anything but rhyme before, very rigid rhymes, and I began to develop schemes and patterns for sounds which were somehow less obvious, but you get them through your ear, if not through the eye. I just happened to learn this from Yeats, and Thomas too, in a way."

After reading several other poems, Sylvia was asked a question which touched upon her inability, despite the piano lessons supplied by her mother, really to appreciate or hear music. Years later Elizabeth Sigmund would describe Sylvia's piano playing as "terrible" and record her dismay because she was so "tone deaf." Sylvia was asked, "Do you hear the music or do you get the image?" She replied:

It's very funny because I haven't an ear for music, but I hear the music in the rhythm, which somehow I don't think about. It's funny. I have a visual imagination. For instance, my inspiration is painting, not music, when I go to some other art form. Ted, what do you think? I mean, I see these things very clearly. I feel, ideally, I would like to be musical without being artificial, which, I think, is sometimes difficult. And to be able to speak straight out, you know, the way you talk, is again terrifically hard, while getting all the richness and allusions in that you get in rhetoric, which, you know, is like eating cake and wanting to have it, I guess.

Sylvia remained ever the conscious artist, and, as this quote shows, was fully cognizant of the need in contemporary poetry to locate and maintain a conversational voice. What is interesting about her extended comments on her own poetry is the studied absence of any significant discussion of content, of motifs and themes. She did respond briefly to individual questions about specific poems, but always in reference to their immediate cause or inspiration, as if technique alone were sufficient for explanation. The poetry speaks for itself, of course; it is the ultimate explanation of its own existence. But there is also a vague impression given that its darker concerns would not quite fit in with the role she was laboring to maintain of professional artist and her whole new image as a brilliant wife of a brilliant poet. The Sylvia Plath giving this reading and interview did not want to appear involved in dying cultures, demonic myths, and the world of repressed imagoes.

Ted Hughes has claimed that Sylvia saved only nine poems from her time at Smith as an instructor; but the interview makes clear that "Poem for Paul Klee's Persius: The Triumph of Wit over Suffering," and perhaps "On the Decline of Oracles" were also written at that time, although the latter might have come from an earlier period. "The Lady and the Earthenware Head" dates from February, 1957. His other remarks are more accurate, as the whole group certainly are "chilling." Sylvia was moving ever nearer to her demonic sense of the world's elemental evil and accepting the poet's function as a visionary one for the damned. In "Poem for Paul Klee's Persius," for instance—many of these poems derive from paintings and sculptures, due to a magazine commission on the topic Sylvia had been offered—the contemporary artist's vision is linked with older "statuary of sorrow" represented by the "Laocoön." The conclusion of the poem and its governing idea is another touchstone, the bald infant dome, "the world fisted to a foetus head."

Art making art, poetry about poetry—the academic self-consciousness of Smith probably made such a course inevitable; but Sylvia continued to deal with the specific concerns of her own aesthetic. In the other nine poems saved from her teaching experience, which maintain and elaborate upon the steady technical progress discussed during her April reading, the darkness of her vision has not lightened, if anything it had increased; but her images now more readily take unorthodox leaps and evolve along lines other than the purely logical. In "The Thin People," for example, the speaker does not hesitate to fly from the broad, socially impressionistic figures of the initial twenty-four lines to the narrative specifics of a mythical old lady's own tale, before returning to an immediate present tense. For the first time, Sylvia was accepting her mind's insidious ingestion of illusions about the world as part of the aesthetic process, and this without hysteria or morbidity. The poems written near the end of her teaching experience certify the wisdom and the relief behind her decision to leave, and the real pleasure she must have felt in finally having assumed wifehood and its reduction of selves before the larger concerns of forwarding her husband's career and eventually bearing his children.

Practical concerns again predominated as the Hugheses found themselves suffering the tedium of finding suitable rooms for the following year. As they were certain that Boston had to be their new home, the problem was again economic—finding a flat that they could afford. Neither of them had "jobs" in the conventional sense, which also meant that landlords would be less likely to approve a lease. Whatever its faults, Smith at least represented a refuge where "nobody cared about money" and where creative aspirations were accepted as part of daily life, regardless of their ultimate suffocation under bureaucratic procedures.

Sylvia knew exactly what she was abandoning, more so than Ted, and must have felt uneasy. Her brief teaching career had certainly been "a success" by any objective standards, and she had made many new friends. She was also returning to a Boston she knew and loved, where old friendships could be revived, as with the Plumers (Marcia and her husband) and the Davisons. But the prospect was vague in a way that went against what Paul Roche has characterized as her "thorough" and "thoroughly analytic and synthetic mind."

Poetry is written for the whole man; it sometimes
scares those who want to hide from the terrors of
existence, from themselves.

THEODORE ROETHKE

13

You Died Like Any Man

The Hugheses did manage to secure a reasonable flat, another tiny,
low-rent set of rooms. Sylvia once remarked to Elinor Klein during a
later visit, "Isn't this silly? Teddy can't even stand up straight here."
Located in Louisberg Square at 9 Willow Street, a part of Boston's
Beacon Hill area, suite 61—Sylvia used the ironic "suite" designation in
her letters—had the advantage of a superb view of the harbor from its
small windows, as well as an abundance of light and air. Once again the
young couple set about vigorously transforming a commonplace apartment into something of their own, installing pictures, bookcases, books,
and other personal effects. Ted made himself a rough desk from two
planks, which he arranged in a window niche, and Sylvia brought along
her grandmother's desk for her own writing. She told a *Mademoiselle*
interviewer that she had "a fetish about my grandmother's desk with an
ivy and grape design burned into the wood."

The interview had taken place soon before leaving Northampton,
although it would not appear in *Mademoiselle* (along with a photo of the
couple and a poem by each of them) until January 1959. In talking about
her marriage Sylvia said, "The bonuses of any marriage—shared
interests, projects, encouragement and creative criticism—are all intensified." Her remark is not all public relations, however, as it echoes
an earlier observation by Paul Roche, who had noticed at Smith that Ted

and Sylvia shared "intense, passionate feelings for the same things." What is especially interesting about the otherwise bland interview is Sylvia's insistence upon the artistic difference between herself and her husband: "In the morning we have coffee (a concession to America) and in the afternoon, tea (a concession to England). That's about the extent of our differences. We do criticize each other's work, but we write poems that are as distinct and different as our fingerprints must be."

That last sentence, or slight variations of it, will be repeated by Sylvia again and again in her correspondence and conversations, as if she remained determined that her art, already subject to Ted's strong influence, would not disappear into his altogether. She told Myron Lotz later in the year, for instance, that "we lie together but we write poems as different as our fingerprints." The difficulty was a real one for her as she remained committed to her husband's career and her own image as ideal wife. For their poems, despite all their alleged "difference," they are obviously deeply in debt to each other, although it becomes nearly impossible after a while to isolate exactly who was indebted to whom. Images and motifs, often identical or only slightly altered, crop up continuously, and are obviously borrowed from or inspired by the other's efforts. Ted was leading the way certainly, drawing Sylvia out from behind her curtain of stiff method; but his own poetry was also benefiting from her unique imagery, as is evident in "Pennines in April," which appeared in *Mademoiselle* with the interview and which reflects Sylvia's fierce reaction to seascapes and recent concern for the artist. It also uses a climax that seems right out of several of her earlier poems: "In a still, fiery air, hauling the imagination,/ Carrying the larks upward."

What made the relationship even more delicate at this time was Ted's growing success. He had had a book published to good reviews and was completing a second. He was also finishing a book of children's stories, which was already accepted for publication; and thus he decided—now that his brief teaching career was at an end—not to look for work. Sylvia was the one who would eagerly find a job to supplement their small savings and whatever money came in from their poetry sales and rare readings. But she had at last cracked open *The New Yorker*'s golden door, as two of her longest poems had been accepted there just before she left Smith. The money she received for "Mussel Hunter at Rock Harbor" and "Night Walk" (the original title of "Night Shift") was enough to pay three months' rent.

And yet Sylvia did have to work, if only to relieve a temporary writer's block and find new material. Early in October she secured a position as secretary to a psychiatrist at Massachusetts General Hospital

—which must have triggered a whole series of dark memories—and she would remain there for two months. Although this would prove a fertile field for themes—leading to two of her better short stories, "The Daughters of Blossom Street" and "Johnny Panic and His Bible of Dreams"—the hospital depressed and irritated her. Further, it served to remind her of a submissive feminine function she could not escape and the ancillary waste of her education. One happy result of the employment was renewed contact with Myron Lotz, whom she met at the hospital one day soon after her arrival. He had graduated from Yale in June, after coming in first on Part II of the National Board of Medical Examiners' Exam and winning the coveted Campbell Award; and now he was at "Mass. Gen." as a resident intern on a fellowship. Like Sylvia five years before, he was reaching a dangerous peripety, and by December would himself be in McLean's, torn by a suicidal depression. An odd sidelight to his sad incarceration was that he was put in the same locked ward with Robert Lowell, whose class Sylvia would audit the following year at Boston University.

Sylvia and Mike were glad to see each other, all traces of past bitterness were gone, and she invited him to dinner at the Louisberg flat. He accepted and showed up accompanied by a young lady friend, whom he later described as "not very bright." The dinner was a pleasant and informal affair, although Mike recalls getting somewhat drunk during the course of it. He found Sylvia's husband congenial and hospitable, but could not imagine him ever "dancing around the room." There seemed to be a "certain somberness about him." One incident in particular stands out in Mike's memory, and it is revealing of the fact that Sylvia was not as easy to live with as the public picture seems to suggest at the time.

During a casual conversation, Mike mentioned to Ted that his present companion was content with her female destiny and just wanted to make the right man a good housewife someday. "My God, snap her up!" Ted exclaimed.."You don't find many like her." Sylvia's reaction to this statement is not recorded, but she must have sensed the implications. She was laboring hard—perhaps too hard—to conform to the expected pattern. Peter Davison, whom they would see fairly often during their year in Boston, recalls that she was "very worried about marriage, about what should she do as a wife, about cooking and baking and how can you live with a man, etc. She generally made a big thing about it." He also sensed undercurrents of insecurity behind the mask: "I believe her feelings about marriage and children were anxious and intense."

This kind of response to the ordinary events of daily life had to create a certain amount of tension in the Hugheses' home, despite Sylvia's heroic attempt to absorb herself in her husband. She was probably sincere enough, but her ego was surely as great as her husband's; and to pretend otherwise was to permit Ted to enlarge his own self-image at her expense, though frequently with her connivance. For example, Ted had contacted Stanley Kunitz, then a relatively obscure but respected poet, and went often with Sylvia to his house for long discussions about poetry. Ted spoke freely and passionately on occasions, but all Mr. Kunitz can remember of Sylvia is a silent figure lost in the background.[1]

Similarly, in November of 1958, Ted and Sylvia were at Peter Davison's tiny apartment to meet Robert Frost. Six people crowded into the small room, including a photographer and a reporter from *Life* magazine, while Frost delighted in another chance to demonstrate his own rustic image. Davison, who was under some strain as host, recalls vividly that both Ted and Sylvia "were very silent, Sylvia more than Ted, as Frost held the floor." This silence continued during a final walk around the block and the subsequent farewells. Meeting an idol, a near folk-hero, was of course partially responsible for Sylvia's silence—a silence which went against her grain; but it also seemed to derive from this insistence upon self-effacement, especially in Ted's presence.

On the other hand, they continued to share their dedication to poetry. As Peter Davison notes in talking about his own poetry at the time, Ted and Sylvia "worked very hard at it, were far more advanced poets than myself." They were also always generous in sharing their knowledge: "I went up to Willow Street with the first poems I ever wrote, and they made very useful suggestions, about metrics, which lines they liked and didn't, etc., especially Ted." Ted was deep into the poems of *Lupercal*, expanding the bestiary begun in *The Hawk in the Rain*; and Sylvia worked steadily to produce a body of verses that would refine and continue the breakthrough evident at Cambridge and Smith. She had enough poems for a volume, but none of the publishers she approached was interested. Even Peter Davison's firm, the Atlantic Monthly Press, would reject the collection, although the magazine itself, which she constantly flooded with material, remained open to her.

In the title poem of that first collection, Sylvia had begun to confront the idea that evil comes from the self, which, in turn, derives from its own past, its own childhood, not the past childhood of all mankind. History is not being denied totally, but merely subjugated to the realization that biography has a more pertinent pattern to reveal, namely, that self-revelation might be the only universal left in the twentieth-century. As a poem, "The Colossus" is another transitional piece, a curious mid-point between the two phases of Sylvia Plath's poetic development. In terms of basic techniques and language, it belongs firmly to the first phase, although here and there, especially in the last stanza, the concise, knife-like sentences suggest the staccato rhythms of *Ariel* and *Winter Trees*—as do the tentative investigations of a huge Electra complex.

It is the personal elements that give the poem its power, fierce emotional energy, and sense of relentless purpose. This is definitely not the still-life pattern isolated so consistently in the past, although it is the natural offspring of the artistic method initially experimented with in "Hardcastle Crags." Psychologically, the poem is a reliable indicator of Sylvia's growing realization that her father's ghost would not stay buried. This also had been abundantly evident in "Full Fathom Five" and, more recently, in "Man in Black"; and it was likewise becoming obvious that her entire poetic career was geared towards this confrontation:

> Thirty years now I have labored
> to dredge the silt from your throat.

Since Sylvia was only twenty-six at the time, the thirty is a metaphor. For the mythical context of three still remained central to her cosmos, as it did to that of fairy tales, legends, and Christian allegory. Thus, from the beginning, however honest her exposure of self, it would always entail this governing air of magically endowed significance. She would reveal her deepest secrets and feelings, but always in terms of a self-created myth about herself. The bitch goddess was precisely a creature with links to unseen forces and profound subterranean patterns. Sylvia's concept of life as art or disguise had not changed; it had merely been transferred to the psychological level of truths robed in witch's shrouds and queen's gowns. This was because she saw that modern man as programmed by Freudian theory (after the death of God) had to find salvation in another context of belief—even if that meant a turning towards black magic and astral projections. In this sense, she and her whole poetic career foreshadow the tremendous surge in the 1960's towards the dark arts and a rejection of an "absurd" universe—which is, after all, a rational, humanistic concept—in favor of a more vague but more reassuring occultism. This is what defines her poetry and gives it that special imprint of genius: its tendency always to foreshadow the future.

But these things come later, when they take on a more organized pattern after the return to England and the release of her imago in all its black glory by Ted's infidelity. Sylvia herself was introduced to astrology and other "mystical" machinery by her husband and his sister Olwyn. They had always been fascinated by such things, while at the same time insisting upon maintaining a certain distance between their interest and any actual belief, sometimes treating the whole matter with sophisticated humor. David Compton has confirmed that Ted's and Olwyn's dabblings in the occult were never more than that. Yet, on the other hand, Clarissa Roche claims that Ted often worked out the best astrological dates for sending out material to editors, which nicely complemented "Sylvia's witch propensities"; and Olwyn sent Sylvia a copy of *Scorpio*, an illustrated French book on Sylvia's birth sign, soon after the Hugheses settled in Boston.[2] At the end of a letter to Olwyn in December 1958, Sylvia thanked her sister-in-law for the book and asked her to burn a candle for her.

Sylvia, of course, would find in such bizarre possibilities a new conceptual framework for her life and art—a badly needed spiritual code to replace lost religious impulses. Yeats himself, idol for both Hugheses, had devoted much of his imaginative life to supernatural phenomena of one kind or another and used them frequently to buttress his autobiographical themes.

But to return to "The Colossus," the speaker is centrally concerned with an actual colossus, which she cannot comprehend but feels a fearful affinity with. The shift from the natural animal monstrosity touched upon in "Sow" and "The Bull of the Bendylaw" to the mechanical disaster envisioned in "Night Shift" has been caught in flight. Her colossus is both, since it is conceived of as possessing "immense skull plates" and "bald, white tumuli" for eyes; but his brow consists of "weedy acres," and "Mule-bray, pig-grunt and bawdy cackles" issue from his "great lips." The combination of pastoral and mechanical images reaffirms that deadly universe in which the mindless order of a machine finds fullest expression in nature's jungle morality.

The suggestion of an actual ruin (the literal can never be ignored in any of Sylvia's poems), perhaps at Knossos, also introduces the classical themes of "Lament" and many other previous poems. All three possibilities—classic ritual, tribal cult, modern machine monster—come together to form the titanic but lifeless statue of her father. He is the adumbration of total evil, but still there is a lingering ambivalence. She is aware of his power and size without knowing her own relationship to him: "I shall never get you put together entirely." This revelatory and pathetic insight leads her to consider him as an oracle of old,

"Mouthpiece of the dead" or "of some god or other"; but she cannot be sure. Her only hope of finding a clue to his meaning lies in her own peculiar metaphorical behavior. Besides clearing his throat of silt, she had mended his skull plates and cleaned out his eyes, like a woman (Antigone?) preparing a body for burial. She is ever aware of her unnatural reaction to him as lover and father: "A blue sky out of the Oresteia/ Arches above us." The gestalt is consciously Freudian—as is the next poem in this sequence.

"The Beekeeper's Daughter" is unique because, for the first time, Sylvia gives public expression to the hate side of her relationship with her father. Never before had she dared in her poetry, except tentatively and under disguise, to admit to the image of her father as domineering brute. After analysis, of course, she had told Nancy Hunter and others the new truth: her father was a tyrant whom she wished dead and then felt terribly guilty about when he did die. There is more truth in this picture than in the saintly deceptions of earlier years, but it too is incomplete. For it does not take into consideration the fierce rage Sylvia felt (and continued to feel unconsciously) towards her father precisely because he had died and abandoned her.

Finished with myth-making once and for all in "The Colossus," or at least myth-making about her father, Sylvia tried in "The Beekeeper's Daughter" to reconstruct Otto humanly—a whole cycle of bee poems still lay in the future. The poem is addressed directly to the father, an innovation that was important to Sylvia's personal voice, as will be seen later; and it presents him as moving among "the many-breasted hives." Her own sting comes in a separate line: "My heart under your foot, sister of a stone." The organizing concept lies in the bee hive itself—in those "little boudoirs" where the drones are kept, "potent as kings" but doomed; and where the queen sits at the center of the universe, "a queenship no mother can contest." Male and female roles seem reversed, but nature's pattern of destruction still remains central: "A fruit that's death to taste: dark flesh, dark parings." It is clear that Sylvia has retained her conviction of the universe's evil design, but she has also added the evil of masculine domination over woman's freedom and identity.

Otto Plath was not only being resurrected in his own reality, but he was also being integrated with the pattern of male repression Sylvia saw in operation all around her. He was the symbol of the vast personal and social pressures that had distorted her life from its conscious beginnings in Winthrop; he was the cause for her retreat behind masks and prime instigator of the endless insecurity propelling her existence into a series of depressions and manic explosions. Yet it was therapeutically a healthy sign that she could now release the hatred in a more direct fashion and admit to "unseemly" feelings of bitterness towards her dead father. Perhaps buoyed by the cleansing revelations of "The Beekeeper's Daughter," Sylvia wrote "Electra on the Azalea Path" and coolly cast herself in the role of mournful daughter still ensnared by a destructive Electra complex. It is another attempt, doomed from the start, to go home again, this time to the cemetery behind the church in Winthrop where Otto was buried. If she lies to herself in this poem, Sylvia had at least shifted closer to some ultimate insight by conceding her hatred of her father and accepting the premise of her new life with Ted.

Their marriage seemed to be thriving at the start of the new year of 1959. Economic pressure would lessen considerably in the spring when Ted won a Guggenheim, and Sylvia did not have to work. She was free to pursue literature in a way she had never been before, except during those idyllic stays at Benidorm and Rock Harbor. Ted, in fact, often seems to have disappeared during the spring, but people who did see them together at their small apartment have attested to the apparent happiness of their home. Peter Davison rarely visited them after November of 1958, as he was then seeing much of his future wife Jane Truslow, but when he did his reaction was invariably favorable. He was particularly taken with Ted: "I was struck by him and amused. He had a very funny, wonderful sort of Yorkshire humor, full of curious information."

Marcia also responded favorably to Sylvia's husband, after an initial period of coldness during which she found him "rather aloof." As he came to accept her as Sylvia's closest friend, Ted displayed another side to his personality. She found that he was "an incredibly fine raconteur who told lengthy and delightfully funny stories about Yorkshire," and she characterized him glowingly as "a charming, charming person." Marcia realized that part of his "superior attitude" resulted from a real shyness in the presence of strangers, although "there were a lot of things about America and Wellesley which Ted found repugnant."

This repugnance, which was partially the outgrowth of normal home-sickness, helped convince Sylvia that America was out of the question as a permanent residence. She agreed, no doubt reluctantly in light of her hatred for English weather, that they would return to England late in the fall. Another matter that bothered Sylvia far more was their inability to have children. Marcia had been delivered of a set of twins in the spring; and Sylvia generously, and perhaps with a touch of envy, made the trip to Marcia's house twice a week to help feed and bathe the babies and otherwise get "very much involved." As Marcia recalled, "At that time, she was very concerned because she hadn't conceived, and they were talking about whether they ought to see a doctor." The Hugheses apparently did seek medical advice with positive results, but Sylvia must have felt a little desperate. Babies were absolutely essential, "a part of Sylvia's wanting to experience everything life had to offer," as well as necessary emblems of her mental health and new life. Perhaps this helps explain the insistence upon herself as a stone—an arid thing—in the poems about her father from this period, an extension of the bald infant heads that had always dominated her imagination.

After planning to return to England—and a letter of Sylvia's suggests that the decision had been made by December of 1958—the Hugheses decided that they had to see more of America before leaving. They intended to spend the three months of summer on a cross-country camping trip. Before that, however, Sylvia joined Robert Lowell's poetry seminar at Boston University, having been drawn there by Anne Sexton and George Starbuck, two other poets who were auditing the course.

Great poets are often proverbially ignorant of life. What they know has come by observation of themselves; they have found within them one highly delicate and sensitive specimen of human nature, on which the laws of emotion are written in large characters, such as can be read off without much study.

JOHN STUART MILL

14

That Landscape of Imperfections

The first five or six months of 1959 were also months of frustration and discontent for Sylvia, who fretted under the constant rejections of her volume of poetry and worried about the possibility of being sterile. But they were also months of intense excitement and creative production as a result of Lowell's class and of Sylvia's initial exposure to the basic techniques of what has been called "confessionalism." Also in Anne Sexton she had found another friend—one who shared her own drive for poetic success, her Wellesley background, even her lapses into suicidal depression.

The routine was unvaried but stimulating. Along with George Starbuck, Sylvia and Anne Sexton attended Lowell's seminar in the morning, staying in the background for the most part, though occasionally making comments and submitting one of their own works for class analysis—a step which Sexton has vividly described as "sometimes letting our own poems come up, as for a butcher, as for a lover." [1] After class the trio would take Sexton's car and go to the Ritz Hotel and its plush bar, where they sipped martinis and munched on the free potato chips. Three young poets on the edge of success, commercial and/or personal, and under the spell of their own internal dramas, must have made for odd but exciting company.

Death seemed to be a natural topic of conversation. But talk of death in that lush setting did not generate a depressing mood. Instead, aided perhaps by the martinis and a residue of "negative capability" left over from the classroom, it had an opposite effect and reconfirmed their own identities, "as if death made each of us a little more real at the moment." Sexton has written that she and Sylvia "talked death with burned-up intensity, both of us drawn to it like moths to an electric light bulb"; and, after her friend's suicide, Sexton would complain in an elegy, "how did you crawl into,/ crawl down alone/ into the death I wanted so badly and for so long"—a bit of prophetic self-indulgence and self-revelation.

After their stint in the Ritz each day, the three poets invariably, if sometimes unsteadily, departed for the Waldorf Cafeteria, where they could buy a complete dinner for 70 cents. None of them was in any particular hurry to get home. Starbuck had recently divorced his wife and Sexton's only obligation was to appear at her psychiatrist's office by seven o'clock. Sylvia was also pretty much on her own as Ted, according to Sexton, "was either able to wait or was busy enough with his own work." In class itself, none of them hesitated to speak their mind or to criticize one another's poetry. Sexton has characterized Lowell's reaction to Sylvia's poems as positive and claimed he said that "he liked her work and that her poems got right to the point."

Sexton disagreed vigorously, although she admitted that "I was too determined to bet on myself to actually notice where she was headed in her work." She felt and told Lowell—probably with the advantage of some hindsight, since her memoir was written years later—that Sylvia's poems "dodged the point and did so perhaps because of her preoccupation with form." Also she believed that Sylvia "hadn't then found a form that belonged to her"—though in that case it is possible Sylvia had not shown her any of the father poems or the few striking successes she had achieved at Cambridge, such as "All the Dead Dears," "resolve," and "Hardcastle Crags," where form and matter had been merged with near perfection.

Robert Lowell's recollections of Sylvia, preserved in the brief Preface he wrote for the American edition of *Ariel*, are somewhat different from and less dramatic than Sexton's.[2] He found her "willowy, long-waisted, sharp-elbowed, nervous, giggly, gracious—a brilliant tense presence embarrassed by restraint." He was aware of the mask and what it hid, at least partially: "Her humility and willingness to accept what was admired seemed at times to give her an air of maddening docility that hid her unfashionable patience and boldness." He remembers the poems she submitted were "somber, formidably expert in stanza structure, and had a flair for alliteration and Massachusetts' low-tide dolor," and concedes that none of it "sank very deep into my awareness. I sensed her abashment and distinction, and never guessed her later appalling and triumphant fulfillment."

At the time, of course, Lowell was working his own *purgatorio* into a confessional form—stimulated, no doubt, by the poetry of a former student, W. D. Snodgrass, and by Anne Sexton's contemporaneous efforts. But he had a greater effect on Sylvia than he could have realized, not only by encouraging her awareness of the possibilities inherent in confessional verse, but in further enlarging that "Massachusetts' low-tide dolor" he talks about. One immediate result was "Point Shirley," which Ted Hughes has characterized as a deliberate attempt on Sylvia's part to capture Lowell's seashore grays. The dolor, for Sylvia, was real, as was the intense sense of corruption engendered by the ever-present sea which dominates the poem: Sylvia's grand and frightening mother, an enemy that runs against "both bar and tower," the "sea in its gold gizzard," "the sluttish, rutted sea," the sea that "Eats at Point Shirley," "A dog-faced sea" and, finally, Sylvia's absolute evil, "the black sea." And the nature of this sea, so obsessively denigrated, finds a metaphorical correspondence in the hardness of surface attitude and reality, the emphasis on stones and gritted waves, which are linked with the hardness of her grandmother's wash "snapped and frozen here." Remoteness, the poet's cold eye, certainly seems suitable to such a landscape, but Sylvia's task is more human, though Herculean: to squeeze the milk of her grandmother's love "from these dry-papped stones." Breasts play an important part in this poem, and in many poems to come, dry, hard, arid breasts, the moon in different guises, symbols, always, of sterility and of a loveless mother.

Sylvia's experimentations at this time were not, however, always concerned with the private mythology of a private life. On several occasions, notably in "The Times Are Tidy" and "Aftermath," the former coming some time before "Point Shirley" and the latter immediately after, she did attempt to bring her brush to bear upon a broader social canvas, a reflection of her growing political awareness and her conviction that an interior drama must ultimately find some external counterpart. Both poems were at least attempts to sketch in a wider spectrum, to move away from the self. They also might be viewed as Sylvia's way (perhaps a rationale) of certifying her dismay with America, making her forthcoming voyage to England more sensible. Furthermore, the idea of grafting a social sensibility to a personal voice was valid and would help save Sylvia's final work from the self-indulgence so evident in Anne Sexton's later verses.[3] But for now, while still not yet sure of that voice, she had to fail, particularly since in neither poem did Sylvia risk revealing a naked self, or any self for that matter.

In the very next poem she wrote, "Two Views of a Cadaver Room," a potent near-masterpiece based on an Auden poem, she convincingly demonstrated what such a mating could do for her aesthetic. The visit to the hospital under Buddy Willard's guidance had never left her mind—she referred to it again and again over the years, as several friends have testified—and in particular the foetus in a bottle remained buried like a fang in her imagination. Now she was ready to use it as a central motif, but had wit enough to realize that it required a balancing reality—artistic in nature since she was still creating art about art—one that would make lucid the connection in her mind between the dreadful scene in the hospital and the impulse towards poetry. The result was a "split" poem in which two scenes are juxtaposed, the banal and the classical, which sum up man's fall from grace and beauty, from innocence itself.

"Suicide Off Egg Rock" is not as effective as "Two Views of a Cadaver Room," its remoteness too restricting and "unreal" in the end, but it does provide another brave attempt at merging personal despair with social significance, as the first four lines make abundantly clear:

> Behind him the hotdogs split and drizzled
> On the public grills, and the ochreous salt flats,
> Gas tanks, factory stacks—that landscape
> Of imperfections his bowels were part of—

The images certainly give vivid reality to the combination of Coney Island tawdriness and industrial wastes, internalizing them in the suicide's bowels and stressing an ambiance of man-made ugliness. The "landscape of imperfections" is America synopsized in a phrase, the objective correlative Sylvia was seeking for her personal sense of alienation and anguish, but by transforming her persona into a male, probably to achieve distancing, she helps destroy the poem's immediacy. Only in "Mushrooms," an odd and attractive little poem written later at Yaddo, would she reduce the extraneous matters to a core truth, shove her consciousness directly into the eye of nature itself. Though strongly influenced by Emily Dickinson, "Mushrooms" is closest in spirit to Theodore Roethke in that it assumes a vegetable identity in the murky realm of preconscious infancy. In form, a lean and whimsical form Emily would have appreciated, the poem never misses a beat, sounds simulating sense in a felicitous merger of eye and ear: "Our toes, our noses/ Take hold on the loam,/ Acquire the air." Anthropomorphic mushrooms have freed Sylvia's lines of clutter, suggesting the success of "resolve," perhaps because the concept had a simplicity of design that required no convoluted parentheses of layered reflections and cross references.

The menace, which Sylvia obviously wanted to instill, does not ever find a dark enough tone, but there is a child-like joy in the actual process of making the poem that comes through. If in the end there is no threat, the last three lines do justify what preceded them, do certify and sustain the images of mushrooms as human masses, the crowd in "Aftermath," without reaching too far:

> We shall by morning
> Inherit the earth.
> Our foot's in the door.

The play upon the prediction of Jesus that the meek would inherit the earth is ironic without being brilliantly so, yoking Sylvia's real distance from the rest of ordinary humanity with her prevalent consciousness of a threatening nature and man.

The three-month tour of the United States turned out to be a happy interlude for Sylvia. While traveling with Ted through many of the states, and parts of Canada, she would not write a single poem, though she did continue her sketching. She and Ted were alone again, free of nagging financial concerns and other social pressures; and they were also meeting nature on its own terms as campers. It seemed somehow appropriate that during this expedition into America, Sylvia should finally become pregnant.

Yet if she was happy at this time, other fears must also have emerged. First there was the terrifying prospect of birth, which had always haunted her; and she also had to face the possibility that motherhood might intrude upon her art. Yet the poems which later deal with this trip, such as "Sleep in the Mojave Desert," "Two Campers in Cloud Country," and perhaps "Crossing the Water," are merely token expressions of the stock feeling of being lost in vast places.

But the story that resulted from the trip, "The Fifty-Ninth Bear," is another fantasy revenge—and this time on Ted. Again, as in "The Wishing Box," a wife is seen in a passive, somewhat resentful relationship to a stronger husband. The heroine is Sadie, whose plain name is an amusing contrast to her great imaginative faculty, while Ted takes life under the vengeful name of Norton—his character in the story being somewhat similar to a friend's in its amused, superior tolerance of his wife's child-like incapacities. The second paragraph of the story gives a good account of what the Hugheses actually saw and possibly experienced during their stay in the park, and it also indicates some insight gained by Sylvia into the sensitivity behind Ted's calm façade—its hidden fear of what lay within his visions of a brutal nature:

Norton dallied then, letting his wife drift on ahead. Her slender, vulnerable shape softened, wavered, as the mists thickened between them. She withdrew into a blizzard, into a fall of white water; she was nowhere. What had they not seen? The children squatting at the rim of the paintpots, boiling their breakfast eggs in rusty strainers; copper pennies winking up from cornucopias of sapphire water; the thunderous gushers pluming, now here, now there, across a barren ochre-and-oyster moonscape. She had insisted, not without her native delicacy, on the immense, mustard-coloured canyon where, halfway down to the river, hawks and the shadows of hawks looped and hung like black beads on fine wire. She had insisted on the Dragon's Mouth, that hoarse, booming spate of mud-clogged water; and the Devil's Cauldron. He had waited for her habitual squeamishness to turn her away from the black, porridgey mass that popped and seethed a few yards from under her nose, but she bent over the pit, devout as a priestess in the midst of those vile exhalations. And it was Norton, after all, bareheaded in the full noon sun, squinting against the salt-white glare and breathing in the fumes of rotten eggs, who defaulted, overcome by headache. He felt the ground frail as a bird's skull under his feet, a mere shell of sanity and decorum between him and the dark entrails of the earth where the sluggish muds and scalding waters had their source.

Anyone who has actually visited the Devil's Cauldron in Yellowstone National Park knows how accurate and vividly realized Sylvia's description of it is; but the key element is her return to a portrait of two extremes, a male and female character in complete opposition, like the aging brother and sister in "Sunday at the Mintons."

As a story, "The Fifty-Ninth Bear" effectively sets up the human antipodes of Sadie as dreamer, child, innocent, who "took games seriously" and had bet her husband they would see fifty-nine bears—the number being her "symbol of plentitude"—and Norton as a firm father figure and apparent pragmatist with mystical inclinations. Norton believes he has "a certain power" over nature, which he could will to move and exist. Yet Sadie, who has a way with animals and depends on Norton, is becoming increasingly disappointed with him for not living up to that image. Despite that, "More and more during the second year of their marriage she seemed unwilling to go anywhere without him."

No man could bear such clinging self-effacement. Norton even thought of himself as a widower because his wife seemed too frail to outlive him; though during their love-making he became the child nursing at her breasts. When the fifty-ninth bear turns on him—the language is all from Ted Hughes' poetry—he hears Sadie's final cry but could not tell "whether of terror or triumph."

Ted and Sylvia returned to the East in early September and by September 9 were living in Yaddo, the well-subsidized retreat for artists and writers at Saratoga Springs, New York. The Hugheses were thus granted another extension of their tour—freed from financial concerns and given another respite together before the arrival of the baby and their attempt to find a London home. Pauline Hanson, who was the resident secretary at Yaddo during their stay, recalls: "The two poets were here from September 9 to November 19, 1959. They were very much fond of each other, very quiet, kept much to themselves. Pleasant, hard working and appreciative of the kind of life Yaddo offered them. Our office files for them show no letters from them after they left Yaddo. I believe that from here they were to return, briefly, to her home, before leaving, then, for England. They did have good visits here—they spoke warmly of this, both of them, when they left." [4]

The magnificent grounds, complete with old statuary, ponds, fountains, and the endless stretches of woods, must have had a great impact upon them, particularly as they had just come from the wilder regions of the United States. Here, in all its autumnal glory and sense of lush decay, was nature in the guise of a dying empire—dominated, for the most part, by silence and often grey skies, increasing amounts of rain, threats of snow, temperatures hovering down close to Sylvia's winter world.

The many free hours together and long walks daily through the dying vegetation and among corroding public monuments made the mystical seem a proper and sensible approach to art and self. Ted speaks of their devoting much time to devising and playing with "exercises of meditation and invocation." One of the latter led directly to "Mushrooms," which was written during their stay. Also, much more significantly, under Ted's influence Sylvia began re-reading Theodore Roethke's work and for the first time understood how his flight into a pre-conscious self and internalized sense of the organic world related to her own search for an authentic voice. In the keystone of his art, in the so-called "greenhouse" poems, she would discover a piece of her own past and comprehend that a confessional voice had almost inevitably to have its tap roots in the primitive arena of animism which childhood recreates.

But the immediate influence was nature itself—nature in the grandeur of another fall, and seen always against the backdrop of the Victorian mansion and its age's lost values. Ted finished *Lupercal* and had the satisfaction of knowing that it would be brought out in the spring by Faber and Faber. He was also working on several stories dealing with Yorkshire, two of which would appear in the *London Magazine* and all of which were typed up by Sylvia from his final drafts—she continued to act as agent and secretary for both of them and to carry on the bulk of their fairly extensive correspondence, including her own lengthy letters to relatives and friends. In October Sylvia had been notified of John Lehmann's acceptance of "The Daughters of Blossom Street," which must have cheered her, since she still clung to the hope of becoming a professional short-story writer for specialized magazines.

The central event of Sylvia's life at this time, however, was that she was again writing poetry—taking immediate advantage of the fall setting to shape a series of elegiac lyrics and fitting herself into the darkening mood of Yaddo's nearly deserted landscape. During one of their hikes through the woods, the Hugheses came upon two dead moles on the path. The small, delicate bodies and clenched, almost human hands struck to the heart of Sylvia's sense of personal hurt and universal corruption. "Blue Moles," the poem that resulted, displays her unique imagery to good advantage as, in the first stanza, the two dead creatures near an elm root are seen as "out of the dark's ragbag," "Shapeless as flung gloves," and "Blue suede a dog or fox has chewed." It concludes with a summary condemnation of fate's accidental evils: "Blind twins bitten by bad nature."

The second section of "Blue Moles" takes the process of anthropomorphizing nature one step further, closer to Theodore Roethke, as the poet, from her night bed, enters "the soft pelt of the mole" and participates vicariously in its constant battle for survival. Here is another effort, like "Mushrooms," to equate a certain segment of animal or vegetable life with human existence. Sylvia views the underground lairs as "mute rooms" and speaks of roots and rocks as "fat children." Finally, she merges the mole with her interior self: "Down there one is alone." In the last stanza, a horrific truth emerges, though a familiar one to both Sylvia and Ted Hughes. The moles themselves are envisioned as eaters of life, who will never find the "heaven/ Of final surfeit." Sylvia's personal happiness also seems at issue, as she restlessly searches for an ultimate good or truth or simple joy which her intellect knows is impossible to attain: "What happens between us/ Happens in darkness, vanishes/ Easy and often as each breath."

Invocations, meditations, incantations, all the magical resources of childhood drove Sylvia's art at Yaddo to express what the ending of mythical realms actually meant to her, and what the end of her own childhood had to do with fall and the decline of once-credible oracles. Autumn into winter, the beloved and hated season of her art, provided an exterior analogue for the failure of an aesthetic to take root in the historical and metaphysical past. In the next poem, "Flute Notes from a Reedy Pond," another actual place reconfirms the absence of Godhead and meaning. Coldness settles on the land and the pond as summer's umbrellas "Wither like pithless hands"; and, frighteningly, "There is little shelter" from nature's cold truth. Nature is reduced to the mere process of eating—an artless oral compulsion of "frog-mouth and fish-mouth" that draws all value down into "a soft caul of forgetfulness."

The only poem written at Yaddo which does not seem to fit in with the others, although it is concerned with endings of a sort and nature's cruel sway, is "A Winter Ship." It seems wholly the product of some recollection from the past—perhaps a visit to Gordon Lameyer's ship, which suggested to Sylvia another method for contrasting human creativity with nature's awesome power. The poem may also have a vague connection with the ship of Orestes in "The Colossus"—a mythical vessel that could never again land at shore.

"A Winter Ship" is not a successful poem, but it has returned to a concern with lovers confronted by reality. Love is an illusion that must succumb to the temporal powers of flesh and mind. As a part of the Yaddo group, the poem at least goes beyond autumn to the stasis of winter death, although the fact that it had to find inspiration in the past might imply that Sylvia could not or would not imagine herself and Ted as the lovers involved. Their love was still special enough to escape autumn's perennial warning. "Mushrooms" came next, and it represented a return to Roethke's vision and fear of the organic world; but human despair needed a more concrete symbol, and Sylvia found it in the blackened rubble of a burnt-down spa near the estate's grounds. Its abandoned ruins echoed the decaying woods and the death of something human.

Sylvia was obsessed with the death of her own myth about a Satanic monster and saw the rubble of "The Burnt-out Spa" as the remains of an "old beast," "A monster of wood and rusty teeth." As she looks through the rubbish, she finds human parallels that suggest her reaction to the fallen idol of her father in "The Colossus." The collapsed structure is seen in terms of "his body" and "his carcass" and she describes the in-roads of nature as intruding upon "his bones" and "His armor-plate, his toppled stones." Like an archeologist, she pries among "Iron entrails, enamel bowls,/ The coils and pipes that made him run." Irony resides in the fact that the small surrounding dell now eats "what ate it once"—a pat evocation of tooth-and-claw existence; but life remains. A spring emerges from the wreckage like a tongue from "the broken throat, the marshy lip." The oracle does still speak, then, but what it says is not clear.

Leaning over the rail of a bridge, the speaker gazes down into the water of this spring and encounters a "Blue and improbable person"— her double in the magic mirror of a father-shadowed past—who "is gracious and austere." The poet refuses to recognize this other self, who is the real artist in her and the offspring of the myth of the father: "It is not I, it is not I." And yet she also appreciates the unreality of the other's existence, where no "animal spoils on her green doorstep"—a wonderful touch that appears misplaced at first but reminds the reader that a child is involved. Alas, the stream that keeps her shut off from this unreal other self "Neither nourishes nor heals." It is a sad poem when read with some knowledge of its creator's life; in the end it is an admission that no amount of icon-destroying creativity could ever make Sylvia well again, and that even her art's new honesty somehow could not dispel the father's ghost and her inner disease.

A spa was both her dead father and the poet's dead hopes for any human dignity; but it was a manor garden at Yaddo in the grip of autumnal decline that brought death and birth into a penultimate union and inspired the finest poem written during these two and a half months. How important it was to Sylvia herself might be gauged from the fact that she chose "The Manor Garden" to begin *The Colossus* collection, putting it before "Two Views of a Cadaver Room," as if signaling the reader that it most effectively betokened the book's *raison d'etre*. It is both a freer poem than the preceding Yaddo exercises and closer to an incantation in its leaps from image to image and idea to idea. It also suggests Emily Dickinson gathering her garden world and her intense personal fear of death into a bouquet of hope and art against heaven's blank door.

The first stanza provides season and place:

> The fountains are dry and the roses over.
> Incense of death. Your day approaches.
> The pears fatten like little buddhas.
> A blue mist is dragging the lake.

In five short sentences the poet wastes no time in establishing her poetic reality—the end of life (water) and art (roses), the sweet smell of death (burning leaves), the approach of new life and a new vision (buddha pears) and the immediate reality of a blue mist, which is seen as searching for a body in the water. The simile of the third line has also stressed the governing principle of birth in death, as pears ripen in autumn; but now the emphasis has subtly shifted from negative to positive elements.

The new life that is coming—Sylvia's own child and her aborning poetic voice—is seen as arriving through "history" in the second stanza and through myth in the third—ruined, fallen myths, "broken flutings," that continue to survive in nature alone, in "white heather, a bee's wing." But the fourth stanza is puzzling with its allusions to "Two suicides, the family wolves,/ Hours of blankness," which seem to relate both to an actual womb and to the metaphorical death of parents entailed by any birth, as well as to the Roman legend that Romulus and Remus were suckled by wolves. Also, Sylvia's two suicide attempts might be implied—the unconscious one when she was a child crawling towards the sea and the deliberate attempt in the crawl space under her house.

Magic dominates the universe of the poem, as it had partially (with the reference to omens) in "Electra on the Azalea Path." Stars and spider prepare for the coming of destiny's infant. Even the worms leave "their usual habitations." In the last two perfectly realized lines, the importance and uncertainty of the birth is certified: "The small birds converge, converge/ With their gifts to a difficult borning." It is now clear that Sylvia has raised her own life to the level of myth and insists upon her pregnancy as a central drama in a universal theatre; but this fact must not obscure the equally significant development in her art. Besides becoming a mother, Sylvia was on the brink of discovering her personal idiom; and she could not help but see these as dual aspects of the same interior self.

As October ended and the Hugheses' stay at Yaddo was coming to a close, the sense of endings found further confirmation in winter's descent. Along with it came Sylvia's birthday. She was twenty-seven years old, pregnant at last, headed for life in a foreign country, and reaching full poetic stature. Internal storms and contradictory impulses must have raged in the conscious and unconscious regions of her mind. Her sense of myth and man's primitive roots was enlarged by reading Paul Radin's collection of African folktales, and linking this primitive world with the interior, animistic world of childhood—a union which became inevitable with her continual rereading of the poetry of Theodore Roethke. At one point, after reading *The Colossus*, Anne Sexton in a letter would even accuse Sylvia of "trying to out-Roethke Roethke."

All of these factors resulted in "Poem for a Birthday," which Ted has since explained was "a series of poems she began as a deliberate exercise in experimental improvisation on set themes." Improvisation was wholly new to Sylvia—a relaxing of control and disguise which she could never have faced before, despite her husband's urgings; but now she came to see it as a path which was essential for any movement away from method into creative madness. The birthday is a birthday in truth, and the poem envisions Sylvia's breakdown and electro-therapy as symbols of another birth that involved a loss of that earlier self.

Sylvia's circle was thus complete, but with the profound difference that now she realized her poetry could give her bitch goddess the freedom of expression she could not give her in real life. The first phase of her poetic development came to an end with "The Stones." Method had given way to madness in the only way method can: by becoming a part of that madness, such an integral and almost unconscious part that it would no longer interfere with content. When Ted and Sylvia left Yaddo for Wellesley, to spend a few weeks with Aurelia before sailing to England, they were more nearly equal than they had ever been in the past, Sylvia having matured enough in her art to leave Ted (and Theodore Roethke) behind.

Far too many critics have tended to dismiss the first phase of Sylvia's development entirely, that is, have dismissed almost all of its verse, as would Sylvia herself in a year or two—but one cannot afford to be so casual. Sylvia had already, by the end of 1959, written a handful of poems which are simply too valuable to lose, a handful of poems—and had not Randall Jarrell said that was enough to qualify for "major" status?—which remain as important as anything she would write later. I am speaking of "All the Dead Dears," "Black Rooks in Rainy Weather," "Night Shift," "The Colossus," "The Manor Garden," "The Beekeeper's Daughter," "Watercolour of Grantchester Meadows," "Two Views of a Cadaver Room" and "Poem for a Birthday," particularly "The Beast," "Witch Burning" and "The Stones." These are solid works, often brilliant works that mate a unique personal vision, admittedly negative or Gothic, with a nearly flawless craft. Other poems such as "Electra on the Azalea Path," "Hardcastle Crags," "resolve," "Words for a Nursery," "Suicide Off Egg Rock" and "Point Shirley," are also too close to some ultimate beauty to abandon altogether.

It is innate in the female psyche to bring blood, conception, birth and death into close connection with one another.

Helene Deutsch

15

A Clean Slate

When the Hugheses arrived in England in early December, Sylvia was already five months pregnant and probably in the grip of mounting anxiety. She did not have a real home as yet and was in a foreign country far away from her mother, who among other things had warned her against the dangers of natural childbirth. Worse, the English weather was settling into its wet, gray winter chill, and she and Ted had to live temporarily in Yorkshire with Ted's family. She still found the Hughes clan difficult to deal with and resented their casual ways; in a letter to Marcia she remarked on Mrs. Hughes' penchant for putting unwashed pots into the oven and cupboard, an unfair charge that did not take cognizance of Mrs. Hughes' advancing arthritis. But Mrs. Hughes and her husband, a congenial carpenter, were not a major problem.

Ted's sister Olwyn, though always pleasant to Sylvia as letters between them attest, was a bit of a problem. Large, strong, highly intelligent, she had apparently never met any man to match her brother in either masculinity or intellect. Years later, she would admit to different people that she had never loved any man but Ted. As Clarissa Roche has observed, the Hugheses were a very close family, and Ted and Olwyn in particular; and any outsider must have felt uncomfortable in their presence. Sylvia often did, though she tried not to show it, as perhaps she was just a shade unsure of where Ted's loyalty would ultimately reside in the event of an overt struggle for his love.

In the next few years, Sylvia would frequently accuse Ted and Olwyn of what she called "intellectual incest"; and, again according to Clarissa Roche, in moments of anger would go much further and omit the adjective. The poem that seems to relate to Olwyn, admittedly written after the break-up with Ted, "Amnesiac," is absolute in its shrill condemnation of her. But such fierce and openly antipathetic sentiments were still in the future as the two women maintained an air of polite friendship towards one another. Whatever hostility did emerge usually did so in the disguised form of mocking, playful condescensions. Only in letters to friends back home did Sylvia reveal her true feelings about the Hughes family.

If for no other reason, overcrowdedness alone caused the stay in Yorkshire to be unbearable for Sylvia, and it was not made any more palatable by the habitual visits of relatives in the area. She could not wait for Ted and her to return to London and search for their own flat, but when they did so on New Year's Day the experience turned out to be neither as easy nor as pleasant as Sylvia had anticipated. Instead it became another Northampton nightmare of going from agent to agent without the least success. Moreover, the weather was especially intolerable, with periods of cold rain alternating with blasts of freezing wind. For two long weeks Ted and Sylvia scoured London from end to end by subway, bus, foot, and, on rare occasions, taxi. The only redeeming note was a growing friendship with the W. S. Merwins, who had been but slight acquaintances earlier. The American poet and his British wife Dido welcomed the young couple into their home and tried to help locate agents and potential landlords for them. It was Dido Merwin who found an apartment in Chalcot Square that she thought might be suitable. Ted and Sylvia went to see it and were delighted by the location and reasonable rent; it was one street off Regent's Road in what was known as the Primrose Hill section of London, only a few blocks away from Regent's Park and its beautiful zoo.

The three-story building, one in a row of somewhat dilapidated houses facing a green, was in the process of being renovated. The new landlord was converting it from a neglected tenement for Irish laborers into a series of modern flats. Unfortunately, the rebuilding was not completed, but that did not deter the Hugheses from immediately signing a three-year lease. (During the two weeks they had to wait before moving into their new home, they resided with another young couple—a Welsh poet married to a German girl named Helga and their two-year-old daughter—who lived in a condemned but soundly constructed dwelling not too far away.) Sylvia was now ecstatic. For three years at least they would have a home of their own, or until they could afford to buy a larger, more permanent one; and they would be living in London near one of its great parks.

When they actually moved into the Chalcot Square flat, however, on February 1, they had to confront the familiar tedious chores of transforming an empty apartment into a home. This time they had the additional problem of doing so under siege in a structure which was not yet finished. Various workmen were constantly hammering away inside and outside, erecting scaffolds, discovering flaws in the walls, fixing pipes, and in general interrupting their sleep and work patterns day and night. Physically exhausted from their search and the whole bother of moving, the Hugheses were too tired to do anything the first few days but rest and reflect upon their good fortune, go out to eat, and take long walks in the park. When they did begin fixing up the flat, the first thing Ted and Sylvia did was to cover the ugly floorboards in the kitchen, bathroom, and hallway with marble-black linoleum. It was easy to wash and kept out some of the many drafts that entered the flat despite the new walls and window frames. The floorboards in the bedroom and parlor, which were badly scratched, were covered with three layers of paint.

Other improvements included painting the walls white and buying a big double bed, a gas stove, and a refrigerator. The Merwins kindly loaned them tables, chairs, and some china from their attic until Ted and Sylvia could buy their own in secondhand shops; and Ted put two huge bookcases in the alcove off the parlor. He also made two chairs for himself and Sylvia, which they frequently had to carry around as the stream of workmen flowed in and out of the flat—all this causing Sylvia to compare their situation to that of the hero in Ted's short story "Snow," where an unnamed madman imagines he has crashed in the arctic and has only his chair to keep him sane and in contact with the past. This story, by the way, and two others, "The Rain Horse" and "Sunday," would appear in a Faber and Faber anthology later in the year.[1]

But after a couple of hectic weeks the workmen departed and Sylvia, who had been too exhausted to write, settled down into the routines of home-making that always soothed her. Soon she would feel strong enough to return to poetry, although she would write only one poem, "You're," before the baby arrived in April. The flat was cozy, if still too chilly at times; and it had the advantage of much airy space and light.

The kitchen in back was sunny for the most part, and the parlor had two large windows overlooking the square. And although the bathroom was tiny, the hallway was big enough for a bureau. The third-floor location gave Sylvia a sense of peaceful detachment from the outside world. Above her in the attic dwelled an old woman artist—a rent-control tenant who could not be moved out and who lived, according to Sylvia, on gin and pineapple juice. Sylvia reacted with unkind distaste to the idea of the old woman's flat being buried under twenty years of accumulated detritus amid endless pots of rainbow hyacinths.

The greatest drawback of the flat was its lack of an extra room for the baby. Sylvia wrote to Marcia that the baby would thus have to sleep with them, "Freud and Spock to the contrary," since it would be at least two years before they could consider finding a larger place. Ted's Guggenheim was stretched thin already and money remained a major difficulty. Not too surprisingly, the baby preoccupied her. She was uneasy and tense, though convinced it would be a strong baby boy. They had registered too late with the National Health Service for that organization to locate a free hospital bed for her, and she would have to have the baby at home with the help of a midwife—the very term "midwife" went against her entire American background. Fortunately, Dido Merwin had introduced Sylvia to her own doctor, John Wigg, who put her in the care of his young assistant, whom Sylvia found both attractive and capable. He promised to stand by in the event she needed him during the actual delivery, and she went to relaxation classes at a clinic to prepare for her ordeal. Her mother's warning against natural childbirth still haunted her, but she was relieved somewhat when told she would be given whiffs of anesthesia and other mild sedation to help lessen the pain.

Sylvia was also comforted by the fact that she would not have to spend twelve long days in the hospital, which was standard practice in England at the time, and could have Ted at her side throughout. Also she was provided with a free pint of milk each day, and received reduced prices on milk and medicines at the stores. Economy was important, and Sylvia looked with ironic humor upon the reality that the baby whose conception she had had to pay for was going to be delivered free. The baby itself as idea and approaching fact was another matter. Myron Lotz, who had returned to Oxford, visited her before April and remembers that "she had this fantastic premonition and fear that the child would be born dead, with the umbilical cord around its neck, a horrible fear of the death of her child." And yet he also recalls that she "seemed reasonably well adjusted" to the entire pregnancy.

Of course, for a pregnant woman to have harbored such fears is hardly abnormal. Yet Lotz (now a doctor) unhesitatingly labelled Sylvia's fear as "definitely pathological." This raises again the spectre of Sylvia's obsession with dead infant skulls and her consistent linkage of babies with sterility and death itself. It also summons up the possibility of a deep, carefully repressed feeling of hostility towards the unborn child.

At best, Sylvia had always been ambiguous about childbirth, and the addition of another obstacle between her and her art had to have instigated many moments of intense, if hidden, despair. There was a life growing inside her, and that life threatened her own both literally and figuratively. But the event itself remained essential, as she well knew, as well as positive and wonderfully "normal" in its own right. Later, after Frieda and Nicholas were born, Sylvia would desire more and more children—reasserting an earlier determination to breed a race of "giants."

For now, things were less certain. But her time and energy, perhaps fortunately, were too engaged for much quiet reflection or anxiety. She ran the flat efficiently and calmly, did the cooking and laundry, and continued to send out Ted's and her own manuscripts. Her only real regret was that she would have the baby in England, away from her mother and close friends like Marcia. And economic difficulties lessened somewhat when Ted's first book, *The Hawk in the Rain*, was given the 1960 Somerset Maugham Award. They planned to use the money for a three-month trip to southern Europe either that winter or the next.

Sylvia's work, too, earned some money for them. Before she left Yorkshire, she had been told by Olwyn about a contest being sponsored by *The Critical Quarterly*, which had been receptive to Ted's poetry. She submitted a poem called "Medallion," which had probably been written several months earlier, and was notified in January that she and another poet, Alan Brownjohn, were to divide the prize. Her share came to nearly eight pounds. The poem saw print later in the year in a slim supplement, *Poetry 1960: An Appetiser*, appearing in the back section under "Prize Poems," while Ted's "Hawk Roosting" was unaccountably included in "Poems of the 1950's," along with pieces by Philip Larkin, R. S. Thomas, Thom Gunn, and others.

As the baby's kicks could not be entirely ignored, Sylvia's imagination was poked into action. "You're" is nothing more than a strand of associative responses to the reality of a foetus, but its art is certain and fascinating to contemplate. Addressed to the unborn babe, it begins with an exterior description that sees the bud as already born, "Clownlike, happiest on your hands"; but then it turns inward and remains a portrait of an unborn child: "Feet to the stars, and moon-skulled,/ Gilled like a fish." Sylvia's ambiguity about the foetus is evident in the odd mixture of the horrific and the whimsical—as in the connection between her own child's head and those moon-barren skulls glowing in a hospital jar. Dodo, spool, owl, turnip are the images in the first stanza and these lead to a touching climax of "O high-riser, my little loaf"—a play upon the old expression, "one in the oven." Sylvia then returns to the idea of foetus as fish—"our travelled prawn" (a reference to the Hugheses' recent trip through America and back to England)—which homes "Like a sprat in a pickle jug." This jar, however, has none of the terror of a specimen jar. It contains not something that is still and dead, but rather "A creel of eels, all ripples." In the end, a mathematical image brings the playful sequence to an appropriate close: "Right, like a well-done sum./ A clean slate, with your own face on."

"You're" is essentially a joyous celebration of the life process, that other extreme of nature's order which helps make the reality of "Medallion" bearable. In it the poet gambols through her own field of talent without care for the fatal pits she knows are still there. Sylvia herself was generally happy as the birth approached, and that sense of joyful expectation was intensified when the publishing firm of William Heinemann accepted *The Colossus* for fall publication. At last she would have a book in print and could legitimately bear the title of poet. Book and child were dual symbols of important completions in the autobiography Sylvia Plath was carving from experience. They were also proof that she could maintain two supposedly antagonistic roles, those of mother and poet, and thereby create life as well as literature. And her husband's book, *Lupercal*, also appeared in England just before the birth. This too was taken as another sign of achievement and essential success. Not only did it appear, but it got excellent reviews and transformed Ted Hughes into a major figure in British poetry. Soon he and Sylvia would be introduced to London's literary set and be taken up by Eliot and Spender.

Though still convinced, like Ted, that English poetry in general was a dull affair, Sylvia found her attitude towards literary England changing considerably with the acceptance of *The Colossus*. She realized that the presses and magazines were kinder and more open to poetry than in America, where the commercial drive remained dominant, at least among major publishers. Yet her book would be eventually accepted in America by Judith Jones at Knopf, who had sent the manuscript to Stanley Kunitz for evaluation. He had recommended publication, but suggested the withdrawal of "one or two poems" because of their blatant Roethke cast.[2]

Sylvia's midwife, an Indian woman named Mardi, or one of her two assistants, came every day to check her, and the doctor predicted that the baby would arrive around March 27. Sylvia ballooned to 150 pounds and seemed certain the doctor was correct, particularly as the kickings had increased. Unfortunately, during the final weeks of March she came down with one of her sinus attacks, a miserable cold that kept her in bed for two weeks and left her exhausted. Ted himself was tired and tense from anticipation, worry, and the many extra chores he had to take on, which included cooking. How intense a strain he was under can be seen in an experience which happened to him the day after the birth. He had an appointment that day about a possible reading with George MacBeth, the Scottish poet and producer of many BBC shows.[3] The appointment was important in Ted's eyes because the BBC continued to represent the surest means of promotion for his work. He and MacBeth talked for a while and then decided to have lunch in a nearby restaurant. On the way, they stopped off at a rest room. While standing next to MacBeth, Ted suddenly fell backwards, hit the floor with a heavy thump, and lay perfectly still. After the Scottish poet revived him by opening his collar and slapping his face, Ted explained the triple pressure he had been under—the birth of his child that morning, the lack of sleep, the anxiety naturally instilled by worry over the impression he was making on the producer.

Sylvia had been awakened by labor pains at 1:15 on the morning of Friday, April 1, only an hour after she had with the help of sedatives fallen asleep. Still groggy, she decided to return to bed and telephone the midwife in the morning, but Ted called the woman immediately and asked her to come over as soon as possible. Sister Mardi bicycled over, convinced that only the first stage had begun and she would be able to leave and return in the later morning hours. But Sylvia's pains were increasing in severity and frequency. Thinking it was only the beginning of her ordeal, she asked the midwife for another sedative, but none was available. However, Sister Mardi did call the doctor, who arrived near 5 A.M., but he also had no drug to give her.

All the while, Ted was holding Sylvia's hand and rubbing her back as the intensity of the spasms increased. A few minutes after the doctor's appearance, and after some four and a half hours of labor, Sylvia gave birth to a girl, whom she named Frieda Rebecca. Sister Mardi washed the baby in Sylvia's big pyrex baking dish and put her in the cradle next to the double bed, where Sylvia could admire and touch her. Instead of being one of great agony and possible horror, the whole experience had been unexpectedly smooth. Sylvia delighted in the ease and miraculous "hominess" of it all—the escape from stitches, a depressing ward, and a pile of hospital bills. Before leaving, the midwife told Sylvia not to get out of bed before the next day and to sleep as much as possible. But a few moments after she departed, Sylvia went into the living room and called her mother in the United States. By that afternoon, she was sitting up in bed, eating yogurt with maple syrup, and typing a long letter to Marcia Plumer on her portable Olivetti. The sound of Frieda "dozing and snorkling" nearby was utterly consoling.

Like teaching, motherhood was a role Sylvia had been preparing herself for most of her life, although with much more dread and uncertainty. The reality of it turned out to be much easier to bear than she could have anticipated—the diaper-changing, the nursing, the constant alertness—primarily because Ted did share in the chores. They would spell one another minding Frieda while the other took advantage of the Olivetti. As usual the main problem was lack of space. A. Alvarez, who would be visiting them for the first time a few months after Frieda's birth, has provided a dramatic picture of the physical circumstances under which they labored to produce poetry, keep sane, and raise their child properly:

The Hughes' flat was one floor up a bedraggled staircase, past a pram in the hall and a bicycle. It was so small that everything seemed sideways on. You inserted yourself into a hallway so narrow and jammed that you could scarcely take off your coat. The kitchen seemed to fit one person at a time, who could span it with arms outstretched. In the living room you sat side by side, long-ways on, between a wall of books and a wall of pictures. The bedroom off it, with its flowered wallpaper, seemed to have room for nothing except a double bed. But the whole place had a sense of liveliness about it, of things being done.[4]

The very tallness of Ted and Sylvia had to make such quarters unbearable at times. But, as Alvarez suggests, their energy and good will towards one another, and their excitement over a pretty daughter and mushrooming poetry careers, prevented any serious eruptions of temper. Also, the Merwins again demonstrated their generosity by offering Ted the use of their commodious study while they were away for the summer at their farm in France. Eventually, both Sylvia and Ted would have use of the study. Sylvia visited it in the mornings while Ted watched Frieda, and Ted went there in the evening hours. The Merwins had taken a kind of paternal interest in the younger poets, which was easy to bear since Ted respected the American poet's work and liked him personally, and was particularly pleased by the good omen of Merwin having "Leo rising" in his horoscope.

Friends began dropping in to see the baby and renew old ties. The newly married Davisons—Peter had since wed Jane Truslow, Sylvia's housemate at Lawrence—stopped off during their European honeymoon; and Jane was amazed by the change she thought she detected in Sylvia: "It was quite a surprise to me to see how domesticated she had become with Ted." Jane had, of course, known only the brassy, blonde poet-vamp who returned to Smith after the suicide attempt. Now she felt "everything hung together" for Sylvia and noted that "she seemed more humane and outside of herself than I had ever seen her." Her husband, who had been much closer to the earlier Sylvia, saw something else. "One quality we saw in the London, 1960 visit," he recalled, "was this restlessness, restlessness."

Set against this view were the impressions of several other guests. Wendy Campbell came down from Cambridge for a brief visit, having only time "to rush in and out" and noticing little more than the flat itself, which she described as "painted white and excitingly filled with objects, and photographic blow-ups that made me long to stay and examine it minutely." Later, though, Ted, Sylvia, and Frieda spent a day and night with Wendy at her Cambridge home, and she had a chance to view them at more leisure: "I was interested to see the calm affectionate pleasure with which Sylvia dealt with Frieda. Once more the lack of fuss, the efficiency, the collectedness."

Myron Lotz also dropped in again but remembers very little of the visit, although he took several photographs of Sylvia with Frieda which radiate happiness. George MacBeth, however, who never actually met Ted and Sylvia together at any one time, interviewed Sylvia several months after Frieda's arrival and was not impressed at all. Perhaps out of nervousness, she had reverted to her bright Smith mask—gushing, giggling, making fatuous remarks, and generally behaving like a stereotype of the American coed. Furthermore, she made the mistake of overpraising MacBeth's own poetry in an obvious effort to gain his support. Despite his reservations, however, the Scottish poet agreed to have her read a few of her poems on the BBC late in November.

But it was A. Alvarez who has left the clearest picture of Sylvia at this juncture in her life. As *The Observer*'s regular poetry editor, he had early seen the merit of both Ted's and Sylvia's poetry and printed several of their pieces in the paper; but he did not come to know them personally until the appearance of *Lupercal*, which he reviewed enthusiastically. The paper then wanted him to interview Ted for a more intimate article, and he agreed. Alvarez called Ted and arranged to pick him up at home; they would use the time of their interview to push their babies through the zoo grounds.

His impression of Sylvia seems accurate enough, if a bit superficial, reflecting as it does both the image Sylvia herself wanted the world to have of her at that moment and Alvarez's own common male tendency to dismiss wives as mere background figures on their husband's stage: "In those days Sylvia seemed effaced; the poet taking a back seat to the young mother and housewife. She had a long, rather flat body, a longish face, not pretty but alert and full of feeling, with a lively mouth and fine brown eyes. Her brownish hair was scraped severely into a bun. She wore jeans and a neat shirt, briskly American: bright, clean, competent, like a young woman in a cookery advertisement, friendly and yet rather distant." After the walk through the zoo with Ted, Alvarez had the embarrassing experience of discovering that Mrs. Hughes was actually Sylvia Plath, the poet whose work he had been responsible for printing in *The Observer*. It was embarrassing for both of them because she had to inform him of the fact and thank him for having accepted "Night Shift" a year before. Not only was Sylvia embarrassed by the incident, but "also depressed." Here was proof that her selfless efforts to promote her husband's career could and did help retard her own. Alvarez saw the Hugheses a few more times in the next couple of months, though it was Ted who became his friend and drinking companion. During the summer, he and Ted did a program for the BBC and returned to pick up Sylvia and Frieda to take them to the local pub for a quiet celebration. Standing around the pram on the sidewalk and drinking their beer, Alvarez saw Sylvia in a different light. Now she seemed to him "easier, wittier, less constrained than I had seen her before. For the first time I understood something of the real charm and speed of the girl."

On November 20 Sylvia read for the BBC on the Third Program's "Poet's Voice" series, which was devoted to "New Poetry." She did the reading well enough to guarantee future work with the BBC and had to have been pleased with her performance—she took as much care in reading her poems as in writing them, as the recordings of her readings from *Ariel* convincingly demonstrate, by adopting accent and tone to the poetry's brittle, highly intense persona. She had to also be pleased in November when *The Colossus* appeared.

The English reviews of the Heinemann edition were generally

favorable, though usually hedged by reservations, none of them serious. Don Moraes in *Time and Tide* did not like Sylvia's tendency to play with words, or the book's sense of being too long; but he praised her control of craft and concluded that *The Colossus* was "one of the best first books for a long time." In *The Manchester Guardian*, a shorter review by Bernard Bergonzi emphasized the influence of John Crowe Ransom—especially in "Spinster"—which was deemed all to the good, and had kind words for Sylvia's "fastidious vocabulary," her feel for the right word in the right place. Peter Dickinson's very brief comment in *Punch*, more blurb than review, linked Sylvia's potent symbolism to "a good surrealist painting" and found her outlook gloomy but her poetry "exhilarating to read."

A. Alvarez was out of the country at the time, having left for America in the autumn; but *The Observer* sent *The Colossus* on to him for review, which he did in the December 18 issue. This was the review Sylvia read with the most interest. He wrote: "She steers clear of feminine charm, deliciousness, gentility, supersensitivity and the act of being a poetess. She simply writes good poetry. And she does so with a seriousness that demands only that she be judged equally seriously." His reservations, valid ones, had to do with the absence of a personal voice. To him, as he explains in his memoir, *The Colossus* "seemed to fit the image I had of her: serious, gifted, withheld, and still partly under the massive shadow of her husband. There were poems that had been influenced by him, others which echoed Theodore Roethke or Wallace Stevens; clearly, she was still casting about for her own style."

Alvarez's review also touched upon the brooding sense of danger and of lurking horrors in Sylvia's poetry: "It is this sense of threat, as though she were continually menaced by something she could see only out of the corners of her eyes, that gives her work its distinction." Months later, in February of 1961, when Sylvia saw Alvarez again, she thanked him for the review, "adding disarmingly that she agreed with the qualifications." Her appreciation of *The Colossus*'s real limitations was no pose, but the perceptive response of a poet who knew where she had been and where she had failed, and who was determined to push on.

As the year 1960 came to its end in the form of another gray and wet English winter, Sylvia was once again oscillating between extremes of one sort or another. The cold, damp weather led to several more sinus attacks, and she was still attempting to write poetry, which had become a disappearing wisp in the wind of housekeeping and mothering. Also she was pregnant again, and that of course meant more ambivalence as she viewed her situation at varying times as either subjection to female function or as a sign of beneficence from mysterious forces because the baby was due to be born around the time of Ted's birthday. Set against these conventional experiences were the exhilarations of a first book printed and favorably reviewed, an American edition scheduled for the spring, a successful appearance for the BBC to be followed by a joint interview with Ted early in the next year, and continued acceptance of her poetry by a wide range of important magazines in England and America.

The restlessness Peter Davison saw in Sylvia was still there, but the year as a whole had been one of happy beginnings.

> . . . the absurd man, when he contemplates his
> torment, silences all the idols. In the universe
> suddenly restored to its silence, the myriad wondering
> little voices of the earth rise up. Unconscious, secret
> calls, invitations from all the faces, they are the
> necessary reverse and prize of victory. There is no
> sun without shadow, and it is essential to know the
> night.
>
> ALBERT CAMUS

16

I Am Two People Now

Camus was speaking to and for Sylvia's generation about the need to persevere in the face of despair, not by retreating to theism or other outmoded orthodoxies, but by exploiting the very horror which so frightened mankind. Sylvia could and would do this by translating the bitch goddess into artifice and defining her terrors in terms of Hiroshima and Auschwitz; and finally, like Camus, she would come to the realization that the artist must always "serve suffering and beauty."

But it was only when tragedy struck twice that the universe's seemingly evil design again reasserted itself in Sylvia's life and she realized what her course must be. In February of 1961 she became ill and was rushed to the hospital, where she soon lost her unborn second child. The sorrow of the situation was intensified by a total lack of anticipation. Frieda had arrived so easily and so well; the second was expected to be even easier. Announcements had been sent out to relatives and friends and a search begun for newer, larger quarters. Suddenly it was all ended, without meaning. The doctors had no idea of what had gone wrong.

Then, three weeks later, sharp, stabbing pains exploded in her lower abdomen, and she was once more rushed to the hospital—this time to have her appendix removed. It seemed to Sylvia as if the malignant universe were punishing her for daring to be happy and prosperous.

Actual pain had always frightened her, though she suffered it courageously, and now she had been hospitalized twice within the space of
several weeks. While in the hospital for her appendectomy, another
father almost came near. Theodore Roethke, who was the prime cause of
her poetry's new direction, was in London at the time. The incident has
been related by Allan Seager in his biography, *The Glass House: The
Life of Theodore Roethke*:

> He and Beatrice continued to see their London friends and about this time
> Ted lunched at Charles's Restaurant in Jermyn Street with Eric White, the
> head of the Poetry Book Society and the author of the great biography of
> Stravinksy. He told Ted about the plight of Ted Hughes and Sylvia Plath.
> They were living next door to W. S. Merwin and his wife. Merwin had to go
> to America and he had asked White to keep an eye on them. Hughes did not
> keep accounts and at that time was nearly destitute—Sylvia Plath was in a
> hospital for an operation and Hughes was trying to keep house with their
> year-old child. White called him and told him not to worry, that money would
> be forthcoming from the BBC and the Arts Council. Ted, who admired the
> work of both Hughes and Sylvia Plath, was immediately concerned and wanted
> to send her flowers but, he said, he was leaving England and would not have
> time, so he gave White some money and asked him to do it for him. Later, he
> tried to get Ted Hughes a job at Washington.[1]

This was early in March—Roethke departed on March 5—and Sylvia
was undoubtedly touched by the flowers, as well as reminded of her
poetry's new voice and vision. The two hospital experiences led directly
to several fine, biting poems, one of which, "Tulips," would be included
in *Ariel*. It would be satisfying to think that the flowers which figure in
the poem were those sent by Roethke, and perhaps they were; but for
the speaker in the poem, the flowers are symbolic of the outside world
she has left behind, that of health and summer: "The tulips are too
excitable, it is winter here." From this commences the monologue of a
withdrawn self that had surrendered to winter nothingness and the
peace of "I am nobody."

As in "The Stones," Sylvia has adopted a passive role which reduces
her to a thing being worked on by others. Bitterness seeps through and,
with the loss of identity, complaints that she is "sick of baggage," which
cruelly includes "husband and child" in the photograph at the side of the
bed, where they catch onto her skin like "little smiling hooks." There is
no love here, as in "Candles," but only the narcissistic self on its journey
into myth. Sylvia compares herself to a "thirty-year-old cargo boat."
Thrice the cock crowed, and she concedes that sickness and fear have

"swabbed me clear of my loving associations." This is not an abnormal but a common experience, which is why Sylvia always speaks so intimately to other women's hearts—speaking the unspeakable, and bringing out into the open those terrible but normal thoughts which many women experience (and feel dreadfully guilty about) during the course of their lives.

The nothingness of her state was soothing by reason of its freedom from the emotional demands of others; and consequently it has a chaste ease of remoteness that is drug-like: "I am a nun now, I have never been so pure." She tries to communicate the peace of it (like being near death or receiving a communion wafer) and its freedom ("you have no idea how free") and its silence. But the tulips, and the sentiment behind their presence, disturb the drift into nothingness. They are alive and breathe through the gift paper "like an awful baby," too red in contrast to the winter death of hospital and withdrawal into self. She drowns again because of these "dozen red lead sinkers around my neck," but it is an unwelcome, painful contrast to the drowning in the fourth stanza, where she had sunk into forgetfulness "and the water went over my head."

"In Plaster" was written at the same time and in the same place. The woman in the bed next to Sylvia's was wrapped almost completely in a plaster cast—sealed-off in such a way that suggested the sort of double self Sylvia had always found intriguing and all too applicable to her own divided consciousness. She had no difficulty in imagining herself as the woman: "I shall never get out of this! There are two of me now." The new "absolutely white" person represented by the cast is contrasted favorably to "the old yellow one" and offers, like the nun-state of "Tulips," freedom from human needs and demands. The anxiety Sylvia had always experienced behind her mask can now speak out: "I was scared, because she was shaped just the way I was."

The rage of these poems is not yet complete, which helps explain the lack of an efficient form; but it is clearly evolving, and abetted no doubt by the fear and actual pain Sylvia was experiencing. Other poems from this period, such as "Face Lift," "Heavy Women," and "I Am Vertical," reflect the same voice still muted by the masks of wife and mother. For now, though, she was squarely within the traditional lyric mode and her "I" was not yet confessional. She was pregnant and living in London, in pursuit of a successful career, and partner to a man whose own career was reaching new heights. But Ted was not happy.

As Alvarez has noticed, Ted Hughes at this time was "fretting to leave London" and yearning for the rural simplicities he had known as a boy. Sylvia must have felt equally trapped in their small flat, particularly with another baby coming—a fact she disclosed publicly only several months later. But Yorkshire had been impossible, as its grim industrial coldness was too much for her, so a compromise had to be reached. Finally they agreed to buy a house in Devon. Devon was south enough to have a warmer climate and only thirty miles or so from the beaches at Cornwall and the sea Sylvia loved, while it was also rural enough to satisfy Ted's desire for the country diversions of fishing and hunting, and for pleasant isolation from the city's frantic pace and the social impositions of a highly competitive literary world.

During a joint interview Ted and Sylvia had given on the BBC in January, they both stressed the smallness of their flat and the difficulty of trying to write while cramped in small quarters with an infant. Elizabeth Compton, wife of the mystery-writer and playwright David Compton, wrote to offer the Hugheses free board. The Comptons lived in a ramshackle farmhouse in Devon which had neither running water, electricity, nor indoor toilet—yet it was in the heart of the farm country and perfect for serious writers with limited means. The Hugheses never answered the letter, but perhaps the invitation played a part in their decision to consider Devon for their permanent home. For that was what Sylvia wanted above all—a permanent home where she could raise her children without pressure and develop a sense of roots.

The BBC interview is also interesting for what it revealed about Sylvia's current literary tastes. She conceded to having been "stunned" during college by Auden and Yeats and Thomas, but now confessed that she had gone over to Blake, which certainly suited her move towards dark mysticism and the nursery-rhyme fervor and directness that characterize many of the poems written from August 1962 onwards. Wyatt, Roethke, Lowell, Sexton, and Blake were to be her mentors, and not the mainline stream of modernism represented by Yeats, Pound, Eliot, Crane, and Auden, though Yeats would never disappear entirely from her life and art.

Other bits of information that emerged from the interview included Ted's isolating, in a playful way, their different temperaments—his silences compared to her "noisy" behavior; and Sylvia's admission that the money had run out and they needed a lamp. She also talked a little about her approach to poetry, notably her tendency to take off from visual images; and she explained how Ted's interest in animals had led to memories of her father, then to bees, and finally to the image of beekeeping. Behind this lay her tale of having believed in magic until the age of nine as embodied in the standard childhood symbols of Santa Claus, Superman, and the like; and then slipping into unhappiness, or reality, and trying to escape through her introverted diary stories and poems. Speaking partly the truth and partly myth, she claimed she adjusted at sixteen or seventeen, but did not mention her suicide attempt and breakdown.

Poised against this was the childhood reminiscence of Ted—again part myth, part truth. He recalled having hunted with his older brother Gerald and having been used as a retriever by him to bring back the shot animals, and spoke of his love for hunting and for his brother, and how he hated the broken bodies in his hands, and was moved by the plight of the animals, and yet how insidiously he was drawn to participate in the ritual of their destruction. But Sylvia interjected a different view here and insisted upon her husband's sensitivity and gentleness—as seen in the "fact" that he could no longer shoot rabbits. Ted did feel the animals' anguish and could imagine himself in their place, as both *The Hawk in the Rain* and, particularly, *Lupercal* demonstrate, but he was also drawn by an impulse to carnage.

The interview was thus not entirely candid, and the talk between the young couple bubbled along rather too happily. Sylvia read "Mushrooms," and Ted told of having been a script reader and a night watchman for a rose gardener. Sylvia gaily mentioned how Ted went off at nine in the morning to do his writing while she did everything else—cooking, cleaning, taking the baby to the zoo. There is no hint of resentment, but the mere mention of the situation is itself a form of condemnation. She called herself a housewife. She had read his poetry before their meeting; he had spent the next three months, and all his money, courting her. Lately, he had introduced her to Beethoven—she admitted to being tone-deaf and that the viola, piano, and school orchestra had been forced upon her—and his last quartets, which she responded to with enthusiasm. Sylvia stressed that her poetry developed from "the sensuous and emotional experiences I have" and that she had always admired masters of practical experience, found most artists narcissistic, and believed that if she had not become a poet she would have been a doctor.

What is important in the interview was Sylvia's statement that she now found poetry "absolutely essential" and that "the actual experience is a magnificent one." Also, she believed herself to be "absolutely fulfilled" when she had written a poem. This was not mere gushing public relations, but a definite milestone in Sylvia Plath's career. It was first of all in sharp contrast to her previous German bricklayer approach to poetry and helps to explain the amazing difference between the poetry of the first phase and that of the second. In a later interview

Sylvia would describe this change as a shift from a written to an oral style and the discovery of a greater sense of listening to her own poems, rather than viewing them simply as formulas and forms on a page of paper. There was more to the shift, of course, but this attitude of joy and celebration in the very act of writing remained at the root of every poem Sylvia wrote after "The Stones"—even the seemingly most bitter poems of hate and despair.

Part of the joy stemmed from greater control of form or voice and a feeling that the major consideration was no longer how but what. Refinements were still to come—the final mating of Roethke and Sexton in child-like metronomic lines—but they too were inevitable offshoots of content. Blake, and her own early tendency to make esoteric and thus mythify her references, would help her here. For now, nothing seemed beyond her. Spurred by the double tragedy of miscarriage and appendectomy, and the possibility of a permanent home, which was another ambiguous situation for her; and anchored in the success of *The Colossus* and a new pregnancy, Sylvia was writing with determination, energy, and happiness. Several of the poems touch upon Frieda. One of them, "Morning Song," was sent to Alvarez at *The Observer* and he gladly printed it in the May issue. This was followed in five months by "Mojave Desert"—it was in 1961 that Sylvia wrote "The Fifty-Ninth Bear."

"Morning Song" opens with a delightful image—"Love set you going like a fat gold watch"; but this apparently pleasant comparison casts a few minor shadows when read with an awareness of Sylvia's dislike of "fat" and her fearful younger consciousness of a mechanical, clock-like universe. These uneasy elements are reinforced by the second line's allusion to the baby's "bald cry," which finds a disquieting elaboration in the second stanza: the baby is seen as a new statue in "a drafty museum"—a threatening statue whose nakedness "Shadows our safety" while the two parents stand around "blankly as walls." This is no crooning hymn to life, no sentimental celebration of a daughter's birth, but a chillingly precise attempt to describe metaphorically Sylvia's actual reaction to Frieda's birth and invasion of her life.

The poetry Sylvia was writing during the first five or six months of 1961 included several fine poems about the American camping expedition, while "The Babysitters" was a tender recollection of Sylvia's trip with Marcia to Marblehead and the little island off its shore years earlier; and she also wrote around this time the equally tender "Candles." There was also a poem called "Insomniac" that Sylvia entered in the annual Cheltenham Festival Poetry Competition. In August she would be notified by Eric White, the same good friend who had earlier tried to solicit Theodore Roethke's aid for the Hugheses, that the poem had been awarded first prize. As the Festival's organizer, he also invited Sylvia to donate her work sheets of "Insomniac" to the British Museum, which she gladly and proudly did—a fitting gesture since the poem was apparently written in that institution's reading room.

Ted and Sylvia were now winning prize after prize, along with several grants, and becoming involved in London's literary life. Not only had Eliot and Spender opened their homes to them, but other contemporary poets such as George MacBeth, Edward Lucie-Smith, and W. S. Merwin were an integral part of their social life. Sylvia also kept in touch with Anne Sexton through the mails; Thom Gunn, whom both Hugheses respected highly, had been a friend of Ted's since Cambridge; and Philip Larkin was also an acquaintance. It was a delicate, often highly valuable tissue of connections that should have made these years in London a culmination of all their career dreams. But Ted still wanted farms and streams and trees around him, and Sylvia found herself becoming overly critical of the "big names" now that she was able to observe them at close quarters. Perhaps London reminded her of her *Mademoiselle* experience in New York, where crass favoritism and subtle snobbism kept the glittering ferris wheel turning. Her essential Puritanism and romantic concept of the poet's lofty mission no doubt made her a harsh critic of those who did not live up to her standards.

They finally found a lovely house in Devon, a big thatched cottage with over two acres of land in a small village named "Croton," fifteen or twenty miles away from the cathedral city of Exeter. Both of their parents had lent them money, which supplemented their own savings, and they were able to purchase it with only a small mortgage. Not only was it a joyous conclusion to cramped flats and endless economic pressures, but the house was only four hours from London by train and within an hour's drive of beaches north and south.

Money also continued to come in. Sylvia appeared once again on "Poets in Partnership" for the BBC in March and then introduced a "Living Poets" preview on July 8. This later was an offshoot of the Mermaid Poetry Festival which she and Ted would attend as invited readers. Held in the Mermaid Theatre in London, the Festival ran from July 16 to 23 and was organized by the Poetry Book Society in conjunction with the Arts Council of Great Britain, under the direction of John Wain, another of the Hugheses' poet-friends. The long list of participants included most of England's established, as well as younger poets, along with select groups of European and American poets, critics, and translators. There were also twelve specifically commissioned poems (the money donated by Arthur Guinness Son & Co.) from twelve different native poets, and Sylvia and Ted were among them. The only restriction on these works was length: they had to be between 50 and 200 lines. Sylvia submitted "Tulips" and Ted "My Uncle's Wound"; and they read their poems, which were also printed in the Festival's Souvenir Program, at the theatre on Monday, July 17. Ted read in the afternoon with Clifford Dyment and Geoffrey Hill, and Sylvia read at night, along with Ted again and six other commissioned poets. It was obvious that Ted was considered the more important poet.[2]

But Sylvia's reputation was growing. The *Critical Quarterly*'s first thin supplement of the year before, *Poetry 1960*, which had published Sylvia's prize-winning poem, sold an impressive 12,000 copies. This success made the magazine decide to try to repeat its achievement in 1961 with another supplement to be specifically American in character and entitled *American Poetry Now*. Sylvia was invited to be its editor—a job she happily accepted and tried to handle with judicious fairness, though it was a difficult task when so many of the contemporary poets were friends and she had only twenty-two pages to work with. Sylvia emphasized in her brief preface that *American Poetry Now* "is a selection of poems by new and/or youngish American poets for the most part unknown in Britain. I'll let the vigour and variety of these poems speak for themselves."

Despite her earlier envy she included three poems by Adrienne Rich; two by W. D. Snodgrass, one of confessionalism's true founders, although she was not really convinced of the power of his work as a whole. But Sylvia also put in "Fools Encountered," a prosaic bit of rhymed pleasantness by E. Lucas Meyers, Ted's close friend, for no accountable reason; and she gave W. S. Merwin almost three pages. The other selections were less controversial, and quite eclectic in fact, with academics and more radical poets evenly represented: Daniel G. Hoffman, Howard Nemerov, George Starbuck, Barbara Guest, Denise Levertov, William Stafford, Louis Simpson, Richard Wilbur, Robert Creeley, and others. She had also tried to obtain permission to reprint a poem by Gregory Corso but did not succeed. All in all, it was a credible collection that demonstrated Sylvia's always keen awareness of trends and traditions in American poetry. Ted once told his sister Olwyn that he had not really known about American literature until he met Sylvia.

Another happy interlude for the Hugheses came in June when they were able to take a holiday in France. Aurelia came over from America to take care of Frieda. Sylvia and Ted spent the time at Berck-Plage, a resort area on the coast north of Rouen. It was a pleasant time for both of them, except for a visit to a nearby convalescent home for the disabled. The vision of those crippled bodies sitting helplessly in the sun, surrounded by the sea and healthy young bodies, was too close to her own fear of the universe's malicious indifference. Ted himself has since written of the incident: "It was one of her nightmares stepped into the real world"; and in the poem born of the incident Sylvia speaks with horror of "things" glittering on "the balconies of the hotel"—steel wheelchairs and aluminum crutches—while children rend the air "with hooks and cries."

Dylan Thomas heard trees scream aloud when they were struck, and Theodore Roethke went running to his wife's arms when startled by a wounded mouse. Sylvia was always finding unremitting reminders of flesh's frail limits, and could not quiet that anxious feeling that happiness would never be pure and untouched by inner knowledge of threatening oblivion and past sorrows. Perhaps, though, Devon might be the answer—a return to nature and simpler rural ways; a return, in a sense, to childhood's Eden domain, with Sylvia playing Aurelia (mother and daughter) to Ted and her children.

Side by side with the human race there runs another race of beings, the inhuman ones, the race of artists who, goaded by unknown impulses, take the lifeless mass of humanity and by the fever and ferment with which they imbue it turn this soggy dough into bread and the bread into wine and the wine into song . . . A man who belongs to this race must stand up on a high place with gibberish in his mouth and rip out his entrails.

HENRY MILLER

17

Lady of the Shipwrecked

It was on September 1, 1961, when the Hugheses officially moved into Court Green, their large Devon cottage at the heart and summit of Croton. Thatched roof, white walls, an acre of daffodils that flowed in a yellow sea to a curving street and a wall of granite, behind which lay the churchyard cemetery, "the wall of corpses," seventy apple trees, large wooden doors, many large, stark rooms, a courtyard, a cobbled hallway, a huge country kitchen—these were some of the impressive features of Sylvia's new, and supposedly final, home. She was determined that it would be a happy and creative home, and liked the fact that the town's small center was only a two-minute walk away from her door, the chemist's shop, the post office, the town hall. It breathed ancient traditions and promised sturdy roots. When she discovered that the big old church which faced her across the sloping front yard dated from the twelfth century, she was enraptured. Here was a medieval sense of the past no New England edifice could ever hope to duplicate.

The town of Croton itself she found depressing to contemplate in its "cement-gray" plainness; and A. Alvarez, who would be visiting the Hugheses the following year, has left a vivid description of it: "By Devon standards it wasn't a pretty village: more gray stone and gloom than timber, thatch and flowers. Where the most perfect English villages give the impression of never having been properly awakened, theirs seemed to have retired into sleep. Once it might have been a center for the surrounding countryside, a place of some presence where things happened. But not anymore. Exeter had taken over, and the life of this village had drained slowly away, like a family that has come down in the world."

At summer's end, when Ted and Sylvia arrived, the thick foliage hid the town from view, except for the imposing church, and it was a veil which Sylvia did not particularly like. It made her feel isolated from humanity, especially at night, and she would rejoice when her old nemesis winter arrived to strip the trees and reveal her neighbors' houses and tiny stores. The town and the empty house were depressing, but she could do something about the latter. For what they thought was the last time, the Hugheses set about instilling their presence in a vacant structure. Dirty floorboards, which Sylvia deemed a typical English vice, had to be covered; and carpets which she hoped would arrive by Christmas, were ordered for the upstairs bedrooms, hall stairs, and front room or parlor.

Sylvia also stitched curtains and made sheep-skin draft-stoppers on her hand-wind Singer machine, and Ted constructed rough furniture from a plentiful supply of logs. He made a big, crude work table for Sylvia out of elm planks and installed it in her work room downstairs, although later, after her separation from Ted, she would claim that her brother had made it for her during his visit (he had in fact spent several hours smoothing down the as-yet-unassembled planks). Ted also painted the entire outside of the house. But most of the labor had to be done by outside help, plumbers and electricians, which meant more bills. Ted and Sylvia were already deeply in debt from paying solicitor's and surveyer's fees, as well as moving and income tax costs; but the loans from their parents and Ted's rapidly increasing income left them in reasonably good financial shape. They were also helped considerably by Aurelia's continuing generosity as she bought her daughter both a washing machine and a refrigerator, almost unheard of luxuries in Devonshire, as a combined house and birthday gift. To cap their good fortune, on November 6 the Saxton Foundation awarded Sylvia the full grant ($2,080) she had requested to finish *The Bell Jar.*

Despite Sylvia's attestations to the contrary later, money would never again be a major problem. If anything, they lived far better than most of their neighbors. Their house had once been a manor and they would always be regarded by the rest of Croton as members of the gentry. They had a local woman named Nancy come in every day to help with Frieda; and the Hugheses often had other help as well. None of this, however, really relieved them from a great deal of hard work on their own. As late as June of 1962, Sylvia would be painting furniture in white and black, spotting it with her favorite Austrian design of hearts and flowers, and carrying on the annual gardening tasks, such as weeding, mowing and scything. She also did the cooking, and transformed her large kitchen into a typical peasant one, decorated with hanging onions and garlic bulbs and, in honor of Ted's famous poem, an old-fashioned recipe for pike from the middle ages.[1]

Sylvia's relationship with Croton would be pleasant for the most part, due largely to her American friendliness and lack of class prejudice. At first the local people were somewhat disconcerted to be greeted by Sylvia's casual wave and cry of "Hi!", feeling that her position as "lady of the manor" did not permit such displays; but they soon responded in kind and accepted the fact that her American background somehow put her outside normal class distinctions—a conviction which did not extend to Ted, who remained, by choice, a distant figure to most of his neighbors.

Sylvia and Ted appeared as "artists" in the sense of dedicated outsiders, but Ted was the family's recognized or official artist (with Sylvia's full support) who did not have to moderate his moods and behavior to suit external, essentially unimportant obligations. Like many husbands, he left social and business duties to his wife. As she had since their marriage began, though not without reservations and certain key compromises on Ted's part, Sylvia accepted her role as an Edwardian "woman of the house"—contacting necessary repair men, keeping accounts, doing the shopping and cooking, tending the garden, and generally taking care of the annoying particulars which go into the business of maintaining a fairly substantial domestic establishment.

For Sylvia, the role was a comforting and necessary social mode—a way of defining her surface identity in a crisp, straightforward way. The regular pattern of her days at Court Green, however exhausting at times or intellectually demeaning, provided a solid platform for her poetic efforts. They also gave her personal history an ancient past among ancient artifacts and folkways which was safely different from her real past and its array of destructive, rootless traumas. She was "the lady of the manor" and enjoyed being so. When the ladies from the church came in the spring and told her that her daffodils had always been donated to the church at Easter she fell in happily with the idea, graciously invited the ladies in for tea, and smilingly bade them good-day when they departed with armloads of her flowers. Ted, on the other hand, did not like the idea at all. In Sylvia's eyes, though, the donation of the daffodils to the church was important and proper not only because it allowed her the opportunity to play *grande dame* to the town, but because it was another custom that had its origins in tradition—a form of art, after all, in which a kind of immortality is guaranteed. It made her and her family real people in an historical context, while also preserving a basic ritual—theatre for life's spiritual activities. Spirit was central to survival, as were the symbols that proved it. Plato still ruled her mind with his glowing vision of a perfect other world, even if his philosophical approach had been shifted to the less rational plane of rites and signs of mysticism and unseen dark forces.

In the new house, off the kitchen, was a windowless room, fairly large, which disturbed Sylvia. Somehow it seemed menacing, like a tomb, or a closet of ghosts and monsters, but in any case too dark and airless in a dwelling that shook with human voices and lay open to the sun. She felt uneasy when near that room, and her awareness of its existence plagued her sleep. But her practical surface self would have nothing to do with such nonsense, and she turned it into a very ordinary closet with hooks for coats and other garments and put a curtain across its entryway. She would later tell her new-found friend, Elizabeth Compton, that she had "a very eerie feeling that there was another room behind it" and that the room was always there waiting for her.

Coffin or cave, the room was a constant reminder that human happiness had a boundary to it. But Sylvia had lived with that room all her life and would not succumb now. Instead she flung herself into her new reality and, defying the lurking disasters her mind insisted upon seeing, celebrated the earth and its miracles of light: "Smell the earth!" she would exclaim to Elizabeth. "Look at this plant, it's grown so much in two days!" She too was taking root, and admitted that "This is the first home I ever had, the first roots I have ever felt."

The Comptons had been among the first friends Ted and Sylvia made in Croton. Soon after the Hugheses arrived, remembering Elizabeth's kind letter and offer of help, they had contacted the young married couple and invited them to their house for tea. Happy over the prospect of having some intellectual companions in the area, the Comptons eagerly made the long trip, about twenty-five miles, from their primitive farmer's cottage to Croton. They were quite impressed by the house and its beautiful grounds, and recalled in particular the huge, carved front door which was thrown open to welcome them. The meeting was a pleasant success. David, a quiet, gentle man, talked at length with Ted about literature, while Sylvia and Elizabeth became acquainted.

Elizabeth was both intrigued and a little disconcerted by Sylvia, whom she found "honest and direct," perched on the edge of her chair, "tense with excitement," her long hair hanging down freely, and dressed in black stockings and shoes and a long skirt that was then out of fashion. At one point early in their talk, Frieda toddled in and headed for the ashtray where Elizabeth had snuffed out several butts. Hating the smoking habit with a Puritan's icy disdain, Sylvia ordered her daughter to get away from "that nasty, dirty thing," which made Elizabeth feel "small and unsavory," although she appreciated the candor and lack of real malice behind Sylvia's remark. The conversation drifted into politics, and Sylvia asked, "Are you a member of a party?" "Yes, the Liberal," Elizabeth replied, and Sylvia jumped up and shouted with delight to her husband, "Ted, this is a committed woman!"

The whole scene is fascinating and revealing. Sylvia's intensity, which was real, and her dramatic gesture, though no doubt affected to some degree, vividly convey the essence of her existence at the Devon juncture in life and career. She was freer than she had ever been, as the poetry clearly shows, and less inclined to hide her attitudes and emotions; but she was also still playing a role and trying desperately to jam her complex intellect and sensibilities into an earth-mother pattern. She would never once discuss writing with Elizabeth during the course of their friendship, or any other serious subject outside of music and politics, and left literature to Ted. But her political consciousness was legitimate and intense. One of her friends in Croton would be Mark Bonham Carter, the local member of Parliament and an intelligent, well-read man. After her comment about Elizabeth being a committed woman, Sylvia paced up and down while she talked, "enraged in a personal way" by the world's tragedies and the way in which war was tied to money, and expressing a "deep passionate feeling about the American marriage between the military and the industrial complex."

America had been abandoned for good, if with some reluctance—but that reluctance had to find its opposite emotion in distrust and condemnation, and this would foreshadow the progression of emotions that would come with Ted's eventual ouster. She would reach the point where England alone was her native land, with nothing in America missed except ice cubes, and where the past could be attacked as well. And yet there was much more to her political convictions than that, of course, for they were sound, orthodox, liberal opinions that grew out of sincere concern and dismay. The important element is that Sylvia was a political creature at this time—as she had stated quite boldly during the BBC interview and would again in a later article for the *London*

Magazine[2]—who accepted the need to project a personal voice upon an international screen.

The immediate effect was not apparent. The poetry written in Devon before her son's birth on January 17, 1962, is an assertion of terrain that reflects Sylvia's awareness of place as an extension of self. But the personal voice is not surrendered, nor are the recent advances made towards freeing the bitch goddess. In "Wuthering Heights," for example, which probably grew out of a Christmas visit to the Hughes home in Yorkshire, the opening line uses place for a metaphor of self that recalls "Witch Burning" in the cycle "Poem for a Birthday": "The horizons ring me like faggots." A woman is again walking alone through a landscape full of despair and uncertainty and is threatened by death—which, in the second stanza, finds a romantic fallacy. The wind pushes her and everything else in one direction "like destiny" and attempts to "funnel" her heat away, while the roots of the heather invite her "To whiten my bones among them."

Sylvia is questioning the nature and place she is coming to know as a rural earth mother in Croton. Thus, in the third stanza, the speaker looks to the grazing sheep for possible relief from her terrible awareness of death. The pupils of their eyes like "black slots" do take her in; but the experience is empty, or even more frightening, "like being mailed into space." Black eyes, black night, black universe—how inadequate they make her new role seem. The sheep themselves are pictured as standing "about in grandmotherly disguise," which suggests Sylvia's own imitation of the simple values she associated with her grandmother. And how repellent nature's representatives in the sheep are made to seem with their "wig curls and yellow teeth/ And hard, marbly baas."

All roads lead to blackness; and the fourth stanza moves smoothly along "wheel ruts" to the ruined human structure, where "Lintel and sill have unhinged themselves" and where people no longer exist and their names are written on the wind—"a few odd syllables." The wind "rehearses them moaningly: / Black stone, black stone." This is the boundary to happiness again, but a climax is apparently impossible. The final stanza trails off into stillness, while the speaker is conscious of the sky and the grass which, like herself, "is too delicate/ For a life in such company"; and she watches the valley below, "narrow/ And black as purses," where the house lights come on and gleam "like small change." The poem does—sometimes effectively—portray a lost soul's mind at work with the materials of place, and translates personal disease into a universal truth of sorts; and yet the result is an uneven and unresolved private dilemma that hovers too close to self-pity for much impact.

It is transitional, however, another step along the way from "Hardcastle Crags" to "The Moon and the Yew Tree," which would be written several months later, and would provide another insight into the dark room in Sylvia's bright country home and divided mind. That it was written at this time is significant, since the birth of a child was imminent and Sylvia was supposedly in the warm grip of a new life. The cluster of other place poems written about the same time, such as "Blackberrying," "Private Ground," "Finisterre," "I Am Vertical," and several related pieces like "A Life," "Crossing the Water," and "The Rival" series, perhaps emerged in part from Sylvia's earlier loss of her child and several tense situations at home, which involved extreme reactions to minor slights, real or imagined, by guests. There was also the terrible experience Sylvia had at the Hughes home during their Christmas visit. She related the grim details to Elizabeth Compton afterwards; and though they may tell only one side of a complicated story, they do emphasize their importance to Sylvia herself.

According to Elizabeth, the visit went well at first. The Hugheses, including Olwyn, who was again just back from Paris and still friendly to Sylvia, made a fuss over Frieda and tried to provide a true holiday welcome for their new in-law. As usual, Sylvia felt uncomfortable, somewhat like an outsider, and made the mistake of thinking that Mrs. Hughes did not like her because she would not let her wash the dishes or help in other ways. In actual fact, Ted's mother was delighted over her son's choice for a wife and stood in awe of "the great American lady" he had married. It was just that Mrs. Hughes' working-class mentality reacted to the idea of such a person stooping to menial chores. The pleasant atmosphere evaporated during lunch when Olwyn began taunting Sylvia in subtle ways and making fun of her, according to Sylvia. It soon reached the point where Sylvia next made the tactical error of confronting her sister-in-law directly by saying, in effect, that Olwyn did not like her and had never liked her, and that she wanted to know why.

The substance of Olwyn's bold reply was that Sylvia was a spoiled American interloper who had tried to take Olwyn's place in the tightly knit family. "I'm the daughter in this house," she shouted at the stunned Sylvia, "not you!" After several other remarks along the same line, all of which affirmed a deeply held hatred, Sylvia fled the room in tears and ran upstairs to the bedroom she shared with Ted and Frieda. Embarrassed, hurt, lonely, she expected Ted, who had sat through the whole affair in awkward silence, to appear at any minute to comfort her. He never did.

Ted's behavior here has to be considered in light of his past experiences with both women, his sincere commitment to both, and his natural male inclination to regard such outbursts as temporary bouts of female oversensitivity that would resolve themselves if left alone. Life with Sylvia had never been easy, had always been subject to her flashes of intense rage or despair; and he knew enough about her intelligence and tight control to realize that she would manage to pull herself together very soon without his aid. He was torn between the two women, an unwilling victim of their mutual jealousy, but it is doubtful that he remained downstairs out of any conscious conviction that Olwyn came before Sylvia in his life. Quite the contrary, they were both a part of him in such a fundamental way that all such ideas would have appeared absurd.

For Sylvia, however, his failure to come upstairs was nothing less than a rejection of her and an admission that he sided with Olwyn in their conflict. She was devastated. Hours later, when Ted still had not shown up, she decided that more drastic action was necessary; or perhaps she simply felt that she could not bear her husband's blatant betrayal any longer. She marched downstairs without a word and walked outside, heading for the moors. It was a dramatic gesture in perfect keeping with the original *Wuthering Heights*—sincere but romantic, the product of soap opera, a child's flight from a difficult situation.

Mindful of his duties as host, Ted did not follow, at least not right away. It was hours later, after twilight, when he finally realized that Sylvia was not returning and could, in fact, be in danger, not from the moors so much as from herself. He stalked into the darkness, sure-footed among the sea-swells of earth and heather he had known since childhood, and soon located her in a "semi-conscious" state. Gently he guided her back to the Hughes home. What happened next has not been told, but is easy to imagine. There must have followed the usual embarrassed apologies. Olwyn left for Paris and would soon be writing to Sylvia again with facile congeniality, and Ted took his family back to the quieter rhythms of their cottage in Croton.

Without exaggerating the significance of the argument between Sylvia and Olwyn out of proportion, it is necessary to see what a profound effect it had to have had on Sylvia, especially since she was pregnant at the time and in fact less than three weeks away from delivery. It had also (from her vantage point) struck at the foundation of her marriage, which she regarded as sacrosanct, and guarded with the same fearful intensity with which she guarded her children and had, earlier, her possessions. Elizabeth Compton thought "there were areas,

like her marriage, which you just didn't approach, like a radar screen";
and Alvarez would characterize the marriage, as late as June, as "strong"
and "close." The problem was Sylvia's narcissism—her sealed-off retreat
behind the mask of loving wife and mother—that prevented her from
understanding Ted, including his long struggle to escape from the
provincialism and humiliations of a working-class background. As
Elizabeth Compton phrased it, "Sylvia did not see the ramifications" of
the deep brother-and-sister union, nor ever comprehended the peculiarly
English demons dogging her husband's footsteps.

The incident in Yorkshire had undoubtedly affected the bleak
landscape of "Wuthering Heights" and probably had something to do
with "Finisterre," "Blackberrying," and "Private Ground," although all
three touch upon places from the past. It was the recent past in the case
of "Finisterre," which grew out of the June 1961 trip to southern
Europe. Another place poem, "Stars Over the Dardogne," seems
similarly to have originated in a trip to southern France. Sylvia's verses
do not escape the limitations of the place-poem genre, but her unique
voice and their apocalyptic aura of imminent doom save them from
complete collapse into pretension. In "Finisterre" the land's thrust into
the sea is the occasion for another contemplation of extremes, beginning
starkly with "This was the land's end: the last fingers, knuckled and
rheumatic/ Cramped on nothing." Landscape is seen as a human corpse
being eaten by the relentless sea—a concept which finds parallels in
earlier poems of drowned sailors and ship passengers, "Leftover soldiers
from old, messy wars." The language is relaxed and personal. A lonely
woman is walking, weighed down by the horrors of the world and by
mists bearing dead souls: "I walk among them, and they stuff my mouth
with cotton./ When they free me, I am beaded with tears."

Her sorrow here is not private, however, since the first two stanzas
had supplied a vision of wasted human deaths that helps explain the tears.
But the third and last stanza must find a personification or myth to
justify what cannot be justified, namely, nature's cruelty; and it does so
in "Lady of the Shipwrecked," with its echo of both Lowell and
Wallace Stevens. She is a hard mother figure, a reverse Madonna, the
black opposite of tender compassion. Her wings are "marble skirts"; and
she strides toward shore, "three times life size," without paying attention
to the statue of the sailor praying to her or the real peasant woman
praying to the statue. Her mind is elsewhere, on death not life, on chaos
not order, because she "is in love with the beautiful formlessness of the
sea." Sylvia obviously accepts and revels in that negative pull; she still
wants a Satanic myth, only now she is aware that it must come from her

own perverse self. The poem itself is a form of myth-making, though there is a distinct separation here between the suffering heroine and the bitch-goddess figure.

"Blackberrying" also confronts and proceeds along a finger of land jabbed into the sea: "A blackberry alley, going down in hooks, and a sea/ Somewhere at the end of it, heaving." The poem is clearly the mate of "Wuthering Heights" in that it uses the same "wind funnels" and concludes with the same suggestion of metallic obduracy. This time the climax has the wandering persona standing on a cliff's edge to face the night sky over a pounding surf: "nothing but a great space/ Of white and pewter lights, and a din like silversmiths/ Beating and beating at an intractable metal." The images are frequently vivid, as when the brambles are seen as hooks dragging her to this last confrontation with her mind's terrifying awareness of the vacuum space where the universe's heart should be. Madness and suicide almost seem kindly in contrast to such a bleak inner and outer terrain, as Sylvia well knew.

"Private Ground" is no more cheerful, though a weaker poem, and it casts its eye back upon the stay at Yaddo. Here Sylvia returns to the autumnal laments that had initiated the second phase in her poetic development. The grounds of Yaddo again provide a perfect conjunction of cultural and natural images in decline. Thus the incongruous classical Greek statues, bought "Off Europe's relic heap/ To sweeten your neck of the New York woods," are being boarded up against the approach of winter by workmen who are also "draining the goldfish ponds." The next four lines are a brilliant tailoring of metaphor to suit the poem's desire to merge the fall of nature with the fall of man:

> They collapse like lungs, the escaped water
> Threading back, filament by filament, to the pure
> Platonic table where it lives. The baby carp
> Litter the mud like orangepeel.

Water returns to the idea of water. Nature destroys without conscience and leaves behind dying infants. Greece too fell, and Plato died, but his ideas survived, though at what a price: knowledge of corruption, of mortality, Sylvia's personal anguish. The next and last two stanzas move into the persona's own efforts at survival. As "the grasses/ Unload their griefs on my shoes"—a line Sylvia will soon use in "The Moon and the Yew Tree" and had used several times earlier—the figure bends over the drained pond, "where the small fish/ Flex as the mud freezes," and begins to "collect them all" and carry them to a safe new life in a lake. It is a positive action, atypical in the entire Plath canon, but even here there is an image of the lake as "Morgue of old logs and old images." The lake contains the mirror that shines in so many of her poems—a reflection of the double in herself and a convenient symbol for art's peculiar process; but it also reminds the persona and the reader that this act of kindness must ultimately be negated by nature anyway. The lake is a morgue and the fish, like men, will die after all. She did act, however, and tried to defy man and nature—an idea which might be extended to encompass her survival at Croton where she stubbornly and courageously refused to let her fear and despair interfere with her functions as wife and mother.

On January 17, 1962, Sylvia gave birth to a son, again with only the aid of Nurse Winifred Davies and Ted, and again with very little difficulty. The child was named Nicholas Farrar. Mrs. Hughes' family were Farrars and Nicholas Ferrar, founder of Little Gidding, was an ancestor. Nicholas was a healthy baby, dark and quiet, and resembling his father. Sylvia was delighted and greatly relieved. Like many women who have lost a child, she probably had experienced some doubts and guilt about her own ability to produce life (as "Parliament Hill Fields" certainly intimated).

She was now a mother to be envied with her perfect set of children, which gave a male and female balance to her small family. It reassured her of her womanhood and normalcy. She was writing better than ever and was still quite capable of caring for two children. After the birth, she went back to her self-effacing role and kept her Devon home running smoothly along the traditional cycle of seasons. As Elizabeth Compton observed, "she was celebrating life at this stage, really celebrating."

From the beginning, Sylvia had tried to become a part of the life of the village. Neighbors were met and converted into friends, however dull or narrow-minded. The local circle of young mothers was approached, and their conversations about babies cheerfully participated in, if sometimes to the point of absolute boredom. One young mother in particular, Sylvia Crawford, who had three daughters became a fairly close friend, though even she restricted their talk mostly to matters concerning babies. Sylvia yearned for what she called "college-educated mothers" who could discuss such things as politics or literature. Elizabeth Compton provided some relief because of her interest in and knowledge of music, but Ted alone kept Sylvia from being swallowed up by rural ignorance.

The image she did project in Croton, where there would be much sincere grief over her death, was that of a bright, happy, extroverted

American girl with a kind word for everyone. Nancy, the woman who worked with her nearly every day and saw her under the most adverse conditions, has testified to her warmth and happiness. Nancy could remember no scenes, no hints of either intense depression or shrill rage.

Another person in Croton whom Sylvia liked very much and appreciated was the district nurse, who had helped deliver Nick. David Compton has characterized Nurse Davies as "a great deal more intelligent than most of her kind," [3] and Sylvia must have enjoyed the chance she offered to talk about things at a level above the ordinary, as she did in her long conversations with Mark Carter. There is much in Sylvia's role-playing in Croton to suggest a comparison with the image she had skillfully cultivated earlier in her life. For she still worked hard at making precisely the impression she wished to make, kept people at a distance by putting them into categories, and exposed just those features of herself she wanted them to see. The Comptons, for instance, represented art and the simple life to her, that is, a basic, self-sacrificing, traditional vision of the artist as a noble outsider working under primitive conditions in virtual isolation to produce his masterpieces. The very absence of modern conveniences in their home, especially their dependence upon candles for light, appealed to her romantic imagination and helped complete the environment she wished to envision herself and her family ensconced in. When the Comptons spoke of trying to move to more comfortable quarters, she protested in half-serious dismay, "You can't! I like to think of you with your little twinkling lights."

But behind Sylvia's artful façade the motor was run always by the same vague fear that had pursued her all her life. The persistent sense of menace in her poetry was not imagined; it was a part of her daily existence. This meant her children too, as little alter egos, were also vulnerable and that she had to be constantly on guard against dangers to them or to their property. Thus when someone broke Nick's pram, she flew into a rage. When Frieda fell and cried in the garden, she raced out the door in a flurry of concern to bandage and kiss her wound. Everyone who knew her has mentioned her excellence as a mother. David Compton recalls her as a "wholly non-aggressive, wholly family-oriented Sylvia, the American mother par excellence, very much the cliché young American mother, children-oriented, freezer, Bendix, high standards of diet, hygiene. She was good at it, a perfectionist." His wife goes further: "Her children were central, nothing about their lives should be touched, not out of ego but fear, and she could be savage as a leopard in defending her offspring, in being protective. This is why you were wary with her."

And yet neither of the Comptons would describe her protectiveness as neurotic and remark instead of Sylvia's "calm" and "efficiency" in guarding her children's lives and maintaining an "idyllic" family group. She must have paid a high price for exercising this kind of control, but when explosions came and the dam did break on rare occasions, her wrath generally descended upon weekend guests from outside the town. After Sylvia's death, David and Elizabeth Compton lived for several months in the Court Green cottage, showing the house to prospective buyers on Ted's behalf, and they remember finding many letters from weekend guests who had been obviously upset and astounded by some minor incident or another which had inexplicably provoked Sylvia into a shrill fury. One such event would result in a poem called "Lesbos," where Sylvia used her art to exact revenge upon a couple from London who had infuriated her with their demands and subsequent refusal to allow her daughter's kittens into their rented place at Cornwall.

Behind it all, as usual, as part of the gnawing fear, was an absence of belief. The place poems end in nothingness or hardness because that was all her devouring mind could rationally discover; it was the oblivion logic could not avoid. Belief is what she craved—the slightest sign that events had an ulterior significance. She lit bonfires and kept totems of black magic in her study drawer, but more was needed—a positive system of spiritual meaning. She wanted desperately to commit herself to religion, as she had committed herself to politics and art, but found no salvation in the Unitarianism of her upbringing.

In Croton itself there were few real alternatives. The ancient church that greeted her each day across the acre of flowers and whose bells seemed to summon her at dawn and dusk on Sunday both repelled and attracted her. She loved its solid, grim, ancient tradition, its eight bells, and its sound of evening hymns, as well as its old-fashioned ritual—its traditional funeral march through the streets to the church door, the casket trundled along on a cart that rattled ominously over the cobbles, mourners dressed in formal black suits. But she hated its coldness, its solemn, dark remoteness, as epitomized in the stone figures of saints that lined its walls, and its prejudice towards women: she was convinced that the Trinity was a male plot to replace the mother in the normal family unit with a vague spirit, the Holy Ghost.

But in the beginning she did try to become integrated with the church. To her it was *the* church in town, which meant that to belong to any other was sheer social folly. She wanted her children to have the advantage of growing up with the support of a rich religious tradition, as her mother had had in the Catholic Church. Ted was strongly opposed on ethical and class grounds, and despised the idea of his children being subjected to the snobbism and narrow-mindedness of Anglicanism. But Sylvia persisted. As a first step, she attended Evensong on a Sunday evening, and later asked the rector—a small Irishman who had served in Kenya for years—to explain the service to her. She enjoyed the singing and the chanted responses, but the sermon was another matter. She found it depressing and ignorant, and rejected the minister's heavy emphasis upon man's weakness and his need to find salvation through Christ. Nor could her mind abide his blatant appeal to uneducated fears and obsolete dogmas.

To make matters worse, the rector, despite his African travels and presumed sophistication, was essentially rigid and doctrinaire in his response to any kind of intellectual curiosity. Sylvia thought him a bigot, and resented his constant recourse to platitudes and the oppressive dullness of his sermons. She was amused when, after having read her and Ted's books of poetry, he delivered an attack from the pulpit on "educated pagans." But he did come and explain the rites to her, and Sylvia kept up the pretense of being interested, attending Evensong for several months after Nicholas's birth. Eventually, however, the dam broke in this case too, and Sylvia ended up banishing the rector from her kitchen. To gain a clearer impression of the rector and of Sylvia's attitude towards him and his church, it is only necessary to read "The Mothers' Union," a story Sylvia wrote in 1962, along with several other tales for the slicks.[4]

As usual, this particular story is almost strictly autobiographical; and the heroine is named Esther, which is not too surprising since Sylvia was deep into completing *The Bell Jar* at the time. It is a well-developed piece of "fiction" that recalls its author's earlier efforts to tag a moral insight onto the end of her *True Confession* sagas. Like Sylvia, Esther has recently arrived in a small English village, is eight months pregnant, already a mother of another infant, and married to an English writer. Her home is suspiciously like Sylvia's also, "a large, thatched manor farm with its own cobbled court," where the front door, "yellow-painted and flanked by two pungent bushes of box, faced across an acre of stinging nettles to where the church indicated a gray heaven above its scallop of surrounding headstones." The neighbor Rose, an elderly woman who lived a few doors away with her retired husband and was originally from London, has come to take Esther to the monthly meeting of the Mothers' Union, a church group where the local women can socialize and engage in community activities.

Before departing, Esther goes to say goodbye to her husband Tom, and the picture Sylvia provides supplies some idea of how she viewed Ted and Frieda in her Devon world: "Tom was planting berry plants in the newly spaded square behind the empty stables. The baby sat in the path on a pile of red earth, ladling dirt into her lap with a battered spoon. Esther felt her little grievances about Tom's not shaving and his letting the baby play in the dirt fade at the sight of the two of them, quiet and in perfect accord." This was not an idyllic picture perhaps, but quite clearly the image Sylvia loved and wanted to maintain of herself and her family. Though Sylvia was never really Esther, Esther was a real and important part of Sylvia—one of the surface Sylvias she had projected since childhood into her biography and into so many of her short stories.

Esther and Rose are accompanied to the meeting by a Mrs. Nolan, wife of the local pub-keeper, who had lived in the town for six years and still, inexplicably, knew "Hardly a *soul*." They reach the church and enter, along with several other groups of women, and Esther "realized that she had never been inside before, except at night for Evensong." She also felt hypocritical when closing her eyes and pretending to pray. What drove Sylvia to the church becomes evident further on with a reference to the bells and their Sunday ringing: "The bells had made Esther feel left out, as if from some fine local feast."

The next six paragraphs encompass a flashback scene that describes Esther's original introduction to the rector and the church; he had dropped in on her a few days after their arrival. "A small, gray man, with protruding ears, an Irish accent and a professionally benign, all-tolerating smile, he spoke of his years in Kenya, of his children in Australia and of his English wife." There is clearly no attempt to disguise the facts of Sylvia's own experience here; and it is Sylvia who waits a month and then, "still perturbed by the evangelical bells," dashes off a note to the rector asking him to explain the ritual of Evensong to her. He shows up a few days later, and the heroine admits that she has been brought up as a Unitarian, which the rector accepts graciously; but she does not "blurt out that she was an atheist and end it there." In the discussion that follows, Esther admits that she cannot accept the resurrection of the body—but she does not say, however, that she also rejected the more fundamental concept of the resurrection of the spirit. At last the rector asks if she believes in the efficacy of prayer, and Esther's response is a touching insight into Sylvia's desperate desire for belief: " 'Oh, yes, yes, I do!' Esther heard herself exclaim, amazed at the tears that so opportunely jumped to her eyes, and meaning only: How I would like to. Later, she wondered if the tears weren't caused by her vision of the vast, irrevocable gap between her faithless state and the beatitude of belief."

The next sentence helps clarify why Sylvia would feel it absolutely essential to adopt the guise of a Jew in her last poem's fiery assault upon her father and Ted: "She hadn't the heart to tell the rector she had been through all this pious trying ten years before, in comparative-religion classes at college, and only ended up sorry she was not a Jew." At the end of the meeting, the rector departs, after having invited her to the Mothers' Union meeting, and Esther senses a lack in him and his religion. She had not given him the cakes and tea she had prepared especially for his visit, and "Something more than forgetfulness, she thought, watching the rector's measured retreat through the green nettles, had kept back those cakes." The rest of the story, which should be read for its diary value, if for nothing else, condemns the rector rather gently for his awkward sermonizing and forgetfulness and proceeds to the meeting.

When asked by Mrs. Nolan what she did, Esther is pure Sylvia: " 'Oh, I have the baby!' Then Esther was ashamed of her evasion. 'I type some of my husband's work.' " The narrative that follows sharply defines organized religion's most glaring failures in Sylvia's eyes— including its crude concern with money-making—and leads to the ultimate sin of narrow-mindedness when Esther discovers that Mrs. Nolan is not welcomed into the group because she is divorced. At the end, like the parade of earlier teenage heroines, Esther makes the right moral decision by leaving. Rose alone is her friend, separate from the hypocrisies of the rector, his wife, and the other town ladies—Rose may very well be modelled on Mrs. Crawford—and the two march off arm in arm. But the last paragraph is more than a happy ending; it intimates a few deeper currents Sylvia saw emanating from the foreboding church:

The gravestones, greenly luminous in the thick dusk, looked as if their ancient lichens might possess some magical power of phosphorescence. The two women passed under the churchyard, with its flat, black yew, and as the chill of the evening wore through their coats and the afterglow of tea, Rose crooked out one arm, and Esther, without hesitation, took it.

The essence of the story is Sylvia's terrible drive for belief and sense of sorrow that Croton's grim Anglican church could not provide. In 1962 Sylvia would commence a long and involved correspondence with a Jesuit group in Cambridge.[5] The Jesuits no doubt appealed to her because of their reputation for tough-minded intellectualism and because they were the order where Gerard Manley Hopkins, a loved fellow poet and sufferer, had found that religion did not inhibit his poetry.

Nevertheless, astrology was still a major interest, and the Hugheses' bedroom at Court Green had a picture of a witch of sorts on the wall—actually a blown-up print of Isis.[6] And in Sylvia's work-table drawer lay a pack of Tarot cards. Her own study wall had a bulletin board that faced her each day as she wrote, covered with yellowing clippings, mostly from American publications, about the bizarre horrors man is prey to—accounts of bloody rapes and murders. One story in particular, which David Compton recalled, detailed a strange case in the United States that involved a young man with a mother complex. When she died, leaving him alone, he told no one and kept the corpse hidden in the house, where he tried pathetically to bring her back to life with electric shocks. Only when the body decayed to the point of a foul odor blanketing the entire neighborhood did the police arrive to investigate. Sylvia's attraction to the story is not incomprehensible. Her relationship with her mother was deep and ambiguously wounding, and the electric-shock idea had to have appealed to her past experiences.

But that first winter in Devon was a birth of hope and expectations. The seventy apple trees yielded a small harvest, and Sylvia gave birth to Nicholas. She also planned a garden, which Ted resisted initially, not liking gardening, but soon agreed to, since it would save money. And the church did serve its social function. Nicholas was christened there on March 25 in a gown of Limerick linen and lace that Sylvia had borrowed from the bank manager's wife. Also there were many teas with other neighbors, one of whom was a retired major and another the district nurse and midwife Sylvia liked. The gardening and going to teas were important parts of the satisfying ritual involved in planting roots, though the writing was never neglected. The Hugheses reverted to an old schedule in order to give both the opportunity to create without worry about interruptions or responsibility for the children. Sylvia wrote in her study in the mornings while Ted gardened, did carpentry work or other odd jobs, and tended to Frieda, while the baby slept or was minded by Nancy. Then Ted wrote through the afternoon while she managed the house and Frieda. The evenings were free for reading or listening to music as the children slept.

It is not too difficult to see that Sylvia had more to do than Ted, even with Nancy's capable aid, and still acted as secretary and agent for both of them. Also, according to David Compton, Ted occasionally had to take a train into London for business reasons, and would not return until two or three in the morning. He might have been restless under the restraints of rural domesticity at that point in his career. But Sylvia was no less restless, and probably more so since she had to endure the small talk and boring social amenities that went with belonging to the village.

Frieda had been uttering individual words since late summer, and was at that age when motion has a joy all its own. Nicholas was a quiet baby, but he still had to be nursed, his diapers had to be changed, and the house began acquiring that peculiar smell associated with infants. This new reality was part of what Sylvia would try to communicate in her later poems, when she emphasized the usually ignored and unpleasant aspects of being a young mother. It was not only the metaphor of dead infant skulls that she would insist upon, but the daily impact of actual babies—as in "a stink of fat and baby crap" in "Lesbos."

But for now, the pattern was complete, impenetrable, enclosed by a family atmosphere of mutual support and love that kept the bitch goddess in check. Sylvia could play "a plain and resourceful woman" without too much strain, knowing that her study was always there for her to retreat to each morning. The winter was wet, and the many electric heaters insufficient, despite a £25 bill every three months, but somehow the family escaped the usual assortment of colds. Then, early in March, Sylvia came down with chilblains. The nature of the malady was particularly upsetting as she felt that winter had sneaked up on her at the very moment when she thought she had it beaten.

Furthermore, the next few weeks saw the weather turn dark and rainy and drive everyone indoors. Sylvia felt "grim" and worried about everything. Slugs were attacking the garden, and she would have to retaliate with pellets of poison—a thought that was in itself disturbing. And there were small financial worries. Money was going out constantly for house repairs and for the baby's expenses, as well as to pay the usual bills like that for electricity every three months, mortgage, Nancy's salary, and so on. The Saxton money helped, as did the steady trickle of cash from reviews, poetry sales, radio work, and other literary activities, but Sylvia could not wait for the time when their £900 loan from their parents and the modest mortgage was done with completely. Also, she doubted if the garden would ever pay back their investment.

The worries were typical and not really significant, but the chill of winter increased their impact tenfold. She was simply living in the wrong climate, as her sinuses testified often enough. She wrote to Paul and Clarissa Roche and begged them to pay a visit, assuring them of room in the spare bedroom where a double bed was set up. They could not come, and Sylvia must have longed for London and contact with older friends. But with April came whole days of sunshine and the daffodils began to bud in the front yard. Spring had arrived, and Sylvia had survived another winter.

The only bad kind of pain and aberration is the kind
caused by power wanting to come through, and being
pushed back. Then you get suffering, and if it isn't
used to grow, it thumps you right back into the
basement, and the period of playing with one's toes.

LOUISE BOGAN

18

The Moon Is My Mother

April brought its usual portion of showers to Croton, but its airs were
warm and healing. For Sylvia it meant less use of her cocaine spray for
troublesome sinuses and a chance to take the children outdoors. She was
writing with steady concentration, working on *The Bell Jar*, a few short
stories, several poems, and a verse play for radio. The latter had come
about through the request of Douglas Cleverdon, a producer for the
BBC. He had produced Ted's radio piece *The Wound*, which would
subsequently appear in *Wodwo* early in 1962, and naturally thought of
Sylvia doing something similar. She eagerly agreed and was excited by
the chance to write in a different genre.

The result was *Three Women: A Monologue for Three Voices*, which
was completed and sent on to Mr. Cleverdon by early May.[1] No
attempt was made to create an actual dramatic interchange of voices, or
to differentiate among the three women in any significant way,
primarily because such a feat was beyond Sylvia's technical skills as well
as outside her interest. She did not want drama; she wanted ritual. And
the three ladies are not characters but variations on the same personality
and voice. They reflect three Sylvias and three archetypal female roles:
Young Girl, Secretary, and Wife.[2]

As a drama, *Three Women* is often uneven in its effects, the three
voices are too similar in their obsessions and language, and the range of

emotions too narrow to maintain any tension. But there is the same kind of power evident here as in the poetry—a relentless exploration of the negative dimensions of the universe as envisioned by the female psyche. Conception and birth, blood and death, a closer look at the "Heavy Women"—Sylvia's recent experiences of losing a child and giving birth to Nick—all come together in the winter season of a white hospital and a simple plot involving three women before, during, and after childbirth or miscarriage.

The wife sees herself as central, "slow as the world," and "When I walk out, I am a great event"—fertile in contrast to the moon, which passes and repasses "Luminous as a nurse." But the secretary is a victim of men, a pregnant career woman trapped by male "flatness from which ideas, destructions, bulldozers, guillotines, white chambers of shrieks proceed" into "the small red seep" that is death. "I saw a death in the bare trees, a deprivation." And the reaction of the young girl to her pregnancy was no less negative, though calmer, as she is aware of how she had been changed. "The face in the pool was beautiful, but not mine." Now she is suddenly conscious of nature's lurking evil: "I saw the world in it—small, mean and black."

There is no relief from Sylvia's mind or art. The secretary, like Eliot's typist, had found no joy in sex, though she protests that she tried to love and play the passive female role required by society and husband— "tried not to think too hard" and "tried to be natural"—which meant "to be blind in love, like other women." She lived on the surface of romantic delusions, until awakened by conception to reality, white sheets, "a world of snow now," faces of her past miscarriages envisioned as "bald and impossible," "little sick ones that elude my arms." When her babies were born dead, she saw the connection between their dead faces and the "faces of nations/ Governments, parliaments, societies,/ The faceless faces of important men"—a male world of abstractions that is "so jealous of anything that is not flat!"

The two birth experiences, wife's and secretary's, are paralleled, with the secretary conceiving of herself as earth mother "hating and fearing" herself. Sylvia's art is still oral. The earth is a red mouth, an old woman's face, who had been used "meanly" by men; and it promises the revenge of "Lady Lazarus": "She will eat them./ Eat them, eat them, eat them in the end." But images of revenge cannot prevent the secretary from having another miscarriage: "The sun is down. I die. I make a death." And the wife's successful bearing of a son is almost equally unhappy. He is described as a "blue, furious boy" who flew into the room, "a shriek at

his heel," though the blue fades and he is human "after all." She slowly
begins to understand the beauty of a new life, of a mother love:

> What did my fingers do before they held him?
> What did my heart do, with its love?
> I have never seen a thing so clear.
> His lids are like the lilac-flower
> And soft as a moth, his breath.
> I shall not let go.
> There is no guile or warp in him. May he keep so.

The only success in *Three Women*, then, is that of the wife or mother,
which was probably Sylvia's way of certifying her own role. Earth
Mother is triumphant as she nurses: "One cry. It is the hook I hang on./
And I am a river of milk./ I am a warm hill." But *Three Women* was not
a success when it was broadcast on August 19, as is clear from a
"confidential" Audience Research Report conducted by the BBC.³
Many in the audience thought it unconvincing and were critical of the
author's tendency to strive too hard for effect. Others found some
redeeming quality to touch upon, such as the cleverness of the writing,
though a small minority rejected the play completely. Part of the
problem, as Douglas Cleverdon has pointed out, was that "two of the
three readers engaged for the production were, at almost the last
moment, unable to take part, and had to be replaced at short notice;
consequently the voices of the three women were not differentiated as
clearly as they should have been."

But fame was not Sylvia's in Devon in April of 1962; it was Ted's,
and she continued to insist upon the rightness of that situation. When
David Compton had written a serious play he wanted an opinion about,
he turned to Ted; but when he had written a mystery novel, he gave it
to Sylvia to read, which she did and apparently enjoyed doing. As David
has observed, "she colluded in not being the family writer," and his wife
saw this as integrated with Sylvia's search for a mother and father,
especially the latter, "which she did transfer to Ted so much. He had to
be a success for her." Perhaps Sylvia realized that if people saw her as a
poet that would alter their image of her and prevent any deeper
relationship. This was the view held by Elizabeth Compton and her
husband David—that people who saw Sylvia the poet would not relax
enough to see and relate to the other, more normal Sylvia. Literary
hangers-on, most of whom she had left behind in London, Sylvia
despised, later characterizing them bluntly as "bitches and bastards."

Ted himself had similar feelings and told Elizabeth, "I want friends, not admirers, not parasites, just people who know me as Ted."

To extend her domain at Court Green, and perhaps further prove her mental health, if only to herself, Sylvia learned from her midwife, another woman she admired sincerely for her "practical mastery" of a craft, how to keep bees. It was terrifying—the threat of wounds from the actual bees and their link with her father—but she persisted and had her own bee hives at Court Green, tended them efficiently, and gathered the honey with neighbors. She also acquired a horse to ride for pleasure, an old, gentle animal she mockingly named Ariel—although the basic mode of travel for the family was still an old Morris stationwagon. In April, Ruth Fainlight, a poet and later wife of Alan Sillitoe, had paid a visit, which cheered Sylvia up enormously and gave her a welcomed chance to talk about her art with an intelligent woman.

When Sylvia wrote "Elm" in this same month, she dedicated it to Ruth Fainlight, though the poem is in no way a valentine to anyone. It is derived from *Three Women* and had its inspiration in an enormous elm tree actually located on the grounds at Court Green. The elm, or rather a female spirit trapped inside the elm, speaks to Sylvia, or rather is a projection of the inner Sylvia: "I know the bottom, she says. I know it with my great tap root:/ It is what you fear./ I do not fear it: I have been there." The bottom is darkness, where the "Heavy Women"— death itself—took root; and the wind through the branches and leaves is "the sea you hear in me" or possibly "the voice of nothing, that was your madness?" These two extremes are in the shadow of a third mitigating factor—namely, love—which the tree tells Sylvia "you lie and cry after." The next line tells of the absence of even that and suggests that Sylvia was already aware of losing Ted: "Listen: these are its hooves: it has gone off, like a horse."

This lessens the distance between creator and image, and brings Sylvia inside the elm, so that the next stanza is Sylvia speaking: "I am inhabited by a cry./ Nightly it flaps out/ Looking, with its hooks, for something to love." Such a stark statement of despair signals the reader that it and the four stanzas to follow are spoken by the watcher or persona, not the elm—a persona trapped in her own madness and anxiety, haunted by "this dark thing/ That sleeps in me," the bitch goddess is a bird with its "soft, feathery turnings, its malignity." Clouds imply faces, faces of love, shattering moon, urge to destroy "those pale irretrievables." And the next to last stanza is a plea for mercy from the mind's relentless stalking, "I am incapable of more knowledge," which has led to the influence of the bald moon muse, "this face/ So murderous in its strangle of branches." The moon is Medusa, visage of the bitch goddess: "Its snakey acids kiss./ It petrifies the will." At last the culminating horror is nature's repetitions and Sylvia's consciousness of inadequacies: "slow faults/ That kill, that kill, that kill."

The progression itself is suicidal, Sylvia sinking under the weight of her desolation, a desolation that is turning painfully towards an awesome rage at all creation. As in 1953, Sylvia's anxieties and weakening energies were tumbling her towards an explosion, and her unconscious was laboring with awesome might to save the self by directing the rage outward, seeking an objective, legitimate target for the mushrooming fury. "Elm" is a fine poem, though uneven, uncertain of its voice and narrative focus, a rehearsal, a final dress rehearsal for "The Moon and the Yew Tree." What is missing are essential religious echoes and a clear separation of self from impinging nature. "Elm" makes evident the thinning of the line between reality and fantasy. Here metaphor shifts the persona closer to a pantheistic awareness of nature from the inside. It also intimates that Sylvia was accepting the parallels or allegories her conscious mind created as *real* connections, which is part of her black-magic sense that the universe hinged upon *her* every action and thought. Sylvia is a child held in check for too many years, which is why "Daddy" and "Lady Lazarus" and so many other late poems insist upon a nursery-rhyme formula. In "Elm" Sylvia wanted a scheme for self-revelation that would permit conscious art to simulate the actual, but her always shrewd sense of craft must have told her that a more direct confrontation was needed. The important thing is that her mind and emotions were worrying at the problem, partially stimulated, no doubt, by memories dredged up by *The Bell Jar.*

About this time Sylvia was also working on a series of poems about her muse the moon, only one of which was apparently saved, which indicates how intent she was upon defining the precise nature of her gift and the anguish it entailed. In "The Rival" the reference is asserted in the very first line: "If the moon smiled, she would resemble you." Moon and muse, of course, are oral and in constant agony, but the moon's "O-mouth grieves at the world; yours is unaffected." Again the muse is cast as Medusa: "your first gift is making stone out of everything." The comparison of muse and moon continues as muse is seen as "Spiteful as a woman, but not so nervous." The muse is also regarded as a deadly source of dissatisfactions which "Arrive through the mailslot with loving regularity,/ White and blank, expansive as carbon monoxide"—as brilliant a critical summary of Sylvia's late poems as can anywhere be found. The last two lines, separate from the rest for stress, outline

Sylvia's position at this stage in her life: "No day is safe from news of you,/ Walking about in Africa maybe, but thinking of me."

The poem itself is too weak and contrived, but a slightly stronger one dealing with the same topic and metaphor would be written months later, just before the break with Ted. Called simply "The Rival (2)" for want of a better title, it was written in July, according to Sylvia's manuscripts, and was probably the final poem in the series. It maintains the association of muse with moon, but now the metamorphosis is complete—the moon *is* her muse, "the one eye out there" in space—and poetry is still considered in terms of mail. The muse writes "a poison pen letter."

In May Sylvia wrote "The Moon and the Yew Tree," one of several masterpieces from the final phase. Presumably, it began as an exercise on a theme. Ted was struck by the eerie way the moon shone upon the huge yew tree in the churchyard across from their cottage and suggested she translate it into poetry. By midday, the poem was finished. But Ted was "greatly" depressed by it and saw in the allegory of the lost little girl the pattern of night forces tearing away at Sylvia's soul.

He was right to be depressed. The opening two lines of the poem immediately establish the harsh duality of Sylvia's imagination: "This is the light of the mind, cold and planetary./ The trees of the mind are black. The light is blue." The situation is stark. A woman or little girl or both in one stand at night in the churchyard on a misty, full moon night, separated from the cottage "by a row of headstones." The woman's condition is desperate: "I simply cannot see where there is to get to." The opening two lines have thus set up a dilemma, and the metaphors— the personification of the grass as "spiritous mists" and the symbolic tombstones—refine this dilemma into a conflict between an awareness of death and an awareness of the intellect's dangerous remoteness from experience, "cold and planetary."

Traditionally, yew trees are associated with death, so the very title of the poem is setting out the major opposition of extremes—moon (creative ruthlessness and possible madness) *versus* the yew tree (death and oblivion). In the second stanza it is the moon which draws attention; it is closed against Sylvia, the now familiar "O-gape of complete despair." The next brief sentence, "I live here," is a separate statement that applies both to the town and to lunar despair. Religion does not help; the church bells ring out twice on Sunday to affirm "the Resurrection," but conclude "soberly" on "their names" in a pathetic plea for identity.

In the third stanza it is the yew tree which is central and pointing heavenward. "It has a Gothic shape" that lifts the eyes to the moon—the linear progression is important and is reminiscent of several similar attempts to match physical ascents and descents with metaphorical and thematic ones, as in "Black Rooks in Rainy Weather." As she now contemplates the moon, Sylvia herself, and not the bitch goddess in her, has to concede that "The moon is my mother." This is a terrible admission, though one already evident in so many previous poems from "The Rival" series to "Moonrise." But the moon is not "sweet like Mary" and her blue garments unloose bats and owls instead of saints and angels. The tone remains sad, disconsolate, full of yearning for normalcy, sanity, belief in deity. "How I would like to believe in tenderness," Sylvia says, which finds correspondence in the church's statue of the Madonna, "gentled by candles,/ Bending, on me in particular, its mild eyes."

The flight down was quick and terrible. "I have fallen a long way." So the church is seen in Sylvia's mature, secular eyes: "the saints will be all blue," the pews "cold," and the saints only false images, dead, "stiff with holiness." The moon, of course, must have the last female word. "She" can see "nothing of this," being "bald and wild"; but the real horror is the similar failure of the yew tree, its promise of nothing beyond death: "And the message of the yew tree is blackness—blackness and silence."

In discussing the confessional movement and the art of Sylvia Plath, Alvarez has propounded a generally convincing theory to explain the relationship between madness and modern poetry as a resort to "extremism"—a form of literary brinkmanship in which the poet, faced by a fragmented, bestial society, must gamble his own sanity (and life at times) at the extreme edge of interior experience. But Sylvia, like John Clare, remained in control of her art to the very end and accepted the price of her insights and talent. Her last mental breakdown and suicide were not the product of her art, as both Alvarez and Rosenthal have intimated, but the sad gamble of a lost and lonely little girl afraid to confront again the horrors of schizophrenic depression and hospital treatment.

In May of 1962, however, Sylvia was not mad, but she was very tense and tired, and subject to fits of depression, as she always had been, as well as to bouts of physical illness. She fought against them with familiar determination and depended upon her marriage and children to sustain her. She maintained her surface disguises intact. Her days were too full with taking care of the two and a half acres of land they owned, minding the children, tending the bees and garden, cooking, sewing, cleaning, keeping up friendly relations with the neighbors, and trying to complete *The Bell Jar*. Yet "all that we saw was idyllic," David Compton has said.

Tragedy occurred in June. Neighbors next door down the road, an elderly couple living on a fixed income, were in trouble. The husband came down with a fatal illness, and the wife frequently needed Ted's and Sylvia's help during his final days. His death and funeral, which Sylvia attended, disturbed her, and also summoned up memories of the visit to Southern France the year before—the old man dying the same week and month of the trip "almost to the day," as Ted has confirmed.

Two poems were written soon after the funeral, "Widow" and "Berck Plage," and the latter is comparable in stature to "The Moon and the Yew Tree." Complexly structured and evolved, it is always rapid, often merciless in effect. But unlike "The Moon and the Yew Tree," where the subtleties become immediately evident, its surface is seemingly simple and straightforward. "Berck Plage" presents difficulties, but the author cannot be faulted for esoteric obscurity, since the poem's design does not depend upon a background knowledge of specific places and events—the home for the disabled in Berck Plage and a neighbor's death and funeral—for ultimate impact. It is also the longest poem Sylvia ever wrote, and yet the pace never slackens. Divided into seven sections, which are numbered and perhaps ordered deliberately to encompass the "mystical" seven, "Berck Plage" opens with the mother sea as a threat of nothingness—"This is the sea, then, this great abeyance"—a conversational induction that determines the tone throughout and the next line (two-line stanzas predominate and maintain the quick-step rhythm) introduces the wounded "I" who will pull the strings. "How the sun's poultice draws on my inflammation." Pain and nothingness are at the beginning, and the rest of the first section establishes a scene of resort beach and the persona walking with a smile across its miracles of "Electrifyingly-coloured sherbets" and "pale girls" until "A sandy damper kills the vibrations." The horror has arrived in the form of a home for the disabled—tokens of the universe's bald domain and processes, which blind the eye and introduce the priest in sunglasses and black cassock walking "among the mackerel gatherers." They turn their backs to handle their catch—fish which are seen as "black and green lozenges like the parts of a body." The section ends as it began with the sea—now Medusa—that "Creeps away, many-snaked, with a long hiss of distress."

In section two, the black Nazi boot of a later poem starts the action. "This black boot has no mercy for anybody./ Why should it, it is the hearse of a dead foot." But it belongs to a priest reading from a missal during a funeral service, while elsewhere life goes on. "Obscene bikinis hide in the dunes" and later "two lovers unstick themselves." The extremes of death versus life are again placed in juxtaposition. The "I" at the poem's core is still morbidly attracted, like Esther and Sylvia, to brutal, bizarre accidents and tragedies and sees herself drawn "like a long material" (Sylvia thought of herself as "long") into the "still virulence" like "a weed, hairy as privates"—sex remained repugnant.

Section three, set in the past, commences with the home for the disabled. "On the balconies of the hotel, things are glittering." And suicide is presented as one desperate, possible response to a condition beyond the "I's" control as Sylvia remembers her own walk into the sea off Nauset Beach: "Why should I walk/ Beyond the breakwater, spotty with barnacles?/ I am not a nurse, white and attendant." The children, most of all, scratch at her heart "with hooks and cries," but she knows that her heart remains "too small to bandage their terrible faults." They summarize her vision of humanity's appalling situation; man's side is not Christ's, blooming a red resurrection, but "red ribs,/ The nerves bursting like trees." The only chance for meaning seems to lie in art, not religion—"this is the surgeon:/ One mirrory eye." Man looks into the mirror of art only to discover his evil double. The "I," however, cannot escape "facts"—the old villain, "A facet of knowledge"—which brings the poem into the present, where it will stay: "On a striped mattress in one room/ An old man is vanishing./ There is no help in his weeping wife." With his death goes all of art's metaphors and delusions. "Where are the eye-stones, yellow and valuable,/ And the tongue, sapphire of ash."

It should be a question but is not, because Sylvia knew the answer. Oblivion alone lurked behind the white barrier between life and black death. Section four is a calm and reflective rest period along the way, a slow contemplation of the actual preparation for the funeral. The dead man's visage is seen as a "wedding cake" with "a paper frill." The nurses, once so beautiful in their efforts to sustain life, now "are browning, like touched gardenias." The man is complete, beginning and end joined, and Sylvia will not lie: "It is horrible." A child's curiosity makes her wonder if he is "wearing pajamas or an evening suit" under his sheet. His jaw had been propped by a book "until it stiffened"—art's sole and ironically mocked function at this stage—and the next line has the emotional thrust of a dagger: "And folded his hands, that were shaking: goodbye, goodbye."

The earlier sea finds an echo in Devon's green hills at the commencement of section five. "Run fold upon fold far off, concealing their hollows." But the hollows "rock the thoughts of the wife," which are "Blunt, practical boats" full of the necessary details that a survivor has to consider—clothing, china, "married daughters." The poet, however, refuses this way out and concentrates her attention on the single candle flickering in the dead man's open window: "This is the tongue of the dead man: remember, remember." She sees the neighbor mourners as nothing more than "elate pallors of flying iris"—flowers that fade quickly and forget—while the "empty benches of memory look over stones" in the church graveyard. The cemetery, unlike grief and human memory, endures. "It is so beautiful up here: it is a stopping place."

The funeral procession reaches the church in the next section and is met by the priest. His voice "in thin air" addresses the coffin as "the hills roll the notes of the dead bell." The "I" moves to a contemplation of the church walls and wonders at the proper name for its color. "Old blood of caked walls the sun heals,/ Old blood of limb stumps, burnt hearts." This is a recollection of Berck Plage's cripples and an accurate description of the church's actual walls. The widow, with her three daughters, has beauty, but her face, among the flowers, folds in upon itself like petals "Not to be spread again." Nature has triumphed once more. The sky above the funeral scene is "wormy with put-by smiles," and the indifferent "bride flowers"—a second marriage reference—"expend a freshness." Birth, marriage, death are the trinity of a brief mortal span, and the dead man's soul is "a bride" itself, but married to a groom that is "red and forgetful, he is featureless."

The final section of the poem, which covers the procession's movement into the cemetery, returns firmly to the "I" consciousness and her immediate experience—being in a car and shut off by glass from the real world, "dark-suited and still, a member of the party." The priest is again denigrated: "a vessel,/ A tarred fabric, sorry and dull," Sylvia is throwing another stone at her rector. And the flower cart is projected as "a beautiful woman,/ A crest of breasts, eyelids and lips/ Storming the hilltop." Children nearby see the whole procession as "a wonderful thing." For them it is a Sunday thing of sorts, and Sylvia takes advantage of their innocence to present the final scene through her own child's eye. The six mourners and bearers standing in the grass around the casket, "a lozenge of wood," and the empty hole, "a naked mouth, red and awkward." The last two lines pull dying and death into one vivid tableau:

> For a minute the sky pours into the hole like plasma.
> There is no hope, it is given up.

The poem has certainly offered no hope for salvation or resurrection, and yet its despair is oddly not absolute, perhaps because the art itself is so cunningly ordered along its repetitions of key images, and, far more significant, because Sylvia permits herself to be human.

"Widow," the other poem inspired by her neighbor's death and funeral, is not nearly as strong, focussing on the dead man's wife, and trying to create a counterpart to the earlier "Spinster." It is an angry and genuinely feminist poem that savagely protests against the death a husband leaves behind. The woman now must wear widow weeds like a spider in the center of "loveless spokes," while "The moth-face of her husband, moonlike and ill,/ Circles her like a prey she'd love to kill." The repetition of the word "widow" is effective, and Sylvia depends upon several favorite metaphors, such as the play upon the dead man as "paper image" and his wife as "paper now" and the constant variations upon shadows and the space between stars; but the bile stains the art, at least until the final stanza, when the widow's special fear comes wonderfully to life. For now she fears that her husband's soul might be banging silently against a pane of glass, like the angel shown in a stained-glass window coming to tell Mary of her good fortune. "Blinded to all but the grey, spiritless room/ It looks in on, and must go on looking in on."

The bitterness of "Widow" may well stem in part from Sylvia's growing realization that her own marriage might be in trouble. It is difficult to tell, since Sylvia maintained the image of a happy, contented wife, secure in the knowledge of her husband's fidelity, although the poetry said differently. Certainly this is the picture Alvarez had of her and her marriage when he stopped off to see the Hugheses on his way to Cornwall. Sylvia liked Alvarez and his poetry, which she had recently read, though her appreciative reaction to his work might have arisen from sympathy occasioned by his recent divorce.

But Alvarez also sensed a change in Sylvia and thought the birth of her son had something to do with it. Now he described her as "No longer quiet and withheld, a housewifely appendage to a powerful husband, she seemed made solid and complete, her own woman again." She guided him around the house and grounds as if it "were *her* property." But there was no hint of discord, merely a restructuring of extremes: "Ted, meanwhile, seemed content to sit back and play with little Frieda, who clung to him dependently. Since it was a strong, close marriage, he seemed unconcerned that the balance of power had shifted for the time being to her."

Before he left, Sylvia told Alvarez, "I'm writing again, really writing. I'd like you to see some of the new poems."

What was behind Sylvia's awesome fertility of the moment? Something was nagging at her unconscious, stirring up the dark waters where the bitch goddess had her nest, and the only probable answer is that it was an interior sense that Ted was drifting away and her marriage was about to collapse. Later, believing she had occult powers of foresight, she would tell the Comptons that she had been warned by supernatural forces about what was to come. Once while Sylvia was sitting before the fire in the parlor, where some letters were burning, a piece of paper blew out and landed near her foot. On it was written the name "Olga," the name of the woman whom Ted would eventually make his mistress.[4] Sylvia's seemingly uncanny psychic gift was, as Alvarez has noted, in fact "a triumph of mind over ectoplasm."

Whatever forces were at work upon her marriage, including no doubt a hidden jealousy on Ted's part—an awareness that his wife had caught up with him and was very possibly on the brink of surpassing his remarkable achievement, since he was, at least superficially, "writing the same animal poem over and over" in Clarissa Roche's words—Sylvia remained determined to keep the façade firmly in place. Relief of sorts was supposedly on the way. Aurelia was coming to Court Green in mid-June and would stay the rest of the summer.

An Ancient Proverb

Remove away that black'ning church:
Remove away that marriage hearse:
Remove away that place of blood:
You'll quite remove the ancient curse.

WILLIAM BLAKE

19

I'll have your heart, if not by gift my knife
Shall carve it out. I'll have your heart, your life.

STEVIE SMITH

I Am, I Am, I Am

Aurelia Plath arrived at Court Green in early June to find her daughter much thinner than she had ever seen her. June was also the month in which Sylvia wrote a letter to Olwyn, who was still in Paris, and admitted to being extremely weary after three years of bearing, nursing, and caring for her children, and resented the bovine dullness of it all.[1] The same letter speaks of her sinus condition, which had never been cured but had been improved considerably one summer when she had it drained every day; and advises her sister-in-law, who was apparently experiencing similar trouble, to seek a dry climate like that of Arizona or New Mexico. The tone of the letter is gay, of course, and too riddled with obvious superficiality to reveal very much about the inner darkness her poetry was beginning to explore with ever greater confidence and introspective honesty.

That darkness must be conjectured from the poetry and from the few surface events that highlighted the months of June, July, and August—a crucial time in Sylvia's life and art. The arrival of her mother was both a relief and a burden. Her ambiguous attitude towards Aurelia was perhaps best reflected in two letters she wrote a few weeks apart. The same letter to Olwyn speaks happily of Aurelia's arrival, and shows that Sylvia appreciated the fact that she would now have more help with the children and cooking and more time to retreat to her study and write.

There is no suggestion that the visit was anything else but a carefully arranged and joyfully anticipated event. But the other letter, written to the Roches on July 11, gives a much different impression. It claimed that Aurelia had appeared out of the blue to camp on the Hughes doorstep until mid-August and that her presence would transform their serene household into a "hectic" crowd scene. The latter contradiction might, however, have originated in Sylvia's desire to cover up an earlier invitation to the Roches which promised them the use of the big spare bedroom now occupied by her mother. But the "hectic" part certainly reflects her true feelings about her mother's presence, which always inspired mixed emotions, though she did appreciate Aurelia's practical aid with domestic chores.

Despite her marriage and the ocean between them, Sylvia's relationship with her mother had not altered a great deal since her period of intense psychoanalysis in late 1953; that is, she still knew how to "handle" her mother on the surface, how to treat her with coy deference and affected compatibility. But Sylvia also occasionally belittled her mother behind her back, only to pay a heavy price in feelings of guilt and regret afterwards. Though outsiders who met Aurelia only on a few social occasions, the Comptons believed they saw immediately into the heart of Sylvia's deep emotional dilemma, namely, that her real love for her mother was constantly struggling against a certain embarrassment at her more limited horizons. "Her letters are such a heavy weight on me," Sylvia told Elizabeth Compton more than once.

David Compton has observed, "there was no point of contact whatsoever, a performance would be gone through between them, had probably been gone through all the time." He saw Aurelia as "a perfectly well-meaning, unknowing woman who had a received idea to cope with every known eventuality, uncomprehending of anything that ever happened to her or anyone else, all sentimental, all the things Sylvia would detest." He also believed it must have been "hell to live with her, absolutely murder to have lived with that woman at all," although he did stress her generosity and concluded that he "felt very sorry for her and Sylvia." Later, after her mother had departed and the dreaded break with Ted had taken place, Sylvia would write a poem called "Medusa." Here the bitch goddess was permitted to say all the things she had wanted to say but could not when restrained by love and middle-class morality. Medusa herself had been a prime archetype for Sylvia's urge to freeze experience in poetry. The poem retains that concept, but shifts the deadly figure away from self and to the mother, blaming her for creating both Sylvia's muse and the conditions that resulted in the muse holding sway. "I didn't call you at all./ Nevertheless, nevertheless/ You steamed to me over the sea,/ Fat and red, a placenta/ Paralyzing the kicking lovers./ Cobra light/ Squeezing the breath from the blood bells/ Of the fuchsia. I could draw no breath,/ Dead and moneyless."

There is a mistaken notion among some interpreters of Sylvia's poetry that this poem deals with "Olga," Ted's mistress. The reference, for instance, to "kicking lovers" and to being left "Dead and moneyless" could be interpreted as certain signs that Sylvia saw these as fatal effects on the Hughes marriage; and she certainly would feel that Ted's departure had left her in deep financial straits and more dead than alive. In the very next stanza there are the three acid questions: "Who do you think you are?/ A Communion wafer? Blubbery Mary?" Although the allusion to an overweight madonna fit Olga far better than Aurelia, the final stanza and its metaphor of a sea drowning, following a reference to the bell-jar atmosphere of descending madness and remoteness, recalls Sylvia's obsession with the ocean as a mother and a killing womb. But, that last line, set off starkly from the rest of the poem, makes no sense if applied to Olga and not Aurelia: "There is nothing between us."

The confusion may stem largely from the date of the poem's composition, which was after the break-up of the marriage, and from its tone of outraged fury, as well as allusions to Olga in several other similar poems. The forced eviction of Ted did indeed unleash the bitch goddess, but it has to be remembered that this special Medusa had many scores to settle and that her fury, as *The Bell Jar* vividly demonstrates, would never be solely restricted to the immediate cause of her release. Again and again, she would pounce upon unsuspecting figures from her past, friends and relatives and patrons, while driving always towards the ultimate villain, who was of course her father. But along the way she would not hesitate to attack her mother; and in *The Bell Jar* it is Esther's mother, not her father, who emerges as the primary target.

But in June, such emotional extremes were still in the future. For now Aurelia became part of the Court Green family. The early summer was drier than it had been for years and approached drought condition by July. Trucks with loudspeakers would soon be trundling through the streets, warning residents not to use tap water for their gardens. Sylvia and others had to bring water to their drooping plants in buckets from the house, pretending that it was dirty bath and dish water. The only relief June brought was a chance for Ted and Sylvia to take a trip to London as guests of the BBC, which paid fees and train fares. It was their first trip to the city together since the initial move into Croton and a holiday of sorts that would provide both of them with a needed rest from the demands of children and home.

Ted would appear on a program called "Children's School Hour" to discuss birds, while Sylvia was a guest on "The World of Books," speaking directly to the topic of "Poets' View on Novel Writing"—an appropriate enough subject since *The Bell Jar* was progressing steadily towards completion. On August 1, Sylvia would send in a final progress report to the Saxton trustees, explaining that sixteen chapters of the novel were already finished, about 221 pages, and by summer's end the completed manuscript would be in the hands of Heinemann, who accepted it without delay. Thus her comments on a "Poets' View of Novel Writing" were given in light of an actual situation—and yet her talk is not very revealing.

Like many poets, Sylvia loved the idea of the novel's looseness—Henry James' "baggy monster"—which appeared as such a relief after so many years of laboring within the compressed confines of verse. She spoke of her poetry in terms of a door opening and shutting on an outside scene, so quickly done that only a glimpse could be gleaned of a garden or a person or a dragonfly or a heart or a city; and she tried to illustrate what she meant with a reference to Pound's famous two-line imagist poem, "In a Station of the Metro." She also liked the idea that the novel could accommodate itself more readily to commonplace things in life: "I never put a toothbrush into a poem," she told the interviewer, and then went on to talk about the origins of "The Moon and the Yew Tree." "I did put a yew tree in," she said, "and that yew tree began, with astonishing egotism, to manage and order the whole affair." By the middle of the poem, she had "contemplated it with tender melancholy."

The Bell Jar, however, is anything but a "baggy monster," with its prose lean and to the point, ideally suited in tempo and vulgate structure to its heroine. The only problem, as with many previous stories, is an occasional lapse into the language of a highly perceptive different self. And yet Esther is supposed to be an "A" student from a prestigious college, unlike the other heroines in the stories for the "slicks," where their educational antecedents are either deliberately vague or non-existent. The dilemma was a familiar one for Sylvia as she tried to structure her novel around the inherent possibilities of an evil double, using a naïve alter-ego, her bemused view of herself at the age of twenty-one, to create a kind of American *Candide* in drag. She was striking out against the dual demon of a woman's repressed role in the male-dominated American social and business system and the collapse of the American dream into the false values of a commodity culture.

The Bell Jar is autobiographical because, as I have consistently maintained, Sylvia's narcissistic imagination was almost totally incapable of inventing narrative and characters. She depended exclusively upon her own experiences for fictional incidents, very often changing only the climax to fit her preconceived notion of a morality tale. *The Bell Jar* is no different in that respect, the climax, which might be seen as the suicide of Joan, Sylvia's evil double, being the only purely imagined event in the book. Jane Anderson, upon whom the character of Joan Gilling was very loosely based, did not commit suicide. In fact, she returned to college and went on to become a highly respected psychologist.

Every other event and character in the novel are drawn from actual experiences and from people who had figured in Sylvia's life—but Sylvia was a superb craftsman and very frequently altered the *time* of the events to suit her book's thematic progression. Her brother, for instance, did go to Germany (though neither to Berlin nor on the Experiment in International Living), but it was several years after Sylvia's suicide attempt. These shifts in time, however, were always minor, so that the basic linear plot is almost an exact recreation of Sylvia's slide into depression, possible suicide and subsequent recovery at McLean's. The major difference between *The Bell Jar* and Sylvia's autobiography resides in the tone of the novel, in its need to get revenge upon all the people in Sylvia's life whom she had ever had to depend upon for either financial or psychological support. Not that Sylvia's insights into these people were not valid, but that the concentration is always upon the limits rather than the potentialities or real strengths of their very human existences.

Thus, the portrait of Buddy Willard is a cruel caricature pointedly accurate at times but purely uni-dimensional. The comments of Marcia Brown, Philip McCurdy and others have clearly certified that rigid, joyless, "bland" side of his personality, which Sylvia despised and held up for public ridicule, but nowhere does the novel touch upon other elements in his make-up, which have been equally attested to—the kindness, the generosity, the concern for other people that resulted in his becoming an excellent physician. Similarly, the treatment of the Willard family as a whole, the continuous crucifixion of Mrs. Willard, a double for Mrs. Plath, who, in turn, was one of the doubles Sylvia most feared becoming herself, too often depends upon the spot-lighting of actual flaws to the exclusion of other, more redeeming characteristics. However true the profile of her that emerges in the novel, and Myron Lotz insists that it is completely accurate, mentioning her constant pleas of poverty and martyrdom complex, it never goes beyond the narrow, anti-human confines of a profile done in thick charcoal.

There are others tarred by Sylvia in *The Bell Jar*, such as Mary Ellen Chase and Mrs. Prouty, whose only offense was attempting to act as mentors to Sylvia and to offer both moral and real support in the form of time, advice, written recommendations and, in Mrs. Prouty's case, the gift of thousands of dollars. Even Mr. Crockett, whom Sylvia genuinely liked and admired to the end, is dismissed contemptuously in two lines, "the English teacher I had in high school who came and tried to teach me how to play Scrabble, because he thought it might revive my interest in words," a true enough statement in the abstract, but one that leaves out his weekly visits, his warm, paternal interest in her at the worst moment in her life and her great dependence upon him. That is the crux of it, her great dependence upon him and the fact that he had seen her during a period of humiliating nakedness and weakness, stripped of disguises and unable to summon up the Sylvia she had always used in his presence before, the bright, cheerful, energetic teenager who had the world by the tail.

Edwin, on the other hand, seems to get the treatment he deserves as Irwin in the novel, but even here, the climax must fit a certain artistic purpose, and so Esther hangs up on Irwin with the promise of never seeing him again, while Sylvia had actually gone with him for quite a while after the "rape" episode. Marcia Brown, her single consistent friend, is spared any exposure of faults, though she does surface as "Jody" in *The Bell Jar* during the swimming scene, where Esther questions "Cal" (based upon Professor Mel Woody, now a teacher of philosophy at a Connecticut college) about the easiest method for committing suicide—Cal's friend "Mark" was in fact a boy named Dick Lindenwood, whom Sylvia apparently liked and had dated several times. Nancy Hunter does not appear at all, again for structural reasons, the rape incident at Cambridge in the summer of 1954 being shifted back to late 1953 in order to have Esther engineer her own seduction while still at McLean's near the end of the book, part of the climactic evolution of Esther into a truly free soul, free of madness *and* male domination. Nancy was fortunate to escape, since Sylvia's letters about her, portions of which Gordon Lameyer kindly let me read from his unpublished memoir, castigate her as a "boy crazy" manipulator with no heart.

I have been in contact with most of the people Sylvia used in the novel, though several of them, perhaps understandably, have been unwilling to discuss themselves or the book at all, while others were either dead or had little to offer in the way of new information. A few of the characters eluded me, while others such as "Doreen" and "Dodo Conroy" are known to me, but I see no sense in subjecting them to public scrutiny, their identities being generally unknown. The only sure thing is that each character in the novel has a human counterpart, as does each experience of Esther's, and that in most cases these characters are viewed from a very jaundiced, if very sensitive, perspective. All of this, of course, is why Ted tried for seven years to prevent the American edition of *The Bell Jar* from ever appearing; he knew Mrs. Plath may have been concerned, not so much about the unappealing caricature of herself as about those of friends and neighbors, *e.g.*, Mrs. Willard and Mrs. Prouty, the latter having become a very close friend in her last years.

Myron Lotz always maintained *The Bell Jar* was "straight autobiography, like reading a diary or essay Sylvia had written about her life." He also felt that the portrait of Buddy "fit him to a tee," as did the portraits of Mrs. Willard and Mrs. Plath. Robert and Jill Modlin reacted similarly, finding the descriptions of Mrs. Plath, Buddy and Mrs. Willard "unkind but devastatingly true." But Peter Davison, not one of the novel's victims, might not agree. He noted that in *The Bell Jar* Sylvia had been especially unkind to everyone who had ever helped her in any way, which was the exact opposite of her attitude towards them when he knew her in the year or so following her release from McLean's. Then, in a moment of rare candor, while lying beside him after a strenuous bout of lovemaking, she had talked of her various benefactors with gratitude, praising the very nurses she condemns in the novel. He also, however, would not deem the negative image of Mrs. Plath far from the mark.

There is nothing else to say on the matter. It is a delicate situation that has engendered much unhappiness, many people being wounded and perplexed to discover themselves mercilessly belittled in a book by a girl they had once regarded with affection, had even gone out of their way to aid. But it should also be noted that Mrs. Plath's contention that Sylvia never wanted *The Bell Jar* published in America, where it could hurt innocent victims, is simply not borne out by the facts. As Peter Davison indicated to me in an interview, Sylvia did indeed attempt to get Harper & Row to publish it in the States, but they rejected it.

But *The Bell Jar* is more than a personal vendetta; it is a solid, if flawed, minor masterpiece of sardonic satire and sincere protest, an authentic American novel about the disintegration of the American Dream, comparable to *Miss Lonelyhearts* and *The Great Gatsby*, particularly the former, in direction and theme. Sylvia did write the book at great speed, but so did she produce her best poetry the same way, and to a schedule. The sincerity of her subsequent strenuous denigration of the novel has, therefore, to be questioned. Her dismissal of it, for instance, as "mere apprentice work" and, in a letter to the Comptons (to whom the novel was dedicated), as "a nothing" may be seen as the normal efforts of a sensitive author to foreclose possible criticism. Mrs. Plath herself, in a letter to Harper & Row in 1970, has said that Sylvia told her in person that *The Bell Jar* was "a pot boiler really." [2] But it is easy to understand an embarrassed daughter's need to explain away a book in which her mother is virtually the central villain. More interesting, from a critical standpoint, was Sylvia's persistent categorization of her first novel as "a comedy."

A comedy it surely is, though heavy-handed and adolescent at times, as in its British use of appelations to define character—"Dodo" for a woman who bred children like a cow and should be extinct; "Philomenia Guinea" for an absurd lady novelist who wrote slushy romances. But most of the names used are but slight variations upon the originals. The major humor stems always from Esther's naïve reactions during her nearly disastrous tumble into maturity, her continuous surprise at the sophisticated realities of sex and modern urban life—under-tipping the cab driver, describing Buddy's private parts as "turkey neck and turkey gizzards," concluding that she "liked the idea of being seduced by a simultaneous interpreter in New York City." Again and again a key human situation which seems to demand a serious and perhaps profound response finds in Esther the incongruous innocence of a child: "It hurts. Is it supposed to hurt?" she asks Irwin when he is entering her.

The child-like responses of Esther, which are pathetic when not humorous, though they are sometimes both and further proof of Sylvia's artistic distance and ability to be self-critical, are an integral part of the novel's obsessive concern with infants. It is to free herself from their threat, and from the oppressive rule of males, that Esther buys a douche with Dr. Nolan's blessing. But there is an opposite current at work as well, an ironic counter-movement that has Esther herself ceaselessly trying to return to the womb, become a foetus, and thereby escape the world. After launching herself suicidally down the mountain side on skis, Esther hurtles towards "the pebble at the bottom of the well, the white sweet baby cradled in its mother's belly." Depressed by the silence of her hotel room, Esther later slips into a tub of hot water. "When I stepped out at last and wrapped myself in one of the big, soft white hotel bath towels I felt pure and sweet as a new baby." And the suicide attempt, when she crawls into "the mouth of darkness" under her mother's home, is the ultimate "return to the womb" gesture wherein birth and death are mated.

The governing metaphor of the book is itself a sardonic echo of the hospital jar and its foetal specimen, which Sylvia had already thought of back in 1952, the bell jar itself—the sense of a descending, imprisoning, airless, invisible glass jar. It was the perfect symbol for the smothering reality of a developing mental breakdown and the growing detachment first from phenomena and other people and then from self. At novel's end, the bell jar will have been lifted, Esther reborn, her evil self buried with Joan, but the threat remains: "How did I know that someday—at college, in Europe, somewhere, anywhere—the bell jar, with its stifling distortions, wouldn't descend again?"

Dostoevsky is behind *The Bell Jar* from start to finish as Sylvia consciously tried to imitate his treatment of an evil double and make use of all her research on her honor's thesis as well as her knowledge of psychology. But it is as a reflection of Voltaire's *Candide* that the novel makes most sense in both tone and substance. The last name of Esther Greenwood derives from Sylvia's maternal grandmother's maiden name and asserts Sylvia's awareness of Esther as both one of her selves and a limited, maternal female type in the mold of her grandmother. Thus she is to discover, like Candide, that the modern world is a terrible, hypocritical place, which is continually inflicting suffering upon her cloistered innocence.

Yet the humor of her growing disenchantment is always biting in its effects. Like Candide too, she is a victim of her own naïveté—and illness, which is carefully traced with Freudian fidelity to her mother's inadequacies and her beloved father's death when she was young. She is the victim of her society's false values and masculine orientation that has stretched her on the rack of extremes—passive marriage or active career—since birth. Madison Avenue, heart of America's debased Protestant ethic, brings home the falsity of her cultural heritage immediately. Esther's college successes "fizzled to nothing outside" its "slick marble and plate-glass fronts." So does Hilda's ignorant, callous attitude towards the imminent execution of the Rosenbergs: "I'm so glad they're going to die." Masculine domination finds its personifications in Marco, the brutal woman-hater, and in Buddy himself—not to mention Irwin's final male-chauvinist act of using her when she is using him.

At one point, after Esther learns of Buddy's affair with a waitress, she complains, "I couldn't stand the idea of a woman having to have a single pure life and a man being able to have a double life, one pure and one not." This is a major theme running through the book, and it will find expression in many more of Esther's criticisms of men and their world, but it is also a clear reference to the fundamental structure of the novel, namely, its constant dependence upon the idea of doubles, which is further reflected in the endless shifts between past and present, between two Esthers. The double concept is linked with the motif of male chauvinism in that Esther's basic dilemma of selves—whether to choose between Doreen and Betsy, for example, two aspects of herself, Doreen the evil drive for amoral, sensual pleasure (the id?) and Betsy, the conventional male image of womanhood rooted, like Sylvia's grand-mother, in the old-fashioned values of home-making (super-ego?) and, later, whether to choose between Joan, another evil extreme, lesbian career girl cut off from life like the girl in "Spinster," or the modern, liberated model of Dr. Nolan (Dr. Jones) and her brand of sophisticated independence—derives directly from the many males who, throughout the novel, exploit women for their own purposes without ever seeing them as individuals with distinct human identities.

That *The Bell Jar*'s style is so often a parody of *True Romance* writing is, I think, deliberate on Sylvia's part, a realization by her that Esther had indeed mistakenly thought of herself and her life in these vapid terms. On the other hand, Sylvia herself was not that free of her Esther self to be completely removed from the parody, as her other stories attest. The novel is fun, caustic fun, but near the end much of the satire departs in favor of a more direct, more serious and dramatic approach to the tragedy of Esther's flirtation with death. Christ-like, she buries her evil double with Joan, shadow to shadow, "That shadow would marry this shadow and the peculiar, yellowish soil of our locality seal the wound in the whiteness, and yet another snowfall erase the traces of newness in Joan's grave." The whiteness, of course, refers back to the whiteness associated with babies, a new life, now definitely a resurrection, and the insistence of Esther upon her "real" self: "I am, I am, I am." This is the only chant left modern man, the Jewish value of survival for survival's sake, recovery's initial step.

The months of July and August saw the beginning of descent. Months earlier a woman named "Olga" and her husband, a Canadian poet, had paid a visit to Sylvia's home. While there she had drawn Ted into an affair which would shatter forever Sylvia's last illusions—her belief in her marriage and her husband. As the woman responsible, Olga fit the role almost as if she had come right out of one of Mrs. Prouty's domestic melodramas, at least in the eyes of David Compton, who admits to having met Olga only once, *after* Sylvia's death. He claims "she thought Ted would be great in bed" and that she was attracted by the rare combination in him, personally and in his poetry, of strong male drives and literary sophistication.

Olga is a rather tragic figure, one who can no longer testify in her own behalf, having also committed suicide by gas some time after Sylvia's death, killing herself and her young daughter. Near the end of her life she identified with Sylvia so completely that she thought of herself almost as the late poet's reincarnation. Still, it is difficult not to be slightly prejudiced against her in view of the disastrous effect she had on Sylvia's life. I must rely on what little testimony is available from people who knew her; the Comptons have generously provided their impressions, though emphasizing the briefness of their contact.

David has described Olga in mixed terms as a creative, artistic woman—she was apparently a top copywriter—with definite talents of her own. He has also emphasized that she was "a very high powered presence in any room, quite unbearably another Sylvia, in a much nastier way, much cruder in her dominance." He felt that she had been "obvious" in her actions and her pursuit of Ted, "very physical" and "a very crude person visually" in sharp contrast to Sylvia's "great refinement and sensitivity," which does not quite jibe with comments from less hostile sources. Elizabeth's view of Olga was similar to her husband's, and she stressed the very blatant way in which Olga pursued Ted, even flirting with him constantly in his own home. According to her, Sylvia alone remained oblivious to what was happening under her nose, which does not fit either Sylvia's perceptiveness or her jealous attitude towards her husband and children.

Yet in fact Sylvia did know what was going on, as the incident of the paper with Olga's name blowing out of the fire proves, but she could not or would not face the reality of it. Sylvia likely would not believe for a moment that her husband could be attracted to a person so vulgar in her sexuality. Sex, as we have noted, remained for Sylvia something of a mystery.[3] Though, too, at a much deeper level, there may have been a need to recreate the primal scene of Otto abandoning her. At this level, Olga was fundamental—the archetypal death-seducer stealing away the male idol figure.

The real Olga, however, was much more complex, worthy of a biography in her own right. A close poet friend of hers, who wishes to remain anonymous, has supplied valuable background information. Olga was born in Berlin, during the Nazis' rise to power, to a Russian-Jewish, doctor father, and a German-gentile mother. The family fled first to Italy, then to Israel, before finally emigrating to Canada and a permanent home in Vancouver.

Olga's mother was unstable, given to violent outbursts of temper, while her father, a gentle, quiet man, was apparently unable to stand up to her domination. Tragedy occurred when the mother found herself in love with an Englishman, and could not face the moral and psychological ramifications of that love. Instead, with a twisted logic, she forced eighteen-year-old Olga to marry him. Olga refused to consummate the marriage and secured an annulment after running back home. She always believed that these events contributed to her mother's eventual nervous breakdown.

Olga went on to college, but she was unhappy in Vancouver, claiming that the students at the university persecuted her for being "different." She easily fell in love with one of her professors, a distinguished European economist, who married her and took her away from Canada. Later, during an ocean voyage, she met and fell in love with a Canadian poet (now living in England), leaving her husband to marry him, although the parting was congenial. She would continue to visit her former husband, who also lived in England, from time to time, and he remained a friend and possible father figure.

Interestingly, Olga's friend's account stresses her great beauty, her long black hair, dark Russian complexion and "marvellous grey eyes with long lashes." He concedes, however, supporting the Comptons' harsher description, that her figure was on the dumpy side and rested on "heavy legs and thick ankles." In terms of personality, he recalls her as a perfectionist about everything, from her immediate surroundings to her relationships with others, which made her somewhat self-conscious about her minor physical defects—the resemblance here to Sylvia is almost mystical.

In any event, her marriage was already experiencing severe problems when she met Ted, due to a wide variety of personal reasons. She was the family breadwinner, through no fault of her husband, who was seeking a job that would permit him to write as well, but who yearned for domination and security. Her poet friend believes she also possessed a bit of a masochistic streak. Whatever its various causes, she was overwhelmed by the force of Ted's self-contained presence, as well as by his poetry—she had always wanted to be a "real" writer. More important, as the Comptons had also suggested, she found in him a perfect male representative, was aroused sexually as she had never been before, to the point where Ted Hughes became and remained an obsession. Ted, for his part, fell just as deeply in love with her.

A poem Sylvia wrote in July, "Words Heard, By Accident, Over the Phone," though not a very good poem, is a suggestive one. For it intimates that Sylvia knew what was happening to her marriage in a very real way that had nothing to do with black magic or mysterious omens. The central image is of mud pouring from the phone: "Thick as foreign coffee, and with a sluggy pulse." This leads to the opening of the second stanza: "What are these words, these words?" The situation seems clear. Sylvia overheard Ted and Olga conversing intimately on the telephone. The "foreign" pins down Olga specifically as she did indeed have a European background and accent. The only problem comes in the last two lines of the same stanza. "They are pressing out of the many-holed earpiece, they are looking for a listener./ Is he here?" appears to refer to an incident that occurred much earlier, in spring, when Olga had a male co-worker call and ask to speak to Ted. Sylvia, who had answered the phone, was certainly not fooled. There may have been more than one phone call since, as Clarissa Roche has said, "there was a lot of fooling around before Ted actually left."

The poem moves into a potent surrealistic landscape in the third and last stanza. Now the room is "ahiss" (a play on Olga's real name) with menace and the phone is a "tentacle." The final three lines give some idea of the profound psychological impact the call had on Sylvia, and of her stubborn refusal to abandon art even in the throes of a great emotional shock: "But the spawn percolate in my heart. They are fertile./ Muck funnel, muck funnel—/ You are too big. They must take you back!" The ingenuity here, and private allusion, rest upon Sylvia's play with "muck funnel," which suggests a "cunt" that does not stop running and a "mock" vulva because Olga as yet had no children and her many earlier abortions made such a possibility seem unlikely. The idea of serpent is also directly related to the governing concept of adultery and betrayal.

The finest and fiercest poems from the last six months of Sylvia's life, such as "Lady Lazarus," "Mary's Song," and "Fever 103°," will tend always to commence with a private revelation and then fly off into a relentless, surrealistic, frequently schizophrenic pattern of rapid metaphorical associations that do not rely upon a specific narrative focus for cumulative impact, though a narrative framework as such will never be completely discarded. The persona, however, will never be Sylvia, not even a remote Sylvia, but the myth of Sylvia—the fully conscious legend of the bitch self that she would assert with calculated genius.

The circle was almost complete as August came around. It was then that the telephone incident took place. In the evening the phone rang, and Sylvia answered it. The voice was familiar. A gruff male voice insisted upon talking to Ted. No doubt Olga knew full well what she was doing. Sylvia would recognize the ploy, and Olga was now willing to risk an open struggle. Sylvia did as the voice requested and called Ted. Then, as he went to speak, she moved suddenly, viciously, ripped at the cord and pulled the telephone off the wall.

What she did next is not fully clear. Without letting Mrs. Plath know what had happened, and leaving her with Frieda and Ted, Sylvia took the baby and ran from the house, driving off in the Morris stationwagon. In her mind there was only one place in all of Croton where she could find the reassurance and calm affection she desperately needed, and that was the house of the Comptons twenty-five miles away. She arrived in a state of near hysteria, stumbling through the dark yard, pounding at the door, and being admitted by a bewildered Elizabeth.

The Comptons remember that night with frightful clarity. Elizabeth recalls that the words tumbled out of Sylvia as fast as the tears. "We had this happy day," Sylvia told her, "shopping in Exeter, and then this happened." She explained she could no longer stay with Ted. She could not be calmed or placated and refused the offer of a bed upstairs. "Crying, weeping all the time, her hair drenched, she kept wringing my hand, saying, 'Help me! Help me!' We were extremely worried about her." Elizabeth also specifically remembers her saying, "Ted has become a little man. It isn't what he's done, it's that he lied. At least if he had told me straight out, I could have salvaged some respect for him." The perfect marriage was in ruins. Her reaction had to be extreme. "I am destroyed," she insisted again and again. "When you give your heart to somebody, you can't take it back. If they don't want it, it's gone."

David's recollections of the tragic night confirm his wife's for the most part, though he was impressed by the sudden revelation of a side of Sylvia that they had never seen before, which was now in evidence amid all the "undirected hysteria"—namely, her belief in black magic and supernatural powers. "We began to see all the arcane stuff, the mysticism, all the strange forces that she found significant in life, of which we never had a murmur before. She could say things like 'the truth loves me, the truth comes to me,' this level of intense, if you like embarrassing, communication." She also told the Comptons about the piece of paper with "Olga's" name on it and intimated that the powers which ruled her special destiny had been trying to warn her, but that she had been too dense and fooled by Ted to listen to them. Where Ted and Olwyn might have been playing with their astrological talk and mystical lore, mocking themselves in the process, though perhaps uneasily, Sylvia was "not at all." To her "it mattered," and "she allowed it to make important random events," such as Ted's affair.

When Sylvia had been calmed somewhat, the Comptons felt that they could safely leave her downstairs with Nicholas while they retired to bed. Though still weeping and obviously stunned, she was on the point of falling into an exhausted sleep and had recovered enough to see that her infant son was properly taken care of, fed, and put to bed. In the morning, uneasy and concerned, Elizabeth hurried downstairs to see what Sylvia was doing and found her "in a pink dressing gown, her hair in plaits, with her head in a box of recently born kittens. She turned to me and exclaimed, 'Aren't they beautiful! They're new! I haven't seen anything so new!'"

Very ugly emotions perhaps make a poem.
ROBERT LOWELL

T'have seen what I have seen, see what I see.
OPHELIA

20

Cauldron of Morning

Sylvia returned to Court Green the next day, apparently strengthened enough to face the immediate consequences of Ted's defection. But she could not bear the thought of living with him and asked him to leave, after her mother's departure. David Compton has said "it was definitely an eviction." Sylvia's decision, however, would not remain firm, though for the moment it must have given her a sense of being to some degree in control of the situation. There were chores to do and poses to maintain. The Comptons did not see her for several days.

Mrs. Plath, of course, was bewildered and upset. She knew that something terrible had happened, but Sylvia refused to reveal any of the details. Aurelia, in fact, would leave for America without ever really knowing why her daughter had been forced to flee in the night with Frieda to a stranger's house, or why Sylvia and Ted seemed so "glum," although she must have suspected something. Sylvia certainly needed Aurelia at this point, but, as David observed, "we knew she wasn't going to get any sort of the right things said by her mother," which Sylvia herself undoubtedly also realized. Instead, Sylvia sought to present a pleasant mask and, the day after the telephone episode, Mrs. Plath took color pictures of her with the children in the garden. Sylvia is sitting upright on the grass, obviously tense, pale, the strain evident behind the false smile, as if unaware of the two beautiful children with her.

The only two poems which apparently came in August, "Burning the Letters" and "Stings (2)," reflect the fact that Sylvia's attitude in the weeks following Ted's departure was uncertain. Despair and rage had yet to etch themselves clearly upon her imagination. There was a possibility, at least in her mind, that Ted would return and that Court Green could somehow remain their happy home. "Burning the Letters" deals specifically with Sylvia's angry decision to take a pile of Ted's letters and papers from his attic workroom and burn them in the garden, which she did. It is a direct narrative poem that proceeds from a menace-ridden "I made a fire; being tired/ Of the white fists of old/ Letters and their death rattles" to the second stanza's suggestion that literature itself, part of the house's real attic and her mind's interior construction, has mortal limits: "And here is an end to the writing,/ The spry hooks that bend and cringe, and the smiles, the smiles,/ And at least it will be a good place now, the attic."

In the third stanza, she rakes the dying fire: the charred pieces of paper are birds, "black and glittering," then "coal angels" silenced by her act of destruction, though they "breathe like people"; and finally, in the fire's entrails, like a seer, she finds what she is looking for among the remnant food, "yellow lettuces and the German cabbage" (a reference to Olga). She finds an old friend, birth in death, "Involved as a foetus/ And a name with black edges." Hindsight, an awareness that the name on the piece of paper will indeed lead to betrayal, Olga's victory, supplies the fourth stanza with its negative energy. The name wilting at her foot is seen as a "sinuous orchid" that has a slackened vulva in its mixed nest of "root hairs and boredom" and Olga's accent—"Pale eyes, patent-leather gutterals!" The bitch goddess begins to emerge from the shocked Sylvia standing over the dread name of her doom, and taking on the features of nature, "Warm rain greases my hair, extinguishing nothing./ My veins glow like trees." Dogs somewhere "are tearing a fox," an allusion to Ted's "thought-fox" and Sylvia's victim status. But she is not yet in control; regret, sorrow, self-pity still prevail, and Sylvia can only imagine herself as the fox, the butt of fate, not its master. The death-agony of the fox is, "a red burst and a cry/ That splits from its ripped bag and does not stop/ With the dead eye," yoking the victim's pain with her earlier vision of the artist self as a tin eye, blood "Dyeing the air," telling nature "What immortality is. That it is immortal."

The year before, in "The Rival (2)," Sylvia had linked "poison pen letter" with literature, so the connection is not new, and she was never averse to carting a successful metaphor or simile from one poem to another. In July also came "Stings (2)," which Olwyn Hughes has identified as "the first of all the bee poems, which came in a block in October." [1] The time difference between this bee poem and the group that emerged almost two months later can best be ascribed to the profound difference in mood that characterized Sylvia's reaction to the loss of Ted. By October the split would be irrevocable, uncertainty and fear replaced, forever, by undiluted rage and hatred.

This is all too evident in the first stanza, where Sylvia uses the bees as a metaphor for the fearful doubts assailing her own mind. The persona is near the hive, the bees anointing her hair, "assailing your brain like numerals," while she wonders "What fear?" had set them off, "these animalcules"—these manifold and microscopic invaders of her interior world. In the second stanza, Sylvia continues to address herself, warning herself that the bees are "suicidal," are "making a cat's cradle" in the handkerchief she is wearing "instead of a hat," unprotected, like women who come to church unprepared. There is no hope now, "no use running," "black veil" and gloves studded with bees (the veil reinforces the church intimation), and yet, she realizes with a start, "They are fools!" They have become a part of her, the fears, and she can understand that their senseless flight (her flight into disguise?) is not courageous after all, or even intelligent, as they fall to the earth dead, "Ossifying like junked statues."

The August finale was the purest pathos: Sylvia no longer a heroine, all her battles against the world's demands as wife, mother and artist rendered futile by Ted's desertion. It was clearly now a desertion, not an eviction. His absence was too much for her to bear as she contemplated the dull country life around her, cut off from London, cut off from America, trapped among cows and infants and neighbors who had not the slightest inkling of the tangled snarl of emotion in so complex a personality. She felt trapped and abandoned without Ted's reassuring physical presence and the constant challenge of his teeming mind. Her letters back home began overtly to mirror her despair. Clement Moore recalls hearing that her first reaction was "desperation" and that "poor lonely Sylvia wanted her husband back." He also remembers that Aurelia and Warren were quite worried about her and kept in constant touch through the mails, and that her own letters became "extremely black."

In the next few weeks Sylvia's weakened mental condition was exacerbated by a bout of influenza and she collapsed under a double burden of non-stop fevers that soared to 103 degrees at times and an alternating series of teeth-rattling chills. Now bed-ridden and helpless, she was unable to swallow anything but water. Ted apparently returned and Sylvia believed a reconciliation was still possible—though his subsequent actions would certainly indicate that he never seriously considered staying permanently in Croton. Illness was an old enemy for Sylvia, but the intensity of the influenza was even more severe than her much earlier attack of pneumonia and left her weaker than ever.

The poem "Fever 103°," written after the fact and one of Sylvia's finest poetic achievements, is structured around a leap-frogging series of three-line stanzas that return in the end to a familiar pair of lovers and the danger of love itself.[2] Christian and classical myth are joined in the first three stanzas, as are fire and pureness. The "tongues of hell" belong to Cerberus, the three-headed dog that guarded the gate to Hades; and pain is associated with a moral lapse—"the sin, the sin." "Love" is offered as the sin. Metaphorically, all this is tied into the brutal death of Isadora (Duncan), whose fright the "I" can empathize with in her present state of being sick and abandoned—that is, she fears that "One scarf will catch and anchor in the wheel."

Such agony cannot be merely private, the poet insists. The smoke of it can "trundle round the globe/ Choking the aged and the meek,/ The weak/ Hothouse baby in its crib." Her own suffering has thus attained universal dimensions, and the way her poem functions is clear in the next shift from the image of "Hothouse baby" to that of a "ghastly orchid," which is then victimized by amoral science, the atomic bomb: "Radiation turned it white/ And killed it in an hour/ Greasing the bodies of adulterers/ Like Hiroshima ash and eating in./ The sin. The sin." The evil of the world is defined as man's modern invention, which has turned earth into hell and its inhabitants into victims, but this is firmly associated with the private evil of Ted's and Olga's adultery, which is burning away her love. Like the victims at Hiroshima, Sylvia suffers innocently for the crimes of others, as does her own "Hothouse baby."

But "Fever 103°" was not written during Sylvia's illness, or soon after, because the rage was not yet perfectly distilled. Ted's return had generated some hope. It was during this period that the couple who would inspire "Lesbos" came to stay at the cottage. They would stay for two weeks, ostensibly to help with the children, but the entire visit distressed Sylvia. She resented the food that they ate and no less the damage unwittingly inflicted on Frieda's new pram. When the couple finally departed for a holiday in Cornwall, Sylvia was relieved but still worried about the need for someone to care for the children.[3] Fortunately, she was able to secure a reliable, though quite expensive, nanny from a London agency.

"Lesbos" never escapes the confines of its vindictive domesticity and its autobiographical reliance on factual truth and mean emotion. It is petty revenge, gossip, and whining decked out as art. There are, however, occasional lines and phrases, which are unique in their concentration upon the less savory aspects of home life. Here the prosaic elements of cooking and child care are translated into ominous threats: "The potatoes hiss" and "The fluorescent light wineing on and off like a terrible migraine" and a small child on the floor, "Little unstrung puppet, kicking to disappear." Sylvia throws the other wife's own words back at her with contempt: "You say your husband is just no good to you./ His Jew-Mama guards his sweet sex like a pearl." Two women share the secrets of the bedroom, and the alternative to their husbands' inadequacy becomes attractive: "I should sit on a rock off Cornwall and comb my hair./ I should wear tiger pants, I should have an affair."

Yet the end of the first long section introduces ambivalence: "We should meet in another life, we should meet in air,/ Me and you." Its intimation of lesbian thoughts has led to the entire poem being misinterpreted as proof of Sylvia's hidden lesbianism. But the reference is deliberate and the poem itself does not accept or support the fantasy of repressed homosexuality. The theme of the poem is of course lesbianism as an escape from the grubby details of motherhood, but always in terms of sardonic satire; and the Sappho reference is also keyed to a consideration of lyric poetry itself—the price of art having been her famous leap into the sea centuries before. The penis and testicle images deployed so maliciously in the next two sections convey the two essential satirical connotations of verbal and sexual "foreplay" necessary to comprehend the poem's bitchiness. Sylvia's vision of the evil double cannot adjust to the real world of "baby crap" and "impotent husband." The latter as penis is kept around for protection from the extreme negations of self-love and lesbian aridity; it is a mere conductor for female electricity: "the lightning,/ The acid baths, the skyfuls off of you." Double entendres from college have been resurrected; and the "blue sparks," or sperm, are from the wife, who is the active force in contrast to her passive husband.

The connection between art and sex, or between sterile lesbianism and a bald muse, is strengthened in the third section, which moves from the earlier reference to the husband's guarded testicle to "O jewel! O valuable!/ That night the moon/ Dragged its blood bag, sick/ Animal/ Up over the harbor lights." This results in an erection. "Hard and apart and white." But the wife is frightened by reflections of herself and the moon. "We kept picking up handfuls, loving it,/ Working it like dough, a mulatto body,/ The silk grits." It is easy to envision here a tender moment from the past when Sylvia and some woman might have explored one another's bodies like children playing in the sand, while the useless male member, "your doggy husband," was appropriately picked up and carted off by a dog—by simple animal lust. But fantasy and reality are distinctly separated, so that the central division remains between two female extremes, with mere bitterness in between.

The last short section concerns the wife watching the other woman depart and being appreciative of her sensual buttocks, but now aware of their relation to death in birth—"fist of a baby"—and to the fatal womb—"that sea/ Sweetheart." A continued elaboration of testicle imagery leaves no room for delusions: "I am still raw." Even in the agony and bitterness of her uncertain departure from Ted and the security he represented, Sylvia had the wit and bravado to maintain her Puritan rejection of a totally female opposite extreme.

In early September, she still clung to the idea of a reconciliation, which Ted did little to discourage. The arrival of the nanny left them free to take a longed-for trip to Ireland to a fellow poet's house near Galway. A letter to Elizabeth Compton, dated September 8, speaks of "we" with the usual assurance and views the planned week's vacation as a much-needed respite for both of them. She promised happily to see Elizabeth on her return and to bring along bags of potatoes and onions. The mask is back in place. But in Ireland would come the final performance and ultimate rejection that would leave her completely naked and easy prey to the emerging bitch goddess.

The Hugheses departed for Ireland on Tuesday, September 11, apparently without incident. Then came the shock: Ted had no intention of remaining either in Ireland or with Sylvia. That day or the next morning, he departed alone for London and his recently acquired Soho flat. He was returning to Olga and preparing for the divorce. His love was undoubtedly real enough, but he also could no longer abide the restrictions imposed by living with two children and a strained and straining young wife.

In their different ways, Ted and Sylvia had loved one another with great devotion. The Comptons remember the intense nature of that love with vivid clarity. Elizabeth has remarked that the "feeling between them was deep, unspoken, closely tied." They also recall a specific occasion not long before the Olga episode when Ted and Sylvia had descended cheerfully upon them in a surprise visit, bearing gifts and a birthday cake Sylvia had baked for her dear friend. "This marvellous woman" was how she had described Elizabeth to Peter Davison when he visited Court Green. After a while, the Hugheses had wandered off by themselves to stare down into a pond or stream, wrapped in one another's arms, immune from the impinging world, absolutely immersed in each other.

A touching picture, and a true one, with countless reservations: the intrusion of Olga, contradictory social and national backgrounds, the struggle between two enormous egos and their arts, the normal decline of passion, the mutually exclusive demands of fame and babies, the "typical" male desire for freedom from sexual constraints, and, finally, psychological tensions too powerful to remain smothered by the blissful façade of an idyllic, but dull, rural domesticity. Ted has been roundly, and unfairly, condemned for his "betrayal" of Sylvia, emerging as a Dantesque monster from the slimy hellscape of Sylvia's last poems. Robin Morgan, poetaster and shrill feminist, has even called for his murder in one of her verbal afterbirths. The future alone can supply a broader and possibly more equitable perspective.

Meanwhile, biography, if not art, demands a balancing of forces. Ted did indeed abandon Sylvia, and, if nothing else, it was, in Elizabeth Compton's words, "a critical misjudgment of her," betraying a certain amount of insensitivity. The insensitivity, however, had been present from the beginning of the marriage on both sides, Ted's misunder-standing of his wife's female realities poised, always, against Sylvia's continuous miscomprehension of the working-class origins that helped fuel his fierce literary ambitions and define fundamental elements in his character. Sylvia was always on the brink of self-absorption, and Ted may somehow have sensed this and felt rejected in the process. Or the poet in him may have unconsciously goaded her to explore her own psychological depths. On the surface, nevertheless, it looked as though his defection was little more than another act in the conventional marital tragedy: the wife laboring selflessly to make her husband a success, only to have him abandon her when he has achieved it. Sylvia's hurt was genuine and profound, and exaggerated by a weakened physical condition. Taking advantage of the children's absence, she did engage in some sight-seeing, getting as far as Yeats' tower at Ballylea, that impressive symbol of phallic domination and brooding isolation set above the common strife. It must have seemed terribly appropriate to her own dilemma and aspirations: having genius, wanting power through poetry, and yet pathetically alone. But the beauty of the country had a soothing effect and her tortured mind was still capable of appreciating its charm and peaceful ways.

Sylvia returned a week later to Court Green and tried to put together her new life. Ted was gone for good, that much was obvious and unchangeable; but the children and her work remained. The children were her immediate concern as a fierce maternal instinct drove her to protect them as much as possible from the shock of their abrupt fatherless state. She was undoubtedly aware that they would innocently pay the highest price, as she had paid for her father's untimely death the last twenty-two years. In "For a Fatherless Son" she would write to Nick: "You will be aware of an absence, presently,/ Growing beside you, like a tree."

For the children and for her art, Sylvia struggled to maintain appearances. She tended the children, cooked elaborate meals, helped harvest the apples, minded the beehives, shopped among the townspeople as if little had happened, seemingly cheerful as ever. The only signs of distress were her paleness and continued loss of weight, and the tenseness behind the bright smile. Perhaps the clearest indication of hidden tensions was her sudden conversion to smoking—she, the dedicated crusader against tobacco in any form.

But once embarked upon the bulk of the poems that would go into *Ariel* and *Winter Trees*, and a few others not yet collected, Sylvia underwent a drastic psychological improvement. Clement Moore, who was in close touch with Warren at the time, remembers distinctly how the tenor of her letters home changed from September to early October. He himself had written soon after learning of her plight and attempted to cheer her up with reminders from the past. When the reply came in October, it was full of chatty confidence. Moore also recalls that Sylvia related this dramatic alteration in mood directly to the fact that "she was writing again." Further, Clarissa Roche, who would pay a visit to Sylvia at Court Green in mid-November, had a similar reaction. Though Sylvia was undoubtedly still disturbed about Ted's betrayal, Clarissa felt that "she liked the idea" and "was just plain angry with him"—and further that "she had two sides: she could play the role." Part of it, of course, was a return to a familiar discipline. Elizabeth had noted that "she really believed you had to be an extrovert, be cheerful in a male world or be sick."

Because it is extreme in sensibility and subject matter, too close to the bone for comfort, Sylvia's later poetry has repelled many readers.[4] Irving Howe, for instance, in an interesting piece called "The Plath Celebration: A Partial Dissent" (the dissent is far from partial since he eventually relegates her to the category of "an interesting minor poet") tried to articulate what it was about a poem like "Daddy" that upset him and others: "There is something monstrous, utterly disproportionate, when tangled emotions about one's father are deliberately compared with the historical fate of the European Jews; something sad." [5] He is obviously speaking here as a Jew and as a critic nourished on the leftist humanitarianism of the 1930's and 1940's. But on a superficial level, he is certainly right. There is no way that the poetry of an American girl writing from the remote perspective of the 1950's could ever capture the actual, brutal reality of the holocaust.

However, that is not the real issue. Sylvia was not writing from the standpoint of victims alone, but also from the very center of the Nazi consciousness. More important, her poems are not diary extracts. If anything, they are precise, sardonic, reactions to the premise that her father represented the Nazi devil inside the machine of modern madness, the male tyrant and conquering penis triumphant. But Howe's more sweeping indictment is that "in none of the essays devoted to praising Sylvia Plath have I found a coherent statement as to the nature, let alone the value, of her vision."

Sylvia did indeed have a vision: it was to plunge into the depths of self, the dark side of the mind's moon, and hope to touch the bottom of degradation and sorrow. She was a didactic writer from the very beginning, a true heir of Emerson in her conscious effort to reveal human roots of evil, although her emotional and spiritual soul remained indebted most of all to Poe. Her later poems are simply the rich harvest from the dark seeds planted back in Wellesley.

In October and November, the poems came swiftly, easily, at least one a day, sometimes two or three. Her dilemma fed her art and supplied its emotional mood and base, and her allegiance to method utilized it to keep clinical madness at bay. The relief and joy of it must have been extraordinary. Most of the writing was done in the early morning hours, from about four to seven or eight o'clock, while Sylvia listened to Mozart and Beethoven on her phonograph and sipped brandy. Influenced by Sylvia's own description of the time and place—"they were all written at about four in the morning—that still blue, almost eternal hour before the baby's cry, before the glassy music of the milkman settling his bottles"—many critics have assumed a serene interlude, a peaceful, deliberate rising from sleep to confront the muse amid the hush of creation. But such a view ignores the reality of Sylvia's position, the growing depression which the poetry was struggling against, and the poetry itself—its blatant neurotic rhythms. Sylvia did not awake at 4 A.M. out of choice, despite her complaints to Clarissa Roche about her desperate need for "time to write"; she was literally launched into consciousness by her relentless mind and her fierce depressive anxieties. Paula Rothholz has captured the experience perfectly:

> Flung into consciousness
> to impact steel despair
> doll-lids click-up

Slowly Sylvia gained purpose and strength, and experienced the satisfaction of a creator who has finally located her obsessive center. Several months before she committed suicide, Virginia Woolf had attempted to describe this process in her diary, and her situation was remarkably similar to Sylvia's: "These moments of despair—I mean glacial suspense—a painted fly in a glass cage—have given way, as they often do, to ecstasy . . . and so ideas rush in . . . A hint for the future. Always relieve pressure by a flight. Always violently turn the pillow: hack an outlet." [6] Sylvia was following this advice, transforming desolation and self-pity into rage, and depression into mania. The poems themselves are difficult to sort out chronologically. No specific dates have been assigned, but internal evidence suggests the general progression. There are distinct clusters, of course, various groupings around immediate topics, such as poetry about poetry, poetry of direct revenge, poetry of victimhood, but these too can be viewed as part of an over-all pattern.

This pattern is a simple progression from victim through accuser to an ultimate agent of vengeance—the bitch goddess. In other words, the pattern is one of changing responses to Sylvia's peculiar circumstances and the trauma of Ted's betrayal. The variations in methodology are not extreme, and there seems to be two basic lines emerging: the short, rapid, often rhymed lines of "Daddy," "Purdah," "Fever 103°," and the like, which is the prevailing form; and the longer, more conversational lines of "A Birthday Present," "Poppies in October," the bee sequence, and other poems. But the division between the two styles is not always clear-cut, and poems such as "The Munich Mannequins," "Letter in November," and "The Applicant" lie somewhere in between.

The earliest poems, however, namely, those from October, are probably the poems of definition; these are the poems that strive to encompass Sylvia's awareness of her new status as victim. "Mary's

Song," for example, one of the strongest, moves swiftly to establish the burden of womanhood and envisions the speaker's life as one long preparation for sacrifice. This is then linked to the male world's cruel historical impact and its tendency to kill on an increasingly grand scale. Not a word is wasted and the stark tercets adhere to the schizophrenic chaining concepts of the shorter lines. A lamb cooking on Sunday provides an opening statement—"cracks in its fat"—which introduces the notion of a victim—"Sacrifices its opacity . . ."—and transforms a sun-glazed window into a stained-glass scene of "holy gold." To the speaker's eye it is the fire which "makes it precious," and she realizes that this same fire had been used by the church centuries earlier to burn "the tallow heretics" and, in her own century, to oust "the Jews." Sacrifice had led to sacrifice, not to redemption or forgiveness, and now her mind can only see the ashes of the victims. "Gray birds obsess my heart." The irony, for her, lies in a terrible knowledge of man's technology being always capable of two extremes—either to massacre millions of innocent people or to thrust himself into space.

The next line touches upon a favorite image, a burning kind of beauty that always sees fire as purgative: "The ovens glowed like heavens, incandescent." Space ship and oven have become a single entity; the glory of invention and imagination are mated to one ancient blood lust. There is no escaping the concluding three lines, a personal statement that sums up the insights of the previous stanzas and directly relates them to Sylvia's ambitious prance through life as the golden girl. Until now she has been unaware of her true destiny as a latter-day Iphigenia:

> It is a heart,
> This holocaust I walk in,
> O golden child the world will kill and eat.

This poem makes a clear political protest, but in the only manner Sylvia could—through a lyric, metaphoric transformation of personal suffering into a central analogue for the vast, evil, often impersonal forces of the modern world's consciousness: religious hypocrisy, male aggression, technology without ethic.

Sylvia's birthday on October 27 was a bitter ordeal. She was suddenly thirty years old, completely isolated in the far reaches of a foreign country, tied down by two small children, and betrayed by her idealized love. The result was "Ariel," which would be a prototype poem for her second phase, but earlier, in late September, she had written "A Birthday Present," an ironic counter-point to the birth of the bitch goddess described by "Stones for a Birthday," which should perhaps be read in conjunction with "Purdah." What might lurk behind both poems was that curtained room without windows that Sylvia could not wipe from her mind. In "A Birthday Present" the second stanza certainly seems to suggest the curtained darkness as the persona wonders uneasy about her hidden double: "I am sure it is unique, I am sure it is just what I want/ When I am quiet at my cooking I feel it looking, I feel it thinking."

This is almost straight Poe and establishes a mysterious other force that has a voice but is bodiless and menacing to the imagination. The third, fourth, and fifth stanzas allow the other to mock the persona in her domestic chores and her adherence "to rules, to rules, to rules." The mention of "annunciation" introduces an essential religious element and mocks Sylvia as the virgin about to bear the son of God without benefit of intercourse. The persona recalls her first suicide attempt at twenty: "After all I am alive only by accident." But most of the poem concentrates on the overwhelming depression and the sense of suffocating horror which is envisioned as awareness without stop—as the cunt axis of the universe and its deadly processes: "the cold dead centre/ Where spilt lives congeal and stiffen to history."

Doubtless, "Purdah" is the most clearly feminist poem Sylvia ever wrote—a distinct roar of rage over the condition of women—which she naturally related to her own special situation. It suggests that only through murder could men be made aware of womankind's existence, and thus it prefigures the revenge of the bitch goddess in the subsequent poems. The final three lines allude to the assassinations of Caesar and of Danton, and are an ironic response to the myth that commenced the poem, namely, that Eve was taken from Adam's rib only to be made an object of beauty rather than an equal human being. It is a dramatic poem that maintains the proper aesthetic distance throughout and avoids esoteric confessionalism, though the term "bridegroom" certainly had particular significance for Sylvia.

The constant use of religious motifs was a facet of her desperate plight and of her constant need to see or create correspondences between herself and greater spiritual realities. The problem lay in her rational awareness of organized religion's shortcomings and in the absurdity of dessicated mythologies which ran counter to her emotional hunger for a sign of supernatural purpose. In "Mystic," written in the final month of her life, she would confront the problem directly:

> The air is a mill of hooks—
> Questions without answer,

Glittering and drunk as flies
Whose kiss stings unbearably
In the fetid wombs of black air under pines in summer.

The climax is a separate sentence, a declaration of existence and survival: "The heart has not stopped." It is not a very satisfactory poem, but it has fashioned a kind of positive self-containment from the fragmenting negatives of a lost faith. It leaves open the possibility of interest in the supernatural while conceding an absent Godhead and a secular maturity; and thus inexorably it leads back to the black-magic realm of "The Hanging Man," which had come in June 1960 and is Sylvia's purest poetic effort to articulate her psychological depression after her marriage. It is static, incapable of solution, but chillingly organized around "The Hanged Man" *(Le Pendu)* card from her Tarot deck and her vivid memory of electric-shock treatment. Though only consisting of three stanzas, two lines each, the poem gains depth from its familiarity with how the Tarot actually functions.

The card itself shows a man hanging by the leg, his hair touching the earth between two trees, but the poem views the scene upside down: "By the roots of my hair some god got hold of me." This is more than artistic play. When reading the Tarot cards, the reader assigns different, often opposite meanings to a card when it is upside down. Right side up, for instance, in the case of "The Hanged Man" would mean a life in suspension and a possible reversal in one's mind or way of life; but if reversed, as in Sylvia's poem, its divinatory meaning would be quite different: lack of sacrifice, unwillingness to make an effort, failure to give of the self, ego preoccupation, and false prophecy. This, then, is the fundamental thrust of Sylvia's poem—her awareness that her feelings of being suspended in life and near death, and the agony that entailed, related back to her egocentricity. She is chiding herself for not fighting back as well as warning herself of the consequences—more electric-shock therapy—if she did not. By implication there is also the opposite meaning that marriage and motherhood had brought about a change in her way of life and the need for readjustment and rebirth.

The climax of "The Hanging Man," however, refused to place blame and pointed towards the revenge poems upon the horizon: "If he were I, he would do what I did." Revenge was the key to survival. "Amnesiac" and "Eavesdropper" draw neighbors into the circle of Sylvia's new purpose and rage; and "The Tour" is equally unkind to a well-meaning aunt. They are not good poems in any sense, but for Sylvia they were essential. The bitch goddess in her emerged, free at last. In "Amnesiac"

Ted is pictured as having erased the "little toy wife" like a child, then hugging his pillow and wishing it were Olwyn—"the red-headed sister he never dared touch"—and dreaming of Olga to replace her, though Sylvia condemns both women as barren: "the lot are barren." Sylvia believed that Olga was incapable of giving birth and knew that Olwyn was determined to remain unmarried and childless, still a terrible "abnormality" in her eyes.

Coarse sexual allusions dominate the poem, as well as suggestions of incest—"money the sperm fluid of it all." Sylvia was wrongly convinced that Ted's income was increasing and that the Hugheses did not want him to give her any money—and Ted ends up flanked by the two women "like stars" as Sylvia sinks into forgetfulness: "Sweet Lethe is my life." "Eavesdropper" is no less harsh. A female neighbor, however, seems to be the major target, half of an aging brother and sister couple who now occupied the cottage where the old man whose funeral was described in "Berck Plage" used to live. Sylvia paints her neighbor, who was tall, as "one/ Long nicotine-finger" and throws in a contemptuous reference to "your much sicker/ Predecessor" as "A six and a half foot wedding cake." Yet she concedes that he was "not even malicious." The fourth stanza stresses the errant woman as someone who reads Sylvia's personal poetry or diary ("Mirror talk") in her room like a whore and who, in the next stanza, jumps with surprise when Sylvia catches her at it. The neighbor is linked with the rural people she grew up among: "Trundling their utters home." Even her religious background is transformed into a derisive label: "the Low/ Church smile/ Spreading itself, bad butter." The final stanza summarizes her hypocritical pretenses at being neighborly by emphasizing her hidden motive—her eyes scrutinize "the fly" of Ted's pants on a chair while also checking the sleeping eyes of the children "Just to make sure."

How true Sylvia's accusations were is a moot point. The important thing was that she believed they were, and experienced the satisfaction of discharging her rage in print. But Ted and Olga were the main culprits, and their action, their treachery, demanded the greater concentration of poetic energy. A whole series of poems eventually were to center upon Ted and the affair: "A Secret," "Gulliver," "Childless Woman," "Rabbit Catcher," "The Detective," "The Other," "The Fearful," and "Event." The latter probably comes first, in May, since it has Sylvia and Ted, during the period after the Olga visit, still sleeping together, back to back, but separated: "Who has dismembered us?" It is a sad rather than an angry poem, a poignant comment upon the wreckage of their marriage, which has left Sylvia back in the circle of her "groove of old faults, deep and bitter," subject to the "Intolerable vowels" of the moon, and pathetically aware of their altered relationship: "The dark is melting. We touch like cripples."

"The Detective" sees Ted's and Olga's affair in terms of a murder, with Sherlock Holmes narrating the details to Watson. There has been more than a murder, Sylvia having been obliterated, though Court Green—the scene of the crime—remains: "the smell of years burning" and "the deceits, tacked up like family photographs." One clue is a photo of Ted: "look at his smile." Holmes wonders about the weapon used and concludes that "It is a case of vaporization." Poor Sylvia lost her mouth first "In the second year" (her poetry?) when it had been hung out to dry, then the breasts—"two white stones"—which had two children to feed. "But their bones showed, and the moon smiled." At the end, Holmes can only warn, "We walk on air, Watson," and provide a last symbolic setting: "There is only the moon, embalmed in phosphorus./ There is only a crow in a tree. Make notes." Sylvia was indeed obliterated. What she always feared, according to Elizabeth Compton, was that the possessive Olga would even end up using Sylvia's contraceptive.

In "The Other" Sylvia might be merging Olwyn and Olga into a single enemy, though Olga seems the most obvious object. In any case, the two women are condemned for not bearing children: "The stolen horses, the fornications/ Circle a womb of marble." A crime is again condemned, and "Sulphurous adulteries grieve in a dream." But the import of the title becomes clear in the last three lines, where the persona speaks about the "cold glass" that had come "Between myself and myself." The mirror is again installed, and the poem doubles back on itself as a dialogue between two Sylvias, another confirmation of the fact that she was growing more aware that Ted's betrayal had led to the emergence of the bitch goddess. Its conclusion, ironic and cool, also affirms her realization that survival was now assured: "You smile./ No, it is not fatal." But "A Secret," which has been definitely dated from October, despite several obscurities, concentrates totally on Olga. Its form is a dialogue, a favorite device, though often an interior one, and welds her betrayal to an earlier abortion: "An illegitimate baby./ That big blue head!/ How it breathes in the bureau drawer!"

Though weakened by its esoteric gaps, "A Secret" has that air of mounting horror and constant menace that characterizes the best of Sylvia's work. Its progress and explicit terror are keyed to the Gothic idea of the dead blue infant locked in a lingerie drawer like a dirty secret, trying to crawl out. When it does emerge, a parody of birth, foam in her lap, it does so as a "Dwarf baby,/ The knife in your back." The complexity here, deliberate, I believe, among voices, two women speaking but a third presence in command, gives the poem an intriguing ambiguity of event. Whose baby? Who was stabbed, child or woman? Such questions help frame the poem's decided rage and fear, defining Sylvia's fundamental capacity to funnel her dilemma into a dramatic mode, which does, however, tend to dissipate some of its lyric intensity. What is evident throughout is the poet's grafting of her birth in death obsession upon the treacherous act of Olga, while also relating it to the entire scene of an emerging double. Compare this with "The Fearful," written in November, a confessional, sealed-in rehash of the telephone incident that only makes sense when read with biographical fore-knowledge.

Again, the poem is important for its insight into Sylvia's consciousness of the causal relationship between the appearance of the bitch goddess and Ted and Olga's effrontery: after castigating Ted for crawling behind a pseudonym like a worm and Olga for pretending she "is a man, not a woman," the persona claims "The mask increases, eats the worm." Sylvia exulted in the idea that Olga would have no children, her "womb of marble" incapable of reproducing life—what would greatly increase Sylvia's last depression was news that Olga was pregnant. As for Ted, Sylvia was stronger than he, and her estimation of him as "a little man now" found fullest expression in "Gulliver." When Ted returned to Soho and London's literary life, Sylvia particularly resented the fame his poetry had brought him. In the poem he is stretched out and tied down by tiny "spider men," literary parasites, "Winding and twining" him in their "bribes." Yet, she protests, "they hate you," and would, if they could, cut him up like holy relics, store his pieces in their cabinets. Here revenge is no longer a concern, she wishes he could return to the days when he was truly a giant and begs him to "Step off!/ Step off seven leagues."

Like most lyric poets after they have found their voice, Sylvia was writing too many poems, but the astonishing fact is that so many of them succeed. As she edged closer to the core of her obsession and permitted the bitch goddess greater freedom, the pettiness dropped away; and the poem of revenge, gouging deeper into the shadow behind Ted to resurrect Otto, accordingly stepped outside of itself to achieve a ruthless impersonality of purpose and to give the lyric voice a true universality. It is conscious myth-making at a new level, and this explains why several editors would end up rejecting these later poems. Like most authentic talents, Sylvia would find that the ultimate, long-sought-for break-through inevitably meant a temporary loss of public understanding.

The sharpest evidence of this metamorphosis can be seen in "Lady Lazarus" and "Daddy"—the signature poems of the bitch goddess. In them Sylvia finally reaches back to Otto's death and the agony it entailed; life and art achieve a symbolic marriage at last, and the process of myth-making is itself a part of the ceremony. Otto is transformed into the prime Nazi totem of the twentieth century and Sylvia becomes his Jewish victim, while the voice or style is pure fairy tale, Sexton's voice from "Ringing the Bells at Bedlam," the heavy rhymes of Poe, the "simple" syntax of Stevie Smith,[7] the child-like consciousness and pain of Roethke, the religious insights of Blake, all compressed into a metronomic terror that never loses its neurotically repetitive intensity.

"Lady Lazarus" is almost straight drama, constructed out of the recurrent suicidal urge: "I have done it again./ One year in every ten." Fiction and fact are no longer meaningful divisions, and Alvarez's contention that the third attempt could refer to Sylvia's accident in July—she had driven the Morris stationwagon off the road and hurt herself, and later informed the critic it had been "deliberate"—might be accurate but is hardly relevant, though I have the feeling that Alvarez's own penchant for fast cars might have influenced his interpretation, since the site of the crash was an old air field without a tree or any other dangerous obstacle in sight and since Sylvia remained terribly frightened of physical injury.

What is relevant is that the persona has established a ritual of destruction, a religious one which is specifically tied to poetry later in the poem: "Dying/ Is an art, like everything else./ I do it exceptionally well." The bitch goddess is speaking, not Sylvia, and it is her biography which is at issue, the evil double finally being permitted her own say. She is a Jew, a perpetual victim, who has now seen the light and is intent upon shedding her passive role (and her womanhood as well) in favor of a persecutor's robes. The Jew is modern mass man, foredoomed sufferer, prime victim of the twentieth-century's barbarism. For Sylvia the guise was logical and unavoidable. She had always yearned for the Jew's sense of community and always thought of her personal pain in terms of the massacre of the Jews during World War II. When she first met George MacBeth and wished to praise his poetry, one of her initial remarks had been "I see you have a concentration camp in your mind too."

When Sylvia speaks of her survival as a miracle, and compares her face to "a featureless, fine/ Jew linen," she is warning the world of the transformation from Jew to Medea or Medusa. Thus she peels off her mask of passive suffering like a "napkin" and asks, "O my enemy./ Do I terrify?" She sees no end to her resurrections and mocks the audience that has stood by silently while the horrors were being perpetrated—the "peanut-munching crowd" who revelled in her agonies and were sexually stimulated by it, but who cannot now understand her survival. Sylvia lapses deliberately into personal history, inventing details and altering time to suit the governing magic of three. "The first time it happened I was ten"; and then, at twenty, they had "to pick the worms off me like sticky pearls." But she stresses the "theatrical" aspect of the poem and her suicide, which are united in their defiance of death.

She also derides what she considered a gruesome aspect of organized religion—the preservation of relics—and stridently claims that there will be a charge for "a word or a touch" of herself the freak or for "a bit of blood/ Or a piece of my hair or my clothes." Her anger, from the beginning, has been broadening its range, but suddenly it shifts focus and alights upon the primary target—"Herr Doktor," the Nazi scientist, "Herr Enemy," her father's totem. She mocks his "concern" for her and links it with the Nazis shifting through piles of Jewish ashes for valuables to loot: "A cake of soap/ A wedding ring,/ A gold filling." The final two stanzas equate the Nazi scientist with "Herr God, Herr Lucifer"— total power, light and dark extremes merged in the bright fire of his crematorium—before swinging into a scream of fury that promises a phoenix-like revenge: "Out of the ash/ I rise with my red hair/ And I eat men like air." Thus by poem's end the enemy has been enlarged to include all men, and the bitch goddess is presented as a goddess of fire who has adopted a male identity and male weapons to defeat him at his own game of destruction.

Without a doubt, as Sylvia said in an interview, the poem is about "a girl with an Electra complex"; but she had also said earlier, "I must say I cannot sympathise with these cries from the heart that are informed by nothing except a needle or a knife or whatever it is. I believe that one should be able to control and manipulate experiences, even the most terrifying—like madness, being tortured, this kind of experience—and one should be able to manipulate these experiences with an informed and intelligent mind." This is the cool detachment which allowed Sylvia to refer to "Lady Lazarus" and "Daddy" as examples of "light verse" to Alvarez.

In speaking about "Daddy" Sylvia candidly stressed the allegorical intentions behind its inception: "The poem is spoken by a girl with an Electra complex. Her father died while she thought he was God. Her case is complicated by the fact that her father was also a Nazi and her mother very possibly part Jewish. In the daughter the two strains marry and paralyse each other—she has to act out the awful little allegory once over before she is free of it." The references to her own psychological situation are obvious, though patently absurd, as she well knew. Her mother had no Jewish blood, and Otto's whole philosophy was inimical to fascism. He regarded the rise of Hitler in Germany with horror. Sylvia is not Sylvia Plath of Wellesley in the poem; she is an allegorical self whose rages are surrealistic, not confessional, in nature. Most of Sylvia's poetry depends upon a metamorphosis, and the nexus is inevitably a catering to or revulsion from an extreme. She once described "Fever 103°," for instance, as being about "two kinds of fire—the fires of hell, which merely agonize, and the fires of heaven, which purify. During the poem, the first sort of fire suffers into the second."

In "Daddy" Sylvia clearly defines the "Herr Doktor" from "Lady Lazarus" as a father figure, fits him into the mythology of the bitch goddess, and then relates him to the husband figure of Ted. From the start, the Nazi father is rejected by the daughter, who chants in the dark of a possible mental breakdown: "You do not do, you do not do/ Any more, black shoe/ In which I have lived like a foot/ For thirty years, poor and white." The extremes of black and white are established and the mythical thirty years are emphasized as a fairy-tale symbol. Sylvia knew that fairy tales were hidden maps to the unconscious, just as she knew that the second self, the bitch goddess, was a child. Relentlessly the poem repeats old motifs: The dead colossus "Marble-heavy, a bag full of God"; the love for the ocean mother at Cape Cod, "off beautiful Nauset"; the linking of a father figure with Nazis everywhere by reference to Otto's birthplace in the Polish Corridor, "Scraped flat by the roller/ Of wars, wars, wars"; and the silent ghost of a father separated by barbed wire, the German tongue itself, "Ich, ich, ich, ich."

Purgation is the theme and revenge its vehicle. The persona must again re-enact the growth of the bitch goddess from victim to persecutor who sees herself being carted by train "to Dachau, Auschwitz, Belsen." Sylvia's present interest in black magic is contrasted to the lucid coldness of Germanic allegiance to reason and science, which is "not very pure or true" by comparison. This is an ironic turnabout as her "gypsy ancestress" and "weird luck" have combined with her faith in the Tarot deck to make her "a bit of a Jew." Extremes are pitted against extremes, and the result can be nothing less than a total subjectivity: "Every woman adores a Fascist,/ The boot in the face, the brute/ Brute heart of a brute like you."

These three lines touch upon an aspect of feminine reality Sylvia understood and resented—the acceptance of male repression for the security it engendered. It was not rape so much as an ordering of daily existence. After relating the father totem more directly to Otto—"You stand at the blackboard, daddy"—the persona then returns to the myth of Sylvia's life: her pretty red heart bitten in two by her father when she was ten, and her suicide attempt when she was twenty, which Sylvia accepts as an effort to "get back, back, back to you." Recovery came, however, and she was stuck together "with glue," which suggests the putting on again of a mask; and then she married Ted, the only man she could not dominate—"a model of you." The marriage was a bleak extreme of submissiveness: "And a love of the rack and the screw./ And I said I do, I do."

Betrayal was an inevitable repetition of Otto's abandonment: "The black telephone's off at the root." But she no longer accepts either Otto's or Ted's treachery so easily. "If I've killed one man, I've killed two." And both men are pictured as vampires, Ted having drunk her blood for "seven years." In the final stanza, which is frantic and deliberately hysterical, the allusion to a village yokes the village of Otto's birth to Croton, where most of the neighbors sided with her as the abandoned wife:

> There's a stake in your fat black heart
> And the villagers never liked you.
> They are dancing and stamping on you.
> They always *knew* it was you.
> Daddy, daddy, you bastard, I'm through.

That last line is unique, a vulgar scream that conceals its art. The heavy rhymes have jingled home, the neurotic repetitions stressing the "stamping" effect—the stompings of a Nazi boot and a vengeful daughter and dancing villagers—and the allegory achieves far-reaching significance, not in content, but in psychological mood.

The Nazi has been isolated by Sylvia as a father who had to be God, and in so doing became Satan, as a *man* with a will to power who drank blood, as a *man* who loved purity and order more than humanity, as a remote *man* of science who, like Lucifer, thought he alone had the answer and should be master, even if the price was the massacre of his own kind, of his own heart. "Lady Lazarus" and "Daddy," especially the former, will endure because they provide, with true lyric compression and the appropriate language of madness, dramatic insights into the nature of the beast that has made this century one of endless suffering.

For Sylvia the two poems had to have been extraordinary experiences in themselves. They had released the poison of many years and acted as a catharsis for the repressed feelings of hostility she had always harbored against Otto. These and the many other poems written at Court Green during October and November gave her a firm artistic stance at last. And in "Ariel" she created a perfect metaphor for this other self and the art it must produce—a desperate but exciting art that found excitement in a masculine drive for power.

The poem itself has generally been misconstrued. Ariel was the name of the horse Sylvia rode in Croton, and the poem does refer to her near-fatal and involuntary gallop on "Sam" back at Cambridge. But the real difficulty comes from the sexual ambiguity at work and the vagueness of the actual images. Alvarez has commented quite perceptively on the poem's circular movement—a favorite Plath structural device—and on the fact that the images are curiously "substanceless." "You are made to *feel* the horse's physical presence, but not to see it. The detail is all inward." What Alvarez has not seen is the bottom layer of structure—the foundation, which goes back to Sylvia's love for double entendres and which is specifically an outgrowth of her belief that the bitch goddess was male in her drive for power and revenge. "Ariel" must thus be read as an allegory about art which uses the sperm cell as its major metaphor. Its fierce flight towards the ovary is parallel to the gallop on a runaway stallion. At the beginning there is the quietude of waiting for release in a testicle: "Stasis in darkness." The bitch goddess is then presented as "God's lioness" joined to the stallion to reproduce a child: "How one we grow,/ Pivot of heels and knees!" The ride is described thus: "Splits and passes, sister to/ The brown arc." Legs are spread to allow the male entry into the vulva: "dark/ Hooks—/ Black sweet blood mouthfuls,/ Shadows." There is little doubt of a sperm cell spitting from its liquid cloud: "White/ Godiva, I unpeel" and "I/ Foam to wheat, a glitter of sea." But the sperm is destined to fail—"The child's cry/ Melts in the wall"—and yet doomed to try—"And I/ Am the arrow."

The final stanza, and the last separate line, mate sperm with artistic intention. Sylvia wrote at sunrise and realized that she and the sun were "suicidal" in the enormity of their quest—their drive into "the cauldron of morning." It is a brilliant poem that, once and for all, demonstrated Sylvia's keen insight into her own art. She knew exactly what she was doing during those long morning hours of darkness and despair, reversing the death-in-birth obsession that had ruled her life, creating life from the ashes, creating art, not suicide. However intense or seemingly mad her method, she remained in control.

> The artist's 'immediacy' . . . is perhaps nothing other
> than this long productive memory; it reaches further
> than the memory of other people into childhood, into
> the sphere of first experience without 'experience' and
> inhibitions, into all the freshness of the unknown and
> all the terrors of discovery, and thus not only into the
> artist's own childhood but into the childhood of the
> human race.
>
> ERNST FISCHER

21

Words Dry and Riderless

When Ernst Fischer, the venerable socialist critic, talks about the artist's
"immediacy" and relates it to an undying, far-reaching childhood, he is
defining the essence of artistic process, at least during its early stages. He
is also, unwittingly, providing a perfect description of the bitch goddess
poems Sylvia had been driving towards all her life. The relationship
between childhood and myth might not always be clear, but it is
patently dynamic and basic. For Sylvia, as she showed in "Ariel," the
artistic manipulation of childhood material would express itself in a
constant urge towards negative emotions, metaphors of pain, rage,
sorrow. Innate to this was the corresponding erection of the myth of the
bitch goddess or evil double, with Sylvia confronting childhood's past in
the guise of a furious, vindictive little girl.

Myth, like poetry, offered her a means of defense against the
descending bell jar, and she did not hesitate to explore the deepest,
darkest caverns of her unconscious, where childhood and myth have
their lair. It succeeded in that it removed much of the internal pressure
of Ted's betrayal and made her public mask somewhat easier to
maintain. Alvarez noticed that there "was no trace of the poetry's
despair and unforgiving destruction in her social manner. She remained
remorselessly bright and energetic, busy with her children and her
bee-keeping in Devon, busy flat-hunting in London, busy seeing *The*

Bell Jar through the press, busy typing and sending off her poems to largely unreceptive editors." Nor was there any question of a "writer's block," as there had been during the 1953 disaster, primarily because poetry itself was no longer a disguise, which could break apart like the other disguises under the blow of a severe depression. It was a survival tool, a weapon for self-defense, which permitted an interior heroism that became, simultaneously, purgative and strengthening.

"Ariel" demonstrated its paradoxical nature in the central metaphor of stallion and sperm heading for death and possible birth, the artist riding his vision into battle against near-impossible odds. Shortly before that, she had attempted to bring both impulses—the surface thrusts of early traumas and a parallel desire to shape an enduring legend from its chaos—together in a remarkable sequence of poems that had for their locus her bee hive. In "Stings (2)" she had touched upon the bee hive briefly, but that was a tentative exploration, little more than a convenient metaphor to convey a pessimistic view of human fate. In the group of bee poems written in October, the metaphor is elaborated, extended into her father obsession and structured around the myth of the artist her poetry had always tried to formulate.

The inspiration is clear enough, a memory of Otto as bee expert and a daily contemplation of her own hive's activities, which still terrified her despite a growing ability to handle its occupants. But there is another association equally important, perhaps more so. In the *Ion*, which Sylvia knew well and loved, Plato had compared the bee and his honey-gathering task to the artist and his craft. This association made her identification with the queen bee even more natural. In the first of the bee poems, "The Bee Meeting," which records Sylvia's introduction to bees and bee-keeping by her Croton neighbors, the identification does not come until the last stanza, when the climax of horror ends with a chilly question: "Whose is that long white box in the grove, what have they accomplished, why am I cold?" Death and nothingness ("white") are the logical conclusions to the ritual just described. The previous stanzas, while accurately detailing the actual process of removing the "virgins" (future queen bees) from their cells before they can assassinate the old queen, had already established a dual plane of narration, the literal constantly being enlarged by the speaker's personal interpretation of events: the emphasis on an "operation" and the ceaseless insistence upon related metaphors, such as seeing scarlet flowers as "blood clots" and translating the hawthorn scent into ether for its children, as well as the description of the expert as a "surgeon."

Familiar motifs of another kind also prevail, the stress on doubles, on the use of masks, the persona becoming "one of them" when encased in her veil and hat, all the others' identities hidden under the standard gear until the persona cannot distinguish one from another, and a related concern for female extremes, the preoccupation with "virgins"—the hive itself is "snug as a virgin"—in contrast to the central, well-serviced queen, "the murderess" who is destined, when the virgins break through the hymen-thin cell wall, to die and return "into a heaven that loves her." A cycle of nature, to be sure, but one that has many human implications, at least for Sylvia. The rite is an operation upon self, a shifting of identities to encompass art's need for different perspectives, which joins social disguise with a real metamorphosis, and with Sylvia's real "fear" under her own public mask. The last stanza, besides suggesting the ceremonial sacrifice of a virgin, stresses the persona's peculiar state of suffering and mental fatigue, her continued torture upon a rack of extremes: "I am exhausted, I am exhausted—/ Pillar of white in a blackout of knives." She accepts the destiny of Lot's wife, along with her crime of curiosity and defiance of God, but has phrased it in terms of a child's black and white world.

The next poem in the sequence, "The Arrival of the Bee Box," deals again with a literal scene, the delivery of the box of bees she had ordered for her new hive. But Sylvia insists upon the casket imagery employed at the end of "Bee Meeting" and in the very first stanza presents the much-used theme of birth in death, looking upon the bee box as "the coffin of a midget/ Or a square baby." This morbid black humor fits the consistent emphasis upon emotional poles. In the second stanza, the box is deemed "dangerous," though it has only a single grid, which is "no escape" and to which she puts her eye in the following stanza: "It is dark, dark,/ With the swarmy feeling of African hands/ Minute and shrunk for export." At first sight, the slave-trade reference might seem gratuitous, but other historical allusions are to quickly follow and they provide a broadening range of associations. In the next stanza, for example, the bees are viewed as "a Roman mob," the image of irrational power, which is maintained in the next stanza, where the humming is "furious Latin" and where the persona denies being Caesar, though she is aware of her God-like power over the "maniacs" she has ordered: "They can die, I need feed them nothing, I am the owner." She considers a possible escape from the situation she has created, a shedding of responsibility by a flight into other disguises, such as turning into a tree after freeing them or dressing in her proper bee-keeping clothes, "my moon suit and funeral veil." She promises that "Tomorrow I will be sweet God, I will set them free," but the separate last line has other connotations: "The box is only temporary." Its prosaic language suggests that a whole persona is temporary, will be removed, and that the coffin imagery of the opening stanza may result in a resurrection. The poem has certainly enlarged the sequence's frame of reference and might be read as Sylvia's comment upon the ancient sin of hubris; man assuming divine powers over his fellow man, which, historically, had supplied the opposing evils of a tyrant like Caesar and the lawless Roman mob and had, inevitably, developed into the evil of slavery.

The third poem returns to a more personal, and thus more intense, reaction to the bee hive. In the company of a neighbor who is her teacher, the persona is working on her own hive, which she had—as had Sylvia—painted white and decorated with Austrian flowers "with excessive love," trying to nullify its terror by thinking "Sweetness, sweetness," concentrating on its honey results rather than its living reality. But her mind cannot be deceived, sees the "Blood cells grey as the fossils of shells" and wonders if she is "buying wormy mahogany?/ Is there any queen at all in it?" The queen is there, however, incredibly ancient, her wings like "torn shawls," her body used up, gaunt, "bare and unqueenly and even shameful," like Sylvia's at the time, but still majestic in comparison with the persona, who identifies herself with the "honey-drudgers," the "winged, unmiraculous women," the common housewives and mothers all around her, though she insists "I am no drudge." And yet, her marriage had evaporated her "strangeness," and she had "eaten dust/ And dried plates with my dense hair."

Again, Ted's abandonment, the end of her marriage, has freed her to become the bitch goddess, to drop her submissive mask; but she wonders if the other wives and mothers will now hate her, persumably out of envy, "These women who only scurry,/ Whose news is the open cherry, the open clover?" Open thighs, open bodies, internal organs, the conversational topics of her female neighbors are castigated, and in the next stanza Sylvia links the hive and its honey-making feature—following Plato's lead—specifically to her new poetic voice: "It is almost over./ I am in control." She also links it firmly with her old muse, the bald moon, and with the Ariel purity of sexless power: "It will work without thinking,/ Opening, in spring, like an industrious virgin/ To scour the creaming crests/ As the moon, for its ivory powders, scours the sea." The figures of speech are implicitly sexual, virgin as spinster cleaning woman, spreading herself to male scum but nullifying it, moon scouring the sea, all converging in the poetic act which is purgative, painful, and yet somehow productive.

The rest of the eighth and the entire ninth and tenth stanzas deal with a specific event, which had happened months before. Ted, the "third person" in the poem, had approached the bee hive with unconcealed bravado, only to flee in panic when the bees landed on him.

Sylvia had been amused by the incident when it happened, but now, in her bitch goddess role, she judges Ted more severely, connecting his flight from the bees with his flight from her, and realizing that "He was sweet," though a "great scapegoat," and that "The sweat of his efforts a rain/ Tugging the world to fruit." His poetry, in short, is still rich, important to the world at large, and she rejects the idea of revenge against him. The bees wanted his death, were willing to change him into a villain, landing on his face, "Complicating his features," were even willing to die themselves in the act, "thought death worth it," but she is wiser now, knows that the separation had actually resulted in the discovery of her poetic guise, "a self to recover, a queen." The end of the eleventh stanza begins to sketch in a clearer picture of the masculine queen, with "her lion-red body, her wings of glass," and the final stanza is a fierce summary of the bitch goddess in full flight:

> Now she is flying
> More terrible than she ever was, red
> Scar in the sky, red comet
> Over the engine that killed her—
> The mausoleum, the wax house.

Besides making abundantly evident that Sylvia's poetry was an instrument of survival in a psychological sense, "Stings" demonstrates the advance made from "Daddy" and "Lady Lazarus," the abandonment of the Jew-victim role—instead of being in an engine, being dragged off to a concentration camp death, the persona has risen above the machine. Happily, it also has evinced a more healthy and realistic assessment of Ted's betrayal.

"The Swarm," which follows, need not, then, remain trapped in any narrow confessional groove, can take up where the second bee poem left off, seeking historical, religious and social parallels for the persona's private dilemma. It returns to the crime of hubris touched upon in "The Arrival of the Bee Box," although this time the central villain is Napoleon, the archetypal modern dictator, who used people like pawns, "These are chess people you play with." The swarm of bees, which is released but always returns to the hive, where the "man of business, intensely practical" awaits them and their honey, represent Napoleon's conquering army of ordinary citizens, "Like the pack, the pack, like

everybody," their baser instincts, greed, jealousy, the desire to loot, to
prey upon others, being manipulated by the tyrant: "The bees have got
so far. Seventy feet high!/ Russia, Poland and Germany!"

The bees are shot down, however, the Grand Army falls, and
Napoleon is exiled to Elba, while "the white busts of marshals, admirals,
generals" worm "themselves into niches," signaling hypocrisy, dead
history: "How instructive this is!" The dreams are finished, glory buried
in a mausoleum, and it is the practical man of business who survives and
reaps his profits, the man "with gray hands" that are really "asbestos
receptacles." "Pom! Pom!", more shots, and an individual awareness of
danger, of mortality, " 'They would have killed *me!*" But bees have
their own "notion of honor," an id drive, "A black, intractable mind."
The last two lines supply a dramatic metamorphosis: "Napoleon is
pleased, he is pleased with everything./ O Europe! O ton of honey!"
What has happened, of course, is that the persona has suddenly seen that
Napoleon is not the major villain, that the real Napoleon is the man of
business, the amoral, dreamless merchant who milks death of every last
drop of blood to convert it into the the honey of money—by extension,
Krupp, not Hitler, was the mainspring of the Nazi rise to power.

If nothing else, "The Swarm" should effectively put to rest any idea
that Sylvia's poetry remained too tightly bound to confessional agonies
for true transcendence and universality. The final poem in the sequence,
"Wintering," which is as good as "Stings" and for the same reason, a
more intense relationship between self and poetic material, confronts the
logical end of bee-keeping, the storing of the honey. In this case, Sylvia
had chosen to store her six jars in that windowless room she feared "At
the heart of the house." The bottles sit there like "Six cat's eyes" but the
persona is more concerned with the room: "This is the room I have
never been in./ This is the room I could never breathe in./ The black
bunched in there like a bat." A flashlight reveals what it bodes for her,
"Black asininity. Decay./ Possession." It reminds her of the bee hive, its
dark interior where, during winter's stasis, it "is the time of hanging on
for the bees." The connections with her own situation are here more
obvious, her own need to hang on in the winter landscape of Ted's
departure, to overcome the depression which has made her all too aware
of death, decay, the yearning for a black art. A substitute food has to be
provided in lieu of absent flowers, "Tate and Lyle keeps them going,"
an artificial replacement for life.

The bees ball in a black mass, and the persona's mind does likewise,
"black" against the white smile of the snow, depression countering
nothingness, sterility. On warm days, the bees carry out their dead, and

the survivors are pictured as "all women," the queen and her hard-working virgins, who have "got rid of the men," useless drones, "blunt, clumsy stumblers, the boors." Winter, after all, "is for women," who continue knitting in the face of death and decay, in the face of nothingness, stronger than men, more determined, closer to the earth, their source of energy. Like the gladioli, the hive and its female occupants will endure beyond winter: "The bees are flying. They taste the spring."

The cycle is complete from spring through winter, from the first step in bee-keeping to the taking of honey, and the sequence is surprisingly cohesive, though individual poems, such as "Stings" and "Wintering," are manifestly superior to their companion pieces. It has touched upon the rituals of myth, related self to history, unmasked the oppressive masculine culture, and demonstrated how art can emerge from personal disaster—in all, a female power myth to counter the traditional male hubris vented in aggression and money-making. Happily, the last line of the last poem is filled with hope for the future, reflecting its author's own sense of a breakthrough which seemed to guarantee survival.

This optimism was not merely a poetic guise. Throughout the testing period of October and November, as Sylvia wrote poems and kept house, she regained her confidence. Though she continued to regale her friends with letters of martyrdom and outrage, painting Ted as an arch villain who had abandoned her and the children completely, refusing to give them enough money to buy the baby some shoes—which Clarissa Roche has called a definite falsehood—in spite of his fame and supposed riches, she was simply playing out a role, a role she had learned from her mother. In actual fact her major problem was simply loneliness, the need for articulate, educated friends. She had also continued to beseech the Roches to pay her an extended visit, while refusing their offer of a room at their place instead; and Clarissa did arrive for a week's visit in the middle of November. She knew that Sylvia was desperate for companionship.

Clarissa recalls that the day of her arrival was wet, cold, and gray, and that Sylvia was waiting for her at the station, umbrella in hand. They embraced, laughing, and Sylvia exclaimed, "Oh, you've saved my life!" She was to repeat the sentence many times during the course of the visit, and emphasize "the terrible loneliness one has." Clarissa was fully cognizant of the fact that both statements were true and false and that Sylvia remained in steady oscillation between two roles. "She was sort of martyrish," Clarissa has said, "and yet, at the same time, she felt very vindictive towards Ted." One incident which Clarissa believed distinctly neurotic in its overtones was Sylvia's frantic reaction to Clarissa's iron pills. She was deathly afraid that the children might get hold of them and regularly searched Clarissa's pocketbook to make sure the pills were still there.

Sylvia also kept referring to Clarissa as "the earth mother" and saying things like "How marvelous it is to be the earth mother." Clarissa found this ironic since that was the last role Sylvia wanted for herself. And yet she still loved children. Although determined not to remarry, "she wanted more children actually." She also "loved Poles, had this thing about Poles." The result was a half-humorous plan to have a Polish gentleman impregnate Sylvia. Clarissa was acquainted with a rather wealthy, charming, and intelligent Pole, who had once been in the Polish Cavalry and whose Russian wife was unable to bear him children. Clarissa thought he would be an ideal candidate, and Sylvia agreed. They sat down together and wrote him a serious letter outlining their unusual proposal. They went so far as to secure his address, but the letter was never sent.

Clarissa also felt that Sylvia was neurotic about her writing and her need for more time to work on her poetry. Fortunately, a few months earlier, Sylvia's friend the district nurse had secured Sylvia another nurse to act as a helper for seven weeks. This had been a great aid to Sylvia, who found it nearly impossible to get an agency nanny to come so far from London. She had secured one a few days before the nurse's arrival, but the woman had proved to be senile, unclean, and frightening to the children. Sylvia dismissed her after two days. During Clarissa's stay, the nurse was away on vacation, but when she returned Sylvia would have time to pursue her plan to locate a London flat. London had become in her eyes a utopian city, an escape from the cow-trap of Court Green. In London she could get an *au pair* girl without trouble. In London she could get more freelance work. In London she could get the children good free schooling. In London she would have the kind of stimulating company she enjoyed.

This supposed last advantage, however, was a self-deception. As Clarissa herself has observed, "She had this curious contempt for people, she always seemed to have that. People who thought they were close to her she had nothing but contempt for, so that friendship was very limited for her. Having moved into this smart set with Ted, being taken up by Spender and Eliot, had no meaning at all. The consequence was that nobody cared tuppence about her, although she was too forceful to be ignored." Further, like many other suddenly divorced women, Sylvia would discover in London that most of "their" friends had become "his" friends, especially when the husband was as well known as Ted. The situation would be awkward since Ted and Sylvia still worked with the same people at the BBC and elsewhere.

But London was the only answer Sylvia would accept. She had been going to the city every other week, partly to search for a flat and partly to do recording work for the BBC. On August 24 (most of the programs were recorded at least a few days ahead of time) she had read "Surgeon at 2 A.M." for "Poet's Voice." In this poem she was finally able to confront pain from the other side of the bed. On September 7 Sylvia appeared on a program called "In a World of Sound: What You Value Stays." Almost a month later, on November 4, she was a guest of the Third Programme on a show called, appropriately, "The Weird Ones," where she read some of her recent poetry.[1] These appearances were satisfying for her ego, and she liked the idea of the supplementary income. Ted gave her money on a regular basis, her aunt had sent her money, and she was earning small sums from magazines, in spite of several recent rejections.

Sylvia's financial situation was difficult only because she believed it was. She had always been the one to pay the bills and keep the family budget balanced. She had an exaggerated idea of the money Ted was supposedly earning in his new capacity as celebrity-poet and naturally resented the notion of him making vast sums and spending them on Olga, while she had to count every penny. Clement Moore's stepfather had called her in late October to see that she had legal advice, and a formal divorce was presumably being planned; but her letters indicate that she believed $2800 a year was the most she could hope to get out of Ted. She did own Court Green, however, which was a valuable piece of property, and she had plans to rent it during the winter months—when and if she found a London flat she could afford.

The search appeared endless and hopeless. As she had so often in the past, Sylvia found herself walking the streets, looking vainly for "To Let" signs and going from agent to agent. Weeks later she gravitated back to the Primrose Hill section, probably drawn by memories of her stay there, where she had had such great dreams, had given birth to Frieda, and had lost another child. It was while walking down the block around the corner from her old apartment that she noticed a vacancy sign. It was a flat in a row house and near the front door was a blue metal plaque that informed her that Yeats had briefly lived here. She lost little time in looking up the agent in charge, and convincing him not to demand references by paying a full year's rent (on a five-year lease) in advance.

The fact that the building had once housed Yeats himself, whose tower she had admired only a few months before, seemed to her a certain sign that hidden forces continued to guide her destiny. Moreover, according to a letter she wrote to Peter Orr soon afterwards—she had met Mr. Orr, a member of the British Council, at the end of October while reading her poetry for the BBC—when she returned to Devon she decided to test fate further by opening a collected edition of Yeats' plays with her eyes shut. The play was "The Unicorn from the Stars" and her finger hit upon the line: "Get food and wine and whatever you need to give you strength and courage—and I will get the house ready." [2] Yeats' ghost was obviously an ally.

The significant thing was that she had a flat, and just in time to avoid Devon's wet winter and the absence of her efficient young nurse, who would be leaving shortly. If she had been unsuccessful, Sylvia was determined to return to western Ireland for the winter, where she would at least be near the sea and also near the Irish poet she had met a few months earlier. But now none of that mattered. She was returning to London and escaping from the dullness of village routine, although, to quote David Compton, "she had always liked being of the village, the ancientness of it all," and "she did not like the other things the city offered." London obviously could not live up to Sylvia's expectations, especially since its own winters were no less gray and wet than Devon's.

She and the two children did not move into the flat until the middle of December. It was an ideal apartment in many ways as it occupied the two top floors of the building. Further, as it was located around the corner from Primrose Hill at 23 Fitzroy Road, the zoo was only a short distance away and in Regent's Park there was an excellent playground for the children. The apartment had three bedrooms, a large living room, a kitchen where the family could eat on stools at a counter, and a small outside balcony which Sylvia hoped to take advantage of in the spring. There was no central heating, though an electric heater had been installed in the living room wall, which Sylvia supplemented with several portable heaters, lugging them from room to room as the need arose.

On Christmas Eve, at Sylvia's invitation, Alvarez dropped by for a drink. He has described the flat: "It was newly painted, white and chill. There were, I remember, no curtains up yet, and the night pressed in coldly on the windows. She had deliberately kept the place bare: Rush matting on the floor, a few books, bits of Victoriana, and cloudy blue glass on the shelves, a couple of small Leonard Baskin woodcuts. It was rather beautiful, in its chaste, stripped-down way, but cold, very cold, and the oddments of flimsy Christmas decorations made it seem doubly forlorn, each seeming to repeat that she and the children would be alone for Christmas." He went on to observe, "I had never seen her so strained." He linked the strain with that imposed by the holiday itself, but admitted later that he did nothing about it. This was the last time, a full month and a half before her death, that he saw Sylvia.

Between the lines of Alvarez's memoir one may discern a possible romantic entanglement developing, unspoken but apparently pressed on Sylvia's part. After all, she had called him up and asked him to dinner, which must have gone against the grain of her fierce pride, and had visited him several times earlier on her trips down from Devon, when she read her new poems to him and listened respectfully to his critical reaction. Alvarez himself apparently sensed a reaching out by Sylvia, though he never mentions a romantic motive, and consoles himself with the thought that "she was beyond the reach of anyone." However, when he left her flat at eight o'clock, he admits: "I knew I had let her down in some final and unforgivable way. And I knew she knew."

He had failed her, but Sylvia would not have been surprised by that. As the bee poems, particularly "Wintering," demonstrate, she had become convinced that all men carried within them a certain moral and psychological weakness—a narcissism beyond her own because it could not be bridged even by parenthood. Women were the survivors, in her eyes, because the toughness of their love and hate were absolute. The white, winter smile of her new apartment might have been a reflection of the winter world she knew she could and had already overcome. During the course of Alvarez's visit, Sylvia read him "Death & Co.", which the critic took as proof that "the figure she had invoked so often, only to dismiss triumphantly, had risen before her, dank, final, and not to be denied. . . . This time there was no way out for her." This was nonsense.

Sylvia herself has described the scheme of the poem with her usual precision and detachment in an unbroadcast interview: "This poem . . . is about the double or schizophrenic nature of death—the marmoreal coldness of Blake's death mask, say, hand in glove with the fearful softness of worms, water, and other catabolisms. I imagine these two aspects of death as two men, two business friends, who have come to call." She exulted in her schizophrenic vision of the universe, but there is no evidence in the poem that it had reached the point of finality. Quite the contrary, the poem displays an intellect in calm command of its imagination's rich resources. The soft catabolisms were old friends, "worms" being part of her Gothic signature for years; and the deliberate casting of death in two male figures was for her a natural extension of her painful awareness of the man's seemingly innate Judas quality. That the two men were business men also fit her notion of commercial straw men as history's prime villains—a concept which had been more fully evolved in "The Swarm."

The female persona in "Death & Co." is the familiar Plath dualized heroine. One is ascetic, serious, a solemn representative of rational philosophy without a spiritual or emotional base—Aristotelianism carried to its extreme, which meant a cynical, Nazi-like contemplation of the two babies as tiny corpses in a refrigerator, though they are presented in sterile Greek symmetry: "a simple/ Frill at the neck,/ Then the outings of their Ionian/ Death-gowns." The other extreme is complete self-love and self-glorification at the expense of others, especially women: "Bastard/ Masturbating a glitter,/ He wants to be loved."

It is the climax of the poem which convinced Alvarez that Sylvia had reached the blank wall at the end of her journey. The images of frost and dew, which are visual complements of death's dual aspect, lead to "The dead bell/ The dead bell/ Somebody's done for." Alvarez concedes that the bell might have been "tolling for 'somebody' other than herself" but goes on to say that "she didn't seem to believe so." But as so many previous poems indicate, the death here is the death of Sylvia's other self—the passive, Jewish, victim self, which had been superseded by the stark winter figure of the bitch goddess. "Death & Co." is a good example of why Sylvia's poetry should not be taken too literally, although the poem did grow out of an actual conversation with two men, a hated American critic and his homosexual friend, months earlier. As Clarissa Roche once commented, "She always had the last laugh."

Nevertheless she was, in fact, still very lonely. The early weeks of December had involved a great many frantic chores in extremely bad weather, buying furniture, decorating the apartment, working for the BBC, writing poetry and short stories, trying to find an *au pair* girl, seeing authorities about medical treatment for herself and Nicholas, who had a "wandering eye" problem, and nursery school for Frieda. She was also busy submitting material to various magazines in England and America. The proofs for *The Bell Jar* had long been corrected and returned to her publisher, and she waited anxiously for the novel to appear. It would be released on January 14 and, in the meantime, despite her tremendous work load, Sylvia had started another novel.

By the time of her death, about forty to sixty pages of the new book would be completed. Unfortunately, these pages were lost while in Ted's possession. All that remains, apparently, is an outline of the book as a whole. However, in light of Sylvia's strict dependence upon autobiographical data for narrative purposes, the novel doubtless was to have dealt with "Esther's" life and career in a small English village closely resembling Croton—along the lines of "The Mothers' Union." That this is a likely assumption is evident from a letter she wrote to Elizabeth Compton on February 4, a week before her death, in which she alludes to the unfinished novel and claims that David and Elizabeth appear in it as angels. She also requests Elizabeth not to let her pseudonym become known in Croton for fear of libel suits.

Sylvia's physical isolation in London, like her financial problems, was also often more imagined than real. Though it was true that many of her literary friends (those "bitches and bastards" she supposedly did not need) had dropped her in favor of Ted, she still maintained a circle of literary and social contacts that included George MacBeth and Charles Osborne (at the *London Magazine*) and the Merwins, who remained sympathetic and supportive, and several other couples she had known either from Cambridge or America. Alvarez she would not see again, though she did drop him a note in mid-January about "Winter Trees," which had just appeared in *The Observer*, and suggested that they take their children together to the zoo, where she could show him "the nude verdigris of the condor" alluded to in "Death & Co."

She also kept in touch by mail with the Roches, and also with Marcia Brown, who planned to pay her a visit with her family in the spring; and Elizabeth Compton's occasional notes kept her informed of local happenings in Croton. Her mother's letters also continued to arrive with regularity. Ted himself came by at least every week to see the children, but his visits might have increased rather than diminished her loneliness. Her attitude towards him was changing, as the bee poems and several letters to friends intimate; and this change, on the surface, seemed healthy as it evidenced a more realistic evaluation of his actions. But this shift in perspective was also potentially fatal. What had saved Sylvia from surrender to her depression was her rage, which she translated into magnificent poetry. Though childish and extreme, that rage permitted an externalization of despair and the release of suppressed hostility. Now, as she saw Ted each week, the rage was being replaced by a dangerous self-pity. The sight of him now inspired not bursts of outrage but thoughts of "lost edens."

Coupled with this new attitude towards Ted and herself was the continuing drain on her nearly depleted physical resources. She still smoked, worked feverishly, and ate very little. She had lost twenty pounds over the summer, which she could ill afford, and she was again easy prey to sinus trouble and possible pneumonia. Fortunately, she was assigned to the panel of three doctors who had cared for her during her first pregnancy and subsequent miscarriage and appendectomy, and these were men whom she trusted and liked. They sent her for chest X-rays, provided her with tonics to stimulate her appetite, and prescribed sleeping pills—the depressive's sleeplessness was again pursuing her unmercifully. Behind it all hovered a terrible fear: that she would have another breakdown and have to be hospitalized and undergo shock treatments.

Besides the poetry, what sustained her most were the two children, who needed her more than ever. She knew that the loss of their mother, even if temporary, would be traumatic for them so soon after the departure of their father. They made great demands upon her, which she occasionally resented when it interfered with her writing; but those demands provided a necessary routine that prevented any extended periods of self-scrutiny. It is not surprising, then, that several poems deal with the children. What is somewhat surprising, at least in light of Sylvia's growing anti-male obsession, is their concentration upon Nick rather than Frieda. He was the baby, of course. The poems, "By Candlelight," "Nick and the Candlestick," and "The Night Dances," are attempts to offer her infant son compensatory alternatives to the destruction evident in life and art. In "The Night Dances," which would have to be read as an almost pure surrealistic exercise if Ted had not supplied background information about Nick's tendency to launch himself into a little dance in his crib for no apparent reason, the leanness of the lines and the constant metaphorical leaps again depend upon a circular pattern of responses. There is a progression from a smile in the grass to dances in the night, which are compared to mathematical jottings, then to the circle of the "world forever" and the persona's realization that the child's breath and flesh—"lilies, lilies"—prevent her from sinking into despair. "Cold folds of ego, the calla,/ And the tiger, embellishing itself." Here infant and speaker become a merged self.

In "By Candlelight" the baby is compared to a brass statue of Atlas who holds aloft the persona's heavy world; and in "Nick and the Candlestick" he becomes the Christ child: "You are the one/ Solid the spaces lean on, envious./ You are the baby in the barn." But the early stanzas apparently relate to the cellar at Court Green—"An earthen womb"—where preserves and wines were stored. Like "Mystic," the poem is riddled by religious echoes, often in a mocking fashion, and seems to seek a transcendental or spiritual value outside the mythology of Christianity. All the traditional images of Christ are wounding rather than healing; the white newts are "holy Joes" and the miracle of the fishes are "panes of ice,/ A vice of knives." The religion itself is "a piranha" that drinks "Its first communion out of my live toes." The black and white stresses are familiar, of course, as is the concept of a dead womb (the speaker is a "miner" exploring underground for a sign as to how her child could have been born amid such a sterile environment), but the poem shifts back to 23 Fitzroy Road: "Love, love,/ I have hung our cave with roses./ With soft rugs—/ The last of Victoriana."

In an unpublished article called "Snow Blitz," Sylvia tried to describe what the next few weeks meant to her in terms of physical hardship, though the tone is deliberately light and disguises her real anguish.[3] Her children ill with flu, and she herself only recently recovered from a bout with the same illness, she ventured from the flat after the first few days of snow to reach the local chemist's shop and noted that the snow was "untouched. There seemed to be a lot more of it. Bits plopped in over my boot tops as I crossed the unplowed street. The main road had not been plowed either. Random busses and cabs crawled along in deep white tracks. Here and there, men with newspapers, brooms and rags attempted to discover their cars."

The chemist could not offer much hope for the immediate future, pointing out that the number of plows in the city were minimal. But the snow itself was nothing compared to what followed: "The snow hardened and froze. Sidewalks and streets became a rugged terrain of ice, over whose treacherous crevices old people teetered, clutching dog leads or steered by strangers." The cold spell was followed by another deluge of snow, and another cold spell even worse than the first—"the Big Freeze." And yet it would have been relatively easy to handle were it not for the lack of central heating, the exposed pipes, and a series of strikes by electricians, which brought winter indoors. Alvarez, who experienced this terrible winter onslaught himself, has provided a striking picture of its effects:

It was an unspeakable winter, the worst, they said, in a hundred and fifty years. The snow began just after Christmas and would not let up. By New Year the whole country had ground to a halt. The trains froze on the tracks, the abandoned trucks froze on the roads. The power stations, overloaded by million upon pathetic million of hopeless electric fires, broke down continually; not that the fires mattered, since the electricians were mostly out on strike. Water pipes froze solid; for a bath you had to scheme and cajole those rare friends with centrally heated homes, who became rarer and less friendly as the weeks dragged on. Doing the dishes became a major operation. The gastric tumble of water in outdated plumbing was sweeter than the sound of mandolins. Weight for weight, plumbers were as expensive as smoked salmon, and harder to find. The gas failed and Sunday joints went raw. The lights failed and candles, of course, were unobtainable. Nerves failed and marriages crumbled. Finally, the heart itself failed. It seemed the cold would never end. Nag, nag, nag.

For Sylvia, it must have seemed as if the winter landscape in her poetry had been brought home by a malicious nature intent upon exhausting her last reserves of physical and mental energy. If not the final blow to her sinking morale, it certainly helped precipitate it. The day after the second freezing snap had settled in, she discovered her bathtub half-full with dirty water. Hoping it would go away by itself, she ignored the water, but the next day it was deeper and dirtier. To make matters worse, the ceiling in her bedroom, which she had painted herself only a month earlier, was stained by water, drops of which continued to fall on her new rug. She called the agent, but he was not of much help and a plumber was nowhere to be found. Finally the agent told her the leak was probably the result of a faulty gutter on the roof. His assistants put in a brief appearance, but the attic above the bedroom, where the gutter was located, was too small to allow them to reach the trouble. Instead, rather helplessly, they wiped at the stain, which caused the leak to worsen. Their sole solution was to leave behind a bucket to catch the water, and they then departed in haste with vague promises about returning to complete the job, though they never did.

Meanwhile, Nicholas had managed to shake his crib off its retaining screws, but he was unhurt in the fall that followed, though the same could not be said for the crib. The children were still her main concern, as she feared pneumonia if their flu colds were not properly tended. She kept them bundled up and near the electric heater in the parlor wall as much as possible. The agent himself arrived shortly after the departure of his assistants and, with the aid of a moisture detector, investigated the leaking ceiling. He was able to assure Sylvia that the plaster was in no imminent danger of collapse, although he had to warn her that her drinking water supply was threatened as the outside pipes (not having been layered sufficiently by the builder) were frozen solid. He then advised her to turn off the immersion heater in case it burned out the empty tank. Stepping onto the small outside balcony, the agent next peered at the maze of ice-caked pipes. He discovered that the water in the bathtub came not from outside but from Sylvia's own frozen waste pipe, which should have been discharging the tub water into an open drain below.

Before he left, all the agent could suggest was that Sylvia try to heat up the waste pipe, if she could miraculously locate the precise point of clogging, or throw hot water on its entire length. She tried the latter, flinging hot water from her balcony on the pipe. It did no good and the water in the tub remained, but it did seep into the apartment of the tenant below, an elderly painter, who advised her to disregard anything the agent had told her. The situation was desperate and, later that evening, when Sylvia went for a walk through the frozen wastes of Fitzroy Street, she saw an old man getting water from an open tap which had been installed by the city for that purpose. It did not bode well for the future as Sylvia imagined herself making frequent trips up and down the stairs to secure water for drinking and bathing.

But good fortune had not completely abandoned her. A plumber did show up after dark and was able to free the taps, although the tub remained full of dirty water. She and her children did have drinking water, and every day Sylvia emptied the water from the tub and flushed it down the toilet. Like most Londoners she accepted the situation cheerfully, since at worst it represented a temporary inconvenience. But a few days later, the power cuts began to hit home. Sylvia awoke one morning to find the electric heater dead and asked the painter below what had happened. He informed her about the strikes and lent her a hot-water bottle. Still concerned about her children's flu, she wrapped Frieda in a blanket with the water bottle and dressed Nick in his snowsuit. The heater came back on the same day, but failures would strike at frequent intervals in the days ahead as the electricians worked hurriedly to repair burnt-out lines. The result was that Sylvia herself came down with another siege of flu—"that British alternation of fever and chills for which my doctor offered no relief or cure. You either die of it or you don't."

Fortunately, the gas supply never faltered, and a kindly neighbor brought Sylvia several night lights as candles and tapers were impossible to secure. The deadly winter paralysis did not relax its grip until near the end of January, when the snow finally began to melt and the waste pipe unfroze itself and the tub was emptied at last. For Sylvia, the battle was over, but the war had been lost. Her physical fatigue and recurrent illnesses made the ceaseless struggle against a mounting depression almost impossible to maintain. The tonic, the sleeping pills, the need to care for the children—nothing seemed to help. As in 1953, depression was hardening into melancholia which, in turn, drove her to the brink of a schizophrenic psychosis. Even the generally favorable reviews of *The Bell Jar*, which had appeared on January 14, did not bolster up her sagging spirits.

Like most first novels by relatively unknown authors, *The Bell Jar* was destined to be a financial failure, at least so long as it was published under the name of Victoria Lucas. It did receive some critical attention, though that was frequently bracketed with other unrelated novels in brief reviews. Robert Taubman, for example, linked it with Harold Robbins' *The Carpetbaggers* somehow in his review for *The New Statesman* (January 25), although he also appreciated the fact that Sylvia's book represented "the first feminine novel in a Salinger mood." The anonymous reviewer for the *Times Literary Supplement* was more mixed in his reaction. He praised the author's writing style but criticized the book's structural weaknesses, which is an absurd contention about a novel so cleverly put together. Lawrence Lerner's review in *The Listener* (January 31) praised *The Bell Jar* and wisely insisted upon the fundamental political truths inherent in Esther's observations: "There are criticisms of America that the neurotic can make as well as anyone, perhaps better, and Miss Lucas makes them brilliantly." The most negative reaction, fifty words, more spiteful blurb than review, would appear in *The Spectator* by Simon Raven; but since it did not see print until February 15, Sylvia never read it.

She did read the other reviews eagerly and was no doubt bewildered by the consistent refusal of even favorable critics to comprehend what the novel was attempting to do. This too caused her to be further depressed. Several editors had already indicated, through rejections, their conviction that her new poetry had failed to justify its own aesthetic; and now the literary critics from the establishment's leading journals had demonstrated a similar denseness regarding the unique style and vision (which are dynamically intertwined) of *The Bell Jar*. Sylvia must have also felt that her defensive belittling of the novel was the only reasonable course to take, especially since she "did not want to hurt her mother." She wrote to Clarissa Roche and dismissed the book out of hand, promising the second one would be much better and would be dedicated to her.

There is no accurate way to gauge the actual effects of the reviews on Sylvia's deteriorating self-image, but rejection, real or imagined, could only have made her depression more difficult to bear. She was still writing her "dawn poems in blood" and still struggling to go through the normal motions of day-to-day living, which included many concrete plans for the future. Marcia Brown had agreed to act as her American rental agent for both the Devon and the London domiciles, and had sent notices to the colleges in the area, such as Smith, Amherst, and Harvard, which stated that Sylvia wanted to rent the flat furnished for five months in the summer. She hoped to get about $75 a week for it; and the Court Green house, which she thought ideal for a professor on sabbatical, would be let for the other seven months at a lower rate. That would provide her with a solid income to supplement whatever came in from writing and the $2800 a year she expected to get from Ted once the impending divorce suit was finally settled. Real or not, financial pressures continued to harass her, although she soon had the prospect of renting Court Green to an Australian artist and his family.

Earlier in January, Sylvia had done another program for the BBC—a review of Donald Hall's anthology *Contemporary American Poetry*. George MacBeth had selected her for the task because she was an American poet of talent who was *not* included in the anthology—another rejection for Sylvia to bear. She did not, however, let the omission interfere with her critical judgment, and her comments on the anthology remain perceptive and fair. She talked of Robert Lowell's "tightrope walks of a naked psyche" and noted W. D. Snodgrass's similar tendencies, "albeit in watercolors," and praised his poetic voice for being "quiet, colloquial, laconic, wry." She also stressed the obvious "inwardness of images" and subjectivity that often led to the irrational and surrealistic mode in so many of the poets, and singled out Simpson, Merrill, Wright, Rich, Hecht, and Merwin for particular admiration, while pointing out the influence of Pasternak, Trakl, and Neruda upon these writers. Her criticisms are reserved for the poems included by William Stafford, Howard Nemerov, and Richard Wilbur, which might seem a bit odd in light of her earlier allegiance to the last named; but all three did represent a dead past for her—the academic techniques she had long since abandoned. In closing she lamented the absence of any work by Anne Sexton and read, with distinct pleasure, from Gallway Kinnell's now famous "Flower Herding Pictures on Mount Hanodrock."

She had been offered more work with the BBC for early May, which she was forcing herself to accept, and planned to return to Court Green somewhere around May 20.[4] Other plans included finding a specialist to treat Nicholas's eye. Frieda was enrolled in a small nursery school just around the corner from the flat near the end of January and, by February 4, after a week of tearful protests, had seemingly adjusted to the idea of having playmates and being grown-up enough to attend school. But these surface manifestations of a woman fully in control of her life were merely part of the cheerful façade she had always known how to put on.

Though her plans were real and sincere, they have to be seen as last-ditch defenses being thrown up against an overwhelming attack by superior forces. The depression was increasing in severity. The symptoms were all there for anyone to see: the tense restlessness, the chain-smoking, the continued disinterest in food, the inability to sleep, and the subtle lapses into regret and self-pity, which could easily (and did) turn into self-hatred. On February 4, a week before her death, Sylvia wrote letters to both Elizabeth Compton and Clarissa Roche about the recent details of her life—the terrible snowstorm, the children's illness and her own, the German *au pair* she had acquired who was too fussy about her food and too boy-crazy to have any maternal instincts (the girl would soon be fired), the two articles she had just finished for *Punch* and the Home Service (BBC), the plans for renting the two homes and for Marcia's forthcoming visit. The tone of both letters is generally one of hope for the future and cheerful self-confidence.[5]

And yet there are references to a darker mood—to her lack of appetite and general exhaustion; and, in the letter to Marcia, Sylvia alludes to her feelings of isolation and loneliness—her sense of being cut-off from her closest relatives and friends. More significant, in both letters she refers to Ted's weekly visits with an air of distinct regret, sorrow rather than fury, though the letter to Marcia makes clear her resentment of his popularity and carefree new life. She is also saddened by the realization that her two beautiful children would grow up without a father to guide them.

Then her poetry, the last defense, failed her as well. George MacBeth saw her a week or so before she died and recalls that she appeared as bright and energetic as usual; but he also remembers her telling him that she was writing poems "as long and 'as lean as herself." The poems specifically identified by Ted as coming from that final week—"Balloons," "Contusion," "Kindness," "Edge," and "Words"—are, in a way, her extended suicide note. They reek of airless despair, growing desperation, narcissistic self-absorption, and ultimate failure. Worse, the progression is a fatal march from a child's doomed world through a husband's betrayal to suicide and an inadequate art.

"Balloons" is apparently addressed to Frieda, but it is another attempt by Sylvia to distinguish between reality and fantasy, and stresses the unavoidable pain entailed in a child's loss of innocence. The overt subject is the balloons which the two children have been playing with since Christmas—circles again that can be manipulated into metaphors for the persona's changing moods. The balloons, like the children, commence as "Guileless and clear,/ Oval soul animals," who bring joy to a mother's heart "like wishes or free/ Peacocks blessing/ Old ground with a feather/ Beaten in starry metals." For Nick the balloon is the "pink world" he now owns in his innocence; and his bite, though it destroys the balloon world, has left him untouched in his own self-contained sphere of ignorance: "sits/ Back, fat jug/ Contemplating a world clear as water." Nothing seems to have happened; and yet the last two lines, "A red,/ Shred in his little fist," do imply a different perspective—that future pain and loss are in store for the unknowing infant and his sister.

In "Kindness" Sylvia poses the situation of Ted's act of treachery to her and the children. Here she utilizes his radio play about the man who ran over a rabbit and then sold the carcass to buy his wife two roses as a central motif.[6] Roses were perfect symbols, not only for the beauty and innocence of the children, but as Dantesque emblems of art leading to paradise. The basic narrative frame, however, is a return to the double image. "Dame Kindness" is the bitch goddess's *good* double, the cheerful surface Sylvia who speaks out of her mother's mouth: "Sugar can cure everything, so Kindness says." And it was this Sylvia who went about "Sweetly picking up pieces" after the separation from Ted. In the final stanza, which is addressed to Ted, the depressing change in Sylvia's mental state becomes pathetically blatant:

> And here you come, with a cup of tea
> Wreathed in steam.
> The blood jet is poetry,
> There is no stopping it.
> You hand me two children, two roses.

Poetry has ceased to be a weapon for attack or defense and has deteriorated into a wound. The last stanza summarizes what has happened—the narcissistic retreat into an obsessive concern with the ego's wound that has resulted in the end of poetry and life: "The heart shuts,/ The sea slides back,/ The mirrors are sheeted." The body is dead, the womb is open, and the dances of the doubles forever put into storage.

In "Edge" the physical death is imagined in the way a child might imagine himself watching his own funeral. The poem is a final heroic stab at control that is almost repellent in its icy detachment. The suicide begins the poem—death in birth, the only solution, imitating nature's own remote perfection—and is linked with a classical, heartless past. The dead woman is now herself a work of art, though art is an "illusion." Her dead feet seem to say, "We have come so far, it is over." Her children have died with her and are presented as white serpents coiled at her breasts; but in taking them with her, she transforms them into petals of a closing rose and thus makes them part of herself. The last two stanzas shift focus to the moon, the bald muse in "her hood of bone," who has nothing to be sad about because "She is used to this sort of thing./ Her blacks crackle and drag." Art will endure, in other words, including Sylvia's own poetry—the bitch goddess self and myth—despite the death of the other self, the flesh-and-blood mother, the sacrificial lamb, a woman killed by a male reality and culture.

There is nothing left after "Edge" but the finding of the stark suicide note, which is what "Words" is—the last inevitable paragraph in the sequence as a whole.[7] It leaves no way out. Words provide ceaseless echoes, mirror reality and other selves, and bring back the dead: "A white skull,/ Eaten by weedy greens." But now, "Years later," the poet meets them again and realizes the words are "dry and riderless." They are sperm and stallion from "Ariel" only now lacking the juice of life—the blood jet of poetry.

But things were still not that simple. However much her poetry may faithfully have reflected her mental condition at the time of Sylvia's death, there is still one major factor not taken into account, and that is her real love for her children and strong sense of maternal responsibility. This is what would make the suicide something less than what it appeared to be on the surface. For it was more of a gamble than an outcome of her art, as Alvarez has indicated in his memoir and W. S. Merwin has since confirmed to Peter Davison.[8]

During the last week of her life, from Monday, February 4, to Monday, February 11, Sylvia continued to fluctuate wildly in her moods, running mysterious temperatures and terribly aware that a breakdown was imminent. This knowledge, of course, only served to increase her fears and insecurities. The German *au pair* girl was gone and Sylvia missed her help and companionship. The cold weather was another burden and kept her indoors with the children more often than she liked. Her main source of strength and relief was her doctor, Dr. John Horder, whom she talked to frankly about her mental problem and whom Alvarez has described as "a sensitive, overworked man."

It was obvious to Dr. Horder that her depression was getting worse and, during this same week, he had arranged for her to see a therapist; but the therapist's letter never reached her as it had been delivered to the wrong address. By Friday, February 8, after a long talk with Sylvia, Dr. Horder concluded that time was now of the essence and that her depression had reached a dangerous low point. According to the account in the *St. Pancras Chronicle* (February 23, 1963), the only newspaper to carry the story of the suicide, he then approached three different psychiatrists in a desperate effort to find her room in a hospital. But "Two could not provide one and although the third could he did not think it would be suitable for her." Dr. Horder then returned to Sylvia for a further talk. She seemed in much better spirits, having wisely decided to take the children and spend the weekend with friends in another part of London. He was relieved and told her that he had arranged for a nurse, a Miss Myra Norris, to come to her flat on Monday morning. In Alvarez's account, it is an Australian *au pair* girl who was supposed to come to the flat on Monday morning and who found the body; but the doctor's testimony seems more reliable since he was more directly involved in the case, while Alvarez only heard later about what had happened. There may very well, in fact, have been two appointments.

In any case, Sylvia went with Frieda and Nicholas to stay with an American-British couple who were friends, as the internal pressure had become too great. Racked by self-loathing, which she carefully hid beneath the familiar cheerful exterior, Sylvia insisted upon leaving the friends' home on Sunday evening, instead of early Monday morning as originally planned. She put the children to bed and later, about 11 P.M., she went down to ask the painter for some stamps. According to Alvarez, "she lingered in the doorway, drawing out the conversation until he told her that he got up well before nine in the morning."

At about 6:00 A.M., according to Alvarez's memoir, Sylvia "went up to the children's room and left a plate of bread and butter and two mugs of milk." Next she returned to the kitchen and sealed the door and windows with tea towels and cloths to guard carefully against the possibility of any gas reaching the sleeping children. Finally, she turned on all the taps, knelt down as if to say her prayers, and laid her head in the oven. When the nurse arrived later in the morning and was finally able to get in, with the assistance of some workmen, she found Sylvia "lying on the floor of the kitchen with her head resting on the oven." Miss Norris desperately applied artificial respiration until the ambulance arrived, but the St. Pancras University College Hospital would list Sylvia Plath Hughes as "Dead On Arrival."

A suicide kills two people, Maggie, that's what it's for!
ARTHUR MILLER
IN *After the Fall*

Epilogue

The final irony, in a career dedicated to literary irony, was the commercial success and critical acclaim that greeted Sylvia's work after her death, along with her near-deification. The latter took the form of a romantic reading and perverse worship of her suffering, with the result that her biography appears more important than her poetry. But the suicide, in itself, was hardly dramatic. The details are almost trite. Further, Sylvia died in the shadow of her husband as an "authoress" and "wife," and her entire literary production legally became his (in the absence of a will), although a trust fund guarantees that the actual profits accrue to Frieda and Nicholas.

The inquest was held on Friday, February 15, at a coroner's court in London behind Camden Town, and conducted by the Deputy Coroner, Dr. George McEwan. Miss Norris testified and Ted was asked a few questions. According to the *St. Pancras Chronicle*, he said "his wife had lately had mysterious temperatures and nervous trouble." The result was practically automatic. The Deputy Coroner concluded that Sylvia had died from carbon monoxide poisoning, and that "While suffering from depression did kill herself." Alvarez was also at the inquest and had earlier gone to the funeral home in Mornington Crescent to view the body: "She lay stiffly, a ludicrous ruff at her neck. Only her face showed. It was gray and slightly transparent, like wax. I had never seen a dead person and hardly recognized her; her features seemed too thin and sharp." The final irony was Ted's decision (an act of love) to bury Sylvia in Yorkshire, in the Heptonstall churchyard which she had always admired, surrounded by the cold heart of moor country.

Five months after her death, a group of Sylvia's late poems appeared in *Encounter*, including that explosive pair of Freudian exercises, "Daddy" and "Lady Lazarus." The poems were avidly read and discussed in literary circles. Her suicide seemed to have confirmed her pathological art and instigated the kind of cult worship Sylvia herself would have loved. Myth at last. *Ariel* sold in the neighborhood of 5,000 copies—an impressive figure for serious poetry—in the ten months following its English publication. Here unfortunately were people not in the habit of reading contemporary poetry, many of them women, who apparently felt compelled to possess the last will and testament of a frustrated kindred spirit, or who wished to certify their own "normalcy" by comparing their sensibilities to those of a "mad woman."

The people who touched or were touched by Sylvia in her life did not disappear with her death, though several of them remain cruelly indicted in her literature, unable to escape the corrosive pen of a girl who would not be ignored. Aurelia Plath, who still lives in Wellesley, was stunned by her daughter's death. Not informed until three weeks later of the circumstances of Sylvia's death, she at first denied the possibility of suicide, calling Sylvia's friends and neighbors and former colleagues at Smith to assure them that her daughter had died from pneumonia and complications following a severe cold. And when the obituary announcement appeared in *The Townsman*, there was no mention of either suicide or separation:

Mrs. Sylvia (Plath) Hughes, daughter of Mrs. Aurelia S. Plath of 26 Elmwood Road, Wellesley, died in London, England, on February 11 of virus pneumonia. Mrs. Hughes' brother, Warren J. Plath of Cambridge and Wellesley, flew overseas with his wife to attend the funeral on February 18.

The rest of the notice is a summary of Sylvia's career. For Sylvia's mother, such self-deception could not last, of course, as her son would inform her of the brutal facts on his return. In letter after letter to people who had been close to Sylvia, such as Peter Davison and Elizabeth Compton, the one steady refrain is "Why?" Finally accepting the cause of death as suicide, nothing remained for Aurelia but to attempt to pick up the pieces. She soon began a series of summer visits with Sylvia's children in England, later followed by several return visits on their part.

Feeling too much emphasis had been placed on the morbid aspects of Sylvia's character and upbringing—and on the mother's influence—and not sufficient attention paid to the cheerful, happy child she had known and loved better than anyone else, Aurelia has also made an exhaustive effort to reconstruct her daughter's life. In the fall of 1975 her own massive collection of Sylvia's letters, *Letters Home,* was published by Harper & Row. She hopes this will change Sylvia's negative image.

For her brother, Sylvia's loss and subsequent "reputation" has been no less difficult to bear. Loving Sylvia and Aurelia deeply, he has been outraged by the adverse publicity accorded them both and refuses to meet with researchers and critics. He is married, has three children, and holds a position of some importance in the research division of a company that manufactures computers.

In Ted's case, the adjustment has been made difficult by relentless public scrutiny and judgment. The shock of Sylvia's death was followed several years later by the suicide of Olga and the simultaneous death of her daughter, causing him to remark to a friend with genuine despair that "he had the touch of death." He did eventually marry a nurse from Devon and is living with the two children at Court Green.

His poetry has certainly not suffered, the appearance of *Crow* signaling a major advance by England's leading poet. Shortly after Sylvia's death, Ted had asked David and Elizabeth Compton to live at Court Green until he could sell it. He was apparently eager to be rid of the house that had been the scene of of his marriage's tragic failure. When a buyer was finally located ten months later and the sale appeared near completion, Ted came down to Devon with Olga to remove whatever personal property still remained. David recalls that Ted was in a quiet frenzy as he went from room to room, trying to remove his, Sylvia's, and the children's beloved possessions. But in the end, again according to David, Ted was the one "who went under." He departed in a hurry, visibly shaken. The sale itself was never consummated because of local opposition once the town learned that the prospective buyer intended to turn the two park-like acres into a chicken farm.

The literature, meanwhile, is more or less now in print, and its merit cannot be changed or diminished in the years ahead, no matter how much r how wildly the reputation of its creator fluctuates. Perhaps a proper closing observation would be to note that Theodore Roethke died in the same year as Sylvia. Their deaths rounded off an important era in American poetry and brought to a close the first step towards a recovery of the artistic egotism and energy that had characterized Whitman's "barbaric yawp" a century before.

"As things are, and as fundamentally they must always be, poetry is not a career but a mug's game. No honest poet can ever feel quite sure of the permanent value of what he has written: he may have wasted his time and messed up his life for nothing."

T. S. Eliot

Afterword

A MUG'S GAME

As a poet, I have experienced the gut truth of Eliot's biting observation. As the first biographer of Sylvia Plath, I have had to abide its critical convolutions, knowing that the value of her work and the mess of her life have been forever altered in reaction to my efforts, even when deemed inadequate or flawed. From the start, in 1971, when I encountered Plath's poetry in a summer class at Stony Brook University and hurried to the library to track down whatever was available by and about this extraordinary literary force, I relished the idea of tracing the career, analyzing the progress, and evaluating the *oeuvre* of a major American poet's recent existence without regard to a substantial canon of scholarship.

There were opinions around, of course, reviews, brief memoirs, a clutch of essays, pioneer stabs at establishing a vocational pattern, many of which had been herded by Charles Newman into a thick issue of *TriQuarterly* (Fall 1966) only three years after Plath's death, then published in 1970 as *The Art of Sylvia Plath* by Indiana University Press. Several important critics, including A. Alvarez and Irving Howe, had weighed in with their unique slants on the erupting Plath phenomena. *Ariel,* the posthumous collection of Plath's last poems put together by her husband, poet Ted Hughes, had caused quite a stir when it appeared in England (1965) and the States (1966), and Plath's autobiographical novel, *The Bell Jar,* became an American best-seller in 1971, anchored by "A Biographical Note" from Lois Ames.[1]

Alvarez had known Plath well during her final years in England, and later wrote an intriguing account of their friendship as a chapter in his study of suicide, *The Savage God* (1972). His view of Plath and her marriage seemed accurate enough, often acute in the matter of the poetry's specific merits, though marred by an absurd thesis that Plath's "extremist" aesthetic had made suicide almost inevitable.

Howe's position was equally untenable, if more understandable in light of his deep political commitment and Jewish background. Unable to grasp her verses' Blakean dynamic and underlying, sometimes vicious American innocence, he relegated her to the role of a "minor" bourgeois poet who dared to equate her private anguish with the horrors of the Holocaust.

Valid or not, their particular visions of Plath helped stimulate in me a desire to pursue the breath-and-brain entity behind the poetry. There was, to be sure, another potent motivation: the turtle egotism we shared—bred out of similar blighted childhoods—that hinted at the eventual manufacture of a useful mirror construct. Other psychological elements were involved as well, less clear, complexly over-determined, but intent upon conquest, self-inflation, negative intensities. They coalesced around a common need to release suppressed rage against an indifferent universe in the sexually charged, metaphorically cunning language of the personal lyric.

The sweaty blue-collar details of the actual research chore were easier to master. Ames had been named the official biographer, having gained the cooperation of the Plath Estate, which was being managed by Olwyn Hughes, Ted's sister. The poet's mother, Aurelia Plath, appeared a logical starting place, and I wrote to ask for assistance, stressing a lack of interest in priority and a strict focus on the interstices between the life and the art. Her cordial reply alluded to a recent illness and denied the request but wished me and my project well. Over the next two hectic years, as I spent most weekends in New England trudging from library to school and from house to house, tracking down Plath's letters, early stories, public records of scholastic and literary achievements, which had begun at the precocious age of eight with the publication of a newspaper poem, I was increasingly sanguine about that refusal.

The remorseless over-achiever syndrome affirmed by school magazines and local news items, and reaffirmed by the shrewd testimony of teachers, neighbors, and classmates, suggested that Mrs. Plath's maternal drive had been warped by a serious neurosis, a narcissistic need to mold her daughter to certify her own worth. Factor in the death of Plath's professor father in her eighth year, an ostensibly idolized father who had enjoyed having his gifted daughter show off in front of his colleagues, and a sad psychological picture, admittedly still rough, began to emerge of a bright, sensitive little girl forced into lugging around a heavy mask's frozen smile.

A letter from a woman who had given Plath and her elementary school classmates IQ tests revealed that she tested out in the genius category, the 160 range. Psychoanalyst D. W. Winnicott has noted that "a mother can exploit a baby's intellectual function in order to get free from the tie that comes from the baby's dependence," and if that baby happens to have "intellectual equipment that is well above average, the baby and mother may collude in exploitation of the intellect which becomes split off." Complicate this etiological scenario with a significant life problem, such as an ambivalently perceived but powerful father's premature demise, and the child may well "develop a false self in terms of a lie in the split-off mind, the true self being psychosomatic, hidden and perhaps lost." [2]

In Plath's case, the false self perfected a stereotypic golden girl, a chronic winner, earning parental love and social validation but losing contact with rebellious feelings essential to the maturation of a genuine identity. Time and again, friends from Plath's childhood and adolescence told of her excessive enthusiasms, of their conviction that she was playing a part. Her beloved high school English teacher, Wilbury Crockett, a humane but formal figure of unknown depths, found her "very adept at role playing," possessing a precocious capacity both to "seal herself off" from others and to manipulate them "for what they could give her."

As Freud lectured, exaggeration is the surest adit to an emotion's neurotic energy source. The very fact that young friends, unformed and untrained, could sense the artificial quality of Plath's behavior clarions a primal defense-mechanism's blunt operation. The psychic price of such reality-distorting performances is massive repression of a buried self's normal angers, fears, doubts, its instinctual links to empiric reality. But poetry and stories and art works, when not conventional extensions of the mask shaped to elicit approval, can act as release valves, venting the unthinkable. One of the finds I came upon in *The Bradford,* her high school's literary magazine, was "Family Reunion," a deliciously wicked but anonymous poem obviously written by Plath. It gave voice to the contemptuous fury she kept banked beneath an ebullient cheerleader exterior. A classmate reported that Mrs. Plath had been quite upset by the poem, which caricatured recognizable relatives.

And so it went. Information-gathering acquired an impetus of its own as I roamed like Arnold's gipsy scholar from parlor to tidy parlor of the white, middle-class (now middle-aged) survivors of Plath's New England nurture. Materially successful for the most part, conscientious parents and citizens, many of them professionals, they were expressive and candid, surprisingly candid, about sexual aspects of a nostalgically recalled youth. Over glasses of fine sherry, they spoke into my tape-recorder without reserve or apparent evasions. And yet, the world their recollections evoked, for all its American post-war sweetness, its firm Christian faith in progress and the perfectibility of man, which Plath shared to an amazing degree, hovered at an implausible distance above the Hades of outrage, black wit, and sadistic urges reified by the poet's savagely beautiful late poems.

This philosophic distance kept hazy the portrait of the artist being sketched in the back of my mind as their articulate shared memories webbed the gap between us. I had automatically retreated behind my own guise of genial gym or shop teacher, quick to laugh and agree, exuding gratitude for their welcome, though much closer to Plath, the Plath of *Ariel,* than I could ever be to their measured reprises of lives conducted behind sanity's neat hedges. It was a familiar game, after all, played since childhood, echoing Plath's potsy hops down their pleasant streets of white-framed houses and careless, unlocked bicycles. What was absent, and yearned for with Plath's Enkidu-like apparition, was a sturdy epistemological vehicle powered by a legitimate literary quest.

In grandiose retrospect, Plutarch might be seen as archetypal father to that quest, a moralist first, historian-biographer second, ready victim of an anecdote's seduction—I had nursed meticulous scrapbooks of news items from childhood on, then majored in American history at college. But Plutarch was too prone to sacrifice truth on the altar of myth in service to his didactic and narrative appetites. Many centuries later, the modern father of biography rose as an entwined configuration of Boswell *and* Johnson, the former's life of the latter forever imposing eighteenth-century England's giant personality upon the art's expanding canvas—an art Freud crushingly denigrated: "Anyone turning biographer commits himself to lies, to concealment, to hypocrisy, to flattery, and even to hiding his own lack of understanding, for biographical truth is not to be had, and even if it were, it couldn't be used." [3]

Pared repeatedly down to eccentric excess with Shakespearean subtlety, personality alone had to tether that maligned enterprise, which had been shifted by the Renaissance from historic inevitabilities into grand individual gestures and their consequent ambiguities. I had loved Boswell's *Life of Samuel Johnson* as much as I treasured Johnson's own, more lopsided *Lives of the Poets,* but realized that neither could encompass a twentieth-century culture hero's alienated journey into a pathological realm of primal process far below god and country. Johnson had at least taught the value of seamless cross-stitchings, apt quotations aptly applied, but Boswell's accomplishment remained treacherously unique, sly autobiography masquerading as a great man's profile—his close friendship with and ready access to his absorbing subject hardly likely to be duplicated. And theory, structuralist or semiotic, seemed irrelevant to a bardic profession where gesture must always overwhelm rational schemata.

Frankly, theory was never an issue as the poetry, its lucid unfolding design, a rising curve of virtuosity, sharply reflected the impulses of a character divided from Plath's bottom self in the forced march from birth to willed death. Depth psychology, which had enabled me to probe many oblique angles of my own self-portrait in verse, held telic sway, though I was committed to no one school, having found Freud and Jung and their various disciples equally efficacious at times when reviewing contemporaries or re-examining the canon. The more egregious limitations of both, Freud's sexist bias, Jung's unscientific mysticism, were not crucial in an area where pragmatic impressionism, a poet's schooled sensitivity to his discipline's knotty demands, inevitably rendered final judgment.

Plath herself, I learned from *The Bell Jar* and a few letters, had turned to Freud and Jung during the period of her first nervous breakdown and suicide attempt in 1953. "Electra on the Azalea Path" and a number of poems in *The Colossus* (1960), including the title poem's allegorical assault upon her paralyzing ambivalence towards a dead father, elucidate her debt to Freud, even as her search for a mystical alternative to Freud's Enlightenment rationalism (and to contrary religious dogma) gained intensity with her marriage to Ted Hughes. It was Hughes, sharing his sister Olwyn's naughty-girl taste for the occult and dedicated to a Lawrentian feeding of subconscious fodder directly into his poetry, who liberated her from the academic constraints still evident in *The Colossus:* Hughes and the examples of Anne Sexton, Theodore Roethke, and Stevie Smith.

Several trips to England, which included two exasperating but not unuseful encounters with the formidable Olwyn Hughes, helped solidify my impressions of Plath's last years. The simple physical act of following in her footsteps from Cambridge to London to Devon's scenic farm country and back to London roused the empathetic contradictory emotions of an outsider home from the hill. Although one never feels more nationalistic than when in a foreign country, England's impact is far more ambiguous on an American in summoning up a weird compound of alienation and familiarity, having been prepared by book and classroom to embrace the geography of the culture that mothered us all. This might illuminate why Plath so reveled in her Mark Twain Abroad persona in dramatic contrast to T. S. Eliot's stiff attempts to out-English the English, harping on the lack of modern conveniences, playing up her Polyanna openness to people and events regardless of class differences.

But the interview remained my most effective tool, speaking to people who had known Plath in these places during those final years of loss and brilliant achievement. The process itself proved autodidactic as I murmured and nodded through conversation after conversation and learned how to suspend judgment, how to restrain strong natural urges to reciprocate in the ritual of intimacy, even as I maneuvered each witness into revealing as much as possible without sacrificing her or his good will. My crux advantage was the shark-eyed detachment of the artist, which meant the absence of the kind of covert passion and self-interest that has distorted too much subsequent commentary on the Plath situation, though I tried not to deceive myself about my own mixed motives, my own hunger for secondary gains—the Picasso stare of the poet must shift inward before devouring world and time.

It is an unnatural circumstance at best, perched as I was like an amiable condor in my victim's living quarters, engaged in what appears to be a casual exchange of information, swapping reminiscences, while checking off a list of relevant queries in my head that could very possibly culminate in the discrediting of my host's dearest beliefs. Nor can one ever be sure of one's precise quantum impact on the interchange. The same entrenched egotism that permitted me to maintain the necessary distance could also blind me to hidden agendas, concealed antipathies.

Perhaps the most disconcerting case in point was the visit paid on November 6, 1973 to the Aldermaston home of Clarissa and Paul Roche, since divorced. Paul, respected translator of Sophocles, had taught with Plath at Smith College, and Clarissa had retained a friendly connection with her until near the end. They were welcoming in a relaxed way and had many valuable things to say about Plath's teaching period. Clarissa in addition proffered a number of astute observations regarding Plath's frantic last year, especially with respect to an excessive concern over her children's health and safety. I left Aldermaston that night smugly convinced the interview had gone well. Paul struck me as a bit dry, somewhat removed from the human quagmire, though alert to the intellectual facets of Plath's personality. In contrast, the earthier Clarissa was more finely tuned to Plath's discordant sardonic humor and female twists of mind, as well as more instructive anent the specific strains on an American-British marriage.

After *Sylvia Plath: Method and Madness* came out in 1976, I bundled together an anthology of essays and memoirs about Plath for Dodd, Mead, which meant asking Clarissa to write up her recollections for a modest fee.[4] She gladly did so, and did a decent job of it. At no time were our mail exchanges ever less than cordial. Hence, it came as quite a jolt nearly two decades later to discover in Janet Malcolm's long *The Silent Woman* article that Clarissa had regarded me with disdain throughout, deigning to take my check for her memoir only because I offered her "exactly the amount of money" ($300) she needed to get her carpet dyed.[5] This sort of supercilious maliciousness was, fortunately, rare, but it underscores the treacherous undercurrents Plath frequently stirs up (and doubtless swam against) in England's small literary pond.

Repeatedly, English friends of Plath, whether natives or transplanted Americans, refused to be interviewed out of fear of provoking Olwyn Hughes's wrath. One poor fellow, David Compton, telephoned me at my hotel soon after our London meeting—and soon after being contacted by Olwyn—to plead that his comments on the Hugheses and Mrs. Plath not be misconstrued. Upon my return home, I also had a curious letter from Edward Lucie-Smith, respected poet and art critic, in which he (after another Olwyn elbow-nudge) tried to paint as attractive a portrait of Assia Wevill—Ted's late lover—as possible.[6]

All of which points up the innate imbalance of arranged interviews, the person being interrogated so easily lulled by the spell of home fires and an attentive ear into greater candor than intended. A case in acid point is Peter Davison, minor poet and major operator in Boston's Anglophile literary playground, who became exercised when seeing his comments re Mrs. Plath's dull *Christian Science Monitor* world in print. He had been impolitic and regretted it, claiming a misquote; my tape-recorder ruled otherwise. Though sorry about the incident, which was my fault for not getting his corrections into print, and appreciative of his hospitality and his wife Jane Truslow's graciousness, I found my own regrets somewhat ameliorated by the self-regard that had glazed

Davison's every word and snakes through his arctic autobiography, *Half Remembered*, like Poe's engorged worm.[7]

Davison can take solace from the heavy dose of my own medicine I had to swallow when agreeing—eagerly, expectantly—to be interviewed by Malcolm for an article on Plath's biographers. Famed for her fluent, if savage, character assassinations and agressive masochism, which may owe something to her diminutive stature and nurture as a psychiatrist's daughter, Malcolm was then in the midst of being sued for having invented several quotations while interviewing psychoanalyst Jeffrey Masson. In *The Journalist and the Murderer* (1990), she had branded herself and her journalist colleagues as shameless confidence men, "preying on people's vanity, ignorance, or loneliness, gaining their trust and betraying them without remorse." [8]

None of this concerned me, except her notoriety and ready access to *The New Yorker,* where her husband functioned as an editor. Whatever she wrote would surface there first, the magazine having been retooled into a semi-intellectual version of the sensationalist *Vanity Fair,* and was bound to lure a large audience, newspaper chatter. Since both the hard-cover and paperback editions of *Sylvia Plath: Method and Madness* were out of print—I had to loan a copy to Malcolm for her research—and since subsequent biographies had either ignored or trashed it, I was hoping the attention might entice a few publishers into commissioning a revised edition.[9] Rumor had it that Paul Alexander banked a six-figure advance for his pedestrian *Rough Magic* (1991) manuscript.

In letter and in person, Malcolm was cozily sympathetic, gushing, "You got it all right!" in reference to my book, and smelling a vague "conspiracy" rotting behind the fact that copies of it at college libraries she consulted had disappeared, though still listed in their catalogues. Wanting to spare her a possibly disorienting trip into the wilderness of Queens, I agreed to an interview at her posh duplex high above Manhattan's upper West Side. It was a mistake, mostly because I dared not smoke the entire two or three hours. But it was also genuine fun, slouched under the admiring spotlight of my charming inquisitor's gaze as she almost floated, Buddha-fashion, above an opposing couch, pixie-like in her girlishness, expertly poling my overt craving to be heard down whatever canals she had dug in advance.

I departed her aerie with my normal cynicism softened beyond recognition, naively confident that Malcolm, however dazed by literature's mysterious machinery, would provide a fair assessment of the roiled Plath scene, not to mention a more honest perusal of my own contribution to the turbulence. It is a testament to her professional prowess that I could have harbored such delusions, especially after several closing remarks of hers about a return trip to England and Olwyn Hughes, whose company she patently enjoyed. The Brooklyn Bridge extent of my uncharacteristic gullibility can be gauged from my sending her a copy of a 1987 essay, "Sylvia Plath's Metaphors of Madness," to reinforce my response to a question about having any second thoughts or regrets.[10]

Forged in heated reaction to the mushrooming misapprehension of Plath's poetics and position in American literary history, the essay had given me a chance to cover interpretive ground only partially explored by the book. Mostly, *contra* a barrage of misguided academic missiles, I wanted to advance my view of Plath's fundamental poetic strategy in the final phase of her career, to wit, "her manipulation of a Freudian schema and Blakean praxes to escape the inherent entropy of the confessional mode apotheosized in Robert Lowell's *Life Studies* (1959)." It was a matter of distinguishing between the two contending streams of Romanticism that American poetry navigated in the late 1950's and early 1960's. Plath's turn to Blake for symbolic lyric models, which ushered her "confessionalism" into the theater of Nietzsche and Yeats and at odds with Lowell's Wordsworthian striptease, enabled her to escape the debased aesthetic mistakenly ascribed to her by Arthur K. Oberg and Joyce Carol Oates—or so I argued.[11]

Mailing the essay to Malcolm was a waste of stamps, as was a later 'gift' to her: an essay-review of the Linda Wagner-Martin and Anne Stevenson biographies that damned the beautifully written latter for its expedient Hughes bias and inadequate command of Plath's American heritage.[12] Not only was Malcolm incapable of handling Plath's poetry, but *The Silent Woman* evidenced a minimally cloaked distaste for its subject. More relevant, the entire thrust of Malcolm's project, which seduces the reader with its glib autobiographical linkages between the author and Plath as generational avatars of victimized female nerds who went to the right schools at the wrong time (1950's), is yet another passive-aggressive scenario of Alice drowning in her male looking-glass. The mirror in this case is Malcolm's ingenuous fix on modern literary biography, which recalls Freud's scorn and is confused with *Enquirer* journalism, mocked as a species of home burglary and busybody gossip.

The New Yorker's swollen midcult crowd was doubtless thrilled. *The Silent Woman* validated a reactionary condemnation of the increasing media invasions of private territory and simultaneously satisfied the insecure ache for personal significance behind those invasions—and did it with a diarist's reassuring sincerity. But Malcolm's Lucifer-foolish attack upon the throne of biography, though entertaining and clever, occasionally on target, need not concern us here, except to remark how inevitable entwinings of reportage and research vastly complicate the effort to essay a critical biography of a contemporary or near-contemporary writer, particularly when that writer, like Plath, has wrought permanent changes in her culture's psyche.

Friends and relatives remain alive, insisting upon their Rashomon truths, and written documents come wired with restrictions, ticking potential libel suits. In the instance of Plath's estate, Olwyn Hughes—a tall, humorous woman affecting a cosmopolitan Bohemianism belied by her crude contempt for people who run afoul of her sacred mission to keep the Hughes name unsullied and the family coffers full—is a veritable Cerebus unleashed. As her brother's stand-in, she exerts enormous power over the publication of material related to Plath's life and work, especially in England where strict libel laws prevail. Though quite benign in giving aid, comfort, and reprint permissions to pedant toilers in the basement of literature, she has been fierce about controlling biographers. Besides withholding reprint permissions, she never hesitates to fire off letters threatening legal action, which tends to petrify timid institutions and publishers.[13]

During our meetings, she could not have been friendlier, more generous, in spite of an exclusive contract at the time with Lois Ames. Besides supplying several unpublished Plath stories, she offered advice about hotel accommodations and the like, speaking freely in the meanwhile about what a "burden" Plath had been and her mother still was. Money, the hidden clink of coins, supplied the Balzacian subtext of the clan politics, at least as I read them. The mother wanted to edit a hefty volume of her daughter's loving letters to counteract the negative impression of her maternal role limned by *The Bell Jar,* and Olwyn desired to see the novel turned into a film, which meant gaining the mother's approval—the dreadful, unintentionally comic film that did briefly reach the screen in 1979 was foredoomed by Aurelia Plath's veto power behind the scenes.[14]

The malevolent spread of the subterranean battles raging over Plath's golden remains became much clearer after I finished my research and spent the summer and fall of 1974 hammering out what I believed was an adequate first draft. However, discreet inquiries among publisher publicists disclosed that the Ames book was nowhere in sight, though Harper & Row, Plath's American outlet, planned to do the mother's collection of letters. Frances McCullough, my contact at Harper's, a congenial enough woman who served as the firm's editorial liaison with the Plath-Hughes contingents, assured me over the phone that I would be mailed a galley copy of *Letters Home,* which never did arrive. This is the same creature who later attempted (without success) to persuade writers as distinguished as Richard Wilbur and Joyce Carol Oates not to contribute to my Plath anthology.[15]

Regardless, it was plain by then that my biography would indeed have priority. To be honest, this news elated me without occasioning undue self-scrutiny. Guided always by ego and art, I found the idea intoxicating primarily because it appeared to guarantee Establishment notice rarely accorded a serious poet from elsewhere. In fact, the main reason I leaped at Seabury Press's modest advance lay in its courtesan willingness to also publish a collection of my own poems, another first. *Poems About Silence* was more important to me than a premature stab at pinning down Plath's frenetic butterfly zigzag through this veil of acid rain.[16]

A definitive or even relatively complete biography was out of the question in any case. The two largest collections of Plath material—the mother's hoard of early letters, diaries, sundry childhood items, and Ted Hughes's file of letters, journals, manuscripts, and annotated books— were unavailable.[17] Consequently, there were gaps in the story I had to tell, not in its tectonics, but in the push-and-pull fabric of daily existence and of several germane romantic relationships, as with Richard Sassoon and Edward Cohen, that required documentation. In addition, the pure somatic force of Plath's sex drive had been underestimated. And there were stretches of interior geography that I could only guess at mapping, specifically re the depth of Plath's self-awareness, which I assumed was considerable despite blanks of repression and that artificial surface self so easily penetrated by her contemporaries.

The 1982 publication of *The Journals of Sylvia Plath* exposed the agonizing degree of insight accompanying every twist of excess on the road to Blake's Palace of Wisdom: "Read Freud's *Mourning and Melancholia* this morning after Ted left for the library. An almost exact description of my feelings and reasons for suicide: a transferred murderous impulse from my mother onto myself: the 'vampire' metaphor Freud uses, 'draining the ego': that is exactly the feeling I have getting in the way of my writing: Mother's clutch." This was written on December 27, 1958 under the spur of sessions with Dr. Ruth Beuscher, her psychiatrist crutch since her stay at McLean Hospital in 1953. Relying on the lexicon of Dr. Mortimer Ostow, I had posited "schizophrenic melancholia" as the governing mechanism behind the wrath against father, mother, and an unfair world that had been inverted by guilt and depression into a suicidal punishment of self and them.[18]

Because of my profound enchantment with the elaborate interweave between literature and psychology, my keenest regret properly resides here in what now seems an inappropriate label. Today, my hypothesis would isolate a chronic, inherited manic-depressive condition capable of psychotic dilapidation under sufficient stage pressures and complicated by a narcissistic fixation, severe emotional retardation. After reading *Sylvia Plath: Method and Madness,* two psychiatrist friends of mine discerned a borderline pattern, which reaffirms the slipperiness of the field's nomenclature when striving to organize over-lapping manifold symptoms. Depression is key. Linda W. Wagner-Martin's research had uncovered a history of clinical depression among the female members of the Plath line—I hypothesized a genetic component but lacked supportive data.[19] Further, Plath's *Journals* record a recurrent consciousness of the classic bipolar affective disorder.[20]

Confirmation of a more professional nature comes from the diligent spade work of Thomas Bredsdorff, Professor of Scandinavian Literature at the University of Copenhagen, who managed to interview Dr. John Horder, Plath's physician, "in touch with her from mid-December [1962] till the very end, for several weeks on a daily basis." Horder emphasized that Plath "showed absolutely no sign of schizophrenia," insisting "she suffered from an endogenous depression—the depressive phase of the manic-depressive psychosis—and treated her accordingly, by administering antidepressants to her in January." Well aware "that the risk of suicide increases when the anti-depressive drug is beginning to do its job," he kept close tabs on her, "their latest contact having taken place on the evening before she died." [21]

Besides the diagnostic confusion, errors of chronology were also bound to creep in, the most embarrassing anent *The Bell Jar,* which Plath had finished much earlier than she claimed in letters to the committee supplying funds for its completion. The silent rearrangement of his wife's *Ariel* manuscript by Ted Hughes was less a problem: I had used internal allusions to buttress a thematic-tactical reordering of the closing sequence. Other doubts have to do with stylistic and proportional decisions—too many chunks of interpretive gloss lavished on neophyte poems, not enough theoretical framing of the second phase—that would have been corrected given time for a more leisurely revision.

Time, however, had grown precious to Seabury Press with the discovery of our unexpected priority. As a result, I met with my editor for one long alcoholic day of slash and burn redaction that culminated in a delicious Chinese dinner at his expense and a manuscript I convinced myself provided a viable introduction to the life and art of a major

American poet for an educated general reader. Although the bulk of references to psychological texts were removed from the notes to preclude a hostile reaction from the press and the academy, both of which were then perceived as biased against psychoanalytic ventures, the interior focus of my approach stayed intact without disrupting a relatively coherent narrative. Also, in spite of inescapable lapses of human judgment, it strove for objectivity—and I stand by its literary evaluations.

Rather than conclude with a weary and wearying horror story of the petty *comedie humaine* machinations that ensued at the instigation of Olwyn Hughes, Frances McCullough, and Warren Plath to ensure the delay of my manuscript's passage into print, machinations that eventually compelled me to threaten to sue my own publisher (Olwyn's influence?), let me simply reassert a critical biography's redemptive value.[22] What no one ensnared in the Plath controversies can grasp, including revisionist Malcolm, who buys into the infantile game of choosing "sides" in the Plath-Hughes skirmishes, is the necessarily multi-dimensional character of the great white whale such an enterprise must pursue, reflective of literature's own emotive grounding. Only the poetry of Plath, an artful reconstruction of its geneses, sources, evolution, and intentions, might justify a biography's Juggernaut crushing of innocent and not-so-innocent bystanders along the way.

The rest is commerce.

APPENDIX : THE MUG'S GAME

1. Published by Harper & Row, *The Bell Jar* also included several pen drawings by Plath. The review of *Ariel* in Time (June 10, 1966), replete with photos and a reprint of "Daddy," claimed that the British edition "sold 15,000 copies in ten months, almost as many as a best-selling novel, and inspired a vigorous new group of confessional poets." This not untypical review devotes much of its space to profiling Plath's life, a part of the early media response that helped initiate the Plath cult, making it nearly impossible to consider the poetry separate from the life, especially its pathetic end.

2. D. W. Winnicott, *Home Is Where We Start From: Essays by a Psychoanalyst* (New York: Norton, 1986), p. 59.

3. Ernst L. Freud, ed. *The Letters of Sigmund Freud & Arnold Zweig,* translated by Elaine and William Robson-Scott (New York: Harcourt Brace Jovanovich, 1970), p. 127. Freud was responding to Zweig's threat to write his biography and went on: "Truth is unobtainable, mankind does not deserve it, and in any case, is not our Prince Hamlet right when he asks who would escape whipping were he used after his desert?"

4. *Sylvia Plath: The Woman and the Work* (New York: Dodd, Mead, 1977).

5. Janet Malcolm, "Annals of Biography: *The Silent Woman,"* *The New Yorker* (August 23 &30, 1993), 84-159. The article—published in 1994 by Knopf as *The Silent Woman: Sylvia Plath and Ted Hughes*—occupies the body of the special double issue, indicating the continuing appeal of the Plath phenomena and includes a handful of late poems, suggesting the Hugheses were either not displeased by Malcolm's pro-Hughes stance and/or appreciative of the magazine's clout. What I loved most about the production, aside from wonderful moments of unconscious humor, such as Malcolm's schoolgirl mooning over Jacqueline Rose and the comparison of battleship HMS Olwyn Hughes to a mother quail in her "instinct to protect her brother's interests and uphold the honor of the family," was a salute to the selfless unifying role I play as E. M. Forster's Leonard Bast: "In all complicated feuds, there tend to be small pockets

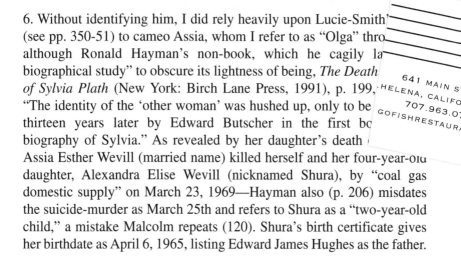

of agreement between the antagonists; members of both sides
together in hating certain people, and Edward Butscher is such a pe
No one I talked to on either side of the Plath-Hughes feud had a
word to say about him" (143).

6. Without identifying him, I did rely heavily upon Lucie-Smith'
(see pp. 350-51) to cameo Assia, whom I refer to as "Olga" thro
although Ronald Hayman's non-book, which he cagily la
biographical study" to obscure its lightness of being, *The Death*
of Sylvia Plath (New York: Birch Lane Press, 1991), p. 199,
"The identity of the 'other woman' was hushed up, only to be
thirteen years later by Edward Butscher in the first bc
biography of Sylvia." As revealed by her daughter's death
Assia Esther Wevill (married name) killed herself and her four-year-old
daughter, Alexandra Elise Wevill (nicknamed Shura), by "coal gas
domestic supply" on March 23, 1969—Hayman also (p. 206) misdates
the suicide-murder as March 25th and refers to Shura as a "two-year-old
child," a mistake Malcolm repeats (120). Shura's birth certificate gives
her birthdate as April 6, 1965, listing Edward James Hughes as the father.

7. The interview with the Davisons—Jane has since died—took place in
their Cambridge, Massachusetts home on March 1, 1974. In spite (or
because) of his considerable ego, Davison's observations about Plath in
his memoir and during the interview were often perceptive.

8. See Janet Malcolm, *The Journalist and the Murderer* (New York:
Alfred A. Knopf, 1990), p. 3. As reported in the New York Times
(November 3, 1994),1,B1, after "nearly 10 years of litigation in which
the case reached the United States Supreme Court once and juries
twice," the suit ended with a Federal District Court in San Francisco
ruling "that while two of five disputed quotations Ms. Malcolm
attributed to Mr. Masson in a 1983 profile of the psychoanalyst in The
New Yorker magazine were false and one of those was defamatory, none
were written with the recklessness required for libel."

9. Alas, even the publisher of the first volume of my Aiken biography,
Conrad Aiken: Poet of White Horse Vale (1988), the University of
Georgia Press, refused the chance to add a revised *Method and Madness*
to their list, claiming financial hardship. Perhaps Malcolm's original
suspicion was right: there is a conspiracy!

10. *Bluefish* III (Spring/Summer, 1987). Demonstrating why I am so despised, an appendix update of Plath studies (61-62) lightly praises ("well worth perusing, if limited in final reach") Lynda K. Bundtzen's *Plath's Incarnations: Women and the Creative Process* (Ann Arbor: University of Michigan, 1983) for its "comprehension of how the poet learned to manipulate a female 'body of imagination' in her maturity, the use of her projected body (a psychic and physical entity) as subject and object, ultimate metaphysical vehicle," dismisses the obsequiously Hughes-tilted *Ariel Descending: Writing About Sylvia Plath* (New York: Harper & Row, 1985), edited by Paula Alexander, as "a thin oleo of the familiar and the unremarkable," and is almost as severe on Linda W. Wagner's *Critical Essays on Sylvia Plath* (Boston: G. K. Hall, 1984), concluding presciently, "Wagner is at work on a biography but appears uncomfortable with her subject's fierce aesthetic."

11. Oberg's "Sylvia Plath and the New Decadence" and Oates's "The Death Throes of Romanticism: The Poetry of Sylvia Plath" can be found in my *Sylvia Plath: The Woman and the Work,* pp. 177-85 and 206-24. Taking his cue in part from Howe, Harold Bloom relegates Plath to the status of minor poet in the mode of Mrs. Felicia Hemans, author of "Casabianca," predicting that a poem such as "Lady Lazarus" will one day be found only in another *Stuffed Owl* anthology—see his incredible introduction to Modern Critical Views: Sylvia Plath (New York: Chelsea House, 1989), which he edited for some obscure reason.

12. "Lives of the Poet," *Georgia Review* (Fall, 1990), 596-602.

13. Olwyn, for instance, unknown to me, wrote a strong letter of protest to the Literary Guild, which had made my biography an alternate selection, with the result that it disappeared from the book club's catalogues soon thereafter. I learned about the incident years later, much too late to do more than shrug.

14. An interesting sidelight to the film's brief career emerged in early 1987 when Dr. Jane V. Anderson, psychiatrist and assistant clinical professor of psychiatry at the Harvard Medical School, filed suit against Ted Hughes and thirteen other individuals and organizations for the "defamation, invasion of privacy and intentional infliction of emotional damage" she endured because of the film—Matthew L. Wald, "Psychiatrist Files a Libel Suit Over Film of Plath's 'Bell Jar,' *New York Times* (January 14, 1987), I, C19. Her attorney, Harry L. Manion 3rd,

argued that the film makers were fully aware that Dr. Anderson had been associated with the character named Joan Gilling in *The Bell Jar,* claiming one of the producers had admitted having a copy of my biography in his possession at the time. The office of the laywer representing Hughes, Victor Kovner, called me to find out how I had avoided being sued by the lady, information I freely shared, but none of it mattered. The trial ended on January 29th when Dr. Anderson settled for 150 thousand dollars from 10 of the 14 defendants instead of the 6 million originally sought, and whatever satisfaction came from the public judgment that she was "unintentionally defamed by the movie"— *New York Times* (January 30, 1987, C13). Hughes was cleared of any liability, though Olwyn, as usual, caused a fuss when interviewed by the *Western Morning News* in Plymouth, England, expressing her fears that the trial would deteriorate into "a feminist vendetta that could ruin her brother." Of Plath, she felt compelled to add, "The truth is, she was terribly possessive, jealous and difficult." *The Boston Globe* (January 24, 1987), 13-14, picked up the story.

15. McCullough's unprofessional behavior was reported to the president of Harper & Row, which may have played a part in her decision to leave that firm for a position at The Dial Press, where she edited *The Journals of Sylvia Plath* (1982), with Ted Hughes acting as Consulting Editor and providing a Foreword—the latter includes an admission that he had destroyed similar journals that ran "from late '59 to within three days of her death" (p.xi). In *The Silent Woman,* p. 163, Malcolm reports: "'Thank you for your copy of the letter to that rat Butscher,' Frances McCullough wrote to Peter Davison in 1976."

16. Although several hundred review copies of *Poems About Silence* (New York: Seabury Press, 1976) were sent out, only three one-paragraph reviews appeared, in contrast to the fifty or sixty fulsome reviews that greeted *Method and Madness* the same year—there would have been more if Aurelia Plath's edition of her daughter's *Letters Home: Correspondence,* 1950-1963 had not been published the season before.

17. The mother's collection, 3,324 items in all, was sold to the Lilly Library of Indiana University in 1977, and Hughes's collection went to the Neilson Library at Smith College four years later, although there are time restrictions on some of the material.

18. Mortimer Ostow, *The Psychology of Melancholy* (New York: Harper & Row, 1970). Among the psychological texts consulted and then removed from the notes was Robert Kastenbaum and Ruth Aisenberg, *The Psychology of Death* (New York: Springer Company, 1972), which, at one point, keenly calculates the kind of insecurity-inducing pressure a child like Plath had to bear, "goaded to conform, to achieve academic excellence, to be productive, to be a joiner, to be a leader. More important still is the fact that parental acceptance and love, which should be a child's birthright, are often made contingent upon his social and academic succsss" (p. 255). Pertinent as well is their earlier report (p. 112) that "the rates of nonpsychotic suicides and of psychosis among people bereaved in early childhood are both unusually high." For a much fuller treatment of the impact of childhood loss on psychological development, see John Bowlby, *Attachment and Loss: Sadness and Depression* (New York: Basic Books, 1980). Plath herself, in a frank letter to Edward Cohen, said "she believed she suffered from schizophrenia, penis envy, and an inferiority complex. She also fought a powerful sex drive"—reported in Paul Alexander, *Rough Magic: A Biography of Sylvia Plath* (New York: Viking Penguin, 1991), p. 89.

19. Linda W. Wagner-Martin, *Sylvia Plath: A Biography* (New York: Simon and Schuster, 1987), p. 110. Aurelia Plath had learned about the strain of depression from her husband's sister but never passed the information on to either Sylvia or her psychiatrist.

20. See *The Journals of Sylvia Plath*, pp. 54-61, 63, 75-80, 93-97, 155, and 163. The entry on page 163, written November 5, 1957, is typical of her response to these bouts: "Brief note: to self. Time to take myself in hand. I have been staggering about lugubrious, black, bleak, sick."

21. Thomas Bredsdorff, "The Biographical Pursuit. Biography as a Tool of Literary Criticism," *Orbis Litterarum*, 44 (1989), 187. Most relevant is Kay Jamison's *Touched With Fire* (New York: The Free Press, 1994). Using her own and the researches of others, Dr. Jamison makes "a literary, biographical, and scientific argument for a compelling association, not to say actual overlap, between two temperaments—the artistic and the manic-depressive—and their relationship to the rhythms and cycles, or temperament, of the natural world" (p. 4). Plath is among her long list of poets, including Lowell and Sexton, who suffered from a severe form of the illness, and Dr. Jamison's comment on the use of psychological analysis in biography merits repeating as well:

"Biographical diagnoses must ultimately, of course, be more tentative than diagnoses made on living individuals, but they *can* [emphasis hers] be done, reliably and responsibly, and with an appreciation of the complexities that go into anyone's life" (p. 59).

22. *Method and Madness* was originally announced as a 1975 publication but was delayed a year when Olwyn Hughes, after I agreed to make most of a long list of changes she wished in the galleys, had Frances McCullough (without my knowledge or approval) send them on to Warren Plath for his approval. The latter's extensive list of requested changes, some of which were absurd, brought about my threat to sue Seabury. I later learned from a friend of the Plaths that a family conference had decided this was the best way to ensure that my book come out after the publication of *Letters Home.*

Note: A slightly different version of "A Mug's Game" appeared in *Biography and Source Studies* (1996), 9-26.

Notes

CHAPTER 1

1. The information is taken from the registration card made out for Otto by his father when he entered the prep school of Northwestern College on September 28, 1903, a copy of which was supplied by the current registrar, O. L. Schlenner.
2. Courses and requirements are taken from the college's bulletin for the time, again supplied by O. L. Schlenner.
3. The only solid piece of evidence of her existence is the January 4, 1932, divorce decree filed in the county of Ormsby, Nevada, where she is simply identified as "Lydia C. Plath." Otto was the plaintiff in the case, but Lydia did not contest the action, although she was represented by a lawyer named Charles S. Nichols. The decree was granted on the ground "that plaintiff and defendant have lived separate and apart from each other for more than five consecutive years without cohabitation with each other."
4. Letter to the author, dated November 20, 1972. All other quotes from Professor Fulton are taken from the same source.
5. Letter to the author, dated March 1, 1973.
6. The interview with Professor Norman S. Bailey was conducted and taped at his New Hampshire home on the morning of March 17, 1973. Unless otherwise specified, all other quotes from Professor Bailey are from this interview.
7. The interview with Professor Elmer Mode was conducted and taped at his Wellesley home on the morning of March 11, 1973. All other quotes from Professor Mode are from this interview.
8. I am assuming it is a literary exaggeration, since the town clerk at Winthrop was unable to supply any records indicating that Aurelia was born from the Shirley Street house. She was born in 1906, but the Schobers are not listed at 892 Shirley Street until 1918.

9. This was originally written by Sylvia for a talk on the BBC in 1962 and was subsequently published in *The Listener* (August 29, 1963). It has since been reprinted in *The Art of Sylvia Plath*, ed. Charles Newman (Bloomington: Indiana University Press, 1970), pp. 266–272.

10. Information supplied by the Superintendent of the Winthrop Public Schools in a letter to the author, dated July 15, 1974.

11. Information relating to Otto's illness and death are taken from an official copy of his death certificate, which was supplied by Winthrop's town clerk.

12. Quoted from an interview with Sylvia and Ted Hughes that was conducted by the BBC and broadcast on January 31, 1961, for the "Poets in Partnership" series. It was entitled "Two of a Kind" and has not yet appeared in print.

13. In a letter to the author, dated August 29, 1974, Doris E. McLeod, reference librarian at the Winthrop Public Library, provided a typed copy of both obituary notices, observing that "It appears our papers did not give him the consideration they should have."

14. "Superman and Paula Brown's New Snowsuit" appeared in *The Smith Review* (Spring, 1955) and has yet to be reprinted.

15. Letter to the author, dated July 31, 1974.

CHAPTER 2

1. Statistical and historical data concerning Wellesley has been largely gleaned from past issues of *The Townsman*, particularly issues covering the years from 1942 to 1950, as well as from various interviews with residents; Philip McCurdy was especially helpful.

2. The interview with Clement Moore (now Henry) was conducted and taped at the Connecticut home of a relative in July of 1973. All quotes from Professor Henry are from this interview.

3. Letter to the author, dated November 27, 1972. All other quotes from Miss Lawson come from this letter.

4. Letter to the author, dated November 16, 1972.

5. Letter to the author, dated November 14, 1972.

6. Miss Lawson was the magazine's adviser during Sylvia's stay at Phillips, and it was she who supplied the author with photostats of its contents. She did not know why Sylvia had not been on the staff, and conceded, "We missed a bet there, I'm afraid." Letter to the author, dated November 30, 1972.

7. In the April 1946 issue, Sylvia had a prose poem called "Spring Song," which was all description and ended with "the pit-pat, pit-pat of spring rain"; and the February 1947 issue printed a story of hers called "A Morning in the Agora," which describes two young women, Lavinia and Chloe, shopping in the ancient Greek market place.

8. The interview with Elizabeth Sigmund, who was Elizabeth Compton when Sylvia knew her, was conducted and taped at her Devon home on July 18, 1974. Unless otherwise specified, all other quotes are from this interview.

9. Letter to the author, postmarked January 4, 1973. In her letter, Miss Humphrey gives the year as 1944–1945; but since this would have been impossible, as Sylvia and her brother (whom she also tested) were then in separate schools, I have taken the liberty of moving the test back a year.

10. Letter to the author, dated January 10, 1973. Unless otherwise specified, all other quotes from Mr. Irish come from this letter.

11. The interview with Dr. "Richard Willard" was conducted and taped at his home on December 2, 1972. All quotes from Dr. Willard come from this interview. The use of a fictional name is at the family's request.

12. Letter to the author, dated October 26, 1972.

13. The interview with Mr. Wilbury Crockett was conducted and taped at his office in Bradford High (now simply Wellesley Senior High School) on October 30, 1972. All other quotes from Mr. Crockett come from this interview.
14. The interview with Philip McCurdy was conducted and taped at his New York City apartment on October 20, 1972.
15. In a letter postmarked February, 1973, Frank Irish definitely attributes "Question" to Sylvia and believes "Family Reunion" must have been hers as well, noting that "No one else, I think, would have been capable of, or interested in, writing 'Family Reunion.'" He was less certain about "Farewell," though other sources indicate it had indeed been written by Sylvia. Philip McCurdy also identified "Family Reunion" as Sylvia's, recalling Mrs. Plath's shocked reaction to it in later years.
16. Letter to the author, dated January 22, 1973.

CHAPTER 3

1. Quoted from Sylvia's own article about Smith, which she wrote while at Cambridge and had published in *Varsity* (May 12, 1956), the university's student newspaper, under the title "Smith College in Retrospect."
2. The interview with Marcia Brown Stern was conducted and taped at her Massachusetts home on March 24, 1974. All other quotes from Mrs. Stern come from this interview.
3. *Smith Weekly Current* (October 19, 1950).
4. *Mademoiselle* (August 1953).
5. *Ibid.*
6. All quotes and information relating to Sylvia's summer jobs while at Smith come from college records, which are located in a Sylvia Plath file at the William Allan Neilson Library (the Sophia Smith Collection).

CHAPTER 4

1. Because of Dr. "Buddy Willard's" unavailability, much information regarding him and his activities comes from the testimony of others or conjecture. Apparently, he was afflicted with or made aware of his tubercular condition sometime in the winter of 1952–1953, though it could have been somewhat earlier. The time can be vaguely established from a letter Sylvia wrote to Dr. Myron Lotz that winter, which alludes to her skiing accident. Furthermore, letters to Marcia Brown from late summer of 1952 indicate that Buddy was still unaware of his illness and still involved with Sylvia, at least to a degree.
2. The interview with Dr. Myron Lotz was conducted and taped at his Virginia home on February 16, 1973. All other quotes are from this interview.
3. The interview with Dr. Robert Modlin and his wife Jill was conducted and taped at their Washington, D.C., home on August 14, 1973. All other quotes from the Modlins are from this interview.
4. Professor Chase was a specialist in the Bible and occasionally gave lectures on its literary aspects for campus groups and at the local bookstore. For a charming, if not very revealing, account of Miss Chase's early life, see her own autobiography, *A Goodly Fellowship* (New York: The Macmillan Company, 1939).
5. The interview with Professor Robert Gorham Davis was conducted and taped at his Columbia University office on February 6, 1973. Despite Sylvia's attempts to impress him, Professor Davis did not recall her very clearly and remembered only having her as a student in his large lecture class. He was aware of her as an

outstanding student and dramatic presence on campus, but could remember very few personal details of their relationship.

6. Letter to the author, dated November 20, 1972. The quote is from a photostat of recollections Professor Gibian had written in October as are other quotes from him, unless specified otherwise.

7. This was the comment of a fellow student of Sylvia who was present during my interview with Professor Davis.

8. Jack Anderson and Ronald W. May, *McCarthy: The Man, the Senator, the "Ism"* (Boston: The Beacon Press, 1952), p. 362. Another Smith student present at the speech (May Targett) vividly recalls the senator knocking over a glass of water in his agitation, much to the delight of his skeptical audience.

9. The poem appeared in the August 6, 1955, issue of *The Nation*, but the year is incorrectly given as 1957 in the bibliography provided by *The Art of Sylvia Plath*, p. 317.

10. Elinor Klein, "A Friend Recalls Sylvia Plath," *Glamour* (November 1966), pp. 168–184. All further quotes from Mrs. Klein, who was Elly Friedman to Sylvia, are taken from this article.

11. In *Letters Home*, ed. Aurelia Plath, a large collection of Sylvia's letters which Harper & Row published in 1975, Sylvia makes clear that Buddy was the actual inspiration for the character of the Minton brother in the story; but I remain convinced that her brother was the unconscious, if not sole, target of Sylvia's pen. The fact that she used a "brother" figure rather than a "boy friend," as she had in "In the Mountains" and would in *The Bell Jar*, certainly suggests the idea was in her mind. More important, from Sylvia's narrow perspective, where all humans occupied stereotyped extremes, the negative, pragmatic qualities of Buddy and her brother were doubtless envisioned as indistinguishable aspects of the same male allegiance to science and practicality.

12. *Seventeen* (March 1953). The quote is from a brief paragraph about Sylvia included, along with a snapshot of her, under the poem, "The Suitcases Are Packed Again."

CHAPTER 5

1. *Sophian* (October 2, 1952). The same issue of this student newspaper noted that the *Smith Review* would be back in business, after a period of bankruptcy, for the new term and with a new editorial board, which included Sylvia. Also the magazine was scheduled to publish Sylvia's prize winning "Sunday at the Mintons" in a future issue.

2. Letter to the author, dated October 26, 1972.

3. *Ibid.*

4. The interview with Gordon Lameyer was conducted and taped at his New Hampshire home on March 17, 1973.

5. According to Lameyer's as yet unpublished memoir, *Who Was Sylvia?: A Memoir of Sylvia Plath During "The Bell Jar" Days*, which he kindly let me read, he had actually missed the Thomas reading at his own college through a misunderstanding.

6. In a letter to Gordon Lameyer, Sylvia admitted that Auden had told her personally that she was "too glib."

CHAPTER 6

1. Quoted by Lotz from a letter Sylvia had written to him from New York soon after her arrival.

2. Laurie Levy, *The Ohio Review* (Spring, 1973), 67–73.

3. The interview with Cyrilly Abels was conducted and taped at her New York City office in August of 1973.
4. Laurie Levy, *ibid.*
5. Sylvia's first visit to New York City occurred during her sophomore year in the company of Marcia Brown, who told me "that year Sylvia came down to visit my mother in New Jersey and I had the astonishing experience of introducing Sylvia to New York City." Interestingly, Marcia thought Sylvia saw New York "with the same sort of almost unbelievable enthusiasm which she approached some other people and situations—sometimes really hard to think it was real."
6. Quoted in *Mademoiselle* (September, 1971), 160.
7. Though she had some familiarity with scientific paraphernalia, Sylvia's conception of the bell-jar metaphor may have derived from a reading of Virginia Woolf's diary or, as a colleague of mine, Newton Nelson, has suggested, from a reading of Anaïs Nin's diary, though whether Sylvia read either is unknown.
8. Quoted in *Mademoiselle, op. cit.*
9. I have not been able to trace the original of "Dr. Gordon."
10. These details, garnered from newspaper accounts, agree almost point by point with the account in *The Bell Jar.* Sylvia slept in the same room with her mother, so it would have been difficult for Aurelia to hide the pills from her for very long.
11. *The Boston Daily Globe*, morning edition (August 25, 1953), pp. 1 and 9. For further details of the search and subsequent rescue, see the evening edition and the two editions for August 26th as well.
12. *The Boston Herald* (August 26, 1953), p. 1. In *The Bell Jar* the remark cleverly fits Philomenia Guinea's Victorian character, though there is always the improbable possibility Mrs. Plath was echoing a communication from Mrs. Prouty.
13. *The Boston Post* (August 26, 1953), pp. 1 and 3.
14. Karl A. Menninger, *Man Against Himself* (New York: Harcourt Brace, 1938), pp. 24–25.

CHAPTER 7

1. The nurse was a friend of Myron Lotz, and it was he who passed her observation on to me. Being in the local hospital must have been particularly embarrassing for Sylvia, since so many of the interns and nurses were either neighbors, friends, or friends of friends.
2. Gordon Lameyer alludes to this anecdote in his memoir.
3. The interview with Peter and Jane Davison was conducted and taped at their Cambridge, Massachusetts, home on the evening of March 1, 1974. Mr. Davison observed that Sylvia's great energy was "distorted, like a bonsai tree," in the various ways it manifested itself.
4. In her memoir, Nancy Hunter Steiner relates an incident (p. 45) Sylvia told about herself during her early days at McLean's, which highlights the despair she felt about her illness: " 'It seems foolish now,' she said, 'but I stormed into the psychiatrist's office and demanded a lobotomy—there seemed little reason to go on suffering and little hope that I would ever recover.' "
5. *Ibid.*
6. Lameyer alludes to the letters and publishes a portion of them in his memoir, and Davison talked about them during the course of our interview. Lameyer, by the way, sent Sylvia a copy of Edmund Wilson's *Axel's Castle* near the end of her stay at McLean's, and it is interesting to conjecture how she may have reacted to this examination of artifices dedicated to detached, mirror worlds. Many of the authors discussed by Wilson were already familiar to her, but it must have been pleasant to see a literature of despair and intellectual elitism so lucidly analyzed.

7. An amusing sidelight to this incident was provided by a neighbor who, noticing McCurdy's car parked for so long in front of the Plath home, called the police.
8. Jane Truslow, of course, eventually became Jane Davison, and Sylvia liked to take credit for having introduced the pair.
9. Wilbur's poem, "Cottage Street, 1953," as yet uncollected, appeared in *The American Poetry Review* (Nov./Dec., 1972), 13.
10. Letter to the author, dated December 12, 1972.
11. During this month she would also attend the wedding of Stanley Kahrl, Lameyer's friend, who was serving with him on the U.S.S. *Perry* at the time.

CHAPTER 8

1. It was a reference to *Rainer Maria Rilke: Selected Poems*, trans. C. F. MacIntyre (Berkeley: University of California Press, 1950).
2. Though I feel Hunter's observation is probably accurate, I have also to speculate about how much of herself she was projecting here as well. In one of Sylvia's letters quoted in Lameyer's memoir, there is a definite conviction on Sylvia's part that Nancy herself was a "user" of boys.
3. Sylvia, of course, was not a virgin, but her menstrual flow remained irregular.
4. The incident is touched upon in Lameyer's memoir, as is a letter she wrote detailing what she believed were Buddy's many faults.
5. Letter to the author, dated January 26, 1973.
6. Sylvia's sex undoubtedly did decrease her chances somewhat. In his memoir, Lameyer quotes from one of her letters in which she describes her humiliating experience during the interview for a possible Fulbright with four male professors. Their questions convinced her that they thought her aim might be little more than acquiring a rich boy friend.
7. The thesis is as yet unpublished, but is readily available at Smith College in the Sophia Smith Collection.
8. Peter Davison, *Half-Remembered* (New York: Harper and Row, 1973), p. 184.

CHAPTER 9

1. For this ten-day vacation, Sylvia stayed in a rented room in a building located across the street from the British Museum, which she used as a study on a few occasions.
2. The interview with May Targett was conducted and taped at her London home on April 18, 1973.
3. Jane Kopp kindly recorded her recollections for me at her Arkansas home sometime in early November 1973, responding to a series of questions submitted in advance. When Sylvia knew her she was Jane Baltzel.
4. Letter to the author, July 6, 1973.
5. The letters between Sylvia and John Lehmann, and between her and Charles Osborne, another editor at *The London Magazine* who became a friend of hers in the last years, are in possession of the Humanities Research Center at the University of Texas and were shown to me with Mr. Lehmann's permission.
6. She cannot be blamed entirely since *The New Yorker*, then as now, was the preserve of big "names" in poetry, despite Robert Lowell's admirable refusal to be included among its pages.
7. Letter to the author, dated November 25, 1972.
8. During her first term at Cambridge, Sylvia had the heady experience of taking a

course with F. R. Leavis, pursuing the History and Theory of Literary Criticism; and another course, on the English Moralists, with Basil Willey. She was also reading Ibsen again, more deeply and completely than at Smith, and was looking forward to taking David Daiches' course on the modern novel next term. Shirley Jackson's *The Bird's Nest* had a "most disconcerting" effect on her as well, which is hardly surprising.

9. The death of the Winthrop neighbor and Sylvia's ride back to Winthrop for the funeral at her mother's side had occurred during her last year at Smith.

10. *The Cambridge Mind*, ed. Eric Homberger, William Janeway, and Simon Schama (Boston: Little, Brown & Co., 1970), p. 301. Alvarez's brief essay, "Sylvia Plath: The Cambridge Collection"—the poems at Cambridge are the group Sylvia submitted during her second year in an effort to improve her grade—is persuasive in its demonstration of Sylvia's professionalism. Another essay in the same anthology by George Steiner called "In Extremis" (pp. 303–307) is interesting for its ability to see Sylvia's link with Poe and Tate and for raising the question touched upon by Irving Howe: did Sylvia have the moral right to don the trappings of a Jew, to link her personal disasters with the plight of the Jews in the concentration camps? Steiner refuses to make a final judgment. One minor note: in the essay Steiner claims he met Sylvia in the summer of 1952 when she came to interview him for *Mademoiselle*. It was the summer of 1953, however, and she did not go to London, but conducted the interview by mail.

11. Dorothea Krook's initial reaction to Sylvia, as described in her as yet unpublished memoir, was less positive: "I noticed a conspicuously tall girl standing in one of the aisles, facing towards me, and staring at me intently. I was struck by the concentrated intensity of her scrutiny, which gave her face an ugly, almost coarse expression, accentuated by the extreme redness of her heavily painted mouth and its downward turn at the corners. I distinctly remember wondering if she was Jewish." Her impression of Sylvia improved considerably during more extended personal contacts: "always neat and fresh, wearing charming, girlish clothes . . . hair down to the shoulders still, but ever so neatly, brushed and combed . . . charming American neatness and freshness is what I chiefly recall . . . she was of course beautiful."

12. *Orlando*, Virginia Woolf (London: Penguin Books, 1946). There are some eleven sections in all which are underlined or bracketed, as was Sylvia's habit. This is one of the few copies of her books not in the Sylvia Plath archives, which remain in the hands of the estate. Efforts to sell the archives to a university library have so far been unsuccessful.

13. Quoted from Eileen Aird's introduction to her study, *Sylvia Plath* (Edinburgh: Oliver & Boyd, 1973), p. 8.

CHAPTER 10

1. The interview with Miss K. T. Burton was conducted and taped at her London office on April 17, 1972.

2. Lameyer discusses the poem in his memoir and identifies what he believes are clear references to their German stay.

3. Many of the Benidorm sketches have been reproduced in Sylvia Plath, *Fiesta Melons* (Exeter: The Rougemont Press, 1971). Also reproduced in this volume are Sylvia's sketches of Withens, a harbor in Cornucopia, Wisconsin, and a Tabac in Paris.

4. Letter to the author, dated June 6, 1973.

CHAPTER 11

1. The letters between Sylvia and Professor Davis have been preserved and are available in the Sophia Smith Collection at Smith.
2. Sylvia's comments on her own poetry come from "Context," a brief essay she wrote in response to specific questions for the *London Magazine* (February 1962), pp. 45–46.
3. In her memoir, Dorothea Krook recalls Miss Chase's visit, and in particular meeting her at a dinner party at the Garden House Hotel, where Miss Chase laughed fondly over Sylvia's two current obsessions: " 'She talks about nothing else,' said Miss Chase, with much pretended exasperation, 'Plato and Mrs. Krook, Mrs. Krook and Plato, Mrs. Krook on Plato, Plato on Mrs. Krook . . . It's hard to know *which* she's talking about, whether it's Plato or Mrs. Krook she admires most.' "
4. Letter to the author, dated April 10, 1974.
5. Letter to the author, dated May 28, 1974.
6. This is quoted from a telephone interview conducted on May 31, 1974. At first I thought Professor Kahrl's memory might be mistaken, feeling that the remark would have most likely been intended for Miss Burton; but in reply to my inquiry on the latter, Mrs. Krook in a letter dated September 9, 1974, reaffirms the probable accuracy of the quote: "As to my having been 'too Aristotelian': I think it's perfectly possible that Sylvia did say this about me (not about Miss Burton!). I was certainly at the time a passionate student of Aristotle, and when I wasn't talking about Plato, I was talking about Aristotle—which maybe she doubtless found tedious. Perhaps this is what Sylvia meant by saying I was 'too Aristotelian': that she found me too enthusiastic about Aristotle for her taste (she cared much less about Aristotle than Plato)."

CHAPTER 12

1. Professor Mode, who also attended the party, did not agree, recalling Ted only as a "congenial Englishman."
2. Ted's essay, "Notes on the Chronological Order of Sylvia Plath's Poems," can be found in *The Art of Sylvia Plath*, pp. 187–195.
3. Quoted to me by Marcia Brown Stern during our interview.
4. Mary Ellen Chase in particular wished her to remain and applied constant pressure, though Howard Rollin Patch and Alfred Fisher must have also been interested in preventing her from "throwing away" her career.
5. The interview with Paul and Clarissa Roche was conducted and taped at their Aldermaston home on the night of November 6, 1973.
6. Letter to the author, dated August 11, 1974.
7. Schendler's comments were reported to the author in a letter from Professor Howard Hirt, who interviewed him in India in the summer of 1974.
8. *Mademoiselle* (January 1959).
9. The letter to Jane was dated February 18, 1958.
10. I was able to secure a copy of the recording from the Library of Congress with the permission of Olwyn Hughes.

CHAPTER 13

1. Letter to the author, postmarked August 17, 1973.

2. I saw the actual book during one of my London visits, a yellow paperback in French with many photos and illustrations.

CHAPTER 14

1. Sexton's memoir can be found in *The Art of Sylvia Plath*, pp. 174–181.
2. See *Ariel* (New York: Harper and Row, 1966).
3. In *The Death Notebooks* (Boston: Houghton Mifflin, 1974), for instance, Miss Sexton's verses often reach the point of unconscious self-parody. Her subsequent suicide does not relieve their self-indulgence but merely confirms the authenticity of its obsession.
4. Letter to the author from Pauline Hanson, the estate's secretary, dated November 27, 1972.

CHAPTER 15

1. See *Introduction: Stories by New Writers* (London: Faber and Faber, 1960), pp. 11–12 and 111–144.
2. See the same letter from Kunitz referred to earlier.
3. The interview with George MacBeth on July 19, 1974, was not taped.
4. This quote and all others from Alvarez in the chapters to follow are taken from his *The Savage God* (New York: Random House, 1972), pp. 3–41.

CHAPTER 16

1. Allan Seager, *The Glass House: The Life of Theodore Roethke* (New York: Doubleday, 1966), p. 271.
2. Details on the Festival were taken from the *Mermaid Poetry Festival Program*, which was issued for the occasion and also contained Sylvia's poem.

CHAPTER 17

1. Elizabeth Sigmund was amused by the split nature of Sylvia's kitchen—its obvious attempt to appear true to some ideal peasant model and the contrasting presence of gleaming American appliances.
2. See "Context," *op. cit.*
3. The interview with David Compton was conducted and taped at his London home on July 20, 1974.
4. Olwyn Hughes permitted me to read a few of these stories, which had been rejected by numerous magazines before Sylvia's death. Their publication would certainly add nothing to their author's reputation.
5. Elizabeth Sigmund told me about these letters, which I have not seen, and stressed how important it was to Sylvia to have someone she could communicate with regarding spiritual matters and how desperately she wanted to believe.
6. Both Ted and Sylvia were admirers of *The White Goddess* by Robert Graves.

CHAPTER 18

1. See his introduction to Sylvia Plath, *Three Women* (London: Turret Books, 1968), pp. 3–5.

2. Sylvia's radio play can be seen as a fascinating attempt on her part to ritualize the three major selves that formed her own character.
3. This confidential report, along with other papers of Douglas Cleverdon, is in the possession of the Lilly Library at Indiana University.
4. Perhaps there were two fires. Clarissa Roche recounts that after Ted's departure, Sylvia would collect her husband's letters and manuscripts from his desk, along with pieces of his fingernails, and burn them in the back yard. She then danced around the fire chanting the proper incantation for casting an evil spell on him.

CHAPTER 19

1. Despite her claim that "I am more myself in my letters," Sylvia's letters were often just other disguises, which only makes this admission the more remarkable.
2. Mrs. Plath's letter is quoted by Lois Ames in her Afterword ("Sylvia Plath: A Biographical Note") to the American edition of *The Bell Jar*, pp. 294–295.
3. During our interview, Mr. Crockett mentioned a vague memory of Sylvia having suggested in a letter to him that Ted was a little too sexually aggressive for her.

CHAPTER 20

1. Letter to the author, dated March 21, 1973.
2. Not enough research has been done on the obvious connection between the delusions of the schizophrenic and the metaphors of the artist; but one important recent study by Dr. Brendan Maher, "The Shattered Language of Schizophrenia," which can be found in *Readings in Clinical Psychology Today*, ed. Barbara Henker (California: R M Books, 1970), effectively demonstrates that the associative chaining evident in the speech patterns of schizophrenics is difficult to follow because the relationships are hidden in the patient's private consciousness, and that the apparently meaningless breaks in syntax and logic are actually responses, often in the form of puns, secondary meanings, and the like, to a distinct interior design. Most significant of all, in my view, is Dr. Maher's observation that "the mental substrata in which certain kinds of poetry are born probably are associative in a more or less schizophrenic way."
3. There is some confusion about this incident. According to Elizabeth Sigmund, the couple in question had been guests at Sylvia's home, but then had moved on to a rented cottage nearer the sea: Sylvia apparently visited them there for a day, as "Lesbos" would seem to confirm, and it was during this visit that Frieda's kittens were forced to remain outside—thus arousing Sylvia's wrath.
4. See Arthur K. Oberg, "Sylvia Plath and the New Decadence," *Chicago Review 20* (1968), pp. 66–73.
5. Howe's essay appeared originally in *Harper's* and has since been reprinted in his collection, *The Critical Point* (New York: Horizon Press, 1973) pp. 158–169.
6. *A Writer's Diary: Being Extracts from the Diary of Virginia Woolf*, ed. Leonard Woolf (New York: The New American Library, 1968), p. 299. This was written slightly more than a year before her own suicide. Under glass, under a bell jar, are seemingly metaphors for the same schizophrenic detachment from experience and self Sylvia underwent. See particularly pp. 171ff.
7. Stevie Smith's *Selected Poems* (Faber and Faber) had appeared early in 1962, and Sylvia was captivated by her odd merger of childish language and vision with Freudian insights. In November of 1962, after securing her address from Peter Orr,

Sylvia wrote to Stevie Smith and received a warm reply. She hoped to meet Smith when she moved to London but never did. See Aird, *Sylvia Plath*, pp. 12–13.

CHAPTER 21

1. George MacBeth told me he had approached Sylvia about including several of her recent poems in an anthology of "sick verse" he was putting together for Penguin. She agreed, apparently amused by the idea.
2. See Aird, *Sylvia Plath*, p. 13.
3. I was generously supplied a copy of this article by Olwyn Hughes.
4. In a letter to the author, dated September 23, 1974, in reply to an inquiry regarding what work Sylvia could have been referring to, George MacBeth writes: "I can't think what her three week job with the BBC in May 1963 would have been. Perhaps she had an enlarged idea of how long it might take to record a programme of her poems which Philip French had in hand!"
5. Elizabeth Sigmund informed me during our interview that Sylvia had also written to Nancy in this last week, requesting her to see that the cat was spayed before her arrival in May.
6. In a letter to the author, dated August 24, 1974, Elizabeth Sigmund tried to sort out the story about the rabbit and the rose: "Did you know the myth about Ted killing the hare (which he told me was Sylvia) and selling it to a butcher and buying red roses for Olga? It really happened, and he told me he dreamed it first, and after wrote a radio play (for Radio 3 BBC) about it. He killed another (sorry—ran over them in his car each time)."
7. According to Alvarez's account, the only actual note found at the scene was a clear cry for help: *Please call Mr. ——*, followed by the phone number. I have rearranged and treated the poems from Sylvia's last week as a sequence. Actually, "Words" was written on February 1, and both "Edge" and "Balloons," the final poems, come from February 5.
8. Ted rejected Alvarez's notion of Sylvia's suicide as a gamble. In the *Observer* for November 14, 1971, Alvarez first put forth his theory, actually an extract from the chapter destined to appear in *The Savage God* and elsewhere. The Hugheses were upset by the article, which was given an entire page under the banner headline of "Sylvia Plath: The Road to Suicide," and feared that it would be read by Sylvia's children and their classmates. Consequently, they caused the *Observer* to cancel the second installment, and Ted had a letter of his printed in the next issue (November 21) in which he denied Alvarez's contention, claiming he had secret information which made the gamble idea untenable, though he refused to divulge its nature.

Bibliographical Note

Since Sylvia Plath's death and the subsequent appearence of *Ariel* in England and America (in 1965 and 1966 respectively), there has been a great deal of confusion and speculation about the availability of Plath material. Much of the voluminous early work had already seen print in a wide variety of "little magazines" and literary journals, where it remained largely inaccessible to the general public, while eight or nine of the later poems have never been published at all. Under the direction of Ted and Olwyn Hughes, the Sylvia Plath Estate saw fit to issue both uncollected and unpublished poems in individual volumes, rather than prepare a complete edition immediately. Many of the poems did not seem worthy of being preserved in book form, but this deplorable situation has also resulted in frustration among students of her work.

Another problem has been the discrepancies between British and American texts, which is no fault of the Hugheses. *The Colossus and Other Poems* was published by William Heinemann Ltd. in London in 1960. Ted Hughes' publisher was (and still is) Faber and Faber; but, according to Rosemary Goad at Faber, the two poets had originally wanted to have different publishers. In any event, when Alfred A. Knopf, Inc., printed the American edition of Sylvia's initial volume in 1962, it excluded nine poems which had appeared in the British edition: "Ouija," "Maudlin," "Metaphors," "Black Rooks in Rainy Weather," "Two Sisters of Persephone," "Who," "Dark House," "Maenad," and "The Beast"—the last four had been sections of the long sequence called "Poem for a Birthday." To complicate matters further, when *Ariel* was published by Faber in England and by Harper & Row in America, the British edition contained three poems not in the American: "Lesbos," "Mary's Song," and "The Swarm."

The two collections of Plath poetry which have since appeared, *Winter Trees* and *Crossing the Water*, both in 1971 and both under the imprint of Faber in England and Harper in America, only confused matters further, as the differences between American and British texts became more pronounced. This has led to rumors that certain poems were being deliberately suppressed in England because of their controversial nature, but a careful check of all four Plath collections in their British and American editions reveals that only three poems have been printed in the United States which have not yet appeared in England: "Amnesiac," "Eavesdropper," and "The Detective," and these are no more controversial than several others already published. Olwyn Hughes and Judith Kroll are now gathering all extant poems for a definitive edition of *The Collected Poems of Sylvia Plath*.

Meanwhile, beautiful limited editions of uncollected and unpublished Plath poems began appearing in England in 1971, mostly under the auspices of the Rainbow Press, Olwyn Hughes' own enterprise. Following is a list of the four titles published in this manner, including identification of those poems which did not appear in any of the other four collections:

Fiesta Melons (Rougemont Press, May 1971), 150 copies. Besides eleven of Sylvia's drawings, the book also contains a brief Introduction by Ted Hughes in which he indicates dates of composition. "Two Lovers and a Beachcomber by the Real Sea" and "Dream of the Hearse Driver" were written in 1951–1952, and the other seven belong to 1956–1958: "Green Rock, Winthrop Bay," "Battle Scene for the Comic Opera Fantasy 'The Seafarer,' " "Complaint of the Crazed Queen," "Southern Sunrise," "Fiesta Melons," "November Graveyard," and "Yadwigha on a Red Couch, among Lilies (A Sestina for the Douanier)."

Crystal Gazer (Rainbow Press, 1971), 400 copies. The year of composition is given for each poem: "Notes on Zarathustra's Prologue" (1950–51), "Mad Girl's Love Song" (1951), "Admonitions" (1950–51), "Go Get the Goodly Squab" (1950–51), "Circus in Three Rings" (1951–52), "Lament" (1951–52), "Alicante Lullaby" (1956), "The Beggars" (1956), "The Goring" (1956), "Recantation" (1956), "Crystal Gazer" (1956), "On the Plethora of Dryads" (1956), "Fable of the Rhododendron Stealers" (1958), and "Stopped Dead" (1962).

Lyonesse (Rainbow Press, 1971), 400 copies. Again, the year of composition is given for each poem: "Mayflower" (1955), "Wreath for a Bridal" (1956), "Epitaph for Fire and Flower" (1956), "Metamorphoses of the Moon" (1953), "A Winter's Tale" (1958), "Owl" (1958), "Electra on the Azalea Path" (1958), "In Midas Country" (1958), "Tinker Jack and Tidy Wives" (1956), "On the Difficulty of

Conjuring Up a Dryad" (1956), "The Snowman on the Moor" (1956),
"Old Ladies Home" (1958), and "The Other Two" (1959).
Pursuit (Rainbow Press, 1973), 100 copies. No dates of composition are
supplied this time, but Olwyn Hughes kindly dated the poems from the
last year or so of Sylvia's life for me: "Dark Wood, Dark Water,"
"Resolve," "Temper of Time," "The Shrike," "The Lady and the
Earthenware Head," "Pursuit," "Doomsday," "Words Heard, By Acci-
dent, Over the Phone" (July, 1962); "Stings (2)" (October, 1962);
"Spider," "The Fearful" (November, 1962); "The Rival (2)" (July,
1961); "A Secret" (October, 1962); and "Burning the Letters"
(August, 1962).

There had also been two previous limited editions done by Turret Books in
London: *Uncollected Poems* (1965), 150 copies, and *Three Women* (1968), 180
copies, the latter with an Introduction by Douglas Cleverdon. The eleven
poems and verse play would subsequently appear in *Winter Trees* and *Crossing
the Water*. Four of Sylvia's poems were published separately as booklets as well.
"A Winter Ship" appeared in 1960 from the Tragara Press, Edinburgh, but the
number of copies printed is unknown, though small. The Sceptre Press
(Surrey) published 100 copies of "Wreath for a Bridal" in 1970 and 150 copies
of "Million Dollar Month" in 1971, while 325 copies of "Child" were printed
by the Rougemont Press (Exeter) in December 1971.

Olwyn Hughes has also confirmed that collections of the short stories are
being prepared. These will be selected editions, but rather generous ones. Most
of the stories had already appeared in print, but there remain several which
were unpublished at Sylvia's death. I was permitted to read three of these, "The
Shadow Girl," which might have originally been "The Shadow," one of the
two stories rejected by *London Magazine* in 1959; "A Winter's Tale," which is
obviously based upon Elinor Friedman's (Klein's) visit to the Hugheses in
Yorkshire shortly after their marriage; and "A Smokey Blue Piano." These
stories are of biographical interest, but of little literary merit.

Sylvia's more interesting and successful stories can be read in the magazines
where they originally appeared, including the solid achievements represented
by "All the Dead Dears" and "Johnny Panic and His Bible of Dreams."
Following is a fairly complete list of published short stories:

"And Summer Will Not Come Again," *Seventeen* (August 1950), pp.
191 and 275–276.
"The Perfect Setup," *Seventeen* (August 1952), pp. 76 and 100–104.
"Sunday at the Mintons," *Smith Review* (Fall 1952), pp. 3–9. This also
was a winner in the *Mademoiselle* fiction contest and was published in
the August 1952 issue, pp. 255 and 371–378.
"Initiation," *Seventeen* (January 1953), pp. 64 and 92–94.
"In the Mountains," *Smith Review* (Fall 1954), pp. 2–4.
"The Day Mr. Prescott Died," *Granta* (October, 1956), pp. 20–23.

"The Wishing Box," *Granta* (January 1957), pp. 3–5. This was subsequently reprinted in the *Atlantic* (October 1964), pp. 86–89.

"All the Dead Dears," *Gemini* (Summer 1957), pp. 53–59.

"The Daughters of Blossom Street," *London Magazine* (May 1960), pp. 34–48.

"The Fifteen-Dollar Eagle," *The Sewanee Review* (Fall 1960), pp. 603–618.

"The Fifty-Ninth Bear," *London Magazine* (February 1961), pp. 11–20.

"Johnny Panic and His Bible of Dreams," *Atlantic* (September 1968), pp. 54–60.

"The Mothers' Union," *McCall's* (October 1972), pp. 80, 126, 128, 130, 142.

I should here express my debt to Charles Newman's invaluable anthology of material about and by Sylvia Plath, *The Art of Sylvia Plath* (Bloomington: Indiana University Press, 1970). An expansion of an issue of *TriQuarterly* (Fall 1966), this collection has been the most substantial work of criticism and biographical information hitherto available. Besides critical essays, *The Art of Sylvia Plath* contains memoirs by Wendy Campbell and Anne Sexton, a biographical sketch by Lois Ames (Sylvia's authorized biographer), Ted Hughes's dating of and comments on many of his wife's poems, and a number of Plath items not readily available elsewhere, such as "Ocean W-1212" and two poems which have not yet appeared in any other collection: "Dialogue en Route" (c. 1951) and "Miss Drake Proceeds to Supper" (1956). Mary Kinzie's "An Informal Check List of Criticism" is both accurate and thorough; and the bibliography by Mary Kinzie, Daniel Lynn Conrad, and Suzanne D. Kurman (pp. 305–319), though incomplete and marred by minor errors, is quite adequate.

As for *The Bell Jar*, it was first published under the pen name of Victoria Lucas in 1963 by William Heinemann Ltd., and then reprinted by Faber and Faber under Sylvia's own name in 1966; but the American edition did not appear until 1971 under Harper and Row's imprint, and this included Lois Ames' "A Biographical Note" and "eight previously unpublished drawings." Sylvia's other prose, her slightly fictionalized memoirs, have only appeared in magazines: "Superman and Paula Brown's Snowsuit," *Smith Review* (Spring 1955), pp. 19–21; "America! America!", *Punch* (April 3, 1963), pp. 482–484; and "Ocean W-1212," *The Listener* (August 29, 1963), pp. 312–313, reprinted in *The Art of Sylvia Plath*, pp. 266–272. "Context," Sylvia's written response to a question about her writing and what she was reading at the time, appeared in the *London Magazine* (February 1962), pp. 45–46. Other autobiographical comments can be found in "Poet on College Time," *Mademoiselle* (August 1950), pp. 52–53, and "Four Young Poets," *Mademoiselle* (January 1959), pp. 34–35 and 85. See also "A Friend Recalls Sylvia Plath," Elinor Klein, *Glamour* (November 1966), pp. 168–84.

Lastly, Sylvia had appeared for the BBC on a number of occasions, and following is a list of the programs, including the dates of broadcast:

November 20, 1960, *Third Programme* ("New Poetry"). Sylvia read "Candles" and "Leaving Early."

January 31, 1961, *Poets in Partnership* ("Two of a Kind"). Joint interview of Ted and Sylvia.

March 19, 1961, *Poets in Partnership*. Continuation of above.

July 8, 1961, *Third Programme* ("Living Poets"). Sylvia introduced.

July 7, 1962, *World of Books* ("A Poet's View of Novel Writing").

August 24, 1962, *Third Programme* ("Poet's Voice"). Sylvia read "Surgeon at 2 A.M."

September 7, 1962, "In a World of Sound: What You Value Stays."

November 4, 1962, *Third Programme* ("The Weird Ones"). Sylvia read.

January 10, 1963, *New Comment* ("Contemporary American Poetry"). Sylvia reviewed Donald Hall's anthology.

August 19, 1963, *Writers on Themselves* ("Ocean W-1212").

September 23, 1963, "The Poetry of Sylvia Plath: A Tribute"— Alvarez commentary, bits and pieces of other interviews, etc.

Index

Aaron, Daniel, 223, 227
Abels, Cyrilly, 102–4, 103, 121–22, 164
"Admonitions" (Plath), 49, 50
"Aftermath" (Plath), 243
"Alicante Lullaby" (Plath), 191
"All the Dead Dears" (Plath), 203–5, 242
Alvarez, A., 179, 224, 260–63, 267, 270, 274–75, 282, 298, 302–3, 335, 339, 341, 350–53, 355–56, 362–63
"America! America!" (Plath), 31
"Amnesiac" (Plath), 254, 331–32
"And Summer Will Not Come Again" (Plath), 37
Anderson, Jane, 47, 51, 56
"Applicant, The" (Plath), 328
"April, 1948" (Plath), 33
"Ariel" (Plath), 339, 341, 342
Ariel (Plath), 211, 235, 242, 262, 266, 326, 329, 365
"Arrival of the Bee Box, The" (Plath), 345–46
Arvin, Newton, 44, 127, 137

"Babysitters, The" (Plath), 57, 270
Bailey, Norman, 6
Baldwin, Frances, 22
"Ballade Banale" (Plath), 63
"Balloons" (Plath), 360–61
Baskin, Leonard, 223–24, 227
"Bee Meeting, The" (Plath), 342, 343–44
"Beekeeper's Daughter, The" (Plath), 238, 239
Bell Jar, The (Plath), 5, 7, 13, 18, 45, 46, 62, 63, 65, 77, 102, 104–5, 109, 148, 163, 296, 341–42, 352, 358
    completion of, 275, 287–89, 292, 299, 304–18
    Plath's breakdown and, 112, 117, 120–21, 125

"Berck Plage" (Plath), 299–302, 332
Bergonzi, Bernard, 263
"Birthday Present, A" (Plath), 328–30
Bishop, Elizabeth, 153, 164
"Bitter Strawberries" (Plath), 38–39, 70
"Black Rooks in Rainy Weather" (Plath), 203, 213, 298
"Blackberrying" (Plath), 280, 282, 283
Blackwell, Betsy, 101–2
"Blue Moles" (Plath), 248
Bond, Sarah, 25
Bottsford, Barbara, 25, 27, 39
Bowen, Elizabeth, 44, 104, 108
Bradford High School (Wellesley, Ma.), 30–39
Brawner, Phil, 79–81
"Brown, Gloria," 161–62
Brown Plumer, Marcia, 42–43, 45, 48, 52, 53, 56–58, 60, 81, 107, 110–11, 127, 128, 131, 132, 145, 147, 151, 152, 171, 177, 231, 239–40, 253, 256, 260, 308, 309, 353, 359
"Bull of the Bendylaw, The" (Plath), 63, 212, 225, 237
"Burning the Letters" (Plath), 320
"Burnt-out Spa, The" (Plath), 249–50
Burton, K. T., 182, 187, 196–98, 207
"By Candlelight" (Plath), 354–55

Cambridge University, 168–88, 197–218
Campbell, Wendy, 179, 184, 206, 217, 261
"Candles" (Plath), 266–67, 270
Carter, Mark Bonham, 278, 285
Chase, Mary Ellen, 44, 68, 73, 83, 132, 182, 202, 207, 227, 309
"Childless Woman" (Plath), 332
"Circus in Three Rings" (Plath), 74–75
Cleverdon, Douglas, 292, 294

Closer Look at Ariel, A (Hunter), 144
"Colossus, The" (Plath), 212, 235
Colossus, The (Plath), 35, 179–80, 237, 250, 258, 262, 270
Compton, David, 237, 268, 277, 285–86, 290, 299, 303, 305, 311, 313, 314, 316, 319, 350, 353, 366
Compton, Elizabeth, 268, 277–78, 280, 281–82, 284–86, 294, 303, 305, 311, 314, 319, 324–25, 333, 353, 360, 365, 366
"Confusion" (Plath), 360
"Conqueror Worm, The" (Poe), 75
Corwin, Norman, 33
Cox, Catherine, 24
Craig, Anna C., 22
Crockett, Wilbury, 30–31, 34–37, 39, 54, 102, 123, 127, 218, 309
"Crossing the Equinox" (Plath), 91
"Crossing the Water" (Plath), 245, 280
"Crystal Gazer" (Plath), 200

"Daddy" (Plath), 296, 328, 335–38, 345
"Dance Macabre" (Plath), 172
"Daughters of Blossom Street, The" (Plath), 234, 248
Davis, Alice Norma, 52
Davis, Robert Gorham, 44, 68–69, 127, 202
Davison, Peter, 123, 124, 147, 160–65, 167, 173, 180, 188, 194, 218, 231, 234–35, 239, 261, 264, 310, 325, 362, 365
"Day Mr. Prescott Died, The" (Plath), 179
"Death & Co." (Plath), 351–53
"Death of Myth-Making, The" (Plath), 180
"Departure" (Plath), 190
"Detective, The" (Plath), 332, 333
"Dialogue en Route" (Plath), 63, 83, 93
Dickinson, Peter, 263
"Disquieting Muses, The" (Plath), 11, 12, 228–29
"Doomsday" (Plath), 93, 134, 335
Dostoevsky, Fyodor, 37, 44, 131, 135, 137, 151–58, 312

Drabble, Margaret, 187
"Dream of a Hearse-Driver" (Plath), 49, 50–51
"Dream with Clam Diggers" (Plath), 210, 213, 214
Duckett, Eleanor Shipley, 68

"Eavesdropper" (Plath), 331, 332
"Edge" (Plath), 360, 361-62
Edwin (Plath's lover), 148–49, 309
"Electra on the Azalea Path" (Plath), 239
Eliot, T. S., 91, 209, 258, 268, 271, 348
"Ella Mason and the Eleven Cats" (Plath), 194–95
"Elm" (Plath), 295–96
"Epitaph for Fire and Flower" (Plath), 195–96
"Epitaph in Three Parts" (Plath), 155
"Event" (Plath), 332

"Face Lift" (Plath), 267
Fainlight, Ruth, 295
"Family Reunion" (Plath), 39
"Famous Poet" (Plath), 202
"Farewell, The" (Plath), 33
"Faun" (Plath), 180
"Fearful, The" (Plath), 332, 334
"Fever 103°" (Plath), 316, 322, 329, 337
"Fiesta Melons" (Plath), 190
"Fifty-Ninth Bear, The" (Plath), 245–46, 270
"Finisterre" (Plath), 280
"Fireside Reveries" (Plath), 24
Fisher, Alfred, 68, 227
"Flute Notes from a Reedy Pond" (Plath), 248–49
"Fools Encountered" (Plath), 272
"For a Fatherless Son" (Plath), 326
"Forsaken Merman" (Arnold), 13
Frost, Robert, 79, 235
Fulbright fellowship, 157, 158, 174
"Full Fathom Five" (Plath), 236

Gaige, William, 32
Gardner, Isabella, 153, 164
Gary, Rex, 116
Gibian, George, 69, 96, 127, 135, 151–52, 156, 158–59, 168, 207

"Go Get the Goodly Squab" (Plath), 49, 51–52, 77, 196

"Goring, The" (Plath), 191

Gove, Bradford, 117

Gowans, James, 176

Graham, Paul G., 151

"Green Rock, Winthrop Bay" (Plath), 221

Guisey, Louise, 27, 61, 140

"Gulliver" (Plath), 332, 333

Half-Remembered (Davison), 160, 163

"Hanged Man, The" (Plath), 331

Hanson, Pauline, 247

"Hardcastle Crags" (Plath), 210, 211, 213, 225, 236, 242, 280

Harvard Summer School, 139, 146–51

Hawk in the Rain, The (Hughes), 191, 202, 207, 209, 224, 226, 235, 257, 269

"Hawk Roosting" (Hughes), 257

"Heavy Women" (Plath), 267, 295

Henderson, Isabel, 168, 169

Horn, Rosalie, 222

Hughes, Edward (Ted), 183–85
   in U. S., 219–52
   marriage to Plath, in Cambridge, 188–93, 197–218
   Plath's break with, 305–60
   return to England, 253–303

Hughes, Frieda Rebecca, 259–60, 270, 272, 275, 285, 288, 290, 302, 319, 349, 354, 357, 359, 363, 364

Hughes, Nicholas Farrar, 284, 290–91, 318, 354, 356, 357, 363, 364

Hughes, Olwyn, 192, 237, 253–54, 257, 272, 280–81, 304, 321, 332, 333

Humphrey, Dorothy H., 27

Hunter, Nancy, 94, 130–31, 134, 135, 139, 143–52, 154, 157, 161–62, 171, 309

"I Am Vertical" (Plath), 267, 280

"Ice Age" (Plath), 153, 171

"In a Station of the Metro" (Pound), 307

"In Plaster" (Plath), 267

"In the Mountains" (Plath), 89, 91

"Insomniac" (Plath), 270–71

"Invitation" (Plath), 88

Irish, Frank, 25, 27–28, 33, 36, 37

Island, The (Plath and Ventura), 33

Jamison, Andrew, 143, 144

"Johnny Panic and His Bible of Dreams" (Plath), 234

"Jones, Ruth" (psychiatrist), 124–25, 127, 137, 148, 152, 158

Kahrl, Stanley, 214–15, 218

Kazin, Alfred, 141, 151, 156–57, 159

"Kindness" (Plath), 360, 361

Kiser, Althea, 37

Klein, Elinor, 129, 130, 140, 169, 173, 177, 181, 191–93, 222, 232

Kohn, Hans, 136, 139

Kopp, Jane, 168, 170–71, 174–78, 182–85, 199, 207, 209, 217–18, 227

Kramer, Art, 80, 82

Krook, Dorothea, 179, 182–83, 186, 196–97, 199, 201, 215

"Lady and the Earthenware Head, The" (Plath), 230

"Lady Lazarus" (Plath), 293, 296, 316, 335–39, 345

"Lady of the Shipwrecked" (Plath), 282

"Lament" (Plath), 78, 205

Lameyer, Gordon, 74, 94, 99, 111–12, 114, 122–23, 125, 129, 130, 141, 144, 146, 147, 149, 150, 155–57, 160, 164, 180, 185, 187–88, 214, 309

Lawson, Helen, 22

Lehmann, John, 172, 248

Lerman, Leo, 108

"Lesbos" (Plath), 286, 291, 322–24

"Letter in November" (Plath), 328

Letters Home (Plath), 366

Levy, Laurie, 101, 105

"Life, A" (Plath), 280

Lindenwood, Dick, 309

Lotz, Myron ("Mike"), 64–66, 87, 91, 95–97, 107, 111, 129–30, 132–34, 139, 147, 150, 160, 166, 176–77, 233, 234, 256–57, 261, 308, 310

"Love Is a Parallax" (Plath), 154

Lowell, Robert, 213, 234, 240, 242–43, 268, 359
Lupercal (Hughes), 224, 235, 247, 258, 262, 269

MacBeth, George, 259, 261, 271, 335, 353, 359, 360
McBey, Robert P., 116, 119
McCurdy, Philip, 29–30, 32–34, 37, 53–54, 59, 74, 87, 91, 105, 111, 125–26, 130, 132, 138–39, 143–45, 147, 150, 158, 202, 224, 308
McLean Hospital (Belmont, Ma.), 122–25, 310
"Mad Girl's Love Song" (Plath), 74, 93, 108, 122
Mademoiselle (magazine), 47, 71, 75, 79, 86, 91, 99, 101–9, 160, 227, 232
"Magic Mirror, The: A Study of the Double in Two of Dostoevsky's Novels" (Plath) 158
"Man in Black" (Plath), 236
"Manor Garden, The" (Plath), 250
"March" (Plath), 23
"Martyrdom of Bishop Farrar, The" (Plath), 202
"Mary's Song" (Plath), 316, 328–29
"May Week Fashions" (Plath), 178
"Medallion" (Plath), 257, 258
"Medusa" (Plath), 13, 305–6
Merwin, Dido, 254, 255, 260–61, 353
Merwin, W. S., 254, 255, 260–61, 271, 272, 353, 359, 362
"Metamorphosis" (Plath), *see* "Faun" (Plath)
Meyers, E. Lucas, 184, 185, 187, 199, 210, 272
Miller, Jonathan, 172
Mode, Elmer, 7, 8
Modlin, Jill, 97, 133, 310
Modlin, Robert, 64, 65, 97–98, 133, 310
"Moon and the Yew Tree, The" (Plath), 52, 280, 283, 296, 297, 299, 307
"Moonrise" (Plath), 298
"Moonsong at Morning" (Plath), 154–55
Moore, Clement, 49, 142, 321, 326, 349

Moore, Marianne, 153, 209
Moraes, Don, 263
Morgan, Robin, 325
"Morning Song" (Plath), 270
"Mother's Union, The" (Plath), 353
"Munich Mannequins, The" (Plath), 328
"Mushrooms" (Plath), 190, 244, 247–49, 269
"Mussel Hunter at Rock Harbour" (Plath), 219–20, 233
"My Uncle's Wound" (Hughes), 272
"Mystic" (Plath), 330-31, 354

"Nick and the Candlestick" (Plath), 354
"Night Dances, The" (Plath), 354
"Night Shift" ("Night Walk") (Plath), 212, 224–25, 233, 237, 262
Norris, Myra, 363
"Notes on Zarathustra's Prologue" (Plath), 49, 50, 83

"Ocean W-1212" (Plath), 8
"October" (Plath), 24
"Olga" (Hughes' mistress), 303, 306, 314–17, 320, 324–25, 332, 333, 349, 366
"On the Decline of Oracles" (Plath), 180
"On the Difficulty of Conjuring Up a Dryad" (Plath), 180
"On the Plethora of Dryads" (Plath), 180
O'Neil, Pat, 54, 140
"Other, The" (Plath), 332, 333

"Parliament Hill Fields" (Plath), 284
"Pennines in April" (Plath), 233
"Perfect Set-Up, The" (Plath), 73, 85
Pitt, Valeria, 186, 198, 209
Plath, Aurelia Schober, 7–8, 12, 13, 15–16, 19–21, 58, 60, 65, 80, 142, 149, 150, 162, 164, 252, 303, 365–66
    Sylvia's first breakdown and, 109–21, 125
    Sylvia's marriage and, 189, 202, 218, 224

Sylvia's relationship with, 35, 45, 73, 83, 156, 273, 290, 304–6, 309–11, 319–21
Plath, Ernestine Kottke, 3
Plath, Otto Emile, 3–13, 29
Sylvia's relationship with, 3, 10, 15, 19, 79, 98, 113, 123–25, 146, 155, 181, 237–39, 249, 334–35, 337–39
Plath, Sylvia, 209, 218–20, 231–43
at Cambridge, 166–88, 197–218
childhood of, 8–10
divided personality of, 67, 125
first breakdown of, 119–25
at Harvard Summer School, 139, 146–51
life in Wellesley of, 20–40
at *Mademoiselle*, 86, 91, 99, 101–9
relationship with father of, 3, 10, 15, 19, 79, 98, 113, 123–25, 146, 155, 181, 237–39, 249, 334–35, 337–39
relationship with mother of, 35, 45, 73, 83, 156, 304–6, 309–11, 319–21
return to England of, 253–303
separation from Hughes of, 297, 315–60
as Smith student, 41–100, 127–37, 151–62
as Smith teacher, 202, 222–31
suicide of, 360–66
See also specific listings for poems
Plath, Theodore, 3, 4
Plath, Warren Joseph, 8, 12, 19, 21, 22, 25, 26, 28, 57, 90, 111, 116, 118, 119, 127–28, 142, 321
"Poem for a Birthday" (Plath), 251, 279
"Poem for Paul Klee's Persius: The Triumph of Wit over Suffering" (Plath), 230
"Poets on Campus" (Plath), 108
"Point Shirley" (Plath), 243
"Poppies in October" (Plath), 328
"Private Ground" (Plath), 280, 282, 283
Prouty (Higgens), Olive, 45–46, 64, 66, 112, 118, 121, 143, 174, 309, 310, 313
"Purdah" (Plath), 328, 330
"Pursuit" (Plath), 195

"Rabbit Catcher" (Plath), 332
"Rain" (Plath), 23
"Rain Horse, The" (Hughes), 255
Randall, Helen, 61, 86
"Recantation" (Plath), 200
Rich, Adrienne, 135, 272, 359
Richards, I. A., 137
"Rival, The" (Plath), 296, 298
"Rival (2), The" (Plath), 297, 320–21
Roche, Clarissa, 223–24, 237, 253–54, 291, 303, 305, 326, 328, 347–48, 352, 360
Roche, Paul, 223–27, 231, 232, 291
Roethke, Theodore, 247, 248, 252, 263, 266, 270, 273, 335, 366
Rossiter, A. P., 198

S———, Richard, 129–30, 140, 141, 147, 155, 175–76, 187
Salter, Elizabeth, 187
Schendler, Sylvan, 226
Schober, Aurelia Greenwood, 7, 119, 177, 189
Schober, Dorothy, 7, 12, 15
Schober, Frank, 7, 12, 16, 17–18, 189
Schober, Frank, Jr., 7, 12
"Sea Symphony" (Plath), 25
Seager, Allan, 266
"Second Winter" (Plath), 96, 153
"Secret, A" (Plath), 332–34
Sexton, Anne, 240–44, 268, 270, 271, 335, 359
Shapiro, Norman, 138, 143–45
Shawber, Anne, 106
"Shrike, The" (Plath), 216
Sitwell, Edith, 34, 71
"Sleep in the Mojave Desert" (Plath), 245, 270
Smith College, 39
Plath student at, 41–100, 127–37, 151-62
Plath teacher at, 202, 222–31
"Smith College in Retrospect" (Plath), 178
"Snow" (Hughes), 255
"Snow" (Plath), 210–12, 225, 237
"Snow Blitz" (Plath), 355
"Snowflake Star, The" (Plath), 24
"Snowman on the Moor" (Plath), 194, 211

"Soliloquy of a Misanthrope" (Hughes), 216
"Soliloquy of the Solipsist" (Plath), 216
"Southern Sunrise" (Plath), 190
Spender, Stephen, 209, 258, 271, 348
"Spinster" (Plath), 153, 179, 181, 194, 263, 302
"Spring Parade, The" (Plath), 23
Starbuck, George, 240, 241, 272
"Stars Over the Dardogne" (Plath), 282
"Stings (2)" (Plath), 320, 321, 343, 345
"Stones, The" (Plath), 266, 270
"Stones for a Birthday" (Plath), 330
"Strumpet Song" (Plath), 180, 181
"Suicide Off Egg Rock" (Plath), 244
"Suitcases Are Packed Again, The" (Plath), 83
"Sunday" (Hughes), 255
"Sunday at the Mintons" (Plath), 71–73, 79, 89
"Superman and Paula Brown's New Snowsuit" (Plath), 17
"Swan, The" (Plath), 345, 346

Targett, May, 47, 168, 169, 206
Teasdale, Sara, 37, 153, 200
Teltscher, Henry O., 108–9
"Temper of the Time" (Plath), 70, 190
"Thin People, The" (Plath), 230
Thomas, Dylan, 34, 51, 70–71, 74, 77, 79, 92, 135, 164, 185, 188, 194, 204, 229, 268, 273
"Thoughts" (Plath), 75–76
Three Women: A Monologue for Three Voices (Plath), 292–95
"Times Are Tidy, The" (Plath), 243
"To Eva Descending a Stair" (Plath), 83–84, 93, 225
"Tour, The" (Plath), 331
Truslow Davison, Jane, 128–31, 157, 218, 239, 261
"Tulips" (Plath), 266, 267, 272
"Twelfth Night" (Plath), 88
"Two Campers in Cloud Country" (Plath), 245
"Two Lovers and a Beachcomber by the Real Sea" (Plath), 75, 78, 160
"Two Views of a Cadaver Room" (Plath), 244, 251

"Vanity Fair (Plath), 195
Ventura, Mary, 33
"Verbal Calisthenics" (Plath), 96
"Victory" (Plath), 25

Walker, Nanette, 67–68
Wallace, William, 25
"Watercolour of Grantchester Meadows" (Plath), 203, 252
Weller, Sue, 144
Wheeler, William Morton, 5, 6
White, Eric, 271
"Widow" (Plath), 299, 302
Wilbur, Richard, 108, 135, 140, 272, 359
Willard, Addie I., 19
"Willard, Bill," 54–55, 58, 60, 87
"Willard, Buddy," 28, 47–64, 87–89, 95, 99, 132, 140, 151, 244, 308, 310
"Willard, Mildred," 54–55, 58, 60, 65, 310
"Willard, Richard," 27–29, 33, 34, 48, 53–54, 59, 64
"Willard, Ronald," 54
"Winter Ship, A" (Plath), 249
"Winter Sunset, A" (Plath), 23–24
Winter Trees (Plath), 211, 235, 326
"Winter Words" (Plath), 153
"Wintering" (Plath), 346, 351
"Wishing Box, The" (Plath), 216–17, 245
Woeber, Mallory, 170, 173–74, 176, 180
Woolf, Virginia, 114, 190, 328
"Words" (Plath), 360
"Words Heard, By Accident, Over the Phone" (Plath), 315–16
Wound, The (Hughes), 292
"Wreath for a Bridal" (Plath), 194–95
"Wuthering Heights" (Plath), 279, 282
Wyett-Brown, Bart, 184

"You're" (Plath), 255, 257–58